VISUAL QUICKPRO GUIDE

Mac OS X Server 10.4 Tiger

Schoun Regan

Peachpit Press

Visual QuickPro Guide
Mac OS X Server 10.4 Tiger
Schoun Regan

Peachpit Press
1249 Eighth Street
Berkeley, CA 94710
510/524-2178
510/524-2221 (fax)

Find us on the Web at: www.peachpit.com
To report errors, please send a note to: errata@peachpit.com
Peachpit Press is a division of Pearson Education.

Project Editor: Rebecca Gulick
Editors: Whitney Walker and Jill Marts Lodwig
Technical Editor: Joel Rennich
Production Coordinator: Kate Reber
Copy Editor and Proofreader: Liz Welch
Compositor: WolfsonDesign
Indexer: Emily Glossbrenner
Cover Production: Sandra Schroeder

ISBN 0-321-36244-6

9 8 7 6 5 4 3 2 1

Printed and bound in the United States of America

Good friends have a new son.
What to get them? Or him?

This book is dedicated to
Xander Cruz Williams.

Acknowledgements

First and foremost I would like to thank Joel Rennich, who is a bigger part of this book than most will ever know.

A big thanks to those people who contributed their expertise in various areas, thereby helping to make the complex easy to understand. They include Victor Alexander, Michael Bartosh, Dave Pugh, Jan Stewart, and John Welch.

Thanks to my editors Rebecca Gulick, Whitney Walker, and Jill Marts Lodwig.

Thanks to my friends Andrina Kelly, Ian Kelly, and Josh Wisenbaker.

Juggling tasks is never easy, and my wife Susan is the gold standard by which all else must be measured. If it were not for her, I would have gone crazy.

I would also like to thank my fellow Mac OS X Server writers Michael Bartosh and Charles Edge. Writing about Mac OS X Server is never easy—so much to cover, so little space and time. We all understand the quest for knowledge and do our best to make it available to all. I feel fortunate to be in such company.

Finally, I'd like to thank the Apple technical writer who tweaked the section in the manual about the uuidgen command for Mac OS X. I have never had so much fun explaining to others how to use this command as I do now.

TABLE OF CONTENTS

INTRODUCTION

Congratulations! You are about to enter the world of Mac OS X Server.

This book covers the most common uses of Mac OS X Server to get you up and running quickly and correctly. It does not attempt to include every possible service and every possible permutation or to anticipate every possible use of Mac OS X Server—that isn't possible—but this solid foundation should take you a long way in your work with Mac OS X Server.

What is Mac OS X Server?

Mac OS X Server is a robust, scalable, and secure operating system that permits the server administrator to share files; run services; protect networks; and store user, group, and computer data. Mac OS X Server is also an integral part of many multiplatform networks, connecting to PCs and Linux boxes with ease. You achieve all this functionality by using a few major applications built right into Mac OS X Server—and, of course, this book!

Why use Mac OS X Server? Why not just share files from another Mac OS X computer or a Windows server?

You'll want to use Mac OS X Server because it was built to help you manage very difficult tasks easily. It works well with other operating systems and can be a file server for older Mac operating systems, such as Mac 8.6 and Mac 9.2, Mac OS X, all versions of Windows, Linux, and Unix systems—all of which makes it very versatile. You'll also want to use Mac OS X Server as a Web server. Since it runs Apache, you'll be running one of the most secure and widely used Web servers on the Internet. You'll want to store all your users and groups on your Mac OS X Server so those users can take advantage of the single sign-on features afforded a Kerberos KDC. Mostly, you'll want to use Mac OS X Server because it was built to be secure, and this above all else is the reason to switch from other server operating systems, which may not be as secure. This book will help you understand how Mac OS X Server can work for you.

Once you've decided that Mac OS X Server will take its place in your network, you'll be happy to know that Mac OS X Server is based on Mac OS X, which is based on Unix— allowing Apple to leverage all the power of Unix for you. Mac OS X Server works by allocating various processes to do the work, and these processes know how to act because they read from their configuration files before they start. To manage these processes, you can use Apple's GUI server administration tools to make changes to the configuration files, or you can directly edit the configuration files via the command line.

What's in this book?

Mac OS X Server can do so much that describing it in one book is a challenge.

While this books discusses Web, mail, NetBoot, file sharing, virtual private networking, DNS, network address translation, QuickTime streaming, and a few other services, there is much more under the hood of Mac OS X—and thus, Mac OS X Server— that is not specifically server related but is important to understand nonetheless.

First, Apple has generously sprinkled open source software throughout Mac OS X and Mac OS X Server. You can consider Apache for Web services, Samba for Windows file sharing, CUPS for printing, FreeBSD for the underlying substructure, BIND for DNS, Postfix and Cyrus for e-mail, Jabber for an iChat server, and so on.

Second, these applications are versatile and expandable, and when a GUI is placed on top of them, they become easier for those attempting to harness the power within them to understand.

Add the server pieces to Mac OS X, and Mac OS X Server shines as a well-balanced collection of open source software controlled primarily by buttons, frames, pop-up menus, and check boxes.

Mac OS X Server also makes use of LDAP, DNS, KDC, ipfw, QTSS, IMAP, SSL, and other technologies commonly known by their acronyms (though maybe not, if you're new to Mac OS X Server, commonly known to you).

Added to the mix are Xserve and Xserve RAID, Apple's entries in the ever-expanding storage market. Xserve provides the first Apple computer designed to be managed without the administrator having to sit directly in front of the server—an approach totally foreign to most long-time Mac users. In fact, Xserve doesn't even come with a video card! (If you want one, you must add it as an option.) The remote administration aspect of Xserve is often what introduces many users to Unix. Powerful, expandable, customizable, dangerous, wonderful, old school—take your pick. If you really want to learn about Mac OS X Server, you need to know a little about Unix.

This book sheds light on these and other technologies to help you make your entry into the Mac OS X Server world. The knowledge you gain from this book is but a starting point for further exploration of a well-designed, solid, secure operating system.

Who should use this book?

In this book, you will learn what Mac OS X Server is, what it can do, and how it works. You will learn the basics of installing, setting up, and managing various services of Mac OS X Server. Novice users of Mac OS X Server will get the most out of this book, while veterans of Mac OS X Server will pick up valuable tips and tricks. No matter what your experience with Mac OS X Server, this book will provide answers to questions you may have about Mac OS X Server.

How to use this book

This book is written as a guide to the basic setup and management of Mac OS X Server. Before you start working with Mac OS X Server, you'll want to install the Mac OS X Server Administration tools on your Mac OS X computer and run Software Update so you can manage your server remotely (these tools can be found on Apple's support Web site, at www.apple.com/support). You'll also want to have the Terminal application handy, possibly placing it in your Dock, and you'll want to know a little about the network on which you're installing Mac OS X Server, such as what IP addresses are used on that network and whether that network is totally off or is connected to the Internet.

You'll also want to familiarize yourself with three main tools: Server Assistant, Server Admin, and Workgroup Manager. Learn how to stop and start services and to change directories in Workgroup Manager, and quickly run through the process of setting up a server.

INTRODUCTION

When you're ready to go, you can use this book in a variety of ways. You can leaf through the chapters and tasks, locating just the tasks that interest you and following them from beginning to end. You can also read the book from beginning to end, following all the tasks along the way. As you will see, Mac OS X Server uses many services, and many of them are interrelated.

Chapters 1 and 2 describe the components of Mac OS X Server and how to install Mac OS X Server on your Mac. Chapter 3 discusses Open Directory, explaining in clear and concise language what Open Directory is and its potential uses with Mac OS X Server; if you are totally new to Mac OS X Server, you may want to read the DNS section of Chapter 6 in conjunction with Chapter 3. Chapter 4 focuses on user and group management, though users of Mac OS X Server in the educational field will appreciate the user, group, and computer management discussions in Chapter 13. Chapter 5 discusses file sharing and access to share points. Chapters 6 through 12 describe the services Mac OS X has to offer. Chapter 6 explores services such as DNS, DHCP, and network address translation. Chapters 7, 8, and 9 discuss, respectively, printing, mail, and Web services. Chapters 10 and 11 describe security and NetBoot. Chapter 12 explains how to set up a QuickTime streaming server.

Note that this book includes some Unix commands, which, in most cases, should be typed on one line. Because some lines are very long, however, they cannot appear on a single line in this book but instead wrap onto subsequent lines. Where this happens, the subsequent lines will be indented and a gray arrow will be used to indicate the line is wrapped.

Additional information and updates

While you are using Mac OS X Server, you'll want to keep track of current updates and tips and tricks as Apple updates its software. Here are some resources:

♦ **www.afp548.com/** is an excellent resource for all sorts of advanced tips and tricks for working with Mac OS X Server.

♦ **www.macenterprise.org/** is the Mac OS X enterprise deployment project.

♦ **train.apple.com/** is the place for information about Apple's training courses.

♦ **www.apple.com/support/macosxserver/** is Apple's support site for Mac OS X Server.

♦ **www.openldap.org/** is the place to go to learn more about LDAP—a must when using Mac OS X Server with many users and groups.

♦ **web.mit.edu/kerberos/www/krb5-1.3/krb5-1.3.1/doc/krb5-admin.html** is MIT's site for information on Kerberos.

♦ **alienraid.org/** is devoted to the use of Apple's Xserve RAID in non-Apple environments.

♦ **www.itinstruction.com/** is devoted to training and education on Mac OS X and Mac OS X Server.

♦ **www.mac-mgrs.org/** is a list serv site devoted to the management and trouble-shooting of Mac OS X and Mac OS X Server. If you can't find the answer anywhere else in the world, do your homework, read the list rules, and get your answers here. This site offers Mac-based community support at its finest.

As for updates, once you have a major version of server software installed and working, you generally won't want to implement the next major version immediately upon release, because issues may arise that make the server unusable—something not acceptable in an environment where the server must be running smoothly 24/7/365. Apple has plans to release its next major update to Mac OS X (Leopard) sometime in late 2006 or early 2007. When Tiger Server comes out, careful evaluation of the initial release will likely reveal incredible additions as well as minor annoyances that will be attended to in updates to come. This is the game we play with all software updates, but in the server market, it's especially important that careful evaluation and prudence rule the day. This book incorporates updates that occurred during its writing and is as correct as it can be up to version 10.4.6.

PLANNING AND INSTALLATION

One of the biggest decisions you're likely to make about Mac OS X Server 10.4 is how to use it to best serve the needs of your particular environment. Servers generally hold and distribute the crux of the information that flows throughout an organization. How many client machines will there be? What platforms must you support: Mac OS X? Windows? Linux? What services will you run? On what type of machine will you install Mac OS X Server? If you use Xserve (Apple's rack-mountable server), will you be adding a hardware RAID card? How about Fibre Channel and an Xserve RAID? Will you be adding two or three servers to your mix? How should you divide the workload? Will this be an upgrade instead of a new install? What about DNS? Who's the domain admin?

These questions and others are part of proper planning before you install Mac OS X Server. Knowing exactly what your requirements are will assist you in making the correct decisions. Once the planning is complete, it's time to decide how to partition your disks, if necessary, and then format them using the style of your choice. After the formatting is finished, you can install the server software.

Installing Mac OS X Server 10.4 is easy—almost too easy. You'd think that a server system this powerful would require all day to install. But as long as you meet Apple's hardware requirements, the installation should take place without a hitch in about 30 minutes, depending on the hardware configuration. You'll need to decide where to install Mac OS X Server and whether to install it onsite or from a remote location. Apple's Xserve mounts in a rack and doesn't contain a video card (so you can't connect a monitor to it, although you can purchase one separately), thus making remote installation, configuration, and management a necessity. Another option for the Xserve is an internal RAID card, allowing you to configure hardware RAID with your Xserve. You can also attach a separate RAID system to the Xserve. Apple's foray into the RAID array is called Xserve RAID, a hardware RAID array system that can be used with Apple's Xserve and other platforms as well. Regardless of the hardware, you'll need a few things prior to installation.

Planning Your Deployment

Think about what Mac OS X Server can do—offer various services such as file sharing, storing user data, and running a Web server—and then think about what you want it to do. **Table 1.1** lists the possible services that Mac OS X Server offers, to help you choose the ones you wish to implement.

Keep in mind that all these available services tax your RAM, CPU, and hard disk(s). If you have a newer computer, you could run several of these services on one machine; but with older computers, you're more limited. Your budget may only allow for a single Mac OS X Server, or you may have been asked to install Mac OS X Server on a much older Macintosh with just the bare system requirements. In later chapters, we discuss which services tax server hardware the most and which are likely to work fine on older Macintosh computers.

Table 1.1

Major Mac OS X server services

SERVICE	DESCRIPTION	YOU MIGHT IMPLEMENT THIS SERVICE WHEN...
Application Server	Runs Java servlet or Tomcat applications directly from the server	You have qualified applications that must run from the server.
AFP File Sharing	Shares files over the Apple Filing Protocol to other Macintosh computers	Users need to share files with both older and newer Macintosh operating systems.
DHCP Server	Offers IP addresses and associated information to other computers and devices	Mac OS X Server is needed to offer addresses to all other devices, regardless of operating system.
Domain Name Server	Directs requests for listed fully qualified domain names to be directed to given IP addresses	You want the server to have a fully qualified domain name, such as afp548.com.
Firewall	Protects the server and network from possible attacks	Protection of the server is paramount.
FTP File Sharing	Allows access to the server via the ubiquitous File Transfer Protocol	Users must transfer files to your server from a variety of operating systems and you aren't too concerned about security.
iChat server	Permits the running of a Jabber server	You want an internal iChat server to which iChat clients can connect.
Kerberos Key Distribution Center	Allows authorization of services without sending the password across the network	The services you wish to offer allow Kerberized connections, thus increasing security.
LDAP Directory Server	Holds user information such as long name, short name, user ID, and preference settings	You want greater management capabilities over all your users.
Mail Server	Used to send and/or receive mail	Users need to send and receive mail.
NetBoot Server	Allows qualified Macintosh computers on the network to boot from a disk image on the server	You have a lab setting and want to boot and/or reconfigure disks on several Macintosh computers at once.
Network Address Translation Service	Acts as a router, sending information from one network to another	You have two network cards pointing to two different networks.
NFS File Sharing	Facilitates sharing with Unix machines	You need to share files with Linux or other Unix machines.
Printer Server	Creates and manages printer queues and quotas	Control over printers is required.
QuickTime Streaming Server	Streams live or prerecorded audio and video content	Video/audio files need to be seen by others locally and over the Internet.
SMB File Sharing	Shares files with Windows computers	Users need to share files with Windows computers.
Software Update Server	Controls Apple Software Updates internally	You want users to have to connect to the internal Software Update server to reduce the load on the outside connection.
Virtual Private Network Server	Permits the secure connection of remote clients	Remote clients need to log in to your server in a secure fashion.
WebObjects	Deploys WebObjects applications	You want to run your custom-built WebObjects applications from this server.
Web Server	Serves up Web sites	There is at least one Web site you want others to have access to.
Xgrid Server	Controls distributed computing to Xgrid clients	Leverage idle computers' CPU cycles to decrease time spent rendering or computing projects.

As you saw in Table 1.1, a variety of services can be run on Mac OS X Server. Some of the more popular implementations of Mac OS X Server are as a Lightweight Directory Access Protocol (LDAP) directory server and Kerberos Key Distribution Center; as an Apple Filing Protocol (AFP), a Server Message Block (SMB), a File Transfer Protocol (FTP) file server; or possibly as a print and iChat server. Other, older, more entrenched servers handle the duties of Domain Name Server (DNS), Dynamic Host Configuration Protocol (DHCP), Web, and email services. It's also likely that a separate server or other network device, such as a dedicated device designed just to protect your network, is providing security services, such as a firewall, network address translation, and/or a proxy service. Other servers probably provide secure remote logins and run as application servers. This doesn't mean you're limited in your deployment of Mac OS X Server. Should you wish to use your server in this fashion, an excellent tool called the Gateway Setup Assistant walks you through those options.

Before you go hog wild, decide carefully what you want to run on your server. Overloading a new server with several services at once makes troubleshooting difficult. Don't misunderstand: Mac OS X Server on a multiprocessor G5 Xserve with 2 GB of RAM can handle just about anything thrown at it. But turning on services without proper planning can lead to a nonsecure server and possible conflicts later.

Throughout this book you'll find discussions about which services demand more of the server than others. Should this server be elevated in the hierarchy of computers in your organization, you might want to utilize a second network card so that you can connect your server to another network, something that is standard on the G5 Xserve and was optional on the G4 Xserve. If you choose to have Mac OS X Server become your Domain Name Server, take great pains to understand the ramifications involved: Incorrectly implementing the DNS can cause many services not to function properly, as you'll see in Chapters 3 ("Open Directory") and 6 ("Network Services Options"). Often an existing DNS is present; making the Mac OS X Server a secondary DNS is an excellent idea in case the first one fails. Allowing your Mac OS X Server to be the path between your local area network inside and the brutally nonsecure and hostile world of the outside Internet requires some education about firewall rules, discussed in Chapter 10 ("Security").

For some, this will be the first time you've installed a server of any kind. Others may be adding Mac OS X Server to a network with existing servers that run a variety of software. Let's look at some popular scenarios that exist today.

A Bit about Unix and Mac OS X Server

Mac OS X and Mac OS X Server were built on top of Unix. This book isn't intended to teach you Unix; however, you should know some basics before you dive into Mac OS X Server. Planning your installation with a nod toward optional Unix administration makes good sense.

Mac OS X Server was designed to be administered either locally or remotely with a few main tools, as you'll see in the next chapter. It was also designed with the option to be administered almost totally from the command line. Understanding a few fundamentals of the command-line structure will help you better manage Mac OS X Server.

The structure of Unix lends itself to the path style of naming, such as /Applications/iTunes, where Applications is a folder and iTunes is the item within that folder. If the folder begins with a slash (/), then you can assume the folder is sitting on the top level of the hard disk or volume. In this book, we'll use this method to describe the location of items.

The main application used to launch a command-line interface is the Terminal, which is located inside /Applications/Utilities. After Mac OS X Server has been configured, the Terminal is automatically placed in the Dock for you.

If you can use a command-line interface while sitting in front of a computer, you can use that interface to manage any other Mac OS X and/or Mac OS X Server system by remotely accessing that computer. Mac OS X Server has a command-line process (a *process* is an application that, in this case, has no user interface) called the ssh daemon (sshd for short) running automatically. This process allows a user to log in to the server from a remote location.

It's easy to log in to your Mac OS X Server from a remote machine. Open the Terminal application, type ssh *server-administrator's-short-name@ip-address-of-the-server*, and press Return. Answer **yes** to the next question about setting up a key, press Return again, and enter the server administrator's password.

You're now logged in to your Mac OS X Server from where you sit, and you can manage things remotely with several command-line tools at your disposal. These tools take a bit of getting used to, but they can often save you a trip to the location of the server to change a setting.

Secondary server scenario

The most common scenario is where one server—in this case, an Active Directory server—is already in place (we'll discuss Active Directory in Chapter 3). The Active Directory server is the primary DNS and the directory data store for the organization. It may also be the application server, the DHCP server, and the print server. Mac OS X Server can fit perfectly into this network by providing file-sharing and chat services for both the Macintosh and Windows computers on the network. Mac OS X Server can also do the following:

◆ Control how the Mac OS X client computer's preferences are handled

◆ Hold the folders where users store their data

◆ Function as an internal Web server (possibly running WebDAV)

◆ Run as a NetBoot server to allow the lab Macintosh computers to boot off an identical system disk every time

◆ Utilize the Software Update Server service to permit Macintosh computers on your network to pull Apple software updates off the internal server, reducing throughput on your precious outside connection

See Table 1.1 for a brief explanation of the services in this list.

AppleShare IP server upgrade scenario

Another common scenario involves upgrading an AppleShare IP (ASIP) server to or replacing it with Mac OS X Server. In this case, the Mac OS X Server is king of the hill, responsible for the directory data store, domain name service, file and print services, DHCP, mail, software updates, and more. The server will likely have more services running than the ASIP server it's replacing, and it will be busy handling requests for all sorts of data. In this case, a fast connection utilizing the Macintosh's Gigabit Ethernet network card(s) will serve you best, because if you have a G5 Xserve, both network interfaces are probably active and can be joined together to provide even more aggregate bandwidth.

NetBoot and Software Update Server scenario

This scenario involves setting up a Mac OS X Server as a school's NetBoot and Software Update Server to provide the initial startup image. It erases the internal hard disk on each machine in the school's labs, and it copies customized, bootable images; each lab receives the appropriate image for its particular task that day.

The server also does double duty as a Software Update Server, providing Apple software updates internally. As an added bonus, this server may also act as the directory data store, allowing students to log in from anywhere in the school and see their home folder.

QuickTime Streaming Server scenario

In this scenario, a server has been set up as a QuickTime Streaming Server and possibly a QuickTime Broadcaster Server. This server's job is to take live input from a camera and stream it out to all employees, allowing them to watch the CEO's latest company announcements. It also streams audio and video content stored as movie files (mandatory safety videos, human resource updates, and meetings recorded earlier so that attendees can gather information they missed) on the server to employees' desktops. All these audio and video streams are, of course, logged to a file so that human resources can document who watched what video and when. The result is a reduction in the amount of time employees spend away from their desks engaging in such mandatory activities.

Each of these scenarios takes proper planning to set up, deploy, and install Mac OS X Server, and they are by no means the only uses of Mac OS X Server. Nor are you pigeon-holed into a particular scenario, running only the configurations mentioned here. The bottom line is that you must carefully evaluate your needs, the role Mac OS X Server will play with respect to those needs, and how Mac OS X Server will grow and possibly take over the duties of some lesser servers.

Megabit and Gigabit

Newer Macintosh computers can communicate with other devices on the network much faster than older ones. Whereas older computers started transferring data at 10 megabits per second, 100 megabits per second soon became the standard. Now, any PowerMac or Xserve you purchase can transfer data at 1000 megabits per second! This transfer rate is called *1 Gigabit per second*; and since it's done over the Ethernet interface, it's commonly referred to *Gigabit Ethernet*.

PLANNING YOUR DEPLOYMENT

System Requirements

The system requirements for Mac OS X Server 10.4 aren't much different from those of Mac OS X Client 10.4. The reason is that Mac OS X Server *is* Mac OS X Client, with four extra packages:

◆ QuickTimeStreamingServer.pkg

◆ ServerAdminTools.pkg

◆ ServerEssentials.pkg

◆ ServerSetup.pkg

You can download and install the QuickTime Streaming Server from Apple's Web site on your Mac OS X Client Macintosh. Called the Darwin Streaming Server, it's identical to QuickTime Streaming Server without the trademark name QuickTime.

You can also install the Server Administration Software package on your client machine. It contains the Mac OS X Server Administration Tools discussed in Chapter 2, "Server Tools." The Server Administration Software package also installs the Server Setup package, which contains the executables used when managing any Mac OS X Server(s) remotely.

That leaves one package. ServerEssentials.pkg is all that separates Mac OS X Client and Mac OS X Server. Inside that package, what makes Mac OS X Server tick?

◆ Apache 2.0 (in case you want to use it instead of Apache 1.x)

◆ Eight extra Apache modules

◆ AppleShareIP Migration, RAID Admin, and Fibre Channel tools

◆ Cyrus (POP and IMAP mail server)

◆ FTP Server Directory

◆ Jabber (iChat server) files

◆ Mailman (mailing list manager)

◆ MySQL Admin tool and associated files

◆ QTSS template files

◆ Server Manager Daemon files

◆ SPAM Assassin and CLAM AV

◆ Squirrel Mail (Web-based email interface)

◆ A few migration files

◆ Additional Startup items: NAT, IPFilter, IPFailover, IPAliases, Mailman, Watchdog, MySQL, Samba, Headless Startup, Serial Terminal Support, and Software Update Server

◆ About 100 additional executables (processes or tools used to manage certain server-based processes)

◆ About 70 edited configuration files for the new Startup items

Table 1.2

Hardware requirements for Mac OS X Server 10.4		
	APPLE REQUIREMENTS	REAL-WORLD REQUIREMENTS
Macintosh type	MacMini, eMac, iMac, PowerMac G3, PowerMac G4, PowerMac G5, Xserve	PowerMac G4, PowerMac G5, or Xserve
Hard disk size	4 GB	80 GB
RAM	128 minimum, 256 high demand	1 GB minimum
Other	Built-in FireWire	Built-in FireWire, Gigabit Ethernet

As you can see, the only things absolutely necessary to make a Mac OS X Client a Mac OS X Server are the executables, the configuration files (almost all stored in the hidden /private/etc and /private/var directories), and the Startup items. The other items are needed to utilize some of the services that run on Mac OS X Server, but there is little difference between the two.

The hardware requirements for Mac OS X Server are listed in **Table 1.2**. Keep in mind that although Apple has a set of hardware requirements, this table includes a column of real-world requirements.

Apple doesn't support Mac OS X Server on PowerBooks or iBooks, although it works on those machines. If you just want to install Mac OS X Server and test the services with one or two client machines attached to a small network, running the server software on a portable Macintosh works fine. However, don't assume that AppleCare will help you with any of your software problems if you're running on a laptop.

✔ Tip

- Mac OS X Server works more reliably when it's plugged into an active Ethernet connection as opposed to an AirPort or FireWire connection.

SYSTEM REQUIREMENTS

Partitioning Choices

You've planned the services to run on your Mac OS X Server and chosen the hardware on which the server will reside. It's now time to decide whether you wish to partition the disk.

Partitioning your disk allows you to easily reformat one partition while keeping software or data on the other. However, partitioning may waste valuable disk space and be less secure, depending on the way the partitions are formatted. You might want to partition a disk to separate the data from the operating system. Or, you might want three partitions: one containing the operating system, one containing the data, and one to back up the data or the operating system. There is no right or wrong way to proceed when you're dealing with partitions. However, with respect to Mac OS X Server, you undoubtedly know the value of backing up your data to another physical location; so, having a local partition for backup probably won't be useful. Having a second local backup disk that you can boot from in case of hardware failure is a more likely scenario.

You have the option of partitioning the disk whether you're installing Mac OS X Server on a Mac with a single disk or multiple disks, such as a RAID array. For example, you may have an Xserve RAID or an Xserve that supports hardware RAID (the G5 Xserve has an option to support hardware RAID via an optional internal hardware RAID card).

Clarifying Some Terms

Now is a good time to look at some terminology to ensure that you understand this book's geek-speak (**Table 1.3**).

Table 1.3

Computer terminology regarding disks		
TERM	MEANING	EXAMPLES
Storage device	Any item connected to your Macintosh that can store information. Storage devices may have the ability to be partitioned.	FireWire hard disk, iPod, USB hard disk, Flash cards, USB storage device, PC storage cards.
Drive	A storage device that's physically connected to the computer and that has or can read from spinning platters or disks.	Hard disk drive, CD-ROM drive, SuperDrive.
Disk	A storage device or the part of a storage device that actually stores data. Sometimes used to describe a partition.	CD-ROM disk, hard disk, or external disk, such as a Zip disk.
Volume	A logical section of a disk that can store files. Volumes are always partitions, even if a disk contains only one partition.	If a hard disk is partitioned into three volumes, each volume appears as a separate icon on the desktop.
Media	Items that store information and that generally are disposable and plentiful.	CD-Rs, CD-RWs, DVD-Rs, DVD-RAMs, floppy disks, Zip disks.
RAID	Redundant Array of Independent Disks. Makes several drives act and look like a single drive. Levels of RAID exist.	Since RAID arrays are multiple disks, examples generally involve additional internal hard disks or preconfigured external RAID systems such as Xserve RAID from Apple.

RAID Review

RAID stands for Redundant Array of Independent Disks. The concept is easy to understand: Take two disks, make the operating system think they're one disk, and you can perform digital magic.

For example, if the operating system thinks it has one big disk, you can have the RAID software write the same information to both disks. The reason to do this is clear: redundancy of data (fault tolerance). If disk one fails, disk two has the identical data. This is known as RAID level 1. **Table 1.4** describes some popular RAID levels.

RAID systems must have at least two disks but can have several, based on the configuration and your budget. RAID can be software based or hardware based; hardware-based RAID is more versatile.

Apple's support for RAID involves both software and hardware RAID. The Disk Utility application can do software RAID on disks, and hardware RAID is supported by Apple's Xserve and Xserve RAID. The G5 Xserve can hold 3 disks, and the G4 Xserve can hold 4; the Xserve RAID can hold up to 14 disks over two controllers and is managed by an application called RAID Admin.

Table 1.4

RAID levels and their uses

RAID NUMBER	RAID NAME	IMPLEMENTATION	ADVANTAGES	DISADVANTAGES
0	Striping	Writes small amounts of data to each drive, switching back and forth	Speed	If one disk dies, all data is lost (no fault tolerance)
1	Mirroring	Writes identical data to both drives	Fault tolerance; hot swapping of disks, if supported	No gain in disk space
3	Striping with parity	Writes to each disk, and writes a parity check to a separate disk	Speed	Usually involves a move to hardware RAID
0+1	Mirrored striping	Two sets of striped arrays	Speed; fault tolerance	Somewhat expensive
5	Distributed parity	Writes data to each disk; parity is written across the disks	Extremely fast read rates; fault tolerance	Somewhat slower writes; three-disk minimum to implement
10	Mirroring	Mirrored array is striped across two RAID controllers	RAID level 1 advantages over two controllers	Four-disk minimum to implement
30	Striping with parity	Parity and striping across two controllers	RAID level 3 advantages over two controllers	Six-disk minimum to implement
50	Distributed parity with striping	Writes data to each disk; parity is written across disks across two controllers	RAID level 5 advantages over two controllers	Six-disk minimum to implement

✔ Tips

■ Remember, partitioning a disk erases all the data on that disk!

■ Separating your boot volumes from your data volumes, if you have the luxury of enough space to do it, will make system recovery much easier and may improve your system's speed.

■ It isn't necessary to create several partitions from your disk. Many people run their server software on a nonpartitioned disk.

When you're setting up Mac OS X Server for the very first time (not doing any sort of upgrade), you boot from the server DVD. Once you've booted off the Mac OS X Server DVD, you have access to the disk(s) via Disk Utility on the DVD and remotely via ssh. If partitioning is something you want to do, you'll probably run Disk Utility and partition the disk(s) in this manner.

To partition a disk:

1. Boot from the Mac OS X Server DVD.

2. Choose Utilities > Disk Utility.

   The Disk Utility window appears, showing all mounted volumes in the left pane's disk and volume list.

3. Select your disk from the disk list menu. (Note the difference between the physical devices, which are flush on the left side of the pane, and the logical volumes that are contained on the devices, which are slightly indented underneath the physical devices.)

4. Click the Partition tab (**Figure 1.1**).

5. Choose the number of partitions (up to 16) you wish to create from the Volume Scheme pop-up menu.

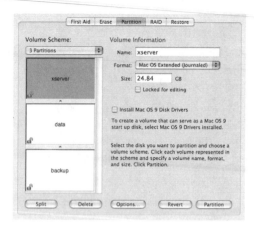

Figure 1.1 Click the Partition tab.

Figure 1.2 Click Partition in the confirmation dialog.

6. Click each partition in the map below the pop-up menu, and give it a name, format, and size.

   You can format the partitions in a variety of ways, depending on their final use:

   ◆ Mac OS Extended (Journaled)

   ◆ Mac OS Extended

   ◆ Mac OS Extended (Case-sensitive Journaled)

   ◆ Mac OS Extended (Case-sensitive)

   ◆ UNIX File System

   ◆ Free Space

   Recall that the minimum disk space required to install Mac OS X Server 10.4 is 4 GB.

7. Click the Partition button, wait for the confirmation dialog, and then click the Partition button in the confirmation dialog (**Figure 1.2**).

8. Choose Disk Utility > Quit Disk Utility.

   You have now partitioned your disk into individual volumes.

Command-Line Partitioning

diskutil is a useful command that lets you partition a disk when a Mac OS X Server is booted from a DVD. When Mac OS X Server boots from the DVD, the ssh daemon is running, meaning you can see it and connect to it via the command line. Once you've connected, diskutil can be used to partition, format, and name disks and volumes. To learn more about diskutil, type diskutil from the command line.

PARTITIONING CHOICES

Disk Formatting Options

Disks and partitions can be formatted in a variety of ways depending on how you wish to use them (**Table 1.5**). Mac OS X Server prefers to format a disk as Mac OS X Extended (Journaled).

Formatting as Mac OS X Extended (Journaled) is your best bet, because adding case sensitivity may cause problems with Classic and SMB mounts. Mac OS Extended (Journaled) adds built-in protection for the directory; the journaling process keeps track of which blocks on the disk were written to last. In the case of an unexpected shutdown or hard crash, the system only checks the integrity of the blocks listed in the journal instead of having to run a diagnosis of the entire disk.

✔ Tip

- For more information about journaling, please refer to http://developer.apple.com/technotes/tn/tn1150.html#Journal.

Table 1.5

Disk formatting options	
FORMAT	USE
Mac OS Extended (Journaled)	HFS+ with constant directory backup (journaling)
Mac OS Extended (Journaled + Case Sensitive)	HFS+ with constant directory backup (journaling), plus added case sensitivity
Mac OS Extended	Hierarchical File System Extended Format (HFS+)
Mac OS Extended (Case Sensitive)	HFS+ with case sensitivity only
Unix file system	Case sensitive, but can't be a boot volume for Mac OS X Server; no support for resource forks
Free space	Unformatted space used for Linux or some other operating system
Mac OS Standard	HFS only; used for backward compatibility with older Macintosh operating systems
DOS	Compatible with FAT (Windows) file systems

If you aren't partitioning the disk, you have the option of wiping, or *zeroing*, the disk using a variety of methods. Doing so erases the disk so that any data previously on the disk becomes essentially unrecoverable (although companies such as Drive Savers can *attempt* the recovery of data, albeit for a price). Zeroing a large disk increases the amount of time before an installation can take place, because you'll have to write an amount of data equal to the size of the disk. The options when zeroing a disk are as follows:

◆ Don't Erase Data erases only the directory structure, not the actual data. Using this method allows for the potential recovery of the data. This is also the quickest option, taking only slightly longer than a nonzeroing erase.

◆ Zero Out Data writes to every block on the disk, making recovery next to impossible.

◆ 7-Pass Erase writes random data over every block of the disk seven times. Many government organizations require this option.

◆ 35-Pass Erase takes substantially longer to perform but gives you that Totally Erased And Unrecoverable Data feeling.

Another important choice to make is how you name your disk(s). In days of old, Macintosh users named their disks whatever they wished. Because multiplatform functionality is paramount with Mac OS X Server, you may want to exclude spaces and other characters in the disk name. Although naming your disk "Tiger Server 10.4" is fine, you may find that "tigerserver" or "xserver" works better in the long run. Minimizing the length of the name also offers an advantage in certain areas, as you'll see later.

DISK FORMATTING OPTIONS

To wipe a disk:

1. Boot from the Mac OS X Server DVD.

2. Choose Utilities > Disk Utility.

3. Select your disk from the disk list menu.

4. Select the Erase tab.

5. Select a disk formatting structure from the Volume Format pop-up menu.

6. Choose a name for the disk.

7. Click the Options button near the bottom of the window.

   The Secure Erase Options dialog opens (**Figure 1.3**).

8. Choose the erase options you wish to invoke and click the OK button.

9. Click the Erase button, wait for the confirmation dialog, and then click the Erase button in the confirmation dialog (**Figure 1.4**).

10. When the erase and format are finished, you may wish to run Verify Disk [Verify Disk] from the First Aid tab [First Aid] on your newly formatted disk or volumes.

11. Choose Disk Utility > Quit Disk Utility.

    Your disk has now been erased and formatted and is ready for the installation of Mac OS X Server.

✔ Tips

■ Using the `diskutil` command-line utility to format your disk(s) is perfectly acceptable and is an excellent way to format disks from a remote location on an Xserve booted from the Mac OS X Server DVD.

■ You can erase free space on a disk or volume using Disk Utility or `diskutil`. This is a great way to keep deleted information from being resurrected by unscrupulous others.

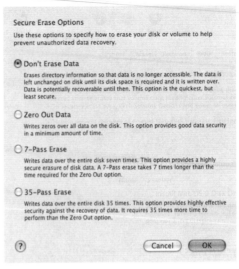

Figure 1.3 In the Erase Options dialog, choose the erase options you wish to invoke.

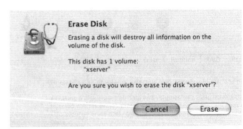

Figure 1.4 Click Erase in the Erase Disk confirmation dialog.

DISK FORMATTING OPTIONS

System Installation

Once the disk has been partitioned (if necessary) and properly formatted, you can turn to the installation of software.

The Mac OS X Server software ships on one DVD. The install can be performed a few ways: You can install the software using the Installer GUI while sitting at the machine or remotely, or you can install it remotely via the command line. Unless the machine has been supplied with a public IP address, automatic discovery of servers is done via Bonjour (Apple's term for its implementation of ZeroConf), as you'll see later. Since most installs are on cleanly formatted disks, let's begin there.

✔ Tip

- You can "trade in" your DVD for CDs by contacting Apple via the company's Web site, if you wish to install Mac OS X Server 10.4 on a computer that doesn't have a DVD drive.

After you boot the machine off the DVD, you're presented with Server Assistant's initial setup screen. However, much more is going on behind the scenes.

First, if there is a DHCP server on the network, your Macintosh has probably picked up an address from it. If the server is doling out public IP addresses, the installation and configuration can start from halfway around the world. If the address is private, installation and configuration can take place from your network. If a DHCP server is absent, the Macintosh assigns itself an IP address in the 169.254.x.x range; this self-assigned address is a function of Bonjour. If this is the case, remote installation can take place from any Macintosh on the local subnet.

Subnetting

A *subnet* is a set of computers and other devices that, by default, only see each other and are separated from other devices. A large organization may subnet its network using a logical divisor, such as one network for finance, one for manufacturing, and one for sales. Or it may choose to subnet based on location: Cleveland, Akron, and Canton. A subnet is often referred to as a *local network*.

Second, the ssh daemon is running, meaning you can access the machine remotely via the command line. This only works via the built-in Ethernet (and serial on Xserve) interface on the Macintosh that is to become the server. If you wish to install the server software while sitting in front of the Macintosh that's booted from the DVD, you're all set to install and configure your server—you won't need the information required next (except the server software serial number for configuration), although you should be aware of the remote install procedures.

IP Address Review

The Internet is made up of millions of devices communicating with each other in a flurry of activity, all so you can send and receive email, chat with others, visit the Peachpit Web site, and so on. In order for this communication to take place, computers must all be talking the same basic language: Internet Protocol (IP). The protocol most associated with this is Transmission Control Protocol (TCP). The combination is often expressed as TCP/IP.

Let's review the addresses, because a good understanding of IP addressing will help you understand how to implement Mac OS X Server in your environment. IP addresses come in three main ranges—A, B, and C (there are more, but this book will stick to the first three)—and two types—routable and nonroutable. The three primary IP address ranges are

◆ A: 0–127

◆ B: 128–191

◆ C: 192–253

Each range includes a set of IP addresses that the Internet doesn't care about. (There is much more to the story here. This discussion is only concerned with the basics.) These are often referred to as *nonroutable* or *private* address ranges. They are as follows:

◆ In the A range: 10.x.x.x

◆ In the B range: 172.16.x.x

◆ In the C range: 192.168.x.x

If a computer or device has any address in these ranges, it can't (without the help of another device) communicate directly with another computer or device on the Internet. You should know whether your Mac OS X Server will have an IP address the rest of the world can see (a *public* IP address) or if it will only be used inside your organization, possibly with a nonroutable address (a *private* IP address). This will make a difference when you attempt to communicate with other devices on the Internet.

Before you run away from your soon-to-be-server to do the remote installation, you need three things:

◆ *Server software serial number*—The 29-digit array that allows you to configure and use Mac OS X Server software. Note that unlike Mac OS X Server 10.3, Mac OS X Server 10.4 checks across the network for other servers running under the same serial number.

◆ *Ethernet address*—A unique, 12-digit address that is used, in this case, to identify the server when installing remotely. It can be found in several places, depending on the model of Macintosh involved. You may want to write down both Media Access Control (MAC) addresses when installing on a G5 Xserve (G5 Xserves have two Ethernet cards, hence two MAC addresses).

◆ *Hardware serial number*—The first eight digits of the hardware serial number are the root password used to authenticate your access to remotely install and configure that server. On older Macintosh computers, root's password is *12345678* (yes, it's typed correctly). This serial number can also be found in several locations, depending on the Macintosh model.

Prior to booting the server from the DVD, you should install the Server Administration Tools on the client machine from which the remote installation will take place; remote installation and administration can't take place without this package being installed.

✔ Tip

■ You need to install the tools, not just copy over the Server folder from a machine where the tools are already installed—that approach won't copy all the pieces you need in order to install Mac OS X Server.

Let's examine three installation methods: local, remote GUI, and remote command line.

To install Mac OS X Server locally on an erased disk:

1. Boot the Macintosh from the Mac OS X Server DVD.

2. Choose the language appropriate for your installation and click the arrow button in the lower-right corner of the screen.

3. Click the Continue button ⟨Continue⟩ on the Welcome window (**Figure 1.5**).

4. Scroll through and read the Important Information window for any additional information.

5. Scroll through the license agreement and click Agree to accept it (**Figure 1.6**).

Figure 1.5 Once Mac OS X Server has finished preparing the installation, you'll see a Welcome window.

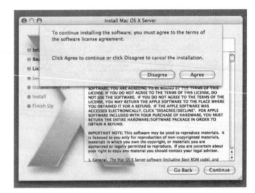

Figure 1.6 Scan through the License Agreement and click Agree in the acceptance dialog.

SYSTEM INSTALLATION

Bonjour

Apple wisely added ZeroConf (Zero Configuration) support to Mac OS X and Mac OS X Server back in version 10.2. It called the implementation *Rendezvous*. In Mac OS X and Mac OS X Server 10.4, the ZeroConf implementation is now called *Bonjour*. Bonjour does three main things:

◆ Assigns an IP address automatically if no DHCP server is present to provide an address. The IP address assigned is in the 169.254.x.x range.

◆ Shows the name you gave your computer instead of the IP address when others browse the local network for your computer.

◆ Provides the discovery of other Bonjour services on the local network.

Although Bonjour isn't configurable (remember, it's nothing more than ZeroConf), it will be important in later chapters, especially those dealing with file sharing.

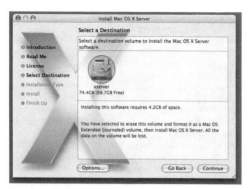

Figure 1.7 The destination window shows a disk or volume in the list.

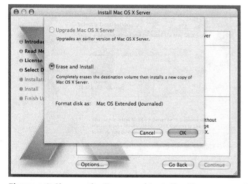

Figure 1.8 Choose the Erase and Install option.

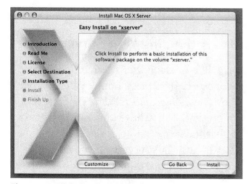

Figure 1.9 Click the Customize button.

6. Choose the destination disk or volume, and click the Continue button (**Figure 1.7**).

   or

   By clicking the Options button, you can choose to Upgrade or Erase and Install (**Figure 1.8**).

   Note that unlike on Mac OS X, you don't have the option to archive the current installation and install a fresh copy of Mac OS X Server.

7. Click the Customize button to remove or change components to be installed (**Figure 1.9**).

   You may wish to remove print drivers and additional languages here (**Figure 1.10**).

8. Click the Install button to begin the installation.

   After installation is finished, Mac OS X Server is ready for the setup stage.

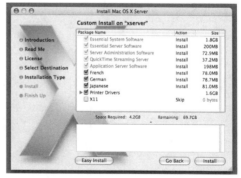

Figure 1.10 Customize your installation package.

To install Mac OS X Server on an erased disk from a remote Macintosh using Server Assistant:

1. Boot the Macintosh from the Mac OS X Server DVD.

2. On your remote machine, navigate to and launch /Applications/Server/ Server Assistant ▧.

   The Welcome screen appears, with three options (**Figure 1.11**):

   ◆ Install software on a remote server

   ◆ Set up a remote server

   ◆ Save setup information in a file or directory record

3. Choose "Install software on a remote server."

   The Destination window opens (**Figure 1.12**).

   Provided you're on the same subnet, you'll see your Mac OS X Server(s) listed with an IP address, hostname, Ethernet hardware address (commonly known as the MAC address), and status. If your network includes more servers, you may need to locate your server by identifying and matching its MAC or Ethernet address. The Status column indicates whether server software can be set up on that machine.

Figure 1.11 The Welcome screen appears when you launch Server Assistant remotely.

Figure 1.12 The remote destination screen shows a computer in the list.

Finding Your Server

The IP address in the Destination window can be the 169.254.x.x Bonjour style with a hostname of *localhost*; or, if a DHCP server is present, it may have an IP address and subsequent hostname designated by the DHCP and DNS servers on your network. If you're in New York and you're setting up a server in Los Angeles, you can choose the Server at IP Address option in the Destination window and type in the real-world IP address of the machine booted off the CD in Los Angeles.

SYSTEM INSTALLATION

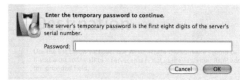

Figure 1.13 Enter the server's password in the authentication dialog.

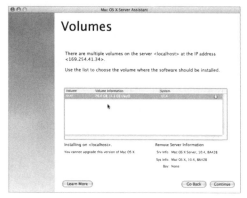

Figure 1.14 Choose a volume on which to remotely install Mac OS X Server.

Figure 1.15 Click OK to erase and format any incompatible software.

4. Click the Continue button.

An authentication window opens, asking for the server's password (**Figure 1.13**). Enter the password, click the OK button, and wait for authentication to take place.

5. Click through the following screens:

- ◆ The Language preference window.

- ◆ The Important Information window. It's a good idea to read all the information here before proceeding.

- ◆ The License Agreement and Agree windows.

6. In the Volumes window, decide which volume to install the server software on (**Figure 1.14**).

This window shows the name of the volume, the format of the volume (including space available), and the current system, if any. A system check is initiated automatically. Should incompatible software already exist on the disk or partition, a window appears (**Figure 1.15**). In most cases, the "Erase and format" option is already chosen for you.

continues on next page

7. Click OK to continue.

An Installing window indicates the software is being installed (**Figure 1.16**).

After installation is complete, a dialog signals a restart of the remote server off the disk or partition.

An Installation Status window indicates that the software has been successfully installed (if installed from DVD—if not, further installation from CD #2 must take place) and the administrator can proceed to setting up the server (**Figure 1.17**).

✔ Tips

■ Keep the server DVD in a safe place. If you're managing a server remotely, it may be a good idea to keep the DVD in the tray and/or affix the server serial number stickers to the DVD cover.

■ Apple has provided almost every GUI tool with a command-line equivalent. If you wish to install via the command line, you can do so. Booting from the DVD runs the ssh daemon, so you can discover and connect to the Macintosh with a command-line interface. To do such an installation, you should install the Server Admin Tools on the Macintosh from which you wish to discover and install the server software.

Figure 1.16 Wait while installation is in progress.

Figure 1.17 The Installation Status window shows the IP address and hostname of the volume on which the server software was installed.

Packages and the Installer Command

Packages are collections of files that are placed on a disk. A package can contain all the files necessary for a certain application to run. Packages can also contain other packages. For example, the OSInstall package is a metapackage, which means it has instructions to install other packages.

The `installer` command is used to install packages via the command line. Some of the Unix flags include:

◆ Setting the language.

◆ Listing all packages inside a meta-package.

◆ Allowing older versions of packages to be installed over newer ones. This option is useful when you need to install an older update because the latest update caused issues with your computer.

◆ Showing installation progress via verbose output.

When you're using tab completion in the Terminal, take care to remove the trailing slash from an installer package or meta-package (.pkg or .mpkg), or the `install` command won't function.

To install Mac OS X Server on an erased disk from a remote Macintosh using the command line:

1. Boot the Macintosh from the Mac OS X Server DVD.

2. Open the Terminal application on your remote Macintosh.

3. Run the command-line tool `sa_srchr` by typing in

   `/System/Library/ServerSetup/`
   `sa_srchr 224.0.0.1`.

   This command searches out your local subnet and returns information about any Macintosh booted from a Mac OS X Server DVD.

4. Locate the IP address in the returned information.

5. Type in `ssh root@the-IP-address-you-saw-in-step-four`, and authenticate using the Mac OS X Server's hardware serial number or `12345678` as the password.

6. Run the installer command by typing in

   `installer -pkg /System/Installation/`
   `Packages/OSInstall.mpkg -target`
   `/Volumes/name-of-your-volume`

   The computer on which you're installing Mac OS X Server will reboot after a successful installation.

✔ Tip

■ Always write down the Ethernet address(es), hardware serial number, and server software serial number, and keep them handy in case you need to reinstall Mac OS X Server.

SYSTEM INSTALLATION

Viewing the Installation Log and Installed Files

Log files are a critical piece of the computer administration architecture. Mac OS X and Mac OS X Server keep log files in various locations:

- /var/log/

- /Library/Logs/

- *your-username*/Library/Logs/

You can view these log files locally with the Console application located in /Applications/Utilities/. Currently, the Console application doesn't allow remote viewing of log files; if you wish to view the log files on your server from a remote location, you must ssh into the server and read the files via the command line using a command like `tail` or `cat after the installation`.

Log files are especially useful during the installation process. When you're installing locally, you have the option of viewing errors during installation or viewing everything taking place during the installation, from the mounting of disks to the cleaning up of temporary files (which takes place after all packages have been installed). To view the install log remotely, run the `tail -f` command on the system log after the installation. Doing so may show any errors that might have cropped up during the process.

Figure 1.18 An initial ssh connection results in this key pair information.

Figure 1.19 You can view the Installer Log from a local installation.

To run the tail command on the system log:

1. Open the Terminal application on the remote Macintosh.

2. ssh into your server prior to clicking the Install button in the Server Assistant:

   `ssh root@your-server's-new-ip-address`

   The first time you do this you'll receive a message asking if you want to create an ssh key pair. This is a standard part of ssh. Type yes and press Return to continue (**Figure 1.18**).

3. Type `tail -f /var/log/system.log`.

4. View the system log in the first Terminal window as the software is being installed on your server.

   You can view the installation log file while installing Mac OS X Server locally by choosing Installer Log from the Window menu (**Figure 1.19**).

VIEWING THE INSTALLATION LOG AND INSTALLED FILES

Server Tools

When you install Mac OS X Server, the Installer application automatically installs a package called ServerAdministrationSoftware.pkg, which is also installed later on any Mac OS X computer, allowing for remote management of your server. Within this package are all the tools needed to manage Mac OS X Server. Some of these tools can only be run from the command line. Some only work with the Xserve and the Xserve RAID. Some are only important if you're moving from an older server version, such as AppleShare IP or Mac OS X Server 1.2.

Of all the tools, two of them—Server Admin and Workgroup Manager—are used to manage almost all aspects of Mac OS X Server. Additional applications found on both Mac OS X and Mac OS X Server fall under the category of server management. This chapter will briefly look at these applications and cover a variety of ways to update the software on your server.

Running Server Assistant

Once Mac OS X Server software is installed on a freshly formatted disk or volume, it must be initially configured. This is the job of the Server Assistant tool, one of the server tools installed with Mac OS X Server.

Before you proceed with the configuration, have a few things handy:

◆ Your server's software serial number

◆ Your server's hardware serial number (needed only for remote installations)

◆ Your server's Ethernet (MAC) addresses (needed only for remote installations)

◆ If you didn't receive a separate Administration Tools CD, the server DVD, which contains the Server Administration Software package (or download it from Apple's Web site)

If you're setting up the server remotely, install the Administration Tools on any Mac OS X computer from which you wish to administer the setup and management of Mac OS X Server.

Now that you have the appropriate information, consider what information is required for initial setup:

◆ Server language and keyboard layout options.

◆ The initial administrator's account.

◆ Name of the computer, in three variations:
  ▲ Hostname (now set automatically)
  ▲ Computer name
  ▲ Bonjour name

◆ Network information such as primary interface, IP address, subnet mask, router, DNS server, and search domain.

◆ Server type and subsequent information:
  ▲ Stand-alone server
  ▲ Open Directory master
  ▲ Connected to a directory system

◆ Services you wish to start.

◆ Date, time, and time zone information.

◆ Whether to save server settings and, if so, how.

◆ Optional entries for the server you are about to set up, entered into the DNS zone files of your organization's existing DNS server (these may be out of your control; consult your network administrator about adding zone entries for your server). Although this information has no window or dialog associated with it, DNS is a critical piece of Mac OS X Server. See Chapter 6, "Network Services Options."

Let's examine each of these items in detail. Understanding what is asked of you in the Server Assistant can affect the future operation and performance of your Mac OS X Server. The screen snapshots you will see in the subsequent sections are from the Server Assistant.

Figure 2.1 Server Assistant is used to do the initial setup of Mac OS X Server.

About server language and keyboard layout options

After the Mac OS X Server software is installed, the initial Welcome screen (**Figure 2.1**) is displayed. Once you select the destination computer and authenticating (**Figure 2.2**), Server Assistant allows you to choose the language (remote install only) (**Figure 2.3**) and keyboard layout (**Figure 2.4**) of your Mac OS X Server. You have several languages to choose from, and multiple keyboard layouts are available for some languages. Next you are asked to enter the software serial number and associated information (**Figure 2.5**).

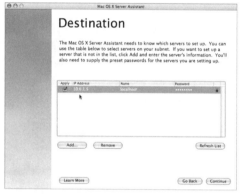

Figure 2.2 More than one server can be set up in the Destination dialog of Server Assistant.

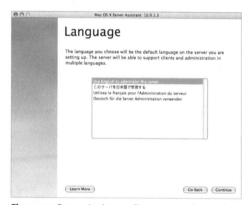

Figure 2.3 Server Assistant allows you to choose the language...

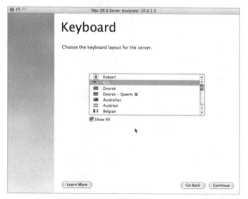

Figure 2.4 ...and keyboard layout of your Mac OS X Server.

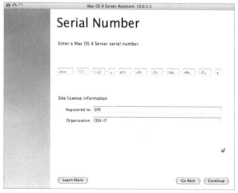

Figure 2.5 The serial number must be entered correctly before continuing.

Creating an initial administrator's account

Any time you install software on an empty disk, you're required to create an initial user account. On a Mac OS X computer, the initial user account, called the *local account*, is also an administrator; it can manage files that regular users can't. Mac OS X Server works the same way, but it initially enables root and gives root the same password as the initial administrator (see the sidebar "Who Is Root?").

Mac OS X and Mac OS X Server create a group for every user, and the group name for each user is the user's short name (**Figure 2.6**). Since you're dealing with Unix, there is already a group called admin. The short name of your initial user should be at least five characters. (Don't use the short name admin.) It's also a bad idea to use "admin" as a name as that's usually the first name picked when attacking a system with a brute-force attack.

Figure 2.6 The initial user account is also a NetInfo database administrator.

Password Practices

You should *pick a password that's difficult to guess*. (Having an easy password on Mac OS X Server is like dangling your data out there for anyone to grab.) You can choose a password that's extremely long, but doing so may cause problems when you log in (you're likely to forget a 48-character password). Choose an 8- to 12-character password that includes letters (both lowercase and uppercase), numbers, and possibly additional characters like an exclamation point or ampersand.

Who Is Root?

Whereas regular administrators have read and write access to some areas of the file system, root (the short name for System Administrator) has full read and write access anywhere on the disk. Root can see all files, change any files, and delete anything, regardless of the owner. Root can also change ownership of any folder or file from anyone to anyone else. Obviously, root privileges are very powerful and, in the hands of a novice, very dangerous.

Many a Mac OS X administrator has logged in as root and inadvertently deleted folders, or created files for others to use, only to find out later that because they created the files and folders as root, others couldn't use them. To be on the safe side, use your root login sparingly.

Logged in as a regular administrator, you can generally place and remove files from locations other users can't access by *authenticating* (entering your username and password) via a dialog that appears when you attempt such a change. Similarly, when you launch the Terminal application while logged in as a regular administrator, you can temporarily get root powers by preceding any command with the word sudo (Super User Do). You have this power for five minutes, after which you're required to enter your password again for another five minutes. If you want full root privileges all the time in the terminal, you can type sudo -s, which will not limit you to five minutes.

You can disable root at any time after the initial setup by opening /Applications/_Utilities/ NetInfo Manager and choosing Disable Root User from the Security menu (**Figure 2.7**), although doing so may prevent the LDAP database and the Kerberos KDC from being created later.

Figure 2.7 Disabling the root user with NetInfo Manager.

Naming your computer

Naming your computer involves three names: the hostname, the computer name, and the Bonjour name (**Figure 2.8**). Each name is used differently. They can all be different, but this can lead to confusion, especially for first-time administrators of Mac OS X Server.

The hostname cannot be set in the Server Assistant in Mac OS X Server 10.4. Instead, it follows a set of rules to determine what the hostname should be. These rules are, in order:

◆ The name associated with the HOSTNAME attribute inside the hostconfig file, which resides in the /private/etc directory

◆ The name pushed down from a DHCP server for the topmost (primary) network interface's IP address

◆ The mapped name inside the DNS server associated with the topmost (primary) network interface's IP address

◆ The machine's link-local or Bonjour name

◆ localhost, if nothing else is defined

The computer name can include letters, numbers, spaces, and special characters and will be seen when users browse the network for your server from Macintosh operating systems, such as Mac OS X and Mac OS 9.

The Bonjour name can include letters, numbers, and dashes and is seen by Mac OS X computers and servers when they browse the network using the Network icon 🌐 under the Local subnet.

✔ Tips

■ You can see a more detailed explanation of the hostname by clicking Learn More (Learn More) in the Network Names window.

■ It's a good idea to spell all names exactly the same, especially if you aren't yet sure how you want to implement Mac OS X Server.

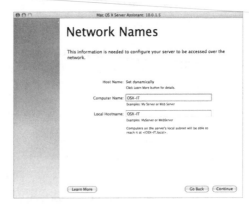

Figure 2.8 Naming your computer involves configuring two names.

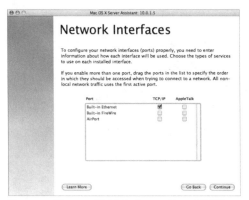

Figure 2.9 Choose which interfaces will run TCP/IP and which interface will run AppleTalk.

Figure 2.10 Provide the required information for each interface that will run TCP/IP.

Network Interfaces

A *network interface* is a way that your computer connects to other devices and computers on the network. It's often the built-in Ethernet interface, but it can be FireWire, AirPort, or a third-party interface card. In System Preferences, these interfaces are called Network Ports. This naming can lead to confusion, since the word *ports* has a different technical meaning when speaking about networking.

About network interfaces and information

Depending on your hardware, you may have more than one network interface that connects to other networks. Xserves come with one or two Ethernet interfaces and a serial port, depending on the revision and options chosen. FireWire interfaces can also be used for networking. And, of course, some computers running Mac OS X Server have AirPort cards.

On initial setup, you can choose which interfaces will run the TCP/IP protocol and which interface (only one) will use the older AppleTalk protocol (**Figure 2.9**). Mac OS X Server's interface won't let you enable AppleTalk on more than one interface at a time.

Should you decide to run TCP/IP on more than one interface, the subsequent dialogs require you to set up each interface with TCP/IP information (**Figure 2.10**), such as the IP address, subnet mask, router, DNS addresses, and search domains. Another option at this point is whether to manually configure or turn off IPv6.

As IPv6 is still an emerging protocol inside the United States, it's not common to find it in use. It is also not something that you would be using without knowing it, so some administrators disable IPv6 in order to simplify network configuration. Typically, outgoing network connections will try IPv6 first, and then default back to IPv4 when necessary. However, there is no current security reason to turn off IPv6, so many administrators just leave it on.

RUNNING SERVER ASSISTANT

An Ethernet tab for each checked network interface allows the reconfiguration of that particular interface's connection to another device. You can force a connection to full or half duplex (if the switch your server is connecting to requires a given setting), set the transmission speed, and specify frame size (**Figure 2.11**).

You can assign more than one static IP address to your Mac OS X Server if, say, you have one IP address on one Ethernet interface that connects to the Internet. You might use a second IP address for your internal network, and that IP address is associated with a second Ethernet interface (as would be the case with an Xserve). If you don't know which IP address you'll need, or you have a Dynamic Host Configuration Protocol (DHCP) server present, set your Mac OS X Server to use DHCP for the time being. (This is a last resort. The initial IP address should never be an address that may change frequently, like one obtained from a DHCP server.) Under most circumstances, Mac OS X Server should have a static IP address. A server that has the opportunity to change IP addresses would, for the most part, be useless.

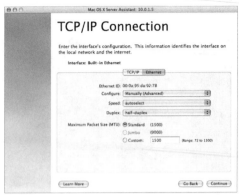

Figure 2.11 The speed of the Ethernet interface(s) can be set.

✔ Tips

- Mac OS X Server won't cooperate if you lack a physical Ethernet cable connection from an active switch or hub to your server. Be sure, at the bare minimum, that you have an active connection via an Ethernet interface.

- Having more than one physical interface active or having more than one IP address on any one physical interface or a combination of both of these is called *multihoming*. A description of multihoming can be found at http://rfc.net/rfc4116.txt.

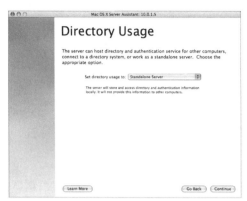

Figure 2.12 Choose your options for initial directory setup.

Standalone Server
✓ Connected to a Directory System
Open Directory Master

Figure 2.13 When you choose the Connected to a Directory System option...

Choosing initial directory usage setup options

Setting up Mac OS X Server's directory service options can seem daunting because some of the options require an in-depth knowledge of the existing directory service infrastructure on your network. However, the options aren't difficult to understand, and this section explains the basics. Your options for initial directory usage are as follows (**Figures 2.12** and **2.13**):

◆ **Standalone Server**—The best option for first-time administrators. It doesn't create a secondary database. If you aren't sure what your needs are with respect to adding users and groups, choose this option; you can always change it later.

All of your user records and their passwords will be local to your system. This option will not create an LDAP or a Kerberos database.

continues on next page

DHCP Options

DHCP servers need to forward the LDAP information to the clients. They do so via an option in the DHCP specifications. If you're working with a non–Mac OS X Server DHCP server, you should tell the administrator of that server to use Option 95 to pass the LDAP information down to the clients.

RUNNING SERVER ASSISTANT

◆ **Connected to a Directory System**—
Places your Mac OS X Server as a secondary server to another, generally larger,
directory server. When you choose this
option, you have four options for connecting to the directory system (**Figure 2.14**):

   ▲ **As Specified by DHCP Server**—
Means your Mac OS X Server's directory information will be passed down
from a DHCP server on your network,
provided the DHCP server is configured to send down that information.
Chapter 6 discusses how to set this
option if you happen to be that DHCP
server. This option is rarely used,
because your server still gets an IP
address from another server; therefore, it's possible that this IP address
could change, rendering your server
inaccessible to others outside your
local network.

   ▲ **Open Directory Server**—Tells your
Mac OS X Server to obtain its directory information from another Open
Directory Server (**Figure 2.15**).
Again, you must configure that server
at the top of the food chain, so to
speak, before you can tell your server
to get information from another
server. You have two options when
attempting to obtain this information:
First is to get the LDAP information
from an Open Directory DHCP server,
and second is to statically define the
LDAP server.

   ▲ **NetInfo Directory**—Tells your Mac
OS X Server to receive its directory
information from an older Mac OS X
Server running a NetInfo shared/
parent database (**Figure 2.16**).

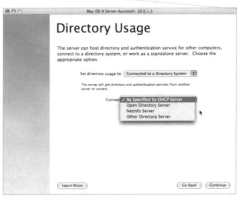

Figure 2.14 ...you have four choices for connecting to
the directory system.

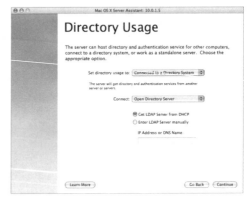

Figure 2.15 Choosing to connect to an Apple Open
Directory and the resulting options.

Figure 2.16 Choosing to connect to a NetInfo parent
database and the three options for connecting to
such a database.

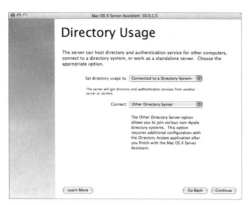

Figure 2.17 Selecting Connected to a Directory System to connect your Mac OS X Server to another directory service.

Figure 2.18 Choosing an Open Directory Master as your directory type isn't recommended at startup.

Jaguar Upgrades

If you're upgrading from Mac OS X Server 10.2 (Jaguar), you'll see one additional option: "Set Directory Usage to no change." This option keeps the NetInfo shared directory domain intact.

▲ **Other Directory Server**—Enables your Mac OS X Server to retrieve directory information from another directory service, such as OpenLDAP on another Unix computer (**Figure 2.17**). Choosing this option generally requires that you configure the Directory Access application to bind to the other directory server, such as Novell eDirectory or Microsoft's Active Directory.

Keep in mind that the four options under the Connected to a Directory System option aren't used by a single Mac OS X Server on a small network without any other directory servers.

◆ **Open Directory Master**—Should not be chosen during the initial setup of your server (**Figure 2.18**)—use Standalone instead. You can promote your Mac OS X Server from a standalone server to a Master any time after setup is completed. You should delay this promotion, because you want to make sure your Mac OS X Server can do both forward and reverse lookups on itself, ensuring the DNS server on your network is set up properly. For more information, see Chapter 3, "Open Directory," and Chapter 6, "Network Services Options."

✔ Tip

■ When you go through the initial setup, unless you're connecting your Mac OS X Server to another, larger directory server or you are completely sure DNS is functioning properly on your network, the best option is to make it a standalone server.

Choosing service startup options

Mac OS X Server can run many services: file sharing, Web, QuickTime streaming, NetBoot, Software Update server, and so on. During the initial setup, you can decide which services should start whenever Mac OS X Server starts up or restarts (**Figure 2.19**). If you don't select any services, you can start them later with the Server Admin tool. This screen is purely a convenience for getting your server up and running as quickly as possible.

However, keep in mind that it is not always the best idea to enable services that have yet to be fully configured, especially with file sharing services.

✔ Tip

■ It's a good idea to start up the Apple Remote Desktop service if you plan to use this method to control the GUI aspects of managing your server.

Setting time zones

Choosing a network time server is an excellent way to ensure that Mac OS X Server always has the correct time. Of course, you must be connected to the Internet to take advantage of Apple's time server, or you can use other time servers (**Figures 2.20** and **2.21**).

✔ Tip

■ Currently, Server Admin will change the time zone city back to Cupertino, CA, regardless of what you choose when setting up the server. Use the Server Admin tool to check this immediately after configuring the server to ensure the time zone is correct, and if not, change it.

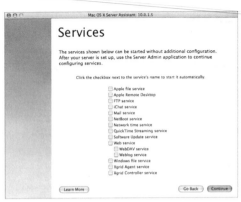

Figure 2.19 Choosing a service will result in that service always being started when Mac OS X Server starts up or restarts.

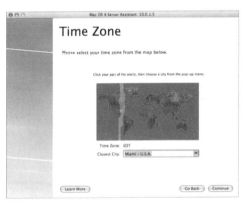

Figure 2.20 Choose from among the server time zone options.

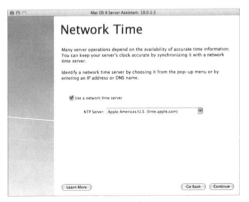

Figure 2.21 Choosing a network time server ensures that Mac OS X Server always has the correct time.

Figure 2.22 The initial welcome screen for remote installations.

Figure 2.23 In the Destination window, choose your server by clicking the check box.

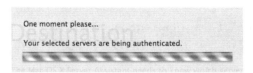

Figure 2.24 Clicking Continue in the Destination window authenticates your setup.

To configure Mac OS X Server using Server Assistant:

1. If you're installing from a remote Mac OS X computer or another server, launch Server Assistant, located in /Applications/Server/Server Assistant.

   or

   If you're in front of the Mac OS X Server, Server Assistant is already running and is ready to set up your server, so skip to step 5.

2. Select the "Set up a remote server" option at the Welcome window (**Figure 2.22**) and click Continue.

   The Continue button appears at the bottom of all the Server Assistant windows. Clicking Continue in each window forwards you to the next window.

3. Select the check box next to your server in the Destination window (**Figure 2.23**).

   The name *localhost* may appear in the Name column if no DNS name has been mapped to that IP address.

   If you have a server with another IP address and that server is not on your local network, click Add and add that server to the Destination list.

4. Double-click in the password field and enter the first eight digits of your server's hardware serial number (newer Macintosh computers) or 12345678 (older Macintosh hardware) and click Continue to show that you are being authenticated to continue your setup (**Figure 2.24**).

   continues on next page

RUNNING SERVER ASSISTANT

5. In the next two windows, choose your language (remote setup only) (**Figure 2.25**) and keyboard layout preferences (**Figure 2.26**), clicking Continue after each screen.

6. In the Serial Number window, enter your Mac OS X Server's software serial number, site license, and organization (**Figure 2.27**).

7. In the Administrator Account window, enter the name, short name, and password of the initial administrator (**Figure 2.28**).

Keep in mind that the initial administrator's password is also root's password.

Figure 2.25 Select the language for setting up your server.

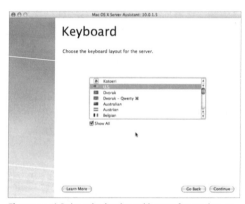

Figure 2.26 Select the keyboard layout for setting up your server.

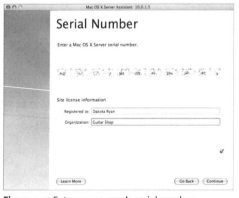

Figure 2.27 Enter your server's serial number.

Figure 2.28 Enter your administrator account information.

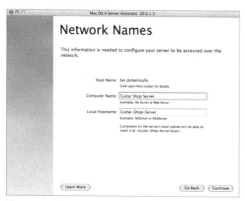

Figure 2.29 Naming your computer involves configuring two names.

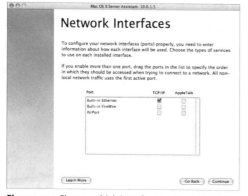

Figure 2.30 Choose which interfaces will run TCP/IP and which interface will run AppleTalk.

8. In the Network Names window, enter the two computer name and Bonjour name for your server (**Figure 2. 29**).

9. In the Network Interfaces window, you'll need to decide whether to activate TCP/IP and/or AppleTalk (**Figure 2.30**).

10. In the next two windows, choose whether you want your TCP/IP connection to be done manually, using DHCP with a manual IP address, using DHCP, or using BootP (**Figures 2.31** and **2.32**). You'll choose a TCP/IP connection method for each selected interface.

continues on next page

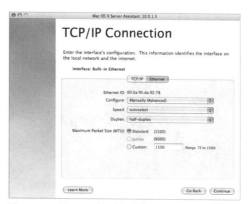

Figure 2.31 Choose a method for TCP/IP connectivity.

Figure 2.32 The speed of the Ethernet interface(s) can be set.

11. In the Directory Usage window, choose a way to implement directory services (**Figure 2.33**).

▲ If you're starting from scratch, you'll likely choose Standalone Server.

▲ If you choose Connected to a Directory System and click Continue, a few options will be available in the Connect to Directory window. Refer to the Initial Directory usage and setup options section for an explanation of these options.

▲ Don't choose Open Directory Master at this point, because it may not set up properly.

12. In the Services window, select the services you want to start immediately after the Server Assistant finishes and the server restarts (any checked services will also start up anytime the server is restarted after setup is finished) (**Figure 2.34**).

Starting unnecessary services can slow down your server and present security risks. Turn on only the services you absolutely need.

13. Set the appropriate time zone in the Time Zone window (**Figure 2.35**).

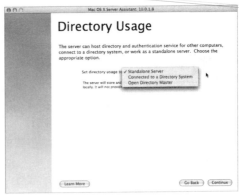

Figure 2.33 In the Directory Usage window, choose a way to implement initial directory services.

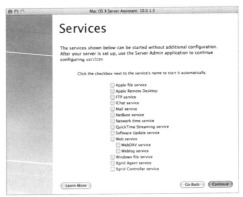

Figure 2.34 Decide which services to start.

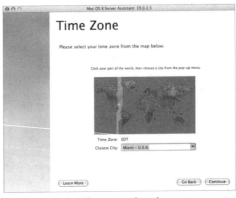

Figure 2.35 Select the appropriate time zone.

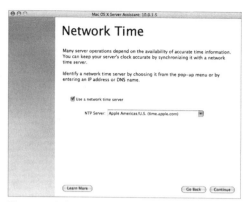

Figure 2.36 Choose whether to connect to a time server.

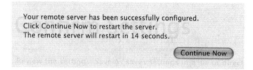

Figure 2.37 The settings were applied successfully. Click Continue Now to reboot Mac OS X Server.

14. In the Network Time window, select the "Use a network time server" check box to provide your system with updated time data and, if you have a local time server, select it from the NTP Server list (**Figure 2.36**).

Before you complete the next step, you may wish to save your settings to a file (see the next section, "Saving Configuration Settings").

15. Finally, confirm your settings and if you are not interested in saving your settings for use later (see the next section), click Apply.

16. In the next window, indicating that the settings were applied successfully, click Continue Now to reboot Mac OS X Server (**Figure 2.37**).

You can now log in and begin exploring Mac OS X Server. If you completed this process from a remote Mac OS X computer, you can begin trying the other server tools.

✔ Tips

■ Mac OS X Server comes in two flavors: a 10-user license and an unlimited user license (defined as the number of simultaneous users that can connect to the server). The serial number controls this license. You can change the serial number any time on Mac OS X Server if you choose to upgrade your server from the 10-user license to the unlimited one.

■ When doing remote installations and configuration, make sure you actually install the Admin Tools rather than copying them from another system, because some of the tools in the System folder are hard to find.

RUNNING SERVER ASSISTANT

Saving Configuration Settings

The Server Assistant's Confirm Settings window gives you the option of saving your configuration settings (**Figure 2.38**). Doing so has several benefits. You can save a small test file to a local USB storage device or iPod and transfer these settings to a clean installation of Server, thus saving you from typing in the information again. You may also want to create a clone of your server or quickly reformat and reinstall your server software after a severe disk failure. In addition, you can save the configuration to another directory server on your network in case a server needs reformatting. You can reformat the server and pull down the initial settings again, saving you from running through the Server Assistant repeatedly. **Table 2.1** lists the possible ways to save your configuration settings.

When you're saving configuration settings, choose the method that best fits your infrastructure. Saving to a text file doesn't allow encryption, so anyone can open the file and see your configuration settings. You can save the file anywhere, but the best idea is to save it on a USB device, an iPod, or another storage device.

Figure 2.38 The server setup Confirm Settings window displays all the options and parameters you've chosen during the initial setup.

Table 2.1

Saving directory data options

SAVING OPTION	SAVE LOCATION	ENCRYPTION?
Text file	Any connected device	No
Configuration file	Any connected device	Optional
Directory record	Other directory server	Optional

Directory Records

When you save your server setup information to a directory record, all the server setup information is placed inside a NetInfo database on Mac OS X or a standalone Mac OS X Server. If you have created an LDAP database on your server (as you will in the next chapter), you also have the option of saving it there.

Figure 2.39 If you save the configuration settings as a configuration property list file, the Ethernet address(es) is used as the filename.

There are several built-in Ethernet ports in the target server.
The MAC addresses are 000a77da7278 000a77f27bff

Do you want to save the settings for each MAC address in a separate file? If not, only one file will be saved, named using the MAC address of the first port listed in the Network Interfaces pane.

No   Yes

Figure 2.40 This dialog asks how you want to dsave the settings for each Mac address.

Save settings
Select Text File to save a record of your settings in a text file.

Select Configuration File or Directory Record to save settings for automatic server setup. If settings are for a specific server, name the file or record using a unique identifier, such as IP address. If settings are for multiple servers, name the file or record "generic".

Select Save in Encrypted Format to encrypt the saved settings, then enter and verify a passphrase.

Save as: ○ Text File
○ Configuration File
◉ Directory Record
☐ Save in Encrypted Format.
Passphrase:

Directory Node: Other...

BSD
LDAPv3   172.16.61.18

Record Name: 000a77da7278

Cancel   OK

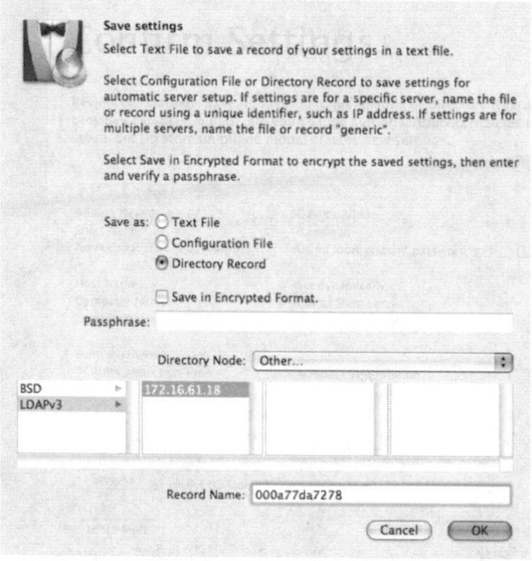

Figure 2.41 You can save the file as a directory record in another directory server.

Another method is to save the configuration settings as a configuration property list file. Doing so allows for encryption of the file, and the Ethernet address is automatically used as the name of the file (**Figure 2.39**). If you have more than one Ethernet address configured for Mac OS X Server, you may see a dialog asking how the file should be saved (**Figure 2.40**). To allow for automatic setup, place the file inside a folder called Auto Server Setup on a removable storage device. You can also change the name of the configuration property list file to generic.plist. When you do this, any server can use the file to configure itself with the parameters contained in that particular property list file.

The third option is to save the file in a directory record. Doing so creates the file inside another Mac OS X or Mac OS X Server. When a freshly installed (and not configured) copy of Mac OS X Server reboots, depending on how the *other* Mac OS X Server on the network is configured, it will discover the configuration plist LDAP directory record on the local network and automatically configure itself (**Figure 2.41**).

In the next exercise, you'll save your initial server settings as a configuration file, which may come in handy should you need to reformat and reinstall your server. It ensures all your initial settings are exactly as they were when you first installed Mac OS X Server.

SAVING CONFIGURATION SETTINGS

To save initial server settings:

1. In the Confirm Settings window, click Save As in the lower-left corner (**Figure 2.42**).

2. In the "Save settings" window that appears, select Configuration File from the list of options and enter a passphrase, if you want to associate one with the file; then click OK (**Figure 2.43**).

3. Insert a USB, FireWire, or another storage device, such as an iPod, if you have one.

   If you don't have one, you can save the file elsewhere on a local or remote volume for later use.

4. Decide whether you wish to keep the Ethernet address as the filename or change the name to generic.plist, an IP address, or a hostname—they can all be used in one manner or another to define a server.

   Keeping the Ethernet address ties that file to the server with that address (**Figure 2.44**).

5. Before you save the file, expand the Save dialog and create a folder called Auto Server Setup at the base level of the device.

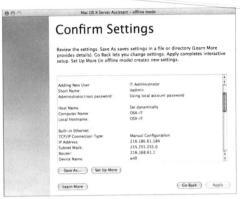

Figure 2.42 The Confirm Settings window is used to save the server configuration.

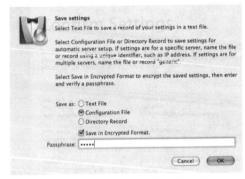

Figure 2.43 You can save the configuration with a passphrase.

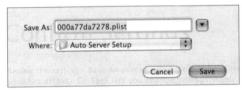

Figure 2.44 Saving the configuration file on a removable USB or FireWire device allows for automatic configuration upon another installation.

6. Transfer the file to a remote storage device if you haven't done so, and save the file inside the Auto Server Setup folder.

7. If you saved the file to your server's hard disk, click Apply to apply the settings.

You do not have to click Apply if the file is saved in a folder called Auto Server Setup on a mounted USB or FireWire device. The Mac OS X Server computer will begin automatically configuring your server.

Reapplying server settings

In some cases, you may wish to erase your hard disk and install Mac OS X Server again from scratch. Doing so means you must go through the entire setup again, which can lead to errors if you are trying to repeat the exact settings that you had before. To reapply the server settings, you first need to install the server software and erase and reformat the disk(s) running it. After the Mac OS X Server DVD finishes its installation, the server will reboot itself and display the Welcome Setup Screen. After the reboot, plug in the FireWire or USB device and the automatic configuration should take place shortly. To encrypt the file from prying eyes, you can supply an initial passphrase when configuring a remote server by choosing Supply Passphrase (Cmd+G) under the File menu of Server Assistant.

SAVING CONFIGURATION SETTINGS

Server Admin Overview

The Server Admin tool is where you start
and stop, configure, and monitor most of
the services Mac OS X Server has to offer.
You can also change the serial number, computer name, and Bonjour name; run Software
Update; set the date, time, and time zone;
and enable a few advanced options (discussed
in later chapters).

Since Server Admin is part of the Server
Administration Software package, it can be
installed on any Mac OS X computer (running
version 10.4). As a result, multiple servers
can be administered from virtually anywhere,
provided the server has a public IP address.

The first time you launch Server Admin, you'll
need to connect to your server. A Connect
dialog will appear within the Server Admin
window. Depending on where you're physically located, you have three options:

◆ A direct connection to the server.

   If you're doing this on the server, the
   Address field contains the Bonjour name
   of the server and the logged-in administrator's long name (**Figure 2.45**).

◆ A connection from another Mac OS X
   Server or Mac OS X computer running
   the Server Admin tool on your local net-
   work/subnet.

   You can click Browse (Browse...) in the
   Server Admin Connect dialog and search
   for your server on your local network, or
   type in the known IP address or fully
   qualified domain name.

◆ A remote connection from anywhere
   around the globe, provided your server
   has a public IP address or fully qualified
   domain name.

   You'll need to have the IP address or fully
   qualified domain name handy for entry
   into the Address field.

Figure 2.45 Enter your administrator name and
password, choose whether you wish to add the
password to your keychain, and click Connect.

Figure 2.46 The main view of Server Admin showing all connected servers on the left.

Figure 2.47 The Server Admin Toolbar lets you add, remove, disconnect from, and refresh your server information.

Figure 2.48 Using the Search function displays only those services with the searched character string.

You'll enter your administrator name and password, choose whether you want to add the password to your keychain so you don't have to type it in later, and click Connect.

Once you're connected, you'll see your server in the left frame of Server Admin (**Figure 2.46**). Clicking the disclosure triangle expands or contracts your server, showing or hiding all the services available on that server. Clicking the server address will display some of the advanced server settings. Alternately, clicking any service shows you that service's settings and options in the right frame of the window.

Across the top is the Toolbar, which lets you add, remove, disconnect from, and refresh your server information (**Figure 2.47**). You can also create a new Server Admin window from the Toolbar, as well as launch the other main server management tool, Workgroup Manager. If you've selected a service, you may also see a Start Service button in the Toolbar. To customize your Toolbar, choose View > Customize Toolbar.

The Search bar permits you to just show services that have whatever letter is typed into the window. For example, typing "we" would only show Web and WebObjects (**Figure 2.48**).

In addition, you have two view options. You can view all your services and their respective status by choosing View > Show Summary, and you can quickly see your users and groups by choosing View > Show User Records (**Figure 2.49**). The former option displays the services and their status horizontally (**Figure 2.50**), and the latter opens a drawer on the left or right of the Server Admin tool that lets you see all the users and groups (**Figure 2.51**).

You'll probably access the Server Admin tool frequently, so you may benefit from adding your server(s) to a Favorites list that gives you menu and keyboard shortcuts to the server(s). To do this, launch the Server Admin tool, choose Favorites > Add To Favorites, and select your server. You can now access your server when launching Server Admin by heading to the Favorites menu and choosing your server or using the Command key and the number associated with your server in the Favorites menu.

Figure 2.49 Choosing the View menu displays options such as Show Summary and Show User Records.

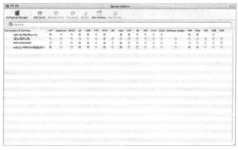

Figure 2.50 Choosing View > Show Summary displays services and their status horizontally.

Figure 2.51 Choosing View > Show User Records opens a drawer on the left or right of the Server Admin tool that lets you see all the users and groups.

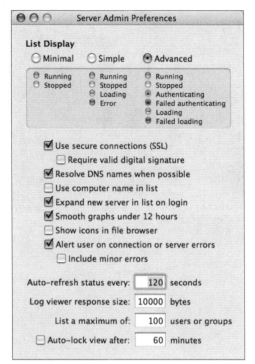

Figure 2.52 You can customize Server Admin in the Server Admin Preferences dialog.

Setting Server Admin preferences

To customize Server Admin to further suit your needs, choose Preferences from the Server Admin menu. Some of the major options available to you are as follows (**Figure 2.52**):

◆ You can change the list display from Simple to Advanced, which will provide you with more information about how services are operating.

◆ You can (although not recommended) disable secure connections, or (better) provide a specific (yours) SSL certificate to be used when creating the SSL connection to your server. The digital signature option is discussed in Chapter 10.

This option is especially important when you're administering a server from halfway around the world.

◆ The "Resolve DNS names when possible" option is used when servers have a properly configured DNS (discussed in Chapter 6).

Server Admin can also be used for the following via the tabs located at the bottom of the window (**Figure 2.53**):

◆ View various log files such as the system.log

◆ Check server network status

◆ Check volume usage information and user/group quotas

◆ Graph CPU usage and network utilization over time

◆ Run Software Update

◆ Change serial number

◆ Enable additional services such as permitting Mac OS X Server to become a network time server and allow the examination of the server via the Simple Network Management Protocol (SNMP)

◆ Change the computer name, Bonjour (localhost) name, date, time, and time zone

◆ Create and manage certificates to be used for various services (certificates will be covered in Chapter 10, "Security")

◆ Use service access controls to restrict access to various services based on user and/or group affiliation

✔ Tips

■ When setting up Mac OS X Server for the first time, the time zone you chose using Server Assistant may not be respected after the reboot and sometimes defaults back to Cupertino. You should use Server Admin to check the time zone and correct it before proceeding to set up other services.

■ If you're working directly on the server, you'll notice that the Server Admin tool is already in the Dock. If you're working remotely, you may wish to add the Server Admin tool to the Dock.

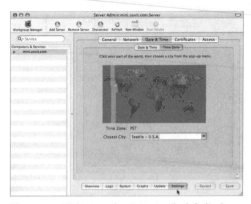

Figure 2.53 Clicking on the server on the left displays the Settings tab for various options when dealing with your server.

Figure 2.54 Choose Settings and then the Access tab to reveal the service access controls.

Figure 2.55 Using Service access controls to limit the users who can log in via ssh.

Figure 2.56 You must restart the ssh daemon to take advantage of the access controls.

To restrict access to the ssh service:

1. Launch the Server Admin tool, located in /Applications/Server, and select your server from the Computers and Services list.

   If you have not already added your server to the keychain, you must authenticate now as well.

2. Click Settings and then click Access in the pane to the right of the Computers and Services list (**Figure 2.54**).

3. Deselect the "Use same access for all services" check box and select the ssh service from the Service list.

4. Click the "Allow only user and groups below" radio button and then the plus button below to add yourself and any other users to Name list (**Figure 2.55**).

5. Click Save to permit only the selected users to log in via ssh.

6. Restart the ssh service by deselecting and selecting the box named *ssh* under the General tab to enable the access controls (**Figure 2.56**).

✔ Tips

- Do not restrict access to services that others may need when using home folders, such as AFP (and if secure connections are being used, ssh). A good way to restrict access to all services is to deny all users access except the server administrator. In this fashion you can ensure all services cannot be accessed unless permission is granted via the services access control mechanism.

- Restricting ssh, while increasing security, can prevent Mac OS X Server from working within an Open Directory Master/Replica scenario. If you want your Mac OS X Server to participate in this process, keep an eye on the system log for ssh attempts and adjust your user's ssh access accordingly.

- If you restrict access to the Login window, you may inadvertently lock yourself out of your own server via the Login window, and not be able to log in to the server at all via the GUI.

Server Admin and Unix

Server Admin has a counterpart in the command line called serveradmin. You can run this tool from the server directly or, when you're connected to the server, from a remote machine via ssh. serveradmin has many options and can be used just like its GUI counterpart. Consult the man page for serveradmin to learn about all the features.

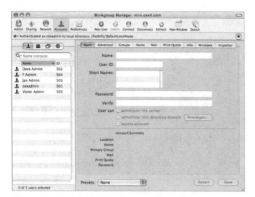

Figure 2.57 Workgroup Manager is another frequently used tool.

Using Workgroup Manager

Workgroup Manager is another tool you'll use frequently when you're managing Mac OS X Server (**Figure 2.57**). The main job of Workgroup Manager is to manage users and groups; add share points such as folders and volumes; create specific network views; and edit preferences for users, groups, and computer accounts. You can access Workgroup Manager directly via Server Admin and vice versa, using the top-left icon in the Toolbar.

Like other tools in the Server folder, Workgroup Manager can be run locally and remotely; the authentication process is identical to that of Server Admin. The first time you launch Workgroup Manager, you'll need to connect to your server. A dialog will appear from the Workgroup Manager window. Depending on where you're physically located, you have three options:

◆ A direct connection to the server.

If you're doing this on the server, the Address field contains the Bonjour name of the server and the logged-in administrator's name.

◆ A connection from another Mac OS X Server or Mac OS X computer running the Workgroup Manager tool on your local network/subnet.

You can click Browse (Browse...) in the Workgroup Manager Connect dialog and search for your server on your local network.

◆ A remote connection from anywhere around the globe, provided your server has a public IP address or fully qualified domain name.

You'll need to have the IP address or fully qualified domain name handy for entry into the Address field.

Address Name Differences

In certain cases, you may see another name in the Address field. This may be due to the TCP/IP information you entered. If you entered a DNS address, you may have a domain name for your server assigned by another Domain Name Server. A *fully qualified domain name* is another name that is related to the IP address you have for your server. This name may be out of your control if you aren't the administrator of that Domain Name Server.

The basics of DNS and Domain Name Server are covered in Chapter 6.

Enter your administrator name password, choose whether you wish to add the password to your keychain so you don't have to type it in later, and click Connect (Connect) (**Figure 2.58**).

✔ Tip

- If you're working directly on the server, you'll notice that the Workgroup Manager tool is already in the Dock. If you're working remotely, you may wish to add the Workgroup Manager tool to the Dock.

The Workgroup Manager Toolbar gives you access to the following buttons (from left to right) (**Figure 2.59**):

- **Admin**, which launches the Server Admin tool

- Buttons that narrow the focus of Workgroup Manager to three specific areas:
  - ▲ **Sharing** settings
  - ▲ **Network** view settings
  - ▲ **Accounts** management, which lets you manage users, groups, and computers
  - ▲ **Preferences** settings for user, groups, and/or computers

- **New User** and **Delete** for account management

- **Connect**, **Disconnect**, and **Refresh**

- **New Window**, which creates a new Workgroup Manager window for the server You might use this option to view users in one window and groups in another.

- **Search**, which when clicked displays a dialog permitting the administrator to display only users based on given set of criteria and subsequently perform batch editing on the results of the query (**Figure 2.60**).

Figure 2.58 In the Workgroup Manager Connect dialog, enter your administrator name password, choose whether you wish to add the password to your keychain, and click Connect.

Figure 2.59 The Workgroup Manager toolbar gives you access to a variety of useful buttons.

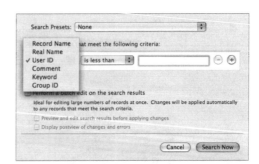

Figure 2.60 The Search button reveals the set criteria and batch editing dialog.

USING WORKGROUP MANAGER

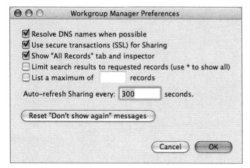

Figure 2.61 The Workgroup Manager Directory drop-down menu lets you select directories you're authenticated to see.

Figure 2.62 Choose Preferences from the Workgroup Manager menu to open the Workgroup Manager Preferences dialog.

In the pop-up menu directly beneath the Toolbar on the left, you can select various directories you're authenticated to see (directories are discussed in the next chapter). By clicking the globe or triangle, you can see those directories (at this point you may only see the local directory) (**Figure 2.61**).

Altering Workgroup Manager preferences

Workgroup Manager has preferences that affect how you'll use this tool, regardless of the server(s) you connect to. Choose Preferences from the Workgroup Manager menu to see some of these important options (**Figure 2.62**):

◆ **Resolve DNS names when possible—** This option is used when servers have properly configured DNS (discussed in Chapter 6).

◆ **Use secure transactions (SSL) for Sharing** (secure connections are discussed in Chapter 10, "Security").

continues on next page

◆ **Show "All Records" tab and inspector**—You can show the Inspector tab (to be discussed in Chapter 4, "User and Group Management"), which lets you see and edit attributes for user, group, or computer accounts on both the local and LDAP databases. This tab becomes incredibly useful when you're doing such advanced editing as adding attributes to users (attributes are discussed in the next chapter). The All Records tab [icons] permits other record types to be edited (such as configuration records, printer records, or mount records, to name just a few). The All Records tab and Inspector should be shown all the time to facilitate and foster constant learning when working with Mac OS X Server.

◆ **Limit search results to requested records** and **List a maximum of () records**—These options become important in large organizations where you have thousands of records. You may wish to show only 500 and do searches for the rest. Chapter 4 covers searching for account records.

◆ **Auto-refresh Sharing**—You can auto-refresh this portion of Workgroup Manager more or less frequently.

✔ Tips

■ In both Workgroup Manager and Server Admin (as well as most other applications), you can use the combination of the Command and comma keys to open the Preferences window.

■ You can show system users and groups, including root and those used by various services by selecting the menu View > Show System Users and Groups. These are hidden by default; you shouldn't change any parameters to the system users and groups unless you're absolutely sure of the result.

Managing Workgroup Manager

Workgroup Manager is used to enter or import user and group information. You can also use it to view and edit accounts not located on a Mac OS X Server. Although this topic is more advanced than this chapter can explore, it's useful to understand how important Workgroup Manager is in your daily dealings with Mac OS X Server.

USING WORKGROUP MANAGER

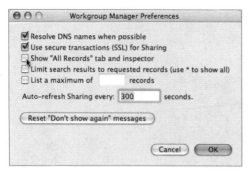

Figure 2.63 The Inspector tab check box in Workgroup Manager.

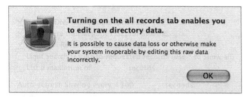

Figure 2.64 A warning dialog tells you that you can lose data or make your system inoperable by editing raw attributes.

To add the All Records tab and Inspector to your view:

1. Launch the Workgroup Manager tool located in /Applications/Server and authenticate if necessary 🛡.

   You don't need to authenticate, although you can.

2. Choose Preferences from the Workgroup Manager menu.

3. In the window that appears, select the "Show 'All Records' tab and inspector" check box (**Figure 2.63**).

4. Click OK to close the Preferences window.

5. A warning dialog tells you that you can possibly lose data or make your system inoperable by editing raw attributes.

   Click OK to dismiss the dialog (**Figure 2.64**).

   If you click the Accounts icon 👤, regardless of account type (user, group, computer), you'll see an additional tab at the end of the account types 👤 👥 🖥 ◉ and an additional tab at the end of the account configuration frame Inspector. This tab will be discussed in more detail in Chapter 4.

✔ Tip

- Add your server to the Favorites menu in Workgroup Manager by launching Workgroup Manager, entering your server information, authenticating, and choosing your server from the Add to Favorites selection from the Favorites menu.

Adding users to your Mac OS X Server

Mac OS X Server can have more than one directory database (discussed in the next chapter). However, you can quickly add users to Mac OS X Server using Workgroup Manager. You'll add users to the local database at this point, but the process of adding them to another directory database is the same.

It is important to note that on Mac OS X you use the Accounts Preference Pane of System Preferences to add users. You can also use this method on Mac OS X Server. In each case, users are added to the local NetInfo database. When a user is created with the Accounts Preference Pane, Setup Assistant (Mac OS X), or Server Assistant (Mac OS X Server), they are added to the local NetInfo database with a user ID of 501 and up. Each user has a group created just for them using the short name of the user. Subsequently, they are the only member in their group. When you use Workgroup Manager to create users on Mac OS X or Mac OS X Server, user IDs start at 1024 and users are members of the *staff* group and do not have a group based on their name. While this does not inherently cause issues, it is worth noting. A good rule to follow is to use the Accounts Preference Pane when dealing with Mac OS X and Workgroup Manager when dealing with Mac OS X Server.

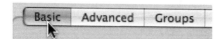

Figure 2.65 Selecting the Basic tab of the User settings in Workgroup Manager.

To add user accounts to Mac OS X Server:

1. Launch the Workgroup Manager tool located in /Applications/Server and authenticate if necessary.

2. In the Toolbar, select Accounts ![accounts icon], and in the Account Types tab, select the User tab ![user icon].

3. In the user settings frame on the right, select the Basic tab (**Figure 2.65**). In the Toolbar, click New User ![new user icon].

4. Enter the following information in the appropriate fields:

    Name—The full name of the user, such as Bob Abooie.

    User ID—Already entered for you in this case. A unique ID that Mac OS X Server (and Client) uses to enforce folder and file permissions.

    Short Names—The user's short name(s). For compatibility with older operating systems, this name should only use letters (usually lowercase) and numbers and be more than five characters, such as bobabooie or abooie. Additional short names can be longer if you wish.

    Password and **Verify**—Passwords should include a variety of characters and both uppercase and lowercase letters. Passwords can be well over 64 characters long; however, this is impractical, and not all computer software that requires authentication can accept such a long character string, such as other authentication systems that keep their own password database.

    continues on next page

Privileges and Permissions

For most purposes (and the purposes of this book), *privileges* and *permissions* mean the same thing: what a user is authorized to do. That may be reading the contents of a folder or opening a file. Mac OS 9 and ASIP use the term *privileges*. Mac OS X and Mac OS X Server largely use the term *permissions*. Apple does use the word *privileges* when dealing with administration of users, groups, and computers, as you'll see in Chapter 4, but this has nothing to do with the ability to access disks, folders, and files.

5. In the Workgroup Manager window, click Save 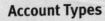.

There are many other options when adding users, as you'll see in Chapter 4.

✔ Tip

■ Both Server Admin and Workgroup Manager will be used to manage Mac OS X Server for the remainder of this book. You might want to take the time to click the various icons in their respective Toolbars and familiarize yourself with these buttons.

Account Types

To switch between user, group, and computer lists, click the Accounts button in the Toolbar and then select the icon that corresponds to the account type.

When you choose each account type, you'll notice the settings (tabs) for those account types change (in the settings frame to the right in Workgroup Manager) based on the account type:

◆ User account settings tabs (**Figure 2.66**)

◆ Group account settings tabs (**Figure 2.67**)

◆ Computer account settings tabs (**Figure 2.68**)

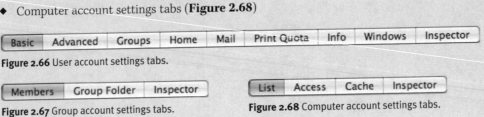

Figure 2.66 User account settings tabs.

Figure 2.67 Group account settings tabs.

Figure 2.68 Computer account settings tabs.

Migration and Compatibility Tools Overview

Not every Mac OS X Server is born from an empty disk. Sometimes previous server versions can't be erased and upgrades must be performed. When you're upgrading a previous version of Mac OS X Server or AppleShare IP, you can take advantage of some tools that not only ease migration, but also allow for the management of older Macintosh operating systems, such as 8.6 and/or 9.2. You may also want to manage services not directly manageable by either Server Admin or Workgroup Manager. Apple provides tools to manage these services.

You will first examine the AppleShare IP Migration tool and later learn how to do an in-place upgrade from earlier versions of Mac OS X Server.

Using the AppleShare IP Migration tool

The AppleShare IP Migration tool is used to upgrade server settings from AppleShare IP (ASIP) to Mac OS X Server 10.4. Specifically, this tool updates users and groups, share points, permissions, and the mail database. It's important to understand, however, that using the ASIP Migration tool is only one step in the series of steps necessary to migrate and update the entirety of your server.

There are two methods: migrating to an entirely new server, or migrating in place by upgrading an existing server to Mac OS X Server. The path you choose will determine how you use the ASIP Migration tool. If you're migrating a server in place, all the functions of the ASIP Migration tool work properly. But if you're migrating to a new server, you can't use the ASIP Migration tool to migrate share points and privileges: Your shared folders must be copied to the new server and configured manually (configuration of share points is covered in Chapter 5, "File Sharing").

Similarly, you shouldn't use the ASIP Migration tool to move user and group accounts to a new server. It's best to export a user and group settings file from ASIP and then import that file directly into Workgroup Manager. (The import and export tools are covered in Chapter 4.)

✔ Tips

- It's strongly suggested that you back up your data and perform a clean installation on an empty, freshly formatted disk whenever possible.

- Realistically, when you're moving to a new server, the only proper use for the ASIP Migration tool is to migrate the mail database. A clean installation is always better than an upgrade.

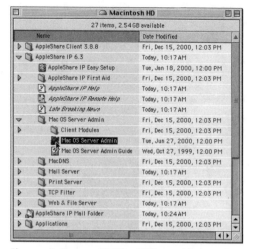

Figure 2.69 To open the Mac OS Server Admin tool, choose /AppleShare IP 6.3/Mac OS Server Admin/Mac OS Server Admin.

Figure 2.70 Connect and authenticate to your ASIP server.

Figure 2.71 Click the Users and Groups icon, and then select Show Users & Groups List from the drop-down menu.

To upgrade from ASIP to Mac OS X Server using ASIP Migration:

1. On your ASIP server, choose /AppleShare IP 6.3/Mac OS Server Admin/Mac OS Server Admin to open the Mac OS Server Admin tool (**Figure 2.69**).

2. Connect and authenticate to your ASIP server (**Figure 2.70**).

   The Server Admin window opens.

3. Click the Users and Groups icon, and then select Show Users & Groups List from the pull-down menu (**Figure 2.71**).

   The Users & Groups list appears.

4. Double-click any user in the list to open an edit window for that user (**Figure 2.72**).

continues on next page

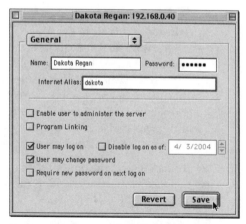

Figure 2.72 In the user edit dialog, it is very important to assign an Internet alias name.

MIGRATION AND COMPATIBILITY TOOLS OVERVIEW

5. Be sure to assign an Internet alias name, which is what Mac OS X Server uses for the user's short name, and then click Save.

6. Install and configure Mac OS X Server. Please refer to Chapter 1, "Planning and Installation," and the beginning of this chapter for installation and configuration information.

7. Choose /Applications/Server/ AppleShare IP Migration to open the ASIP Migration tool .

8. Select the migration options you want by clicking the various check boxes (**Figure 2.73**).

9. At the bottom of the AppleShare IP Migration window, *select either of the following options* to handle duplicate user names:

▲ **Do not migrate the AppleShare user**—Ignores the duplicate accounts.

▲ **Migrate the AppleShare user's privileges and mail to the Mac OS X Server user**—Only moves permissions and mail settings. You'll use this choice when you're moving to an entirely new server and you've already imported the users and groups into Workgroup Manager, but you now need to migrate the mail database.

10. Click the lock icon at the bottom of the dialog, and authenticate as an administrative user.

11. Click Migrate to begin the conversion process (**Figure 2.74**).

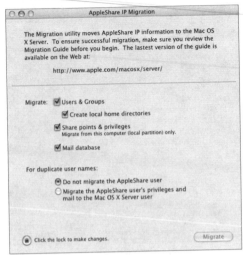

Figure 2.73 Select the migration options you want in the AppleShare IP Migration dialog.

Figure 2.74 Click the lock icon to authenticate and the Migrate button to start the migration process.

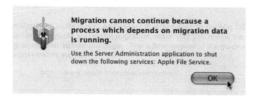

Figure 2.75 A warning dialog may appear if a related service is running while you're using the migration tool.

Figure 2.76 Specify where the ASIP users and groups database file is located.

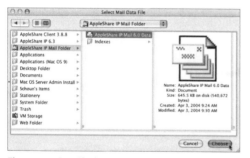

Figure 2.77 Specify the ASIP mail database's location.

12. You may have to use the Server Admin tool to temporarily disable certain services, such as the AFP service, to continue (**Figure 2.75**).

You should disable services to reduce the chance of an error when performing an upgrade.

The Select Users & Groups Data File window opens.

13. Choose System Folder > Preferences > Users & Groups Data File and specify where the ASIP users and groups database file is located; then click Choose (**Figure 2.76**).

14. Specify the ASIP mail database's location, and click Choose (**Figure 2.77**).

Typically this file is located in the /AppleShare IP Mail Folder.

15. The ASIP Migration tool will show a progress bar while it migrates your settings.

When the migration is finished, you should verify the migration process by checking the imported settings from the Mac OS X Server tools. Additionally, a variety of migration log files are located in the /Library/Logs/Migration folder.

✔ Tips

- The ASIP utility will only import users into the local directory. If you need to import users into a shared directory, use the Import function in Workgroup Manager, which is discussed in Chapter 4.

- Always make a complete backup of your ASIP server before migrating or installing a new system. It's also a good idea to set Internet aliases for your user accounts before migration.

- The ASIP user Internet alias will be used as the short name on OS X Server.

Macintosh Manager Overview

Mac OS X Server can support user and group management on older versions of the Macintosh operating system, in case you need to support them. This is good, because Mac OS 9 and Mac OS X are clearly very different operating systems; thus they require different applications for user preference management.

The Workgroup Manager tool is used to manage Mac OS X user preferences, whereas the Macintosh Manager tool is used to manage Mac OS 9 user preferences. Furthermore, Workgroup Manager uses Open Directory to store all user information, whereas Macintosh Manager uses a separate database for managed user preferences.

However, Macintosh Manager still uses Open Directory for user authentication. In other words, you use Workgroup Manager to create and manage all user accounts, but you must use Macintosh Manager to control any user's Mac OS 9 preferences.

To enable Macintosh Manager on an upgraded server:

1. Launch Server Admin and authenticate to the server you intend to configure.

2. Select the server name or address from the service list, click Settings, and then click the General tab (**Figure 2.78**).

3. Select the Enable Macintosh Manager check box in the Settings window (**Figure 2.79**).

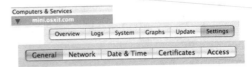

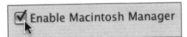

Figure 2.78 Select the server name or address from the service list, click the Settings button, and then click the General tab.

☑ Enable Macintosh Manager

Figure 2.79 Select the Enable Macintosh Manager check box if this is an upgrade; otherwise the check box will not exist.

Macintosh Manager In-Place Upgrade

Macintosh Manager is only available if the version of Mac OS X Server 10.4 is an in-place upgrade of Mac OS X Server 10.3 or 10.2. If that is the case, then you can enable Macintosh Manager.

MACINTOSH MANAGER OVERVIEW

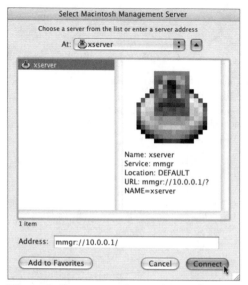

Figure 2.80 You can manually type the server's name or address in the Select Macintosh Management Server dialog.

Figure 2.81 Macintosh Manager has no keychain integration, so you'll always have to authenticate.

4. Click Save.

The Server Admin tool automatically configures the Macintosh Manager share points and database files. The Macintosh Manager service will start up automatically from this point forward whenever the server is restarted.

5. Open the Macintosh Manager tool by choosing /Applications/Server/ Macintosh Manager 🔲.

6. Double-click the Macintosh Manager tool; it will launch and search for the server.

You can also manually type the server's name or address in the Select Macintosh Management Server dialog (**Figure 2.80**).

7. Authenticate with your administrator account (**Figure 2.81**).

Note that there is no keychain integration in Macintosh Manager, so you'll always have to authenticate when you want to manage this service. You're presented with the Macintosh Manager interface. From here, you can import user accounts into the Macintosh Manager database and manage their Mac OS 9 preferences.

✔ Tips

■ The Macintosh Manager tool is the only server tool that will run on both Mac OS 9 and Mac OS X or Mac OS X Server.

■ It's good practice to use Macintosh Manager from Mac OS X, because it's easier to configure certain client-specific settings.

MACINTOSH MANAGER OVERVIEW

MySQL Manager Overview

MySQL (Structured Query Language) is an open source relational database management system that is primarily used on Mac OS X Server as part of a dynamic Web site. The MySQL Manager tool is designed to set up and enable the MySQL service with the default settings. MySQL is complicated and is typically managed using command-line tools and text configuration files. However, free detailed documentation is available at www.mysql.com/documentation/.

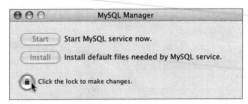

Figure 2.82 Click the lock, and authenticate as an administrative user to set up MySQL files.

To enable MySQL:

1. On your server, open the MySQL Manager tool by choosing /Applications/ _Server/MySQL Manager 🌐.

2. Click the lock icon, and authenticate as an administrative user (**Figure 2.82**).

   You must do this in order to enable the Install button.

3. Click Install to install the default files needed for the MySQL service.

   You must do this in order to enable the Start button.

4. Once the MySQL files are installed, click Start to start the MySQL service.

✔ Tip

■ Although doing so isn't required to use MySQL, installing the Mac OS X Developer Tools (Xcode) is highly recommended. Xcode includes many of the tools used to build Web-based applications.

Figure 2.83 After launching Internet Gateway Assistant, you must authenticate to your server.

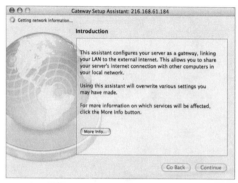

Figure 2.84 The Introduction dialog briefly explains what the Internet Gateway Assistant does.

Gateway Setup Assistant Overview

Mac OS X Server can be used as a virtual private network (VPN) server or a DHCP server, and it can provide Network Address Translation (NAT). While each of these services can be set up separately, Gateway Setup Assistant permits the basic and quick setup of each of these services.

Gateway Setup Assistant is useful when a novice user wishes to quickly provide Internet access through a Mac OS X Server.

To run Gateway Setup Assistant:

1. On your server, open the Gateway Setup Assistant tool by choosing /Applications/_Server/Gateway.

2. Enter your address information, authenticate, and click Connect (**Figure 2.83**).

   The Introduction pane appears (**Figure 2.84**).

   continues on next page

3. Click past the Introduction pane, choose the interface that connects to the Internet (WAN or Wide Area Network) and click Continue (**Figure 2.85**).

4. Choose the LAN (Local Area Network) interface that will provide addresses to an internal network and click Continue (**Figure 2.86**).

5. Choose whether or not to enable virtual private networking (VPN) via Layer Two Tunneling Protocol over IP Security (L2TP over IPSec); if so, decide on the shared secret to be used and click Continue (**Figure 2.87**).

Keep in mind that the shared secret—when typed—appears in clear text.

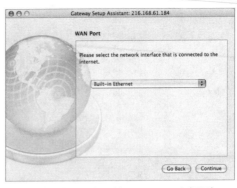

Figure 2.85 Choose the wide area network (WAN) interface that connects to the Internet.

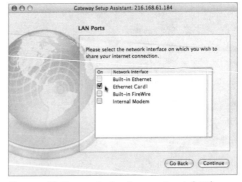

Figure 2.86 Choose the local area network (LAN) interface that connects to the internal network.

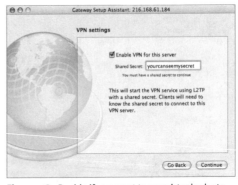

Figure 2.87 Decide if you want to use virtual private networking (VPN) services.

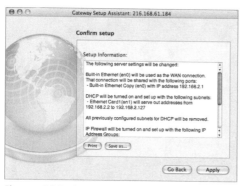

Figure 2.88 Review your settings and save them to a text file before applying them.

6. Scroll through your "Confirm setup" pane and click Save As to save the configuration for backup purposes (**Figure 2.88**).

7. Click Apply to setup basic Network Address Translation and possible VPN services.

✔ Tip

■ While Gateway Setup Assistant is easy to use, it does not permit a more granular set of options. If you use Gateway Setup Assistant, please familiarize yourself with both NAT and VPN at the very least.

Xgrid Admin Overview

Xgrid is software that permits several Mac OS X computers to use their idle processing power to complete tasks deployed by an Xgrid administrator. Xgrid Admin ⚙ works in conjunction with the Xgrid service (set up with Server Admin) and Xgrid Agents (Mac OS X 10.4 computers) (**Figure 2.89**).

Figure 2.89 The Xgrid Admin tool is used to manage Xgrid clients and jobs.

Using Server Monitor

The Apple Xserve hardware has a number of unique features, including a 1U rack mount form-factor, blower fans, and fast-swap hardware. Xserve also includes built-in real-time hardware monitoring and diagnostic tools. The Server Monitor tool is the user interface for this feature.

The Server Monitor tool can run on any Mac OS X computer or Mac OS X Server and monitor hundreds of different Xserves simultaneously. Server Monitor also has the ability to automatically notify you, via email and/or paging services, when there is a potential problem. Initially, there are no Xserves in the Server Monitor list; you must add any computer you want to monitor.

Xserve

Apple introduced the Xserve as a solution for enterprise customers who wanted a rack-mounted solution while still using Apple hardware. The G4 Xserve came with four hot-swappable disk bays and the ability to use Gigabit and/or fiber connections. The G5 Xserve has three available hot-swappable disk bays and similar options for networking. Each Xserve comes with a CD drive for installing the software.

The main difference between the Xserve and running Mac OS X Server on another Apple product is that the Xserve was designed to be managed remotely. You don't generally sit in front of an Xserve to install software or configure Mac OS X Server. While you can purchase a video card for either Xserve (allowing you to plug in a video monitor), you can just as easily manage your Xserve remotely from another room or another state.

If you choose to manage your Xserve remotely, you must to know how to use command-line tools. Installing and initial configuration can easily be done remotely, but you'll use such command-line tools to make changes to the networking structure and base system configuration. If the command-line interface (CLI) isn't your cup of tea, you can purchase an Apple product called Apple Remote Desktop. This software allows you to take control of the mouse and keyboard of another Macintosh. Using this software from a remote Macintosh lets you see the desktop of the Xserve as if you were sitting in front of it.

Another option available to each Xserve (G4 and G5) is the ability to configure the hot-swappable disks in various RAID configurations (see the RAID table on RAID configurations). Not only can you configure the disks, but you can also add the optional Xserve RAID hardware to your Xserve.

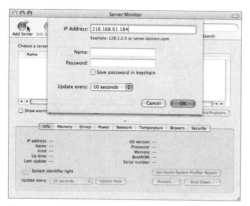

Figure 2.90 In Server Monitor, enter the IP address or name of the Xserve, include administrator authentication information, and click OK.

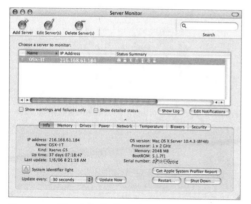

Figure 2.91 The default view of Server Monitor with a server selected.

Using Server Monitor Without an Xserve

Server Monitor can connect to any type of hardware running Mac OS X Server. However, none of the hardware-monitoring features will work. But you can still perform some basic functions available from the Info pane, such as restarting, shutting down, and getting System Profiler reports.

To add a computer to the Server Monitor list:

1. Open the Server Monitor tool ⚠ by choosing /Applications/Server/ Server Monitor.

2. Click Add Server ⚙ .

3. Enter the IP address or name of the server, and include the administrator authentication information (**Figure 2.90**).

   Remember, saving a password to the keychain will automatically log you in to that server from this point forward.

4. Click OK to add the server to your server list.

   Server Monitor will maintain a persistent connection to your server as long as it's in the list. You can repeat the process to add as many servers as you wish to monitor (**Figure 2.91**).

To monitor a server:

1. Select your server from the Server Monitor list, and then select the "Show detailed status" check box to display a more detailed monitoring view in the Status Summary column (**Figure 2.92**).

2. Click each tab in the middle of the window (Info, Memory, and so on) to monitor a specific category.

   Each tab shows a variety of information and statistics about your Xserve. For example, clicking Drives monitors the drives inside the Xserve (**Figure 2.93**).

3. Click the Info tab, and then click Get Apple System Profiler Report to remotely run a System Profiler report (**Figure 2.94**).

   Apple System Profiler, or System Profiler, lets you query a Mac OS X or Mac OS X Server for a variety of hardware and software information.

   The Server Monitor log window appears, and the System Profiler Report is displayed (**Figure 2.95**).

4. In this window, you can click Save As to save the log as a text file for future inspection.

Figure 2.92 Select the "Show Detailed Status" check box for more information about your Xserve.

Figure 2.93 Clicking the Drives tab shows the status of the drives in the bottom half of the window.

Figure 2.94 Click the Info tab, and then click the Get Apple System Profiler Report button.

Figure 2.95 The Server Monitor log window subsequently shows the System Profiler report.

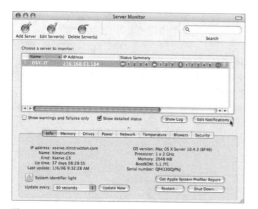

Figure 2.96 Select a server from the Server Monitor list, and then click the Edit Notifications button.

To enable Server Monitor notifications:

1. Select your server from the Server Monitor list, and then click the Edit Notifications button (**Figure 2.96**). The Notifications dialog appears.

2. In the Enabled Notifications section, select the monitoring devices you want to be automatically notified about (**Figure 2.97**).

   These buttons work as toggle switches: Clicking a button switches it between disabled and enabled.

3. In the Email Settings section of the dialog, configure an email account from which the Server Monitor should send its messages (**Figure 2.98**).

continues on next page

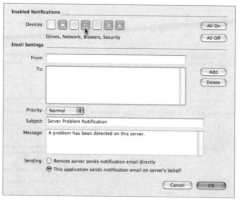

Figure 2.97 Select the monitoring devices you want to be automatically notified about.

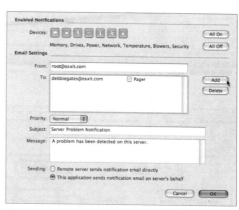

Figure 2.98 Configure an email account(s) from which the Server Monitor should send its messages, and email accounts you want to receive the messages.

USING SERVER MONITOR

4. Configure as many email accounts as you want to receive the messages and set the message priority, subject, and beginning message text.

5. Choose one of the following options to specify whether you want the current tool or the server itself to send the message (**Figure 2. 99**):

▲ Remote server sends notification email directly

▲ This application sends notification email on server's behalf

6. Click OK to save the settings.

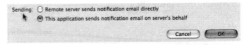

Figure 2.99 Choose an option to specify whether you want the current tool or the server itself to send the message.

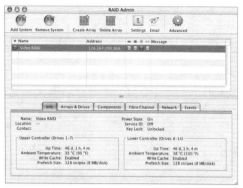

Figure 2.100 The RAID Admin tool lets you view the current settings and configure the Xserve RAID in a variety of ways.

Figure 2.101 The RAID Admin Info tab provides information about the RAID such as the name, location, contact email address, and controller status.

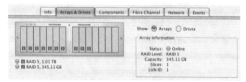

Figure 2.102 The RAID Admin Arrays & Drives tab gives the status of your arrays and drives.

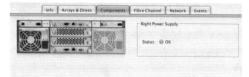

Figure 2.103 The RAID Admin Components tab tells you the status of the installed components.

Additional Server Tools

Mac OS X Server has other server tools that let you set up and configure optional hardware and software, such as RAID, NetBoot, and QuickTime Streaming. These tools are used to manage those hardware configurations and services.

RAID Admin tool setup

The RAID Admin tool 🌰 is used to configure and manage an Xserve RAID array. It lets you view the current settings and configure the Xserve RAID in a variety of ways (**Figure 2.100**).

When you first launch the RAID Admin tool, you're presented with a window that shows all connected Xserve RAIDs. Clicking a RAID array shows information about the array in the tabs within the window. These tabs are as follows:

◆ **Info**—Provides information about the RAID such as the name, location, contact email address, and controller status (**Figure 2.101**).

◆ **Arrays & Drives**—Gives the status of your arrays and drives, such as how the drives are configured and their respective capacity (**Figure 2.102**).

◆ **Components**—Tells you the status of the installed components, such as the left and right power supplies, blowers, RAID controllers, and network cards (**Figure 2.103**).

continues on next page

ADDITIONAL SERVER TOOLS

- **Fibre Channel**—Provides information for each fibre-channel interface (**Figure 2.104**).

- **Network**—Provides information about each Ethernet interface (**Figure 2.105**).

- **Events**—Describes monitored events, if any.

When you create an array, you have several options about how that array is created (**Figure 2.106**). Refer to Chapter 1 for references on the various levels of RAID.

Figure 2.104 The RAID Admin Fibre Channel tab provides information for each fibre channel interface.

Figure 2.105 The RAID Admin Network tab provides information about each Ethernet interface.

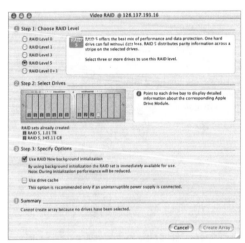

Figure 2.106 When you create a RAID array, you have several options about how that array is created.

Xserve RAID

The Xserve RAID is a configurable double array of disks with one controller for each array. Each array can hold up to 7 disks, with a total of 14 disks and a possible total capacity of 7.0 terabytes. You can configure these disks in a variety of RAID formats depending on your needs. An Xserve RAID also has dual power supplies and dual fans, and it can have dual Ethernet or fibre cards and dual backup batteries. You configure the Xserve RAID using the RAID Admin configuration tool.

Figure 2.107 In the RAID Settings System tab, set up the system configuration.

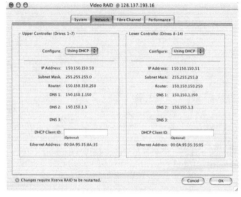

Figure 2.108 In the RAID Settings Network tab, choose whether to use DHCP or manual addresses for each controller.

Figure 2.109 In the RAID Settings Fibre Channel tab, set options such as the speed of the connections and the topology.

To create a RAID array:

1. In the Toolbar, click Create Array (authentication is required) and then click Settings.

   The RAID Settings window opens.

2. In the System tab, set up the system configuration (**Figure 2.107**).

   This includes the name of the array, the location and email address of the contact, the method of synchronizing the time (none, local time, or a Network Time Protocol server), a password, and system alert options.

3. In the Network tab, choose whether to use DHCP or manual addresses for each controller (**Figure 2.108**).

4. In the Fibre Channel tab, set options such as the speed of the connections and the topology (**Figure 2.109**).

5. In the Performance tab, set your specifications (the cache setup for each controller) (**Figure 2.110**).

   Once the configuration is finished, the RAID array is available for use by the Xserve.

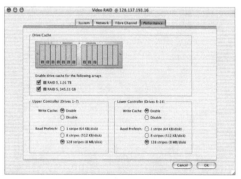

Figure 2.110 In the RAID Settings Performance tab, set your specifications (the cache setup for each controller).

ADDITIONAL SERVER TOOLS

Fibre Channel Utility options

The Fibre Channel Utility lets you change both the speed and topology of the fibre card on the Power Mac or Xserve that's connected to the Xserve RAID (**Figure 2.111**).

You can select each port and change the options. Click Apply to commit the changes to the card.

System Image Utility overview

The NetBoot service is unique in that it shares entire bootable volumes that Macintosh clients can start up over a network connection. You can use the System Image Utility to create and manage special types of disk images known as a *NetBoot* image and a *NetInstall* image. The NetBoot service uses these disk images to provide the remote startup and install services for your Macintosh clients (**Figures 2.112**).

As with most server administration tools, you can run the System Image Utility on any Mac OS X or Mac OS X Server. Likewise, you can use the Server Admin tool to remotely manage the NetBoot service settings. For more information about the System Image Utility and the NetBoot service, refer to Chapter 11, "Running a NetBoot Server."

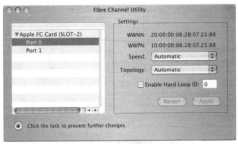

Figure 2.111 The Fibre Channel Utility lets you change both the speed and topology of the fibre card on the Power Mac or Xserve that's connected to the Xserve RAID.

Figure 2.112 The System Image Utility is used to create NetBoot and/or NetInstall images.

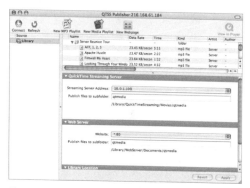

Figure 2.113 The QuickTime Publisher tool is used to manage playlists.

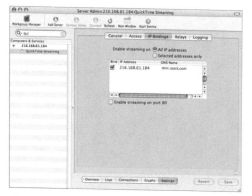

Figure 2.114 Server Admin is used to manage the QuickTime Streaming Server service.

QuickTime Streaming from Mac OS X

You can install the QuickTime Streaming Server on any Mac OS X computer. To do this, either select the QuickTime Streaming Server package in your Mac OS X Server CDs or download and install the Darwin Streaming Server from Apple's Open Source project. Although it's interesting and fun to experiment with the QuickTime Streaming Server/Darwin Streaming Server on Mac OS X, it isn't officially supported by Apple, and you won't receive phone support if you have questions or problems streaming from a Mac OS X computer.

QTSS Publisher overview

The QuickTime Streaming Server (QTSS) is used to deliver streamed audio and video content over your network or the Internet. Apple's QTSS stands out when compared to other streaming solutions due to its open standards compatibility, unlimited streaming capabilities, lack of licensing fees, and unparalleled ease of use. You are literally limited only by disk performance, CPU speed, and network bandwidth. This ease of use is made possible through a variety of comprehensive management tools. One such tool is the QTSS Publisher 🎵, which you can use to manage all of your previously recorded streaming audio and video content (**Figure 2.113**).

The primary objective for the QTSS Publisher is to provide content creators with an easy method of adding and managing QTSS media without having to use the more complicated administration tools (**Figure 2.114**). However, to properly set up a QTSS, you must also enable and configure the server settings via the System Admin tool. Thus, the server administrator can initially configure the QTSS and then delegate the task of populating the server with media to a less experienced user.

This chapter is designed to introduce you to the Mac OS X Server administration tools, so configuration of the QTSS goes beyond its scope. However, this topic is discussed at length in Chapter 12, "QuickTime Streaming Server."

✔ Tip

- QTSS Publisher is used to manage the streaming of previously recorded audio and video content. Use QuickTime Broadcaster to manage the streaming of live audio and video content.

ADDITIONAL SERVER TOOLS

QuickTime Broadcaster overview

The QuickTime Broadcaster tool is used to compress audio and video in real time to facilitate live streaming over a network or the Internet. Typically, QuickTime Broadcaster is used in conjunction with one or more QuickTime Streaming Servers (QTSS) to share this live content with a large number of clients. The number of QTSSs and the amount of network bandwidth through which your broadcast relays directly affect the number of clients that can view your live stream. As expected, the more QTSSs and network bandwidth you have, the more clients you can stream to. Configuration of the QTSS goes beyond the scope of this chapter, but it's discussed at length in Chapter 12.

You need only one Macintosh running QuickTime Broadcaster to create the initial live stream. In fact, you can use QuickTime Broadcaster without being connected to a QTSS to stream content to a few clients.

✔ Tip

■ You can install QuickTime Broadcaster on Mac OS X.

Figure 2.115 The Show Details button expands the QuickTime Broadcaster window.

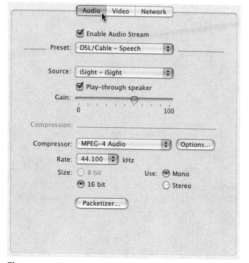

Figure 2.116 In the Audio settings dialog, select the Enable Audio Stream check box.

To set up a simple live broadcast:

1. Connect your audio and/or video source.

   QuickTime Broadcaster is compatible with most audio input devices and digital video devices. This includes Apple iSight cameras, digital video cameras, and analog-to-digital video converters.

2. Open the QuickTime Broadcaster tool by choosing /Applications/QuickTime Broadcaster.

3. When the tool first opens, it shows a compact window with only a few basic settings (**Figure 2.115**).

   Click Show Details to view all the options.

4. Click the Audio tab, and then select the Enable Audio Stream check box (**Figure 2.116**).

   You must select the compression preset and the audio source from the pop-up menus. Several built-in compression presets are good starting points; you can tweak them further with the settings that follow.

   continues on next page

5. Click the Video tab, and then select the Enable Video Stream check box (**Figure 2.117**).

   You must select the compression preset and the video source from the pop-up menus. Again, several built-in compression presets are good starting points; you can tweak them further with the settings that follow.

6. Click the Network tab (**Figure 2.118**).

   Select Manual Unicast from the Transmission pop-up menu, and enter the IP address of the client you're sending the broadcast to.

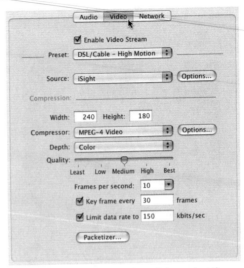

Figure 2.117 In the Video settings dialog, select the Enable Video Stream check box.

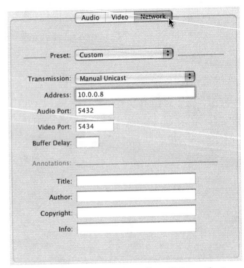

Figure 2.118 In the Network settings dialog, select Manual Unicast from the Transmission pop-up menu and enter the client's IP address.

Figure 2.119 Select Compress from the Preview pop-up menu to preview the video feed with your current settings.

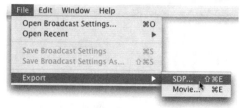

Figure 2.120 Select File > Export > SDP.

Figure 2.121 Click the Broadcast button to begin the live media stream.

Figure 2.122 Double-click the SDP (Session Description Protocol) file to open it.

mybroadcast.sdp

7. Select Compress from the Preview pop-up menu in the main QuickTime Broadcaster window to preview the video feed with your current settings (**Figure 2.119**).

   Verify the settings below the Preview window before you start streaming.

8. Select File > Export > SDP to save the session description file (**Figure 2.120**).

   A Save dialog appears, in which you can choose the destination and name for the session description file. The client uses this file as instructions for connecting to your broadcast.

9. In the QuickTime Broadcaster window, click the Broadcast button to begin the live media stream (**Figure 2.121**).

   Selecting the "Record to disk" check box saves the streamed file to the local hard disk for future streaming.

10. Transfer the session description file to the client computer.

    Double-click the file to open it (**Figure 2.122**).

continues on next page

ADDITIONAL SERVER TOOLS

11. QuickTime Player automatically opens, and the broadcast appears (**Figure 2.123**). There will be a slight delay in the broadcast due to compression time and network overhead.

✔ Tips

■ As your stream is being broadcast, you can also monitor the video feed and connection settings from QuickTime Broadcaster.

■ Click Stop to stop the live media stream (**Figure 2.124**).

■ Each of the tools in this chapter is used to administer, manage, and edit parts and pieces of Mac OS X Server. It's good practice not to authenticate as root when running any of these tools (most tools won't let you, but some will, using both the short name *root* and the long name *System Administrator*). Doing so could have unexpected results such as failure to authenticate later as your administrator account, effectively locking you out of working with your server tools.

Figure 2.123 The QuickTime Player window opens, and you can view the live broadcast.

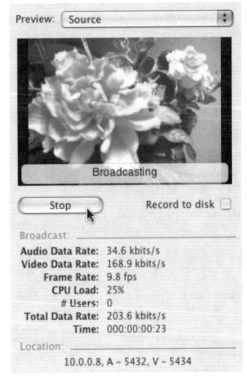

Figure 2.124 Click the Stop button below the broadcast Preview window to stop the stream.

Broadcast Management Options

◆ QuickTime Broadcaster is used to manage the streaming of live audio and video content. Use QTSS Publisher to manage the streaming of previously recorded audio and video content.

◆ Real-time compression and streaming of audio and video are processor intensive. For this reason, QuickTime Broadcaster requires at least a G4-based Macintosh, if not a dual-processor G4 or G5 computer, for best results.

Additional Administration Tools

In addition to the tools discussed here, you may wish to add the following items to the Dock on your server (some items, such as the Terminal, are already on the Dock):

 Activity Monitor—Monitors processes

 NetInfo Manager—Lets you edit data on local accounts

 Console—Lets you view local log files easily

 Network Utility—Checks the network status and connections

 Directory Access—Allows the server to authenticate and connect to other directory types

 Printer Setup Utility—Lets you create printers on your server

 Disk Utility—Lets you carry out permissions repair on your server

 Terminal Utility—Used to manage command-line executables and binaries

ADDITIONAL SERVER TOOLS

OPEN DIRECTORY

A directory service is a centralized store for user accounts, groups, authentication data and security policies. Generally available over a network, this centralized storage facilitates consistent management, since administrative data only has to be managed once, rather than for multiple applications (file servers, mail servers, desktop security, etc.). The term Open Directory refers to Apple's Directory Services architecture—both its components for centrally storing administrative data (generally called Open Directory Server) and the built-in capacity of Mac OS X to access third-party directory services like Active Directory and eDirectory. Because its functionality is specific to Mac OS X Server, this chapter deals primarily with Open Directory Server, as well as configuring Mac OS X Server to access a directory service.

Open Directory Roles

Directory Services are complex. There's no getting around that. Like many of the services of Mac OS X Server, a thorough and complete graphical interface would resemble a jet cockpit, and would be inaccessible to much of Apple's core audience.

Open Directory Server is made up of three underlying services (OpenLDAP, Password Server, and MIT Kerberos). Adding complexity to this is the fact that non-Mac directories typically do not share Apple's goals of simplicity, and integrating Mac OS X Server with them can be quite onerous.

To simplify matters, Apple has introduced the concept of Open Directory roles. An Open Directory role is simply a sort of macro state that defines the configuration of Open Directory Server's underlying services. This well-defined set of configurations brings consistency and predictability to Open Directory Server's complex capabilities.

In general, changes in a server's Open Directory role are activated using the Open Directory module of the Server Admin application. The pop-up menu in the Open Directory's General Settings tab yields four choices (**Figure 3.1**):

◆ When running in Standalone mode, a Mac OS X Server accesses only the local directory—there is no shared directory domain, and the user and group accounts are stored in the server's local NetInfo database. Passwords are stored in the /private/var/db/shadow/hash/ directory. This is what you should choose when setting up a Mac OS X Server for the first time.

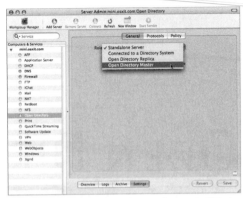

Figure 3.1 Open Directory roles may be manipulated in the General Settings tab of Open Directory within Server Admin.

◆ In addition to its local domain, an Open Directory master hosts an Open Directory shared domain. User and group accounts (along with other directory data) are stored in an LDAP (Lightweight Directory Access Protocol) directory, and authentication takes place using Apple's Password Server. Single Sign-On (SSO) services are provided by an MIT Kerberos KDC (Key Distribution Center).

◆ An Open Directory replica brings redundancy to an Open Directory domain by housing an exact copy of the master's LDAP Directory, Password Server, and MIT Kerberos KDC. In most circumstances, this data is read-only.

◆ When Mac OS X Server is connected to a Directory System, it accesses directory data from Open Directory Server, an Active Directory domain, or some other directory service (including eDirectory and Sun's NIS).

This Open Directory configuration infrastructure is the cornerstone of the Apple Directory Services platform. Its consistent service configuration and directory data provide a foundation on which robust and fairly scalable infrastructures may be built.

Shadow Passwords

Prior to Mac OS X Server 10.2, authentication data was stored as a crypt value in the local NetInfo directory. This wasn't secure, because NetInfo is world-readable and passwords were easily decrypted.

Mac OS X Server 10.2 introduced Password Server, which moved authentication data into a secure, network-available store that was separate from any directories that remained world-readable. Running such a service, though, proved to be overkill for a standalone infrastructure (Mac OS X 10.3), so in 10.4 Apple expanded the 10.3 shadow hash mechanism to support all of Password Server's authentication capabilities.

OPEN DIRECTORY ROLES

Managing an Open Directory Master

An Open Directory (OD) master houses shared identification, authentication, and authorization data for Mac, Linux, and, in some cases, Windows clients. It is the basis of a shared Open Directory domain.

Open Directory Server provides a fairly scalable and, in most cases, reliable infrastructure for small to medium-sized Mac-centric workgroups. Since it is based on open standards and in many cases open source software, it is also an acceptable (although not always ideal) platform for other directory-based applications, such as LDAP-enabled Web portals and document management systems.

To make use of Open Directory Server, however, you first need to create the Open Directory master to house it.

Creating an Open Directory master

As with most administrative tasks, you can create an OD master graphically by using the Server Admin application. This time, you'll work with the Open Directory module.

First, ensure that your server is up to date and that forward and reverse DNS entries are properly configured. If the Mac OS X Server is also a DNS server, refer to Chapter 6, "Network Services Options."

Figure 3.2 The default values when creating an Open Directory master.

To create an Open Directory master:

1. Launch Server Admin, located in /Applications/Server and select Open Directory from the services list.

   See Chapter 2, "Server Tools," for instructions on launching the various tools used throughout this book.

2. Click the General tab and choose Open Directory Master from the Role pop-up menu (see Figure 3.1).

3. In the dialog that appears, specify a name, short name, and password for the new administrator of the shared domain you are creating (**Figure 3.2**).

   Defaults (Directory Administrator and dadmin) are suggested for you. You can override these defaults to make the administrator's name harder to guess.

4. Either accept or enter different Kerberos and LDAP information for your Open Directory domain.

   If your DNS configuration is correct, defaults are supplied for you. Feel free to override them, especially if your DNS environment results in an abnormally long or awkward search base or Kerberos realm.

5. Click Create to close the dialog.

6. Click Save in the Server Admin window.

✔ Tip

- View the slapconfig.log file located in the /Library/Logs directory if you encounter any errors.

What Else Happens When You Create an Open Directory Master?

After you create an Open Directory master, you can open your Directory Access application and select the Authentication tab (**Figure 3.3**).

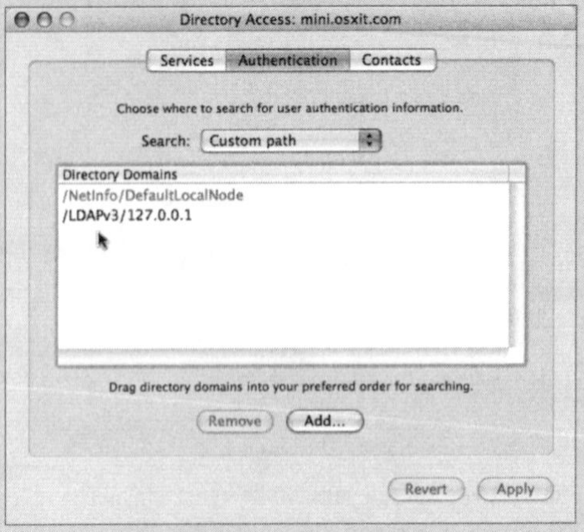

You'll see an entry for LDAPv3/127.0.0.1, which indicates that the Mac OS X Server is now bound to itself. That is, the process that creates the LDAP directory and the Kerberos Key Distribution Center (KDC), discussed later in this chapter, also creates the entry and places it in the Directory Services structure.

The Directory Administrator you create is also added to the admin group in the Server's local NetInfo domain, and a root user (with the same password as the Directory Administrator) is created in the shared domain.

Figure 3.3 The Authentication tab of Directory Access on Mac OS X Server after becoming an Open Directory master.

The directory structure now looks like this:

NetInfo (Local) Domain:

♦ Members of the admin group are

♦ Local root w/same password as...

♦ Your local administrator account

♦ Your LDAP administrator account

LDAP Domain:

♦ LDAP root w/same password as...

♦ Your LDAP administrator account

This duplicity in root, both with the user ID 0, is a bit confusing. Access is granted to folder and file access based on UID, but access to databases is based on generated unique ID. So, the user root may have two distinct passwords—one local, and one LDAP.

Figure 3.4 Authenticating to Workgroup Manager using an administrator name and password.

Figure 3.5 Unlocking access to the shared (LDAP) domain.

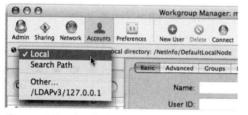

Figure 3.6 Showing the bound domains using Workgroup Manager.

Working with a shared Open Directory domain

To manage user, group, and computer accounts in your shared Open Directory domain, use the Workgroup Manager application to connect to your Open Directory master.

Depending on which domain you want to administer, you either use the local NetInfo administrator's name or the LDAP administrator's name. It's a good idea to use the local administrator's name (**Figure 3.4**), so that he or she can access the local database, and then unlock the LDAP database using the LDAP administrator's username and password.

Because the LDAP administrator's name is added to the local NetInfo admin group, you could add it to the keychain of the user who will be using Workgroup Manager on a consistent basis, if you want. However, for security reasons, you may not want to do this (**Figure 3.5**).

Once both administrators are added, you can choose different directories to administer by viewing the Directory pop-up menu in the upper-left corner of Workgroup Manager (**Figure 3.6**). Actual account management is covered in more depth in Chapter 4, "User and Group Management."

✔ Tips

- In Mac OS X Server 10.4, clicking Workgroup Manager in the upper-left corner of Server Admin results in a Workgroup Manager authentication dialog that specifically targets Server Admin's currently selected server. This is one workaround for Workgroup Manager's annoying habit of trying to log in to the local workstation you're working from.

- You should display the All records tab and Inspector, covered in Chapter 2, as you go through this chapter.

MANAGING AN OPEN DIRECTORY MASTER

99

LDAP Overview

LDAP was designed as a consistent and standardized way to make directory data available over a network, regardless of how or where it is stored. Mac OS X Servers 10.2–10.4.x, Active Directory, and SunONE/iPlanet directory servers are all structured very differently. They all, however, support LDAP access to their underlying data store, and any LDAP client can query them.

So the idea behind LDAP is rather simple— it is an abstraction layer that allows for access to underlying data. The implementation of this idea, however, turns out to be rather complex. LDAP employs a hierarchical structure and odd naming convention, which tends to confuse first-time administrators. Its schema (or rules with regard to the content and format of directory data) can be extremely complex.

In general, an LDAP directory is made up of a hierarchical grouping of entries. Each entry usually contains one or more attributes; for example, a user record should have a short name, numerical user ID, and home directory path associated with it. The user record is an entry, whereas the short name and numerical user ID are attributes.

Each of these attributes has one or more values that actually contain the user data. The directory's schema ensures that particular entries have all of their required attributes, and that the format of those attributes is correct. Numerical user IDs, for instance, should always have an integer value.

The good news is that, in most cases, Apple insulates the administrator from this complexity. Particularly, in an environment where most users are on Apple computers and all are on Open Directory, you'll likely never be exposed to raw LDAP data. Integrating with other directory systems, however, can be more difficult. (Accessing eDirectory,

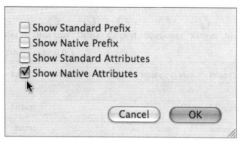

☐ Show Standard Prefix
☐ Show Native Prefix
☐ Show Standard Attributes
☑ Show Native Attributes

(Cancel)   (OK)

Figure 3.7 Showing either Standard (Open Directory) or Native (LDAP) attribute names in Workgroup Manager's Inspector tab.

iPlanet, or other LDAP directories will be covered later in this chapter.)

The main idea behind understanding this very complex and scalable architecture is to keep in mind that Apple maintains two attributes (and their associated prefixes) for every value. That is, every user has at least one short name as well as a long name, a user ID, and a globally unique ID. These are known as attributes, and they each have values typically associated with them. In Open Directory and OpenLDAP, these attributes have different names (**Table 3.1**). In Workgroup Manager, you have an option to view the Standard (Apple Open Directory) and/or native (OpenLDAP) attributes and associative values by choosing Inspector > Options (**Figure 3.7**).

You will notice a few things. First, all three methods of naming attributes are different. Second, Open Directory attributes almost always begin with a capital letter, whereas OpenLDAP names do not. Third, what is not shown are the Apple-specific attributes, such as managed client settings. OpenLDAP has no record of these settings, so Apple has added its own schema set to the OpenLDAP architecture. These can be found by opening the /private/etc/openldap/schema/apple.schema file. Within the scope of this book, it is not possible to handle all the potential permutations resulting from extending or modifying the schema.

Table 3.1

Example attribute names and values

WORKGROUP MANAGER CALLS IT….	OPEN DIRECTORY (STANDARD IN WGM) CALLS IT…	OPENLDAP (NATIVE IN WGM) CALLS IT…	TYPICAL VALUE IS…
Name	RealName	cn	Michael Stanley
User ID	UniqueID	uidnumber	2112
Short Names	RecordName	uid (NOT an error here)	msb
Login Shell	UserShell	loginShell	/bin/bash
Primary Group ID	PrimaryGroupID	gidnumber	20

About Password Server

The next part of an Open Directory master, Password Server, is the part of Mac OS X Server responsible for managing passwords for the shared (LDAP) domain. It is ultimately a process called `PasswordService` and is created when an Open Directory master is chosen from the list of potential server configuration types. It writes out to three log files, which you can access by using the Server Admin tool under Open Directory and choosing the Logs tab. They and their ultimate locations are:

◆ /Library/Logs/PasswordService/ AplePasswordServer.Error.log

◆ /Library/Logs/PasswordService/ AplePasswordServer.Replication.log

◆ /Library/Logs/PasswordService/ AplePasswordServer.Server.log

Using the `mkpassdb` command, you can also back up the database, merge two password server databases, review the mechanisms for handling the passwords, and remove password server slots. Please refer to the man page for more information on `mkpassdb`.

Setting password policies

Password policies (complexity requirements, expiration policies, and password histories) have always been important in governmental sectors. Increasingly, though, a regulatory environment fueled by Sarbanes-Oxley, HIPPA, and FERPA has driven their adoption in the educational and private sectors as well. You can set these policies either globally, using the Server Admin application, or on a per-user basis, using Workgroup Manager. Note that per-user settings override global ones, and that in any case, administrative users in Mac OS X Server 10.4 are not subject to password policy restrictions.

Password policies can be very effective in maintaining compliance with your organization's guidelines but have varying degrees of restriction, as shown in **Table 3.2**.

Table 3.2

User authentication policies

GUI DISABLE ACCOUNTS OPTION	USAGE	PWPOLICY COMMAND-LINE EQUIVALENT
On Date	Disables an account on a set date, such as when a contractor is set to leave a job site	usingExpirationDate usingHardExpirationDate expirationDateGMT hardExpireDateGMT
After a set number of days	Disables an account after a set number of days, such as when a student has access for the number of days in a grading period	maxMinutesUntilDisabled
After a period of inactivity	Disables an account after the user doesn't log in for a set number of days, such as when a user stops using a particular file server	maxminutesOfNonUse
After a set number of failed login attempts	Disables an account after a user or hacker attempts to enter incorrect information a set number of times	maxFailedLoginAttempts
GUI PASSWORD POLICY OPTION	USAGE	PWPOLICY COMMAND-LINE EQUIVALENT
Length Policy	Dictates that a password must be at least a set number of characters long	minChars
Letter Policy	Requires a password to contain at least one letter	requiresAlpha
Numeric character policy	Requires a password to contain at least one numeric character	requiresNumeric
Account name policy	Requires the password to be different from the account name	passwordCannotBeName
Reused passwords policy	Requires a password to be different from previous passwords	usingHistory
Password change policy	Requires a password to be changed after a set number of days, weeks, or months	maxMinutesUntilChangePassword
Be reset on first user login	Require a new password at next login	newPasswordRequired
Allow the user to change the password (in WGM)	Allows the user to change their password	canModifyPasswordSelf
	Requires a password to have both upper- and lowercase letters	requiresMixedCase
	Dictates that a password must be no longer than a set number of characters	maxChars
	Value chosen to reset login after failed attempts	minutesUntilFailedLoginReset
	Compares password against Dictionary	notGuessablePattern

To set global password policies:

1. Launch Server Admin, located in /Applications/Server, select Open Directory from the services list and click the Settings tab.

2. Click the Policy tab and then the Passwords tab (**Figure 3.8**).

3. Configure Password options appropriate to your organization's security policies.

✔ Tip

■ If you follow this procedure on an Open Directory master or replica (replicas will be discussed later in this chapter), it will affect both the shared (LDAP) domain and the local (NetInfo) domain (the policies will be synchronized). However, if you pursue it on a Mac OS X Server that is not hosting a shared domain (as of 10.4.4), it will affect the global policy for the local (NetInfo) domain. You set per-user policies (as of 10.3.3) in the local (NetInfo) and the shared (LDAP) domain. In addition, four other options are available via pwpolicy that currently have no GUI counterpart. These options may not be supported by the local (NetInfo) domain.

To set per-user password policies:

1. Launch Workgroup Manager located in /Applications/Server and connect to your server as a local or directory administrator (**Figure 3.9**).

2. From the "Authenticated as" pop-up menu in the upper-left corner of the screen, choose either a local or shared domain (**Figure 3.10**).

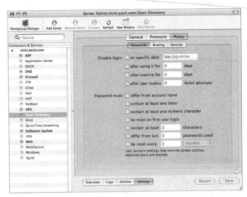

Figure 3.8 Open Directory's global password policy interface.

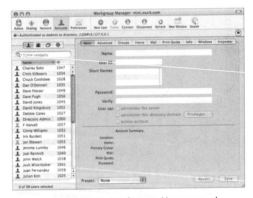

Figure 3.9 Opening up Workgroup Manager and authenticating an administrator.

Figure 3.10 Choosing the shared (LDAP) domain in Workgroup Manager.

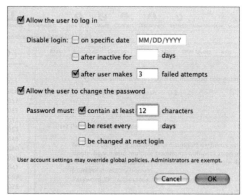

Figure 3.11 User account password policies in the Advanced tab of Workgroup Manager.

3. Select one or more user accounts and click the Advanced pane.

4. Click Options and configure password options appropriate to your organization's security policies. Then click OK (**Figure 3.11**).

5. Compare the per-user policies with the global policies in Server Admin (set in the previous task) to ensure there are no conflicts.

6. Use the `pwpolicy` command to affect other non-GUI policies.

   This example shows how you can require mixed case by replacing *diradmin* with the short name of your shared directory administrator):

   ```
   pwpolicy -a diradmin -v -
   setglobalpolicy requiresMixedCase=1
   ```

7. Enter your shared directory administrator's short name password to authenticate.

   The –v option is verbose and allows feedback to be shown in the Terminal.

8. Type `pwpolicy –getglobalpolicy` to review your new policies.

Storing Password Server passwords

Password Server also has the ability to utilize several methods for storing passwords. The following password storage methods are accessible in the Security tab within the Open Directory service module of Server Admin or by using the NeST command-line tool:

- **SMB-NTLMv2**—Used for Windows ME, XP, 2000, 2003, and higher

- **SMB-NT**—Used for Windows 98 and NT

- **SMB-LAN-MANAGER**—Used for Windows 95 clients

- **MS-CHAPv2**—Used for VPN access

- **GSSAPI**—Generic Security Service Application Program Interface

- **WEBDAV-DIGEST**—Used for WebDAV

- **APOP**—Used for authenticated Post Office Protocol

Each of the methods of storing passwords has its pros and cons. In general, you should turn off the protocols you do not use, especially those that are somewhat unsecure, such as SMB-NT, SMB-LAN-MANAGER, WEBDAV-DIGEST, and APOP.

ABOUT PASSWORD SERVER

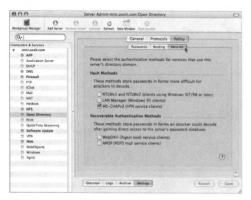

Figure 3.12 Viewing the various password authentication methods in Server Admin.

To disable unsecure password storage methods:

1. Launch Server Admin, located in /Applications/Server, select Open Directory from the services list and click the Settings tab.

   You can leave Server Admin open for the next several tasks.

2. Click the Policy tab and then the Security tab (**Figure 3.12**).

3. Select the check boxes as appropriate and click Save.

   or

   Use the NeST command-line tool:

   ```
   sudo NeST –setprotocols APOP off
   ```

✔ Tip

■ It's not a good idea to turn off GSSAPI authentication using the NeST command, because it may cause unexpected results when using Kerberos for authentication.

ABOUT PASSWORD SERVER

Managing LDAP in Open Directory

LDAP services in Mac OS X Server are provided by the `slapd` daemon—part of the OpenLDAP LDAP implementation. Certain aspects of `slapd`'s behavior are configurable in the Protocols and Policy tabs of the Open Directory module's Settings section within Server Admin.

To set shared (LDAP) domain configuration:

1. Within the Settings section of the Open Directory module, click the Protocols tab and make sure that LDAP Settings is chosen from the Configure pop-down menu (**Figure 3.13**).

   These are basic settings that control the behavior of `slapd`. More advanced configurations are feasible by manually editing the slapd.conf and slapd_macosxserver.conf files in /private/etc/openldap. See the slapd.conf man page for more details.

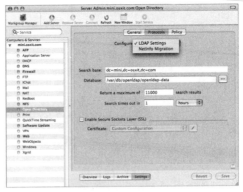

Figure 3.13 Viewing LDAP settings after becoming an Open Directory master.

2. From the following list of options, choose the ones you want to change:

▲ **Search Base**—You can't really change the search base graphically, but it appears here.

▲ **Database**—The location of the database used by slapd, the actual LDAP server process. You can locate the data store on higher-performing or more redundant file servers, such as a RAID array, if you choose. You might also want to segregate it on a non-system volume, in case the system volume is filled by log files or user files.

▲ **Return a maximum of _n_ search results**—Assign a maximum number of records returned from any search. This is useful in preventing denial-of-service attacks that try to review large directories.

▲ **Search times out in _n_**—Setting to discourage loss of service centered around exhausting available TCP sockets. By timing out searches we can ensure that no extraneous sockets are in use.

▲ **Enable Secure Sockets Layer**—Enable ldaps:// connections, and choose among available SSL certificates. This is only marginally useful since out-of-box Open Directory clients do not verify the authenticity of ldaps:// certificates, and since certificates produced by Mac OS X Server's Certificate interface are, by default, not signed by a certificate authority.

Using SSL with LDAP and Open Directory

When you click the Enable Secure Sockets Layer (SSL) check box and choose a certificate (the default certificate is the one that can be chosen prior to creating any customized certificates), you must immediately also inform the Directory Service infrastructure on your Mac OS X Server that you are requiring a certificate. You do this by using the Directory Access application to use SSL for the shared (LDAP) domain.

Once you select this check box and save, anyone using Workgroup Manager to manage shared (LDAP) accounts will be denied. That's because you must first use Directory Access to tell the server to use SSL to see its own shared domain. To do that, open Directory Access on the server (or choose Server > Connect on any Mac OS X computer from Directory Access). Double-click the LDAPv3 service from the Services list and select the SSL check box on the right of the window. Click OK to accept the changes.

You may need to deselect and then select the LDAPv3 service in order to access the Apply button. Then click Apply to notify the DirectoryService daemon to reread the LDAPv3 configuration.

Managing LDAP binding policies in an Open Directory domain

The following LDAP binding and security policies are entirely optional and affect only Open Directory clients. Other LDAP clients are totally unaware of them and may continue to connect anonymously or using clear-text, unsecure credentials regardless of what you do here. In other words, these settings do nothing to secure your Open Directory master.

The first set of LDAP policies are "Enable directory binding" and "Require clients to bind to directory." These revolve around authenticated binding, wherein the Open Directory client uses a Computer account to perform authenticated LDAP queries on the Open Directory master. This behavior is new in Mac OS X Server 10.4. Although authenticated queries could be performed in previous releases, there was no system or standard to provision machine accounts. Again, note that these are client-side policies obeyed only by Open Directory clients, and that these settings do not affect the LDAP server's configuration in any way.

The next set of LDAP policies, discussed in the following task, deal with the security characteristics of the LDAP connection performed by Open Directory clients. Selection of all is required to mark a directory domain as trusted, which is required in order to enforce certain client management policies such as MCX login scripts.

What all of these options really boil down to is that in a default state the entire LDAP component of your Open Directory is available anonymously anyway. So encrypting anything but passwords is a little redundant at this point unless you've implemented a fairly rigorous set of directory ACLs. Therefore, ensuring that passwords are protected is probably enough for most people.

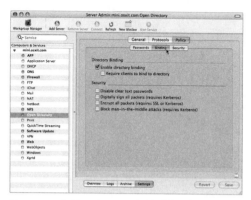

Figure 3.14 Options to securely bind Mac OS X computers to an Open Directory master.

To set bind options on an Open Directory Master:

1. Within the Settings section of the Open Directory module, select the Security tab and then the Security tab (**Figure 3.14**).

2. Click the appropriate check boxes:

   ▲ **Enable Directory Binding**— Permits Open Directory clients to perform authenticated LDAP operations, and alerts them that during initial directory discovery they should permit the creation of a machine account.

   ▲ **Require clients to bind to directory**—Requires Open Directory clients to use authenticated binding. Note that non–Open Directory, generic LDAP clients may still make unauthenticated queries.

   ▲ **Disable clear text passwords**— Ensures that Open Directory clients do not send LDAP passwords in clear text. Clients will select the most secure SASL authentication method available to them: Generic Security Service Application Program Interface (GSSAPI and, in this case, Kerberos) or Challenge Response Authentication Method (CRAM-MD5), but will not fall back to clear-text authentication unless the connection is encrypted by SSL.

   ▲ **Digitally sign all packets**— Cryptographically ensures that every packet is legitimate. Requires Kerberos to work.

continues on next page

MANAGING LDAP IN OPEN DIRECTORY

▲ **Encrypt all packets**—Ensures that no LDAP traffic whatsoever is sent over the network in clear text. Requires either Kerberos or SSL.

▲ **Block man-in-the-middle attacks**—Very similar to "Digitally sign all packets," this option informs the client that it should prevent man-in-the-middle attacks by ensuring the cryptographic signature of the Kerberos authentication operations.

3. Click Save.

Using Kerberos

Kerberos is an open source initiative from MIT and complements the other two pieces of an Open Directory master quite nicely. To put it simply, there are three players in the Kerberos game: a client computer; a computer running a service, such as mail, file sharing, Web, or otherwise; and a computer running as a Key Distribution Center (KDC). All of these interact with each other to provide extremely secure authentication.

System administrators like Kerberos because it offers a feature called Single Sign-On (SSO). When a user logs into a computer that is bound to a KDC, the very act of logging in gets them a ticket from the KDC, which they can then use to prove their identity to that server or other computers running "Kerberized" services without entering a password.

Mac OS X Server running as an Open Directory master is also a KDC. Every time a user is created in the shared domain, a user principal is created for that user. This is the Kerberos way of saying that user can take part in the authentication process. Most services running on a Mac OS X Server can be Kerberized; that is, they can accept Kerberos authentication for their services.

SSL vs. Authenticated Binding

Authenticated binding, which is handled by Kerberos connection on OS X, also encrypts the LDAP communications using the Kerberos service ticket. As such there is no reason to both require authenticated binding and SSL as you're double encrypting the LDAP connections.

The following services can leverage Kerberos in their structure:

- Secure Shell (ssh)

- Apple File Sharing protocol (AFP)

- Sending and receiving email (POP, IMAP, SMTP)

- Windows sharing (SMB)

- File Transfer Protocol (FTP)

- Virtual private networking (VPN)

- Web (HTTP)

- Xgrid (Xgrid)

Kerberos is set up for you when you promote to an Open Directory Master. Once a KDC has been established, you can choose any of the above services from the Server Admin tool (except ssh, which is already tuned for Kerberos) and force Kerberos from the authentication methods of these services. Typically all services are already configured to use Kerberos authentication in addition to standard methods in their default state.

Forcing Kerberos authentication will not allow Mac OS X computers to connect unless they have previously bound to the server via the LDAPv3 plug-in inside Directory Access, or they have manually edited the edu.mit.Kerberos file located in /Library/Preferences on their Mac OS X computers. Problem is, unless they have bound to a server before, this file may not exist, so there is no template for how to edit the contents. That's why a simple bind to the server is easier; it retrieves the information from the server and creates the file on the Mac OS X computer for you.

If you have already set up an Open Directory master and the Mac OS X computer is properly configured to know the DNS information, you can bind the Mac OS X computer to the server and get your edu.mit.Kerberos file, so that you can use Kerberized services.

Kerberos Application

The Kerberos application, located in /System/Library/CoreServices/, is used to obtain, check on, and destroy tickets. One facet of this application that is not initially useful is that it permits the creation of additional realms via which the user can authenticate. The Edit Realms option is located under the Edit menu. If you are not sure how to add a realm, simply copy what you see in the existing realm and change the domain information.

To bind Mac OS X to a Mac OS X Server Open Directory master:

1. Make sure your Mac OS X computer's Network preference pane has the correct information to see the domain name information for the Mac OS X Server by checking the DNS and domain name fields.

2. Launch Directory Access and authenticate using the lock in the lower-left corner of the screen to unlock the icon and permit editing (**Figure 3.15**).

3. Click the LDAPv3 check box (if it isn't selected already) and double-click LDAPv3 to open a plug-in configuration dialog (**Figure 3.16**).

4. Click the Show Options disclosure triangle.

5. Make sure the "Add DHCP-supplied LDAP servers to automatic search policies" check box is deselected (**Figure 3.17**).

6. Click New to open the New LDAP Connection dialog.

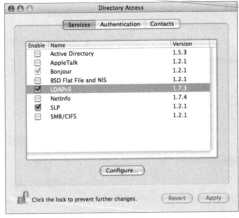

Figure 3.15 Opening Directory Access on a Mac OS X computer.

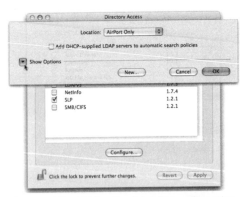

Figure 3.16 The LDAPv3 Plug-in's initial configuration dialog before clicking the Show Options triangle.

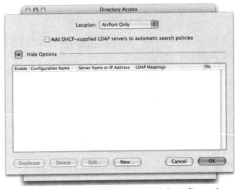

Figure 3.17 The LDAPv3 Plug-in's initial configuration dialog after clicking the Show Options triangle.

Figure 3.18 Enter the name of your Mac OS X Server and click Continue.

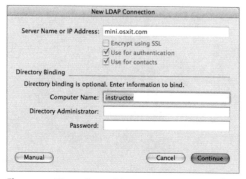

Figure 3.19 You only need to enter a username and password if authentication is enabled on the server.

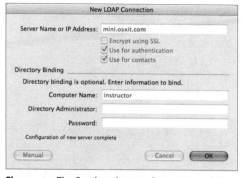

Figure 3.20 The Continue button changes to an OK button as all options are now dimmed and your configuration is complete.

7. Enter the fully qualified domain name of the server and click Continue (**Figure 3.18**).

   There is no need to change the computer name.

8. If you choose authenticated binding, enter a username and password from the shared (LDAP) domain and click Continue (**Figure 3.19**).

9. When a text message near the bottom of the dialog indicates that configuration (binding) is complete, click OK to close this dialog (**Figure 3.20**).

10. In the plug-in configuration dialog, review your LDAP entry and change the configuration name, if necessary.

continues on next page

11. Click the SSL check box if the server is using SSL with LDAP (ldaps://) and click OK to close this dialog (**Figure 3.21**).

12. In the Directory Access window, click the Authentication tab to make sure your server is part of the authentication path and then click Apply (**Figure 3.22**).

13. Open a Terminal window and type id *patrick* and press the Return key on your keyboard.

Use the short name of a user in your shared (LDAP) domain instead of *patrick*. If successful, you are now bound to your LDAP domain and have an edu.mit.Kerberos file.

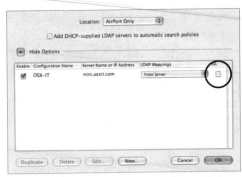

Figure 3.21 Clicking OK returns you to the LDAP plug-ins main dialog.

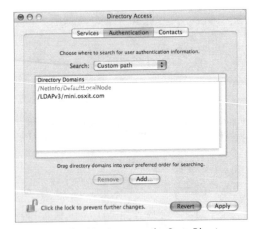

Figure 3.22 Checking to ensure the Open Directory master was added to the authentication search path.

Not the Whole Story

This is just the tip of the Kerberos iceberg. Please refer to one of several Web sites that deal with a more granular level of Kerberos management: www.afp548.com is one of the best.

Also, keep in mind that the LDAP database, the Password Server, and the KDC are all part of an Open Directory master. There are other roles that a Mac OS X Server can become.

Creating and Managing Open Directory Replicas

Prior to Mac OS X Server 10.3, Open Directory Server was not particularly useful to any but the smallest organizations. This was mainly because of its lack of redundancy— Open Directory had no redundancy, so if the single master disappeared, clients would be left without any directory service. Both the client-side behavior and the server-side redundancy have gradually improved with every Mac OS X Server release, and now Open Directory presents a relatively robust, suitably redundant infrastructure for small to medium organizations.

When choosing a role for the Mac OS X Server, the Open Directory Replica option causes the Mac OS X Server to import the necessary data from the specified Open Directory master, thus turning the replica into a secondary copy of the OD master's LDAP, PWS, and KDC.

Creating a replica has several benefits. The most obvious is that it eliminates any single point of failure. Second, having more than one server to authenticate users means that requests for authentication can be spread across several servers, possibly in various areas of the country.

Apple has done a good job making the replica creation process as simple as possible. To create an Open Directory replica using Server Admin, you must first, of course, have an Open Directory master and know the IP address, shared (LDAP) administrator's name, password, and local root password. Also, make sure that your server is up to date and that forward and reverse DNS entries are properly configured. If the Mac OS X Server is also a DNS server, refer to Chapter 6. Password-authenticated ssh logins should be enabled on the master, at least temporarily during the replica-creation process.

To create an Open Directory replica:

1. Launch Server Admin, located in /Applications/Server, select Open Directory from the services list, and click the Settings tab.

2. Click the General tab and choose Open Directory Replica from the Role pop-up menu (see Figure 3.1).

3. In the dialog that appears, specify the IP address of the Open Directory master, the root password on the master, and the username and password of an Open Directory administrator. Then click OK (**Figure 3.23**).

4. In the Server Admin window, click Save and wait for the replication to occur.

   After a few moments, the window will update showing the replication information (**Figure 3.24**). During the replica-creation process, the LDAP and KDC data is scp'd (secure copied, a file transfer protocol based on ssh) over to the new replica. Password Server data is replicated using the Password Server protocol.

5. Check your Open Directory master to make sure that the replica was created and choose how often you wish your master to push information down to your replica (**Figure 3.25**):

   ▲ **Replicate to Clients**—Determines how frequently (defined in the GUI as minutes or days) data is sent to Open Directory replicas. Can be set on a time interval or whenever directory data is changed. If the time interval is less than 60 minutes, data is sent to replicas whenever any changes are made is on the Open Directory master.

   ▲ **Replicate Now**—Forces immediate replication of the Password Server and LDAP data.

Figure 3.23 Information required for a Mac OS X Server to take on the role of an Open Directory replica.

Figure 3.24 Server Admin showing completion of an Open Directory replica.

Figure 3.25 Server Admin of the Open Directory master showing its list of replicas and options for updating them.

✔ Tips

- During this process of replica creation, the master's LDAP server will be temporarily stopped in order to ensure that its exported LDAP data is up to date. This will result in a temporary service outage. So create your first replica as soon as possible. The more user, group, and computer records in your domain, the longer this could take.

- KDC (Kerberos) data is actually replicated and maintained by the Password Server. So the only two replication protocols are critical, Password Server and OpenLDAP.

How Many Replicas?

Sizing an Open Directory environment is highly dependent on your usage pattern and network topology.

As a rule of thumb, however, you should have at least one replica for redundancy and one replica for every 250 to 500 concurrently active users.

For example, a school with 1,500 student machines would be best served with one OD master and three to five replicas (one OD system for every 250 to 375 users). A medium-sized business of 400 client machines could probably get away with just one master and a replica, since office workers typically do not log on and off as much as students do.

It's also a good idea to deploy replicas at geographically remote locations to allow for authentication if the link to the main site goes down, reduce site-to-site traffic, and increase services times for those remote clients.

Because replicas are relatively easy to set up, you can add replicas as needed to reduce load on existing systems and increase redundancy.

Connecting to a Directory System

In all but the smallest organizations, most of the Mac OS X Servers will be neither Open Directory masters nor Open Directory replicas. Instead, your file, Web, mail, VPN, iChat (Jabber), and other services will be configured to access one or more directory domains—Open Directory, Active Directory, or otherwise.

This is the whole point of centralizing directory data. You maintain your user, group, and other administrative data centrally. Mac OS X (and hence Mac OS X Server) is extremely flexible in this regard. Realizing that an Open Directory master is not always the directory service of choice among its customers, Apple has engineered Mac OS X to be one of the most flexible cross-platform directory clients in existence today. Directory Access is the primary method for configuring that access.

When you choose Connected to a Directory Service in Server Admin, you will be directed to Directory Access to configure your connection to the other directory service (although you can also join an existing Kerberos realm as well) (**Figure 3.26**).

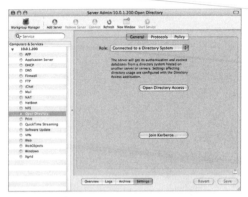

Figure 3.26 Choosing "Connected to a Directory System" from the Mac OS X Server, Server Admin, Open Directory role list.

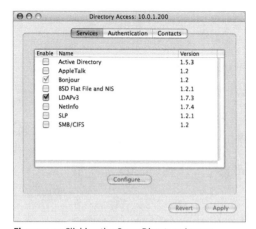

Figure 3.27 Clicking the Open Directory Access button in Server Admin opens the application Directory Access.

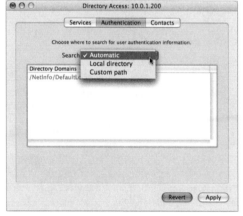

Figure 3.28 Viewing authentication path options from within Directory Access.

Directory Access overview

The Directory Access application is used primarily to connect a Mac OS X or Mac OS X Server computer to another directory service or system.

Directory Access has three tabs: Services, Authentication, and Contacts. In practical terms, the Services tab lists all of the different types of directory services Mac OS X and Mac OS X Server can access, and allows each one to be configured (**Figure 3.27**). The Authentication tab lists the configured directory domains that will be searched for user, group, and other directory data (**Figure 3.28**). The Contacts tab allows configured directory domains to be used for contact information by the Mail and Address Book applications.

To understand how the Directory Access application works, you must be familiar with the concept behind what it does. Since Directory Access is based on a modular plug-in architecture, the application works differently depending on the plug-in used.

CONNECTING TO A DIRECTORY SYSTEM

Let's say you have another Mac OS X Server already in your organization, and you want this Mac OS X Server to see all the users and groups you've created on your first server. Or, you have a Microsoft Active Directory server, and you want to see all the users in that directory service (provided you have the proper access). When you click the Services tab, you can choose from four different methods of connecting your Mac OS X and/or Mac OS X Server to another directory service:

◆ **Active Directory**—Use this plug-in to bind Mac OS X or Mac OS X Server to an Active Directory domain (as you'll see later in this chapter).

◆ **BSD Flat Files and NIS**—Use this plug-in to allow Mac OS X and/or Mac OS X Server to search locally for flat files (/private/etc/master.passwd) containing user and group information and/or allow it to use Sun's NIS, Network Information System (**Figure 3.29**).

◆ **LDAPv3**—Use this option when you're connecting Mac OS X and/or Mac OS X Server to another Open Directory Server or any other LDAP-based directory service.

◆ **NetInfo**—You can use this plug-in when you're connecting a Mac OS X computer to an older parent NetInfo directory, such as Mac OS X Server 10.2 (Jaguar Server) (**Figure 3.30**).

Figure 3.29 Binding a Mac OS X Server to an NIS.

Figure 3.30 Options for binding a Mac OS X Server to an older NetInfo parent domain structure.

Checking authentication paths

Once you've chosen a method and the information is retrieved correctly, you can then have your Mac OS X and/or Mac OS X Server authenticate against that additional directory service.

Whenever a user logs in, Mac OS X and Mac OS X Server always check the local NetInfo directory first. If a user record isn't found in the local NetInfo directory, Mac OS X checks the authentication path for the username and password information, allowing the authenticated user to log in. That search list is handled on the Authentication tab of the Directory Access application (as shown in Figure 3.28).

This can be a multi-tiered situation. For example, suppose you want your Mac OS X computer users to log in to their machines, and their user names and passwords are stored on another directory server, not *your* Mac OS X Server. You don't have to create any entries in the Mac OS X local NetInfo directory. Simply have *your* Mac OS X Server piggyback on that other server for usernames and passwords, and then add computer management using your Mac OS X Server.

✔ Tip

- If you're working on an Xserve or managing your server remotely, you can connect to your server's Directory Access application through yours. To do so, launch your Directory Access application located in /Application/Utilities/, and choose Server > Connect. In the resulting dialog, type in the address or name of the server and the local administrator's name and password, and click Connect. You'll have to reauthenticate every five minutes while this application is open, so it's a good idea to get in, make your changes, save them, and get out.

Accessing an Open Directory domain

If you want, you can use the Server Admin application to begin the process of configuring your Mac OS X Server to access an existing Open Directory domain. This makes sense, since that's where other directory configuration (such as creating an Open Directory replica or master) takes place. Before proceeding with the following task, make sure your Mac OS X Server's Network preference pane has the correct information to see the domain name information for the *other* Mac OS X Server.

To access an existing Open Directory domain:

1. Launch Server Admin and navigate to the Settings section in the Open Directory module.

2. Click the General tab, then choose "Connected to a Directory System" from the Role pop-up menu **(Figure 3.31)**, and click Save.

   Now you can use the Directory Access application for the remainder of your server directory configuration process.

3. Launch Directory Access by running it locally on the server itself or by connecting to your server remotely via Directory Access's Server menu and authenticate as required **(Figure 3.32)**.

4. Follow steps 3–11 in the "To bind Mac OS X to a Mac OS X Server Open Directory master" task earlier in this chapter.

5. Open a Terminal window, type id *paulv*, and press Return.

   Use the short name of a user in your shared (LDAP) domain instead of *paulv*. Your Mac OS X Server is now bound to the other Mac OS X Server's shared (LDAP) domain.

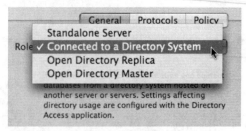

Figure 3.31 Choosing the Connected to a Directory System option within Server Admin.

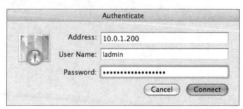

Figure 3.32 Remotely connecting to your Mac OS X Server's Directory Access application.

CONNECTING TO A DIRECTORY SYSTEM

Figure 3.33 Clicking the Join Kerberos button after binding to an Open Directory master.

Joining a Kerberos realm

When a Mac OS X Server is connected to another directory system with a Kerberos infrastructure, you can choose to have your Mac OS X Server join a Kerberos realm. First you must have the KDC's administrator name and password (**Figure 3.33**). Once this has been done, services on your Mac OS X Server can accept tickets from users whose authentication information is maintained on the KDC.

✔ Tip

■ If the Join Kerberos button doesn't work, ssh into your server and execute sso_util:

```
sudo sso_util configure -r XSERVE.
YOURREALM.COM -a youradminsn -p all.
```

This will attempt to Kerberize your server.

Active Directory overview

Microsoft's Active Directory (AD) is one of the most commonly deployed directory services today. As such, integration with it is very important. Apple has engineered the Active Directory plug-in installed with Mac OS X to work well with AD.

Mac OS X is able to access Active Directory natively, without modifying the Active Directory's schema and without any extra software installed on the Mac. This enables AD accounts to make use of Mac OS X Server services like Mail, AFP, iChat, and Weblogs. Mac OS X Server can even store SMB home directories for Windows users.

In addition, Kerberos Single Sign-On is supported by an AD domain in much the same way that it is in Open Directory. Like most other directory services, this configuration takes place mostly in the Directory Access utility.

Before proceeding with the following task, make sure that your server is up to date and that forward and reverse DNS entries are properly configured. An Active Directory integrated DNS server should be listed as the first DNS server for the primary network interface in the Network pane of the system preferences application (**Figure 3.34**). Ideally, your server will also live in the same DNS domain as your Windows systems to facilitate Single Sign-On.

To bind to an Active Directory domain:

1. Launch Directory Access by running it locally on the server itself or connecting to your server remotely via Directory Access's Server menu and authenticate as required (**Figure 3.35**).

2. Select the Active Directory plug-in and click the Configure button.

   or

   Double-click the Active Directory plug-in.

3. In the dialog that appears, specify the fully qualified domain name of your Active Directory domain (not the DNS name or IP address of your AD domain controller).

4. Specify a computer ID (**Figure 3.36**). For Mac OS X Server, this computer ID should correspond to the host portion of the server's fully qualified domain name.

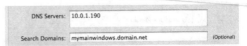

Figure 3.34 Ensuring that the Active Directory DNS is first in the list and that the search domain is set properly.

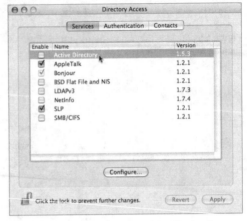

Figure 3.35 Showing the Active Directory plug-in within Directory Access.

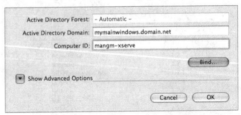

Figure 3.36 Double-clicking on the Active Directory (AD) plug-in within the Directory Access application and entering AD-specific data.

Active Directory Single Sign-On

Once the Mac OS X Server is bound to Active Directory, users should now be able to access your server services that support Kerberos authentication. Note, however, that as of 10.4.3, this procedure will only work if your server exists in the same DNS namespace that Active Directory does. If any errors occur, consult /Library/Logs/slapconfig.log.

Figure 3.37 After clicking the Bind button, you are asked to authenticate as an Active Directory user with write access to the OU specified in the path.

Figure 3.38 A successful bind changes the windows and the default button to Unbind.

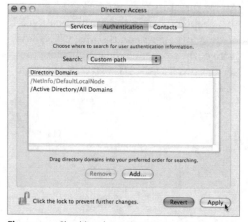

Figure 3.39 Checking the authentication path to ensure Active Directory is indeed in the path.

5. Click Bind. A dialog for supplying the administrative credentials appears (**Figure 3.37**).

6. In the Computer OU field, supply the credentials of a user with full control over the OU or CN and click Bind.

If binding is successful, the Active Directory Domain and Computer ID boxes will become unfocused, and the Bind button will become an Unbind button. The Active Directory bind will then be added to the authentication path (**Figure 3.38**).

7. Click the Authentication tab in Directory Access to ensure that Active Directory is now part of the authentication path and click Apply (**Figure 3.39**).

You may now access AD user accounts in much the same way you would Open Directory accounts: by assigning permissions, accessing Mac OS X Server Services, and provisioning access to Web resources.

✔ Tips

■ If binding is not successful, enable the DirectoryService daemon debugging by executing sudo killall -USR1 DirectoryService. View the resulting log in /Library/Logs/DirectoryService/ DirectoryService.debug.log during a second bind attempt.

■ Common to both the LDAPv3 and Active Directory plug-ins in Mac OS X and Mac OS X Server 10.4 are the "Use for authentication" and "Use for contacts" check boxes, which prevent the extraneous trips to the Authentication and Contacts tabs required in v10.3 and earlier.

Using Active Directory with Open Directory

It's common to need more out of your directory services infrastructure than Active Directory can provide. Although basic Active Directory integration is feasible with no modification to the directory, Mac OS X supports a number of features that are not available on Active Directory. This is the nature of cross-platform integration—a certain level of commonality is feasible, but platform-specific features will generally mean requirements that a single directory cannot provide.

A frequent strategy for alleviating this short-coming is deployment of peer directories. User, group, and other data lives in Active Directory. Mac-specific management data that Active Directory is generally incapable of providing lives in the Open Directory, and Mac clients are configured to access both. As of 10.4.3, Active Directory groups may be nested inside Open Directory groups using Workgroup Manager or the command-line dseditgroup.

By applying Mac OS X managed client settings to the Open Directory group that contains the AD group, users in the AD group are effectively managed, even though Active Directory cannot house Mac OS X managed client attributes. This is often known as the Golden Triangle, one corner being Active Directory, one corner being Mac OS X Server, and one corner being a Mac OS X computer.

To further this scenario, mobile home directories are often created to allow for home directory synching. The goal here is to:

◆ Create an OD master.

◆ Bind the OD master to an AD domain.

◆ Configure Mac OS X computers to bind to both domains.

◆ Synchronize local home directories for each user with directories on the OD master.

◆ Allow user authentication to rely on the AD server.

Before any binding can occur, a machine that can store MCX attributes in records at the user, group, or computer level must be available on the network. Logically, the Mac OS X Server should be promoted to Open Directory master. Before proceeding with this task, first follow the "To create an Open Directory Master" and the "To bind to an Active Directory domain" tasks earlier in this chapter. Then in the Authentication tab of Directory Access on the Mac OS X Server, Active Directory must be listed before the server's own LDAPv3/127.0.0.1 connection.

Figure 3.40 Choosing the shared (LDAP) domain in Workgroup Manager.

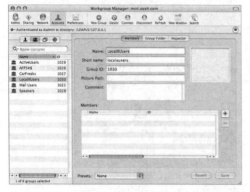

Figure 3.41 Creating a shared (LDAP) domain group.

Figure 3.42 Viewing the user and group drawer, initially showing the same LDAP domain.

To achieve the Golden Triangle scenario:

1. Create the Network mount point by following the "To create a home directory network mount" task in Chapter 5, "File Sharing."

2. Launch Server Admin, start the Apple File Service, and use Kerberos as the authentication protocol.

   For more on the Apple File Service, refer to Chapter 5.

3. Launch the Workgroup Manager tool located in /Applications/Server, and authenticate as the administrator if necessary.

4. Click the directory authentication icon and select the LDAP directory from the "Authenticate as" pop-up menu (**Figure 3.40**).

5. Select the Accounts icon in the toolbar and then click the Groups icon.

6. Choose the New Group icon and enter the group's long name and short name (**Figure 3.41**).

7. Open the users drawer by clicking the plus button next to the members window, and then select the group icon in the drawer.

   The Users and Groups list will open on the side of Workgroup Manager (**Figure 3.42**).

   There are two methods for creating groups from the Active Directory Users. One is to place the individual AD users into groups in the shared (LDAP) domain group. The other is to place AD groups into shared (LDAP) domain group. This second method, discussed here, refers to the new nested groups feature in Mac OS X Server 10.4 and avoids additional administration tasks.

continues on next page

8. Choose the Active Directory Domain from the "Authenticate as" pop-up menu (and type in the AD group you wish to see if necessary by choosing Other from the list) (**Figure 3.43**).

   The Active Directory group shows up in the authentication list (**Figure 3.44**).

9. Select the group that contains all the users who will be using Mac OS X and drag that group into the Members area; then click Save (**Figure 3.45**).

   Your shared (LDAP) domain now has an Active Directory group within its own LDAP group.

Figure 3.43 Choosing the bound Active Directory domain from the list.

Figure 3.44 Typing in the partial name of the group lists only those groups in Active Directory with that name.

Figure 3.45 Dragging the Active Directory group into the LDAP group to make a nested group.

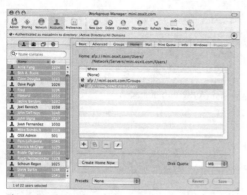

Figure 3.46 Selecting certain users to receive home directories that exist within the Active Directory domain.

10. Select the Users tab in the Active Directory Domain, click the Home folder tab, and select a Home folder path for those users (**Figure 3.46**).

11. Click Create Home Folder at the bottom of the window before you click Save.

It is critical that home folders be created before the users ever log in.

12. Click the Groups tab in Workgroup Manager and select the LDAPv3 group housing the AD nested group.

13. Add mobile home folder options for the group.

Refer to the section "About the Mobile Accounts managed preference" in Chapter 13, "Client Management," for instructions.

14. Follow steps 1–3 in the "To bind to an Active Directory domain" task earlier in this chapter to bind the Mac OS X computer(s).

Remember to use unique names for each computer.

15. In the Active Directory plug-in window, click the Show Advanced Options disclosure triangle.

continues on next page

CONNECTING TO A DIRECTORY SYSTEM

16. Select the "Create mobile account at login" check box and deselect the "Require confirmation before creating a mobile account" check box (**Figure 3.47**).

17. Continue with steps 4–7 in the "To bind to an Active Directory domain" task earlier in this chapter.

18. On the Mac OS X computer(s), complete the "To bind Mac OS X to a Mac OS X Server Open Directory Master" task earlier in this chapter.

19. Reboot the Mac OS X computer(s).

You should now be able to log in to a Mac OS X computer with a username and password that exists on the Active Directory server, have a local home folder created for you based on that account, and have that local home folder synchronized with an identical home folder on the Mac OS X Server.

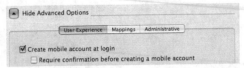

Figure 3.47 Selecting the Mobile home folder options within Workgroup Manager.

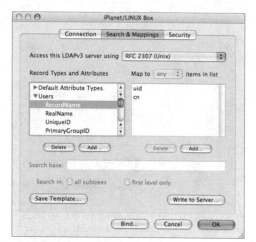

Figure 3.48 Mapping options when faced with binding to another type of directory service.

Accessing eDirectory, SunOne iPlanet, or other LDAP directories

LDAP is a tremendously flexible protocol that shows an extremely wide scope of deployment. Because of this, it's difficult to generalize among different types of LDAP deployments. Even given a single directory service platform (eDirectory, for instance), a wide variety of deployed configurations exist. Because of this, mapping is incredibly important. Mapping attributes is one way to ensure a smoother transition from one directory service to the other.

Although this seems complicated, essentially all you're doing is connecting the dots:

1. Determine the basic access configuration—port number, search base, and whether or not SSL is in use. Also important in some cases are authentication semantics: authentication methods and whether or not authentication is required to access the directory. This has to come from the LDAP administrator, not you. You are attempting to make the Mac OS X Server conform to their directory service, not the other way around.

2. Determine where user records are stored and whether or not sufficient data exists to support the Mac OS X user experience (at a minimum, a short name and numerical user ID should be available). If the attribute doesn't exist on the other directory service, you must either create that attribute or use an empty attribute and match the new name.

3. Configure the LDAPv3 plug-in. Start with the RFC2307 mappings, and customize them according to the research you put into your LDAP directory (**Figure 3.48**).

Accessing or using BSD flat files

The final directory service technology this chapter will look at is Network Information Services (NIS). This technology is still used in certain places, and Mac OS X and Mac OS X Servers can authenticate against it using the BSD Flat File and NIS plug-in. It can also be used to authenticate against flat files that exist on the local disk.

To create a local user outside the NetInfo directory:

1. Choose the Accounts tab from within the System Preferences application to create a user with the Long Name *Back Door* and the Short Name *backdoor* (**Figure 3.49**).

   This creates the home folder directory for the user backdoor (you can use any name that suits you).

2. Open the Terminal application, and type

   sudo mv /Users/backdoor/ /private/var/

3. Press Return, and enter your administrator password when asked.

   This moves the home folder of the user backdoor away from the normal location in the /Users folder and places it in the hidden /private/var directory.

4. Open System Preferences, and delete the user backdoor by clicking the minus button below the list of users and clicking Delete Immediately (**Figure 3.50**).

   This removes the user from the local NetInfo database; however, the home folder for that user has been saved and moved.

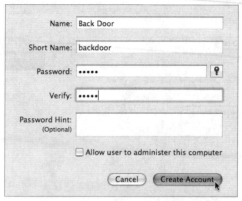

Figure 3.49 Creating an account using the Accounts preference pane in System Preferences.

Figure 3.50 Deleting the just-created account.

Flat Files

Before there were directories to store user information, it was stored (on various operating systems) in plain-text files on the computer. Mac OS X and Mac OS X Server still contain these plain-text files and permit an administrator to add these files in the authentication search path via the Directory Access application. See the task "To create a local user outside the NetInfo directory" for more information.

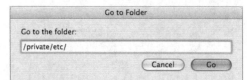

Figure 3.51 Viewing a hidden directory with Go To Folder under the Go menu.

5. Open a new Finder window, choose Go > Go To Folder, and type /private/etc in the resulting dialog (**Figure 3.51**).

6. Open the file, master.passwd, in a text editor, such as vi or pico, by typing sudo vi master.passwd.

7. View the last line of the file, and create a new last line of the file, mimicking everything you see except changing the following:

   ▲ Short Name
   ▲ User ID
   ▲ Group ID
   ▲ Home Folder path
   ▲ Shell type

   For example, in the line backdoor:*: 501:501::0:0:Back Door:/var/ backdoor:/bin/bash, from left to right:

   ▲ backdoor is the user's short name.
   ▲ The asterisk is a placeholder for the password that will be changed later.
   ▲ 501:501 is the user ID followed by the primary group ID.
   ▲ Back Door is the user's long name.
   ▲ /var/backdoor is the path to the home folder, which was moved into /var earlier.
   ▲ /bin/bash is the user shell type.

8. Save the file.

continues on next page

CONNECTING TO A DIRECTORY SYSTEM

9. Open the Terminal, and change the password for your new user by typing `sudo passwd -i file backdoor` and pressing Return.

   Enter *your* password first if necessary, because you started the command with sudo. Then enter and reenter the new backdoor user's password to change it.

10. While you're in the Terminal, type `sudo chown -R backdoor:backdoor /var/backdoor`, and press Return.

    This command reassociates the backdoor user with the backdoor home folder.

11. Open the /private/etc/group file (again using `vi` or `pico`) and add this backdoor user to the admin group, allowing them to have administrative privileges.

    You've created a hidden user inside the local flat file with the same UID and group ID as the local administrator. You must now add the local flat files to the authentication search path.

To add flat-file searching to the authentication path:

1. Launch Directory Access and authenticate by clicking the lock in the lower-left corner of the dialog.

2. Click the Services tab, and click the BSD Flat File and NIS plug-in check box if it isn't already checked (**Figure 3.52**).

3. Click the Configure button to open the BSD authentication dialog.

4. Click the "Use BSD local files (/etc) for authentication" check box and then click OK to close the dialog (**Figure 3.53**).

Figure 3.52 Checking and double-clicking the BSD Flat File and NIS plug-in reveals...

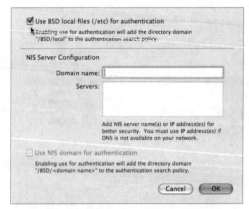

Figure 3.53 ...the check box necessary to allow it to access the master.passwd file.

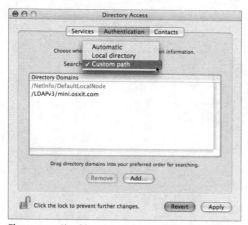

Figure 3.54 Checking the Authentication tab and ensuring that Custom Path is selected.

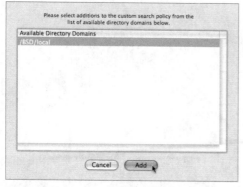

Figure 3.55 Clicking the Add button reveals the newly setup BSD/Local authentication option to add to the path.

5. In Directory Services, click the Authentication tab and choose Custom path from the pull-down menu if not already selected (**Figure 3.54**).

6. Click Add to open a list of Available Directory Domains.

7. Select /BSD/local from the list and click Add (**Figure 3.55**).

8. Click Apply to commit the changes to your Open Directory architecture.

Your Mac OS X Server is now ready to have a hidden user authenticate from flat-file users.

9. Log out, and then log in with your new hidden account.

✔ Tip

■ By making the user ID the same as your initial user, you guarantee that the back-door user will see user 501's files.

USER AND GROUP MANAGEMENT

4

Populating a server with all your users and groups can be a potentially daunting task. You can always use the command line to add users, but within the graphical user interface, there are two additional methods: using the Accounts preference pane or Workgroup Manager. Of the two, Workgroup Manager is the preferred tool used to populate user, group, and computer accounts on Mac OS X Server. While the interface for Workgroup Manager is an obvious holdover from the older Macintosh Manager, it does improve a bit on that design.

Workgroup Manager also includes numerous efficiency-enhancing features. You can quickly make widespread changes by selecting and configuring multiple accounts simultaneously. A User Presets tool can decrease the amount of time it takes to create similar user accounts. Furthermore, Workgroup Manager has an Import option that lets you input new users from many types of external sources.

Before you begin setting up accounts, take time to consider how you're going to organize your users and groups. On Mac OS X Server, groups are used for more than just individual file and folder permissions; they're also used to define access to share points, Web sites, email groups, and managed workgroup settings. Also, if you're configuring users and groups on an Open Directory (OD) master, it's important to consider how your groups will integrate with Mac OS X computers. Remember, any groups in an LDAP directory are accessible to computers that authenticate against your OD master.

If you have anything but local users you can manage specific settings for each user when they log in from a Mac OS X computer that has been bound to the Mac OS X Server on which you're working. In other words, they have *no* account on Mac OS X—only on the server—but they can authenticate and log in. Before you start typing in user and/or group accounts, plan what you want to accomplish. You may find that an organizational tool, such as a group outline or flowchart software (for example, OmniGraffle from www.omnigroup.com), can help you plan the best implementation for your needs).

Configuring Basic User Attributes

Workgroup Manager lets you reconfigure user attributes as many times as you want. Assuming you're a server administrator, you can configure any user account on any database hosted by that server. Otherwise, Workgroup Manager automatically prompts you for administrator authentication when attempting to make changes to a user directory you haven't already authenticated to.

This chapter assumes you've already created additional user accounts on your server. If you haven't, refer to the instructions for creating a basic user account in Chapter 2, "Server Tools."

User ID and More

Each user created on Mac OS X and Mac OS X Server has a number associated with it. This number is known as the User ID number. It contains no text but only numerals, and starts with the number 501 on both Mac OS X and Mac OS X Server. Local NetInfo accounts proceed with 502, 503, and so on, while LDAP accounts start with 1025 and go up. There is an LDAP administrator account whose default user ID is 1000, but that can be changed when the account is set up. If two users have the same user ID, they have access to the same files and folders on the computer that maintains their account information.

In Mac OS X Server 10.4, each user (and group) created also has a globally unique value. Since two Mac OS X Servers each have an account with the user ID of 501, there needed to be a way to distinguish between those two accounts. This basic premise can be extrapolated to groups as well, as groups can contain other groups. Enter the Generated UID, which consists of alphanumeric characters guaranteed—and, with apologies to Dave Barry, I am NOT making this up—to be unique over space and time. Basically, this value is created using the computers hardware (MAC) address and combining it with the 100-nanosecond interval the account was created from October 15, 1582, at 00:00:00. This information can be verified by typing man uuidgen in the Terminal.

Figure 4.1 Open the Workgroup Manager tool, and authenticate as an administrator.

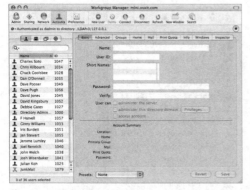

Figure 4.2 Click the Accounts icon and the User tab in Workgroup Manager.

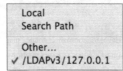

Figure 4.3 Select the appropriate directory database from the pop-up menu.

To configure basic user attributes:

1. Launch the Workgroup Manager tool located in /Applications/Server, and authenticate as the administrator if necessary (**Figure 4.1**).

   You will be using Workgroup Manager for the remainder of the tasks in this chapter. It is assumed you have already logged into your Workgroup Manager and authenticated as necessary.

2. Click the Accounts icon in the Toolbar and then click the User tab in the account types tab (**Figure 4.2**).

   If you've added users previous to this task, they appear in the Name list.

3. Click the directory authentication icon and select the appropriate directory database from the pop-up menu (**Figure 4.3**):

   ▲ If you're working on the local directory, choose Local.

   ▲ If you're working on an Open Directory master, choose /LDAPv3/127.0.0.1.

   ▲ If you're connected to another database, choose Other, and select your database from there.

continues on next page

4. Select the user or users you wish to configure from the user list (**Figure 4.4**).

   or

   You can also create a new user by clicking New User in the Toolbar.

5. In the user settings frame, click the Basic tab.

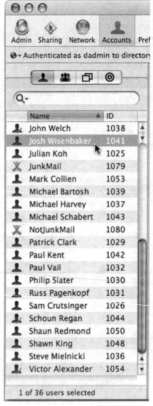

Figure 4.4 Choose a user or users from the selected database.

CONFIGURING BASIC USER ATTRIBUTES

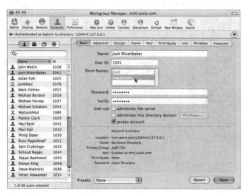

Figure 4.5 Create a user, and configure the Basic user attributes.

6. *Change any of the following* preexisting user account information (**Figure 4.5**):

   ▲ Name (long name)

   ▲ User ID

   ▲ Additional short names

   ▲ Password

   ▲ Administrator settings

   For more on the administrator settings, see the "To change administrative user options" section later in this chapter.

7. When you've finished making changes, click Save.

8. Verify your changes by reviewing the account summary or by testing authentication from a Mac OS X computer.

✔ Tip

■ Click Revert if you made a mistake and don't want to apply the configuration changes (Figure 4.5).

Configuring Multiple Users Simultaneously

There are two ways to select multiple accounts from the user list in Workgroup Manager:

◆ To choose a sequential list of accounts, select an account toward the top of the list and then, while holding down the Shift key, select an account further down the list. Workgroup Manager automatically selects all the accounts between your two selections.

◆ To select multiple accounts in a nonsequential order, hold down the Command key on your keyboard and select multiple accounts. Workgroup Manager adds accounts to your total selection as you click each account individually.

After you've selected all the accounts you wish to change, continue by configuring settings as if you had selected only an individual user account. Click Save to apply the configuration changes to all the user accounts you selected. The only settings you can't apply to multiple user accounts are Name, User ID, and Short Names.

Adding short names

The initial short name of a user in Mac OS X is used as the name of that user's home folder, should they have one. Although you can add more short names, Apple recognizes that changing the original isn't a good idea unless you have a specific reason to do so. That's why the only user attribute you can't change in the Basic tab of Workgroup Manager after you've created a user account is the user's short name. Mac OS X server lets you add several additional short names instead, and once they're configured, the user can use any short name they desire for authentication.

To add short names:

1. In Workgroup Manager, click the Accounts icon in the Toolbar, click the User tab in the account types tab, and click the Basic tab (**Figure 4.6**).

2. Double-click the area directly below the user's original short name.

3. In the text entry field that appears, you can enter an additional short name (**Figure 4.7**).

4. Press Return to activate the Save button.

5. When you've finished making changes, click Save.

✔ Tips

■ You can add more short names by double-clicking the empty space below the last short name in the list.

■ All short names, including any short names that you add, must be unique within the entire system.

■ If you really want to change the original short name, you can effectively do so by creating a new account and moving the user's configuration and files to it. See "Using Presets for New Accounts," later in this chapter.

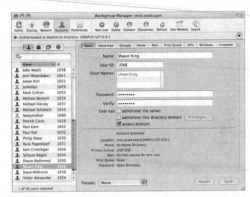

Figure 4.6 Navigate to the user account's Basic tab in Workgroup Manager.

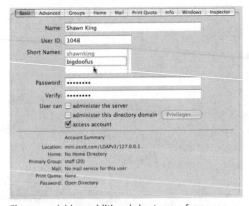

Figure 4.7 Add an additional short name for a user.

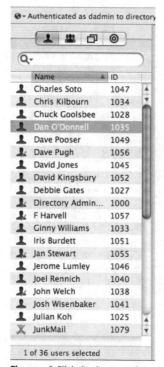

Authenticated as dadmin to directory

Name	▲	ID
Charles Soto		1047
Chris Kilbourn		1034
Chuck Goolsbee		1028
Dan O'Donnell		1035
Dave Pooser		1049
Dave Pugh		1056
David Jones		1045
David Kingsbury		1052
Debbie Gates		1027
Directory Admin...		1000
F Harvell		1057
Ginny Williams		1033
Iris Burdett		1051
Jan Stewart		1055
Jerome Lumley		1046
Joel Rennich		1040
John Welch		1038
Josh Wisenbaker		1041
Julian Koh		1025
JunkMail		1079

1 of 36 users selected

Figure 4.8 Click the Accounts icon and the User tab in Workgroup Manager.

Administrative User Options

Administrative user accounts on Mac OS X Server are very similar to administrative user accounts on Mac OS X. Administrative users can configure any settings or file permissions on both Mac OS X and Mac OS X Server. Essentially, an administrative user account is any user who is also in the admin group. Thus, it's important to restrict administrative user accounts to only those users who require such authority.

From an account management standpoint, administrators aren't that different from other user accounts. In fact, administrative users and regular users are only separated by one check box in the Workgroup Manager application.

This discussion assumes you've already created additional user accounts on your server (refer to Chapter 2).

To change administrative user options:

1. In Workgroup Manager, click the Accounts icon in the Toolbar, click the User tab in the account types tab, and click the Basic tab.

   The user information is displayed (**Figure 4.8**).

continues on next page

2. Click the directory authentication icon, and select the appropriate directory database from the pop-up menu (**Figure 4.9**).

3. Select the user or users you wish to configure from the user list (**Figure 4.10**).

4. In the user settings frame, click the Basic tab.

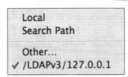

Figure 4.9 Select the appropriate directory database from the pop-up menu.

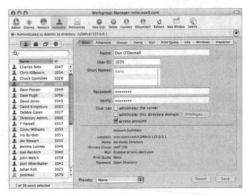

Figure 4.10 Choose a user from the selected database.

ADMINISTRATIVE USER OPTIONS

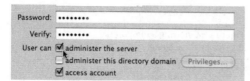

Figure 4.11 If the user account is in a local directory, select the "User can administer the server" check box.

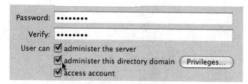

Figure 4.12 If the user account is in a shared directory, select both the "User can administer the server" and the "User can administer this directory domain" check boxes. Doing so...

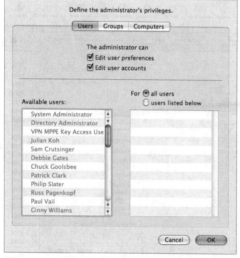

Figure 4.13 ...opens the administrator's privileges dialog.

5. *Do one of the following,* depending on what options you want your new administrator to have:

▲ If the user account needs to manage services using the Server Admin application, click the "administer the server" check box (**Figure 4.11**).

▲ If the user account needs to manage the LDAP database, click the "administer this directory domain" check box (**Figure 4.12**) to invoke the administrator privileges dialog (**Figure 4.13**), and then click OK to accept the default settings.

6. When you've finished making changes, click Save.

This user is now allowed to make changes to all server settings, file permissions, and user accounts.

✔ Tips

- Administrative users can also become the root user by typing sudo -s in the Terminal, pressing Return, and entering their password. This opens a root shell.

- To revert the administrative account back to a regular user account, deselect both administrator check boxes and save your changes.

- An administrative user account in an LDAP directory can administer any computer that authenticates against that directory. In other words, if your Mac OS X computers use the directory server, then server administrators also have administrative rights on those Mac OS X computers.

- You can disable any account by deselecting the "access account" check box. Doing so changes the icon for the user in the user list showing an "X" over their name, indicating that user is unable to log in (**Figure 4.14**).

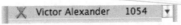

Figure 4.14 Viewing a temporarily disabled user account.

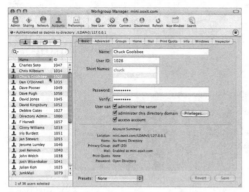

Figure 4.15 Click the Accounts icon and the User tab in Workgroup Manager.

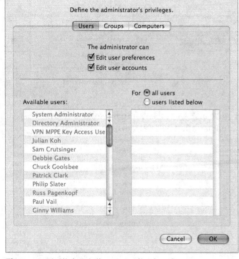

Figure 4.16 Click Privileges to display the administrator's editing privileges dialog.

Restricting administrator directory access

On Mac OS X, every administrative user is allowed to edit all settings, permissions, and user accounts. However, Mac OS X Server gives you more granularity when configuring administrative user permissions. Specifically, Mac OS X Server distinguishes administrators who can configure service settings from those who can configure account settings and share points. For example, server administrators can use the Server Admin tool, whereas directory administrators can use the Workgroup Manager tool for shared (LDAP) accounts, and local administrators can manage local (NetInfo) accounts.

In the previous task, you were instructed to enable unlimited server and directory administration rights for a user account, thus turning it into an administrative account. The following task explains how to restrict an administrator's directory permissions.

To restrict administrator directory access:

1. In Workgroup Manager, click the Accounts icon in the Toolbar, click the User tab in the account types tab, and click the Basic tab (**Figure 4.15**).

2. Verify that the "User can administer this directory domain" check box is selected and click Privileges.

    The administrator's privileges dialog opens (**Figure 4.16**).

3. For this task, select the Users tab. The options are similar for each account type.

    continues on next page

4. To configure the administrator's permissions, *select or deselect the following options*:

▲ "Edit user preferences" lets the administrator edit managed preferences for this account type.

▲ "Edit user accounts" lets the administrator edit account attributes for this account type.

5. Select the "users listed below" radio button (**Figure 4.17**).

6. Drag and drop accounts from the "Available users" column to the right column (**Figure 4.18**).

7. Click OK to accept the changes.

The administrator's permissions dialog closes.

8. When you've finished making changes, click Save.

✔ Tips

■ When it's properly configured, you can safely delegate the task of managing accounts to other users with more time on their hands for such tasks. Keep in mind that every administrator can still become root in the terminal.

■ You can select more than one account at a time while in the administrator's privileges dialog by holding down the Shift or Command key while you make your selections.

■ While you can have granular control over an admin's abilities in the directory when using Workgroup Manager, keep in mind that only the Apple tools respect these controls. Any admin user has full control of their directory domain using the command-line tools.

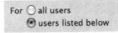

Figure 4.17 Choose the option button that allows an administrator to administer certain users.

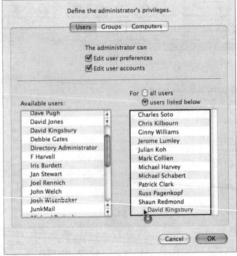

Figure 4.18 Drag users into the field to allow administration by a certain administrator.

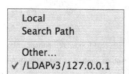

Figure 4.19 Select the appropriate directory database from the pop-up menu.

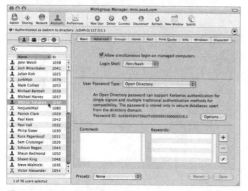

Figure 4.20 Choose a user or users from the selected database.

Figure 4.21 Choose an option from the Login Shell pop-up menu.

Advanced User Configuration

The Workgroup Manager tool affords a variety of advanced user configuration options that you may find useful. For example, you may not want a user to be able to log in remotely via the command line. Or, if they do have remote terminal access, you can dictate what type of shell they use.

This discussion assumes you've already created additional user accounts on your server (refer to Chapter 2).

To configure the shell type:

1. In Workgroup Manager, click the Accounts icon in the Toolbar, click the User tab in the account types tab, and click the Advanced tab.

2. Click the directory authentication icon, and select the LDAP directory database from the pop-up menu (**Figure 4.19**).

3. Select the user or users you wish to configure from the user list (**Figure 4.20**).

4. Click the Login Shell pop-up menu, and then choose a default shell (**Figure 4.21**).

   The login shell permits users to use the Terminal to access the server remotely via the command line.

5. When you've finished making changes, click Save.

   Now, any time this user attempts to launch a command-line interface (generally, using the Terminal application), they will be presented with the shell type defined by this setting.

✔ Tip

■ You can define a custom shell type or script file by selecting Custom from the Login Shell pop-up menu.

Configuring password types

Mac OS X Server 10.4 provides a variety of different password types for different services. The default password type for most users is Open Directory, because it provides the greatest security. (See Chapter 3, "Open Directory," for more information.) Occasionally, though, you may wish to change a user's password from one type to another. The most common reason for doing so is backward compatibility when you have older Mac OS computers that need to connect to your Mac OS X Server.

The password types are as follows:

- **Open Directory passwords** are the default type for Mac OS X Server 10.4, LDAP users. Open Directory provides authentication through a wide variety of other methods, including APOP, NTLMV1 & 2, DHX, CRAM-MD5, LAN Manager, and Web-DAV via Password Server. Open Directory passwords also take advantage of single sign-on features utilizing the built-in Kerberos infrastructure.

- **Shadow passwords** are the default type for Mac OS X and are also used by local users on Mac OS X Server. You can edit the methods of authentication for these local accounts by selecting a user from the local database, selecting the Advanced tab, and clicking Security.

- **Crypt passwords** are the default type for Mac OS X version 10.1 and earlier. This type of password should only be used for backward compatibility and is available to LDAP users. Both local and LDAP users can use this password type.

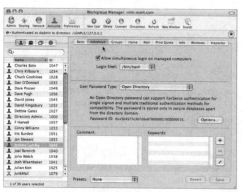

Figure 4.22 Select the Workgroup Manager Advanced tab to change password options.

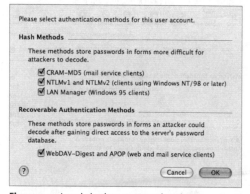

Figure 4.23 Local shadow password options.

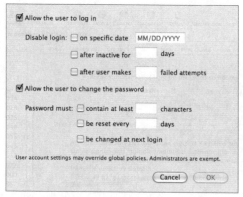

Figure 4.24 Viewing Open Directory user password policy options.

To configure the password type:

1. In Workgroup Manager, click the Accounts icon in the Toolbar, click the User tab in the account types tab, and click the Advanced tab (**Figure 4.22**).

2. Depending on whether the user account is in a local or an LDAP directory, *select one of the following options* from the User Password Type pop-up menu:

   ▲ If the user account is in a local directory, the password is a Shadow Password. Your choice is to set the authentication methods using the Security button (**Figure 4.23**).

   ▲ If the user account is in an LDAP directory, your choices of password types are Open Directory and "Crypt password." Open Directory users have the following password policy options, most of which are self-explanatory (**Figure 4.24**).

continues on next page

ADVANCED USER CONFIGURATION

3. If you chose to change the Open Directory password to Crypt or just select the different password type and then change the password itself, verify a password, and click OK (**Figure 4.25**).

4. When you've finished making changes, click the Save button.

Remember to test authentication from a Mac OS X computer to verify the new password.

✔ Tip

■ When you're changing the password type, you'll be prompted to enter a new user password. However, it can be the same as the old password.

Adding comments to a user account

As an organizational aide, Mac OS X Server lets you add a comment to any user account. This comment is primarily used for administrators to add notes or information about a particular user. However, you can also use comments as part of your search criteria to find a specific account among a large list of users. (User searches are covered in the task "To search user accounts.")

To add a comment to a user account, simply navigate to configure the user's Advanced account attributes as in the previous task, double-click in the Comment field, and enter your comment (**Figure 4.26**). When you've finished making changes, click Save. You can change a comment at any point by entering new text.

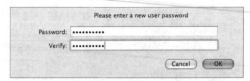

Please enter a new user password

Password: ••••••••••
Verify: ••••••••••

Cancel   OK

Figure 4.25 The password change dialog in the Advanced pane of Workgroup Manager.

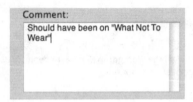

Comment:
Should have been on "What Not To Wear"

Figure 4.26 Double-click in the Comment field, and enter your comment.

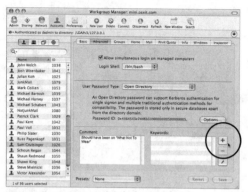

Figure 4.27 Navigate to the Advanced tab in Workgroup Manager and click the plus button to add keywords.

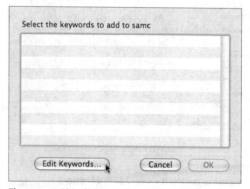

Figure 4.28 This dialog contains any previously added keywords.

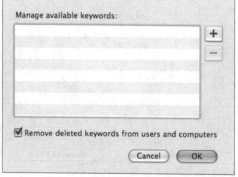

Figure 4.29 The "Manage available keywords" dialog opens.

Adding keywords to a user account

As yet another organizational aide, Mac OS X Server lets you add keywords to any user account. A keyword provides additional bits of information to enable your user to quickly find specific accounts among a large list of users via the search function. Keywords help further define users through categories you create, such as *Temporary worker*, or your personal rating system for each user's computer experience and knowledge.

Say, for example, that you had 50 users. You could rate them with the following keywords: Novice, Intermediate, Expert, Certified, Mac OS X, Mac OS 9, Windows, and/or Unix. You could take that even further by entering application(s) they know well. You could also enter certifications they've received, such as Apple's ACTC and ACSA. These keywords could be combined to allow you to search accounts for users who were trained or knowledgeable in a specific field. (User searches are covered in the task "To search user accounts.") Initially, no keywords are configured.

To add a keyword to a user account:

1. In Workgroup Manager, click the Accounts icon in the Toolbar, click the User tab in the account types tab, click the Advanced tab, and click the plus button to the right of the Keywords window (**Figure 4.27**).

2. Click Edit Keywords in the Add dialog (**Figure 4.28**) and another dialog appears (**Figure 4.29**).

   You must first add some keywords before you can assign them to a user.

   continues on next page

3. Click the plus button and enter your keyword(s) in the field.

4. When finished adding keywords for all users, click OK to return to the Add keyword(s) to selected user dialog.

5. Select the keywords you want to add to the user account, and then click OK (**Figure 4.30**).

6. When you've finished making changes, click the Save button and view the newly added keywords (**Figure 4.31**).

✔ Tips

■ You can always add more keywords at any time, or delete them by clicking the Delete button from within the Edit Keywords dialog.

■ Keywords are case sensitive. In other words, the keyword *Temporary* is different from the keyword *temporary*.

■ You can select multiple items in the Select dialog by holding down the Command or Shift key on your keyboard while you make your selections.

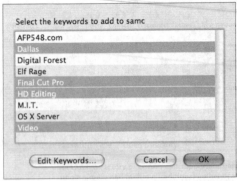

Figure 4.30 Once you add keywords, you can select them to add the selected account(s).

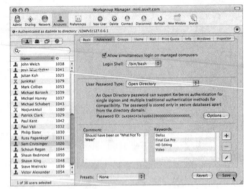

Figure 4.31 View the newly added keywords.

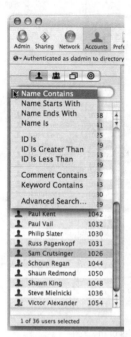

Figure 4.32 Select the spyglass icon to choose the parameter you wish to use from the pop-up menu.

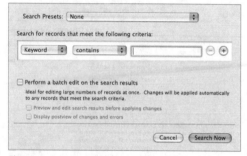

Figure 4.33 Selecting the Advanced Search option opens the Advanced Search dialog.

Searching user accounts

Because Mac OS X Server has the potential to easily host thousands of user accounts, you may find it difficult to locate a specific account in the user list. Workgroup Manager lets you sort through the user list using a variety of search criteria, including Name, User ID, Comments, and Keywords. (For more about adding comments and keywords, see the previous tasks.)

While searching user accounts is useful, performing batch edits on those queried accounts reduces the amount of time an administrator spends making user changes.

To search user accounts:

1. In Workgroup Manager, click the Accounts icon in the Toolbar, and click the User tab in the account types tab.

2. Click the directory authentication icon, and select the appropriate directory database from the pop-up menu.

3. Click the spyglass icon above the user list (**Figure 4.32**) and select the search category you wish to use from the pop-up menu, or click Search in the Toolbar to bring up the Advanced Search dialog (**Figure 4.33**).

continues on next page

ADVANCED USER CONFIGURATION

4. Enter your search criteria in the field above the user list or in the entry field of the Advanced Search dialog (**Figure 4.34**).

As you type, the list—in this case the keyword—is automatically pared down to reveal the user accounts that fit your search criteria (**Figure 4.35**).

5. To bring your list back to its full length, delete the search criteria.

✔ Tip

■ Keyword searches are case-sensitive; name and comment searches aren't.

Figure 4.34 When you choose a search pattern, it appears in the Search field.

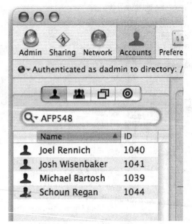

Figure 4.35 View the results of the search in the user's list.

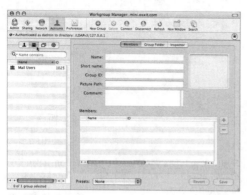

Figure 4.36 Click the Accounts icon and the Group tab in Workgroup Manager.

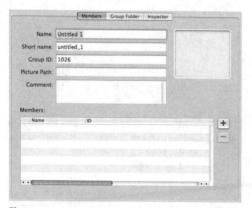

Figure 4.37 Create a new group and all the associated fields.

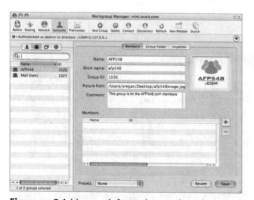

Figure 4.38 Add group information, such as the group name, short name, group ID, picture path, and comments.

Creating Groups

Essentially, a group is nothing more than a list of users or other groups. Nevertheless, groups are used as a means to organize access to file and folder permissions, share points, Web sites, email groups, and managed workgroup settings. Mac OS X Server can also utilize nested groups, allowing groups to contain other groups.

This section discusses initial group configuration; the next section covers adding users to group lists. We discuss implementation of groups in specific services in future chapters.

To create a group:

1. In Workgroup Manager, click the Accounts icon in the Toolbar and click the Group tab in the account types tab (**Figure 4.36**).

2. Click the directory authentication icon, and select the appropriate directory database from the pop-up menu.

3. Click New Group to populate the information in the Members frame with a new untitled group (**Figure 4.37**).

4. Enter a new group name (long name), short name, group ID, path to the image (the image will then appear in the window, and comment (**Figure 4.38**).

   Using the automatically generated Group ID setting is usually acceptable. It's good practice to keep the long and short names the same.

continues on next page

5. Click the plus button next to the Members list.

A user drawer appears to one side of the main Workgroup Manager window (**Figure 4.39**).

6. Click and drag a user account or list of users or groups from the user and/or group list to the Members field (**Figure 4.40**).

7. When you've finished making changes, click Save.

✔ Tip

■ As is the case for user accounts, no two group short names or group IDs should be the same.

Figure 4.39 When you click the plus button, a user drawer appears to one side of the main Workgroup Manager window.

Figure 4.40 Drag users from the users drawer into the members field in Workgroup Manager.

What Is a Primary Group?

Every user belongs to at least one group: their *primary group*. The default primary group for all users on Mac OS X Server is the Staff group (the Staff Group ID is 20). However, you can specify any group as a user's primary group in the user's Groups settings in Workgroup Manager.

You can't remove the user from the primary group's membership. You can, however, change the user's primary group, which removes them from the previous primary group.

The primary group is used to facilitate group membership lookups. Instead of having to iterate all of the group records to determine if a user is a member of a group, the system only has to look to the user's own user record.

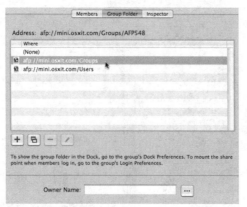

Figure 4.41 Click the Group Folder tab and select a group folder location from the network mount list or...

Figure 4.42 ...click the plus button to specify the server's address, the share point, and the client's mount point.

Assigning group folders

Just as a user can have a home folder, a group can have a group folder. The group folder is used as a common access point for all members of that group. Group folders aren't required for remote login access or any other services; they're convenient locations for shared files. However, group folders must reside inside a share point that your client computers can access. Refer to Chapter 5 for more information about configuring share points.

To assign a group folder:

1. In Workgroup Manager, navigate to the appropriate directory and group list that you wish to have a group folder and click the Group Folder tab.

2. Select the share point where the group folder will reside by *doing one of the following:*

   ▲ If this server has been configured with network mount share points such as sharing the Group folder, select one of those shares from the list (**Figure 4.41**). (If not, see the task "To create additional network mounts" in Chapter 5.)

   ▲ Click the plus button to open the dialog to specify a custom share point in the mount points window that appears. You must specify the server's address, the share point, and the client's mount point (**Figure 4.42**).

   continues on next page

3. To specify an owner for the group folder, click the ellipsis button next to the Owner Name field.

A user drawer appears to one side of the main Workgroup Manager window (**Figure 4.43**).

4. Click and drag a user account from the user list to the Owner Name field (**Figure 4.44**).

5. When you've finished making changes, click Save.

The group folder will automatically be created overnight on the server, provided the server is left running.

✔ Tips

■ You can force the server to create the group folder immediately by entering the following command in the Terminal: `sudo creategroupfolder`.

■ You can use command-line tools to enable disk usage quotas per group account. See the section "Setting disk quotas via the command line" for more information.

■ To delete group members, click the account in the Members list, and then click the Delete button.

■ You can add groups to other groups by dragging one group into the other group and saving the changes.

■ Administrative users are automatically placed in the Admin group user list.

Figure 4.43 When you click the ellipsis button, a user drawer appears to one side of the main Workgroup Manager window.

Figure 4.44 Drag a user account to the Owner Name field.

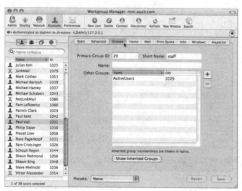

Figure 4.45 Select the user or users you want to add to a group and click the Groups tab.

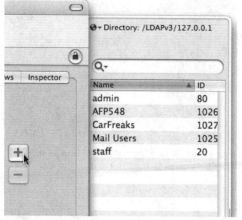

Figure 4.46 Clicking the plus button opens a group drawer to one side of the main Workgroup Manager window.

Adding groups to users

You may find it easier to manage groups by adding groups to users. However, it's important to understand that groups are only lists of user accounts. In Workgroup Manager, when you add a group to a user account, the system is actually adding the user account to that group's user list. This simulation of adding groups to users is another convenience provided by Mac OS X Server.

To add a group to a user:

1. In Workgroup Manager, click the Accounts icon in the Toolbar, click the User tab in the account types tab, and click the Groups tab (**Figure 4.45**).

2. Click the directory authentication icon, and select the appropriate directory database from the pop-up menu.

3. Click the plus button next to the Other Groups list (**Figure 4.46**).

   A group drawer appears to one side of the main Workgroup Manager window.

   continues on next page

4. Click and drag a group or list of groups from the group list to the Other Groups field (**Figure 4.47**).

You can also click Show Inherited Groups to see any groups that your user may also be a member of by the fact that the initial group chosen may be part of another group (**Figure 4.48**).

5. When you've finished making changes, click Save.

✔ Tips

■ To delete group memberships, click the group in the Other Groups list, and then click Delete, which appears as a minus icon.

■ You can show the system groups by selecting View > Show System Users & Groups in Workgroup Manager.

Figure 4.47 Drag a group or list of groups to the Other Groups field.

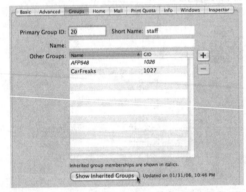

Figure 4.48 Clicking Show Inherited Groups shows all inherited groups for that user or users.

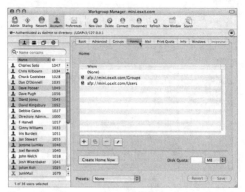

Figure 4.49 Choose a user or users from the selected database and click the Home tab.

Setting the Home Directory

User home directories typically contain all of a user's personal documents and application preferences. They can also be made available over the network, allowing the user to have the same environment and documents no matter what client machine they log into.

Local user home directories are typically stored on a local hard drive. For example, the primary server administrator's home directory is stored in the /Users directory. Most Mac OS X computers keep local user directories in this location as well.

On the other hand, network user home directories must reside on a server configured with a network mount share point to which your clients have access. Network mount share points are like regular server share points, with one very important exception: Client computers automatically connect to network mount share points during startup. (See Chapter 5 for more about configuring network mount share points.)

To create a user home directory:

1. Follow steps 1–2 in the previous task.

2. Select the user or users you wish to configure from the user list and click the Home tab (**Figure 4.49**).

continues on next page

3. To select the share point where the home directory will reside, *do one of the following:*

▲ If this server has been configured with network mount share points, select one of those shares from the list (**Figure 4.50**).

▲ Click the plus button and specify a custom share point. You must specify the server's address, the share point, the name of the directory, and the client's mount point (**Figure 4.51**).

It's easier to create the network mount share, but custom shares are more versatile. See the sidebar "Custom Mount Points" for more information.

4. Click Create Home Now to create the user's home directory immediately (Figure 4.50).

Otherwise, the home directory will be automatically created the first time this user logs in.

5. When you've finished making changes, click Save.

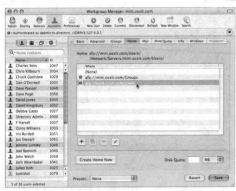

Figure 4.50 Select a home directory location from the network mount list.

Figure 4.51 Specify a custom mount point for the user's home directory.

✔ **Tips**

■ You can also create a home directory by typing sudo createhomedir -a from the Terminal.

■ If users are logging in from Windows computers that require a home directory, the home directory *must* be created prior to those users logging in.

■ It's strongly suggested that you thoroughly test a few network home directories before you implement this feature on a wide scale.

■ You can always change a user's home directory setting in the future. However, if you move a user's home directory location in the Workgroup Manager settings, the server won't move the user's data to the new location for you—you must manually move the user's data to the new location. Be sure to verify the ownership and permissions of the data after moving it to another location.

Custom Mount Points

When you choose custom mount points, you're allowing the mount point to go to another directory or possibly another server. This allows for a greater range of possible locations for the actual home folder. The three options for the custom mount point are as follows:

◆ **Share Point URL** is the URL-style path to the user's home folder.

◆ **Path** is the user's short name.

◆ **Home** is the full path to the location of the home folder.

Setting User Disk Quotas

Mac OS X lets you set user disk quotas that limit the total amount of data a user is allowed to store on the server. These quotas work based on file ownership: Any file owned by a user applies to that user's disk quota.

Disk quotas are applied separately for each volume. In other words, a user with a 50 MB disk quota can store 50 MB of data on each volume to which they have write access.

To enforce disk quotas using Workgroup Manager, the user must have a home folder configured even if you never intend the home folder to be used. See the task "To create a user home directory."

To enable disk quotas:

1. In Workgroup Manager, click the Sharing icon in the Toolbar, click the All tab, select a volume on which to enable disk quotas, and select the "Enable disk quotas on this volume" check box (**Figure 4.52**).

   Typically, you'll select the volume where the user's home folders will reside.

2. Click Save and restart the server to enable quotas for the selected volume.

   This creates the hidden quota configuration files and enables the quota service for the selected volume.

3. Repeat steps 3–5 for every volume on which you want to enforce disk quotas.

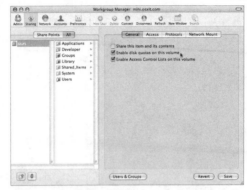

Figure 4.52 From the server volume list, select a volume on which to enable disk quotas; then select the "Enable disk quotas on this volume" check box.

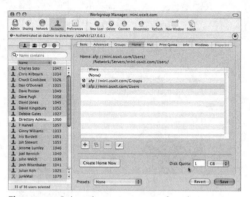

Figure 4.53 Select the user or users for whom you want to set quotas and enter a number size in the Disk Quota field, also choosing MB or GB.

To set a user's disk quota:

1. In Workgroup Manager, navigate to configure the user (or users') Home attributes by clicking the Accounts icon, and then clicking the Home tab on the User tab.

2. In the user list, select the user or users you wish to configure and place a number in the Disk Quota field (**Figure 4.53**).

3. Select MB or GB for the appropriate size of the user's quota.

4. When you've finished making changes, click Save.

   The next time this user logs in via AFP, the quota files will be configured for their account. You can always change the user's quota in the future.

✔ Tips

- When you're using AFP, a malicious user can max out another user's disk quota by filling the other user's Drop Box with large files.

- Quotas set in Workgroup Manager apply only to the volume that a user's home folder resides on.

- Quotas are updated the next time the user logs in via AFP. There is no way in Workgroup Manager to force an update of the quotas, or to make a non-AFP file sharing connection update them.

SETTING USER DISK QUOTAS

Setting disk quotas via the command line

Enabling disk-usage quotas using command-line tools gives you much greater control over quota settings than is available from Workgroup Manager. In fact, there are so many options that this section can cover only the basics.

The following task outlines the generally practiced method for setting quotas from the command line. Note that you must be the super user to configure disk usage quotas.

To set a disk quota from the command line:

1. *Do one of the following:*

   ▲ Log in to the command line as the root user.

   ▲ Log in with sudo -s.

   ▲ Preface every command with sudo.

2. *Do either of the following:*

   ▲ Use the quota files created by Workgroup Manager.

   ▲ Create the quota files .quota.user and .quota.ops.user at the root level of every volume on which you wish to enable quotas, by entering touch /.quota.user /.qouta.ops.user in the command line.

3. Configure the correct ownership and permissions for the quota files by entering chown :admin .quota* and then chmod 640 .quota* in the command line.

4. Update the quota files to reflect the current disk usage by entering `quotacheck <volume name>` in the command line.

5. Enable the quota system by entering `quotaon <volume name>` in the command line.

6. Configure the quota settings for your user accounts by using the `edquota <user name>` command.

This utility uses `vi`, a command-line text editor, to configure the quota settings; consult the man pages for proper use of `vi`.

7. Use `repquota <volume name>` or `quota <user name>` to view the disk quota usage and settings.

✔ Tips

■ Although it isn't recommended, once you've configured quotas using the command-line tools, you can still use Workgroup Manager to configure quota settings.

■ Remember, it's always a good idea to experiment with quota settings on a test account before implementing quotas system wide.

■ You can also configure disk quotas based on group accounts by creating `.quota.group` and `.quota.ops.group` at the root level on any volume.

Quotas Expanded

You can use command-line tools to further edit user quotas—for example, by adding group quotas and/or specifying the quotas as *fixed* (hard quotas) or *malleable* (soft quotas). Hard quotas are implemented immediately, and soft quotas allow users to go over their quotas for seven days after the quota is in place, at which time the soft quota turns into a hard quota. The quota command-line tools are as follows:

◆ **quotaon** and **quotaoff**—Turn the quotas on and off

◆ **repquota**—Summarizes quotas

◆ **quota**—Displays disk quota use and limits

◆ **edquota**—Edits user and group quotas

◆ **quotacheck**—Ensures consistency

Refer to the section "Setting disk quotas via the command line" for more information about using these tools.

SETTING USER DISK QUOTAS

Adding Email to User Accounts

Mac OS X Server provides robust email services based on a Postfix/Cyrus open-source implementation. Primary configuration of the Mail service is available from the Server Admin application. Once the Mail service is configured, you use Workgroup Manager to enable and configure user-specific email settings.

There is much more to configuring an email server than is addressed in this topic. See Chapter 8, "Enabling Mail Services," for details regarding mail server configuration.

To add email to a user account:

1. In Workgroup Manager, click the Accounts icon in the Toolbar and click the User tab in the account types tab (**Figure 4.54**).

2. Click the directory authentication icon and select the appropriate directory database from the pop-up menu.

3. In the user list, select the user or users you wish to configure and select the Mail tab (**Figure 4.55**).

   The default setting for a user's mail is None (disabled).

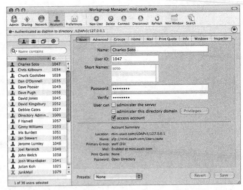

Figure 4.54 Click the Accounts icon and the User tab in Workgroup Manager.

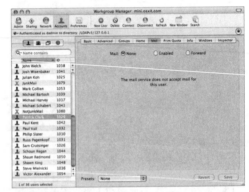

Figure 4.55 Select the user or users for whom you want to configure mail and click the Mail tab.

Figure 4.56 Enable mail for a user with Workgroup Manager and configure the mail server location, mail quota, mail access protocols, and alternate mail store location.

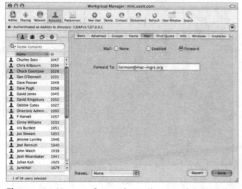

Figure 4.57 You can forward email to another email account automatically.

4. Select the Enabled radio button and if necessary, change the mail server address, set a mailbox quota, set the protocols by which the user(s) will receive their mail, or change where the mail box is stored (**Figure 4.56**).

5. When you've finished making changes, click Save.

✔ Tips

■ If a user leaves your organization, you can forward their email to another email account automatically. Select the Forward radio button and enter the new email address in the Forward To field (**Figure 4.57**).

■ If you decide to change a user's mailbox location, you must first move the mailbox to that location. See Chapter 8 for more information.

■ Setting the Mail Quota to 0 gives the user an unlimited mail quota, as if you hadn't set it at all.

Enabling Printer Quotas

Mac OS X Server lets you limit the number of pages a user can print to any queue hosted by your print server (as defined by the application from which the user is printing). Before you can enforce print quotas, you must first configure the print queues and enable the print server (see Chapter 7, "Printing Services").

To enable printer quotas:

1. Follow steps 1–2 in the previous task.

2. In the user list, select the user or users you wish to configure and click the Print Quota tab (**Figure 4.58**).

   The default setting for a user's Print Quota is None.

3. Click the All Queues radio button and enter a number of pages per number of days quota limit in the associated fields (**Figure 4.59**).

   The default, set at 0, allows this user unlimited printing on all queues.

4. When you've finished making changes, click Save.

✔ Tips

- If a user needs to print beyond their quota, you can reset the quota by clicking Reset Print Quota.

- The Print Service logs available from the Server Admin application show the number of pages and user for each individual print job.

Figure 4.58 Select the user or users for whom printer quotas will be enforced and click the Print Quota tab.

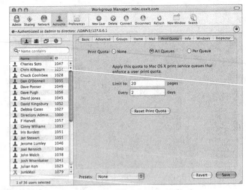

Figure 4.59 Clicking the All Queues radio button shows the default settings, and you can enter a quota limit.

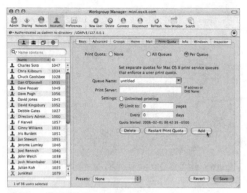

Figure 4.60 Click the Add button to add a specific printer to the managed queue list.

Figure 4.61 Enter a specific queue name and server, and either select Unlimited Printing or specify a pages and days printing limit.

Setting individual print quotas

Since printers range in capacity and capabilities, you may find it useful to set quotas for individual printers. You can do this in Workgroup Manager. Remember, you can only enforce quotas on printer queues set up in the Mac OS X Server print server service.

To set an individual printer's quota:

1. In Workgroup Manager, click the Accounts icon in the Toolbar and click the User tab in the account types tab. Then navigate to configure the user's Print Quota attributes. Select the Per Queue radio button and then click Add (**Figure 4.60**).

2. Enter the Queue Name and the Print Server address in the appropriate fields.

3. Select Unlimited Printing, or specify your own limit for printing pages and days, and click Save (**Figure 4.61**).

4. Click the Add button to set additional queue quotas.

continues on next page

5. Open the Queue Name drop-down list to view all the quotas for this user (**Figure 4.62**).

6. When you've finished making changes, click Save.

✔ Tip

■ If a user needs to print beyond their quota, you can reset it by clicking Restart Print Quota.

Figure 4.62 The Queue Name pop-up list shows all the quotas for this user.

Adding User Information

Another option when using Workgroup Manager is to add user information. This information can then be browsed via any bound client machine with an application that supports browsing LDAP directories. In the case of Mac OS X, this would be the Address Book application. **Figure 4.63** shows the fields available using the Info tab in Workgroup Manager.

Figure 4.63 Enter standard information in the user's Info tab.

Figure 4.64 The Windows tab permits the entry of Windows computer–related options.

Setting Information for Windows Users

Mac OS X Server can be used as a location for authentication information for Windows desktop users. There are a few options within the Workgroup Manager interface that allow for even better integration with Windows users (**Figure 4.64**).

For example, user profiles paths can be set. A Windows user's profile contains registry settings and environment variables specific to that user. By putting this on a network share, the user will have a more consistent experience when logging in on different Windows clients.

Second, similar to that of Mac OS X, a login script can be executed, allowing for such items as servers and printers to be mounted on the Windows user's desktop.

Third, a hard drive letter and path to the user's home directory can be utilized in case the user's home folder is elsewhere on the network.

Understanding the Inspector Tab

The Inspector tab in Workgroup Manager provides unlimited access to the directory database information. It gives you the ability to edit account information outside the confines of the standard user interface. Using the Inspector gives you the power to add, delete, or edit any attribute for any item in the directory database as well as add many new attributes.

However, with great power comes great responsibility. Because you're allowed unfettered access to the directory database, you can very easily mess things up (you can lock yourself out of your own server!). Also keep in mind that any changes you make using the Inspector are made while the directory is live. In other words, you can change an attribute that is currently in use by a user or system process. Needless to say, proceed with caution!

When viewing records in the Inspector, you'll commonly see duplicate entries for the same attribute. For example, when viewing a user record you will find both a RecordName and a uid entry with the user's shortname. You're not looking at two different pieces of data, but instead at two views of the same data (**Figure 4.65**).

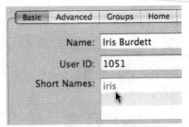

Figure 4.65 View the short name of a user in the Basic tab of Workgroup Manager.

Figure 4.66 The Inspector tab shows the user attributes and their associated values.

Figure 4.67 The attribute view options check boxes.

The uid entry is the raw LDAP information. If you were to look into the LDAP database, you'd find a uid entry for the user, and only a uid entry for the short name. The RecordName is an abstraction that Open Directory makes when reading in the LDAP information. Since OD can work with many different types of data stores that may have vastly different naming conventions, it maps the disparate directory data into a common namespace.

The mappings, which can be modified by using the Directory Access utility, need not pay any attention to the original intended use of the data. For example, you could easily map the LDAP sn attribute for the user's surname to the OD attribute for first name, effectively flipping the name order for that user when Mac OS X's directory services traverse the LDAP database.

To alter attribute names in the Inspector tab:

1. In Workgroup Manager, click the Accounts icon in the Toolbar, click the User tab in the account types tab, select a user account, click the Inspector tab, and click Options (**Figure 4.66**).

   The Show attribute types box appears, showing both attribute and prefix types (**Figure 4.67**).

   continues on next page

UNDERSTANDING THE INSPECTOR TAB

2. Deselect any prefixes and the show Native attributes, so only the show Standard attributes box is checked.

   This only shows the Apple/Open Directory attributes, not the OpenLDAP attributes.

3. Scroll through the attributes, noting the names of the attributes and their associated values (**Figure 4.68**).

4. Click Options again and this time swap the attribute view, showing only the Standard or OpenLDAP attribute names and values (**Figure 4.69**).

Figure 4.68 View the Apple/Open Directory attribute and its associated address value.

Figure 4.69 View the OpenLDAP attribute and its associated address value.

Multiple Values

Here's another fun fact about the wonderful world of directory services. When viewing all the user attributes, keep in mind that for each attribute type, there can be several values. For example, the Apple/OD AuthenticationAuthority attribute, which tells the account what types of authentication it has and where those authentication mechanisms exist, has two values: one for Password Server and one for Kerberos. There is also a small arrow to the left of the attribute's name; click it to reveal all the values for the attribute.

You can create multiple separate values for any attribute by selecting the attribute from the Inspector window and clicking New Value.

Figure 4.70 Double-click a value to make a change associated with the Apple/Open Directory attribute or …

Figure 4.71 …double-click a value to make a change associated with the OpenLDAP attribute.

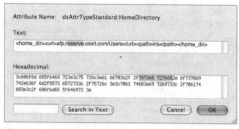

Figure 4.72 You can make changes to more complex values in the attribute editing dialog.

Changing the Home Directory Location in the Inspector Tab

If you must change the user's home directory in the Inspector tab and not in the Home tab, please note you must make changes to the following attribute fields—either Apple/OD or OpenLDAP names:

Apple OD:

- HomeDirectory
- NFSHomeDirectory

OpenLDAP:

- apple-user-homeurl
- homeDirectory

To view or change attribute values in the Inspector tab:

1. Follow step 1 in the previous task.

2. Find the value you wish to edit, and either edit the Standard/Apple OD (**Figure 4.70**) or Native/OpenLDAP categories (they both write to the same location, so editing either is acceptable) (**Figure 4.71**).

   If the attribute's value is long (typically any value that contains XML code), click Edit to make changes. The attribute editing dialog appears, in which you can make changes to more complicated values (**Figure 4.72**).

3. Click OK when you are finished.

4. When you've finished making changes, click Save.

✔ Tip

- When you make account modifications with the Inspector, always thoroughly test your changes before you implement them on a wider scale. In fact, it's a good idea to create test user accounts so you can experiment with changes made using the Inspector.

Adding user attributes

Essentially, there is no limit to the number of attributes a user record can have in either the local or the LDAP directory database provided by Mac OS X Server. You can configure as many attributes as you see fit. Keep in mind that attributes are nothing more than known storage locations for specific user account information, such as additional address lines, middle name, departments, fax numbers, PGP public key, and so on. Apple has 144 preset additional attributes, although only a portion are potential user record attributes.

Adding a custom user attribute to the directory is useful only if a specific system service or feature knows how to use that attribute.

To add user attributes:

1. In Workgroup Manager, click the Accounts icon in the Toolbar, click the User tab in the account types tab, select a user account, and click the Inspector tab (**Figure 4.73**).

2. Click the New Attribute button. An Attribute dialog appears (**Figure 4.74**).

3. From the Attribute Name menu, select one of the preset attribute types (**Figure 4.75**).

   You can also enter a custom attribute type to the right of the menu.

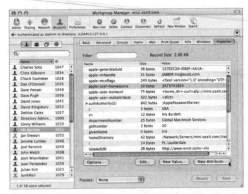

Figure 4.73 Select the user, and click the Inspector tab within Workgroup Manager to click the New Attribute button.

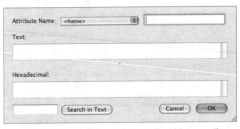

Figure 4.74 Clicking New Attribute to add an attribute to the user account.

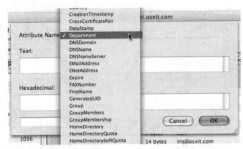

Figure 4.75 Choose an attribute type from one of the many preset attributes.

Figure 4.76 Entering the information in the text field also automatically populates the Hex field.

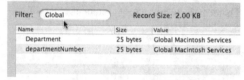

Figure 4.77 Locate the new attribute and its associated value by using the Search field.

4. Enter the attribute's value in the Text field.

   The system automatically populates the Hex field (**Figure 4.76**).

5. When you've finished making changes, click OK to close the Attribute dialog, and then click Save.

6. Locate your new attributes (both Apple/OD and OpenLDAP) and associated value(s) in the Inspector frame, and view the information (**Figure 4.77**).

✔ Tips

- The actual name of the OpenLDAP attribute will vary from the name you chose in the list and the name that appears when it's saved.

- Remember to always thoroughly test directory modifications before you implement them.

UNDERSTANDING THE INSPECTOR TAB

Using Presets for New Accounts

If you've been reading this chapter sequentially, you've probably noticed that there are many settings to configure for a user account. Fortunately, you don't have to configure every single setting each time you create a new user. Workgroup Manager offers a timesaving feature that lets you save a preset for new user accounts.

Once you define a preset, all new users you create will have the same configuration as the preset (the preset must be selected before you create the account). However, even when new users are created with the User Presets tool, you must still configure each user's name (long name), user ID, short names, and password.

To define a preset:

1. In Workgroup Manager, click the Accounts icon in the Toolbar, click the User tab in the account types tab, and select a user account.

   It's a good idea to create an actual account called Preset User. This helps avoid confusion in the future as to which account the others accounts were based on (**Figure 4.78**).

2. From the Presets pop-up menu, select Save Preset.

   A dialog drops down from the title bar, in which you can enter a name for your preset (**Figure 4.79**).

3. Enter a name, and click OK.

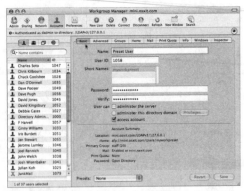

Figure 4.78 Create a preset user for all other yet-to-be-created users.

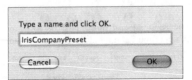

Figure 4.79 Enter a name in the Preset Name field.

Figure 4.80 Select the new preset from the Presets pop-up menu.

"Changing" the Short Name

As previously mentioned, you really shouldn't change the original short name, but you can create a new account and then move the user's configuration and files to the new account.

Simply create a preset using the user's old account as shown in this section and then create a new account using this preset. Next give the new account the same User ID value as the old account. The new account will have attributes and permissions similar to those of the old account.

Note that this solution does *not* move the user's email database or home folder and related files to the new account. You'll have to reconfigure those items manually. Be sure to thoroughly test the new account before you delete the old one!

To create a user with a preset:

1. Within Workgroup Manager, select your custom user preset from the Presets pop-up menu (**Figure 4.80**).

2. Click New User to create a new account that will use this preset.

3. Verify that your preset works by inspecting the attributes on the various account settings tabs: Advanced, Groups, and so on.

   Remember that you must still configure the Basic user attributes to complete this user account.

4. When you've finished making changes, click Save.

✔ Tips

- You can rename and delete presets from the Presets pop-up menu.

- You can also create custom group presets. Repeat all the steps in the previous task; but, in step 2, click the Group icon instead of the User tab.

USING PRESETS FOR NEW ACCOUNTS

5

FILE SHARING

For many organizations, file sharing is the only reason they have a server. Although Mac OS X Server is accomplished at tasks other than file sharing, it stands out as a robust and reliable multiplatform file server by providing file-sharing capabilities via the four most common sharing protocols: Apple File Protocol (AFP) for Mac OS clients, Server Message Block (SMB) for Windows-compatible clients, File Transfer Protocol (FTP) for almost any client, and Network File System (NFS) for Unix-based clients.

For many administrators, the amount of time spent planning access to shared items outweighs the time spent configuring the server. Access to shared items is often a technical and political issue. As a server administrator, you're charged with figuring out how to configure server resources so they fit with your organizational requirements. Therefore, it's a good idea to plan access to your shared items before you try to implement sharing services on your server. You should also set up users and groups before you enable your shared items, because Mac OS X Server uses both Unix-style user and group permissions and access controls to control local and shared file access. (See Chapter 4, "User and Group Management," for more on configuring users and groups.)

When you're ready to configure share points, you have two main areas of concern: setting up and configuring the protocols over which users connect, and the actual share point. This chapter examines both.

Configuring Share Points

When a directory, disk, or volume and its contents are shared via Mac OS X Server, it's called a *share point*. You can also think of a share point as a mount point: When you make a folder a share point, you're defining a shared folder that the user can select and mount on their computer. A user can access various items inside the share point, depending on file and folder permissions.

To make the most of share points, you should have a good understanding of file and folder permissions to facilitate proper access and security within each share point.

At the root level of Mac OS X Server, Apple has a directory called Shared Items. Since Mac OS X and Mac OS X Server are Unix based, you might want to rename this folder Shared_Items, by removing the space or putting an underscore (_) where the space was. (When using certain command-line tools to copy files, a space in the share point name can sometimes complicate matters. You can place your share points anywhere, but Shared_Items is as good a place as any.)

To configure new share points:

1. If the folder you wish to share doesn't yet exist on the server, launch Workgroup Manager and click the Sharing icon in the Toolbar.

   If you already have a folder on the server, you can now skip to step 3.

2. In the Sharing browser within Workgroup Manager that appears, click the All tab to display all the server's local volumes and their contents (**Figure 5.1**).

   The sharing browser works much like the Finder's column view.

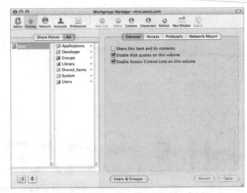

Figure 5.1 Click the All tab and select the folder you want to share.

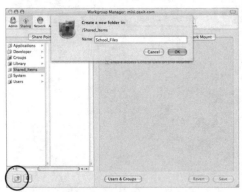

Figure 5.2 Add the folder that you want to share.

Figure 5.3 Select the share point in the All column.

Figure 5.4 Your new share point shows up in the Share Points list.

3. Select the folder, disk, or volume (in this case, your Mac OS X Server volume) that you want to assign as a share point.

4. If it isn't already selected, click the "Enable disk quotas on this volume" and "Enable Access Control Lists on this volume" check boxes and click Save.

   You will be using these options later in this chapter and throughout this book.

5. Click the Shared_Items folder and then click the New Folder button. In the new folder dialog that appears, name your new folder and click OK (**Figure 5.2**).

6. In the sharing browser, select the new folder.

7. Click the General tab and then click the "Share this item and its contents" check box; click Save (**Figure 5.3**).

8. Click the Share Points tab.

   Your newly created share point is shown on the list with the other share points (**Figure 5.4**). You may need to click Refresh in the Toolbar to update the shares shown.

   Although the share point is now set, you'll probably need to configure permissions and file-sharing protocol options (discussed in the following tasks) to fit your needs.

✔ Tips

- It's not a good idea to select an entire disk or volume as a share point because there are a number of files at the root of a volume that should not be user accessible as the system depends on them. These include temporary storage and trash folders.

- You can expand the Workgroup Manager window and show more than just two columns when selecting share points by dragging the column bars at the bottom of each column.

Configuring File and Folder Permissions

Every file and folder on your Mac OS X Server is protected by Unix-style permissions, and/or access controls, sometimes called *privileges*. An entire book could be dedicated to the technology behind file and folder permissions, but they basically boil down to a few simple concepts:

- All items are associated with one owner and one group.

- Only the owner of the folder or file, or an administrative user, can change the permissions.

- All items have permissions defined at three POSIX levels: owner, group, and everybody else (commonly referred to as User, Group, and Other) and access controls, which allow for a much more granular set of permission options (discussed later in this chapter).

- At each POSIX level, you can have one of four basic access settings: none, read only, read and write, or (in the case of folders) write only.

- The permissions most specific to the user attempting to access the file are enforced.

- Permissions define access to an item's contents, not to the item itself.

If you're still confounded by the prospect of Unix-style permissions, you're not alone. Many experienced administrators learned permissions through trial and error. Experimenting with various permissions settings is often the best way to learn, and right now is a good time to start.

Command-Line POSIX Permissions

You can also configure POSIX and ACL file and folder permissions from the command line using the following utilities:

- `ls -l` lists the contents and permissions of a folder, disk, or volume.

- `chown` changes an item's user and group ownership.

- `chgrp` changes an item's group.

- `chmod` changes an item's access rights.

- `chmod -a` changes an item's access rights using ACLs.

Please consult the UNIX man page for chmod to see all the POSIX and ACL options, because they are too expansive to list here.

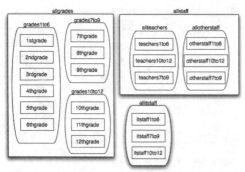

Figure 5.5 Setting up nested groups for logical permissions structure.

Access Control Lists (ACLs) add to the complexity of permission permutations by allowing a larger set of options. They are mainly defined by "allow only" or "deny only." For most purposes, you should not use "deny only," because it will ignore any other permissions under that share point. Instead, simply don't give a user or group access to a share point.

Additionally, ACLs will override POSIX controls. ACL permissions are as follows:

♦ Read

♦ Read/Write

♦ Write

♦ Full Control

♦ Custom

There are two ACL permission levels (Full Control and Custom) that do not exist with standard POSIX level permissions:

♦ Full Control of a share point permits the selected user to handle every aspect of read/write management.

♦ The Custom setting allows a very granular set of permissions, which will be discussed later in this chapter.

When enabling ACLs, planning plays the most critical role in the process. Since Mac OS X Server allows for nested groups, creating smaller groups and then nesting those groups to create levels of control allows for the easiest management of what can be very complex permissions sets.

You can apply ACLs to K–12 institutions, where each grade is a group, schools can be groups, and all students are in one group. Therefore, you have 12 basic groups within three nested groups within one larger group (**Figure 5.5**). Teachers, other staff, and IT staff can be separated in a similar fashion. This allows for some groups to have read-only access, others to have read/write, and still others to have full control.

To Share or Not to Share

You do not have to share a folder to change ownership or permissions on that folder. Often folders on volumes have their ownership and permissions changed even though the folders are not being shared.

To change POSIX permissions:

1. Launch the Workgroup Manager tool located in /Applications/Server and authenticate as the administrator if necessary, and then click the Sharing icon and *do one of the following:*

   ▲ Click the Share Points tab to configure a share point or its contents.

   ▲ Click the All tab to configure any item on a local server volume.

2. From the sharing browser, select the item you wish to edit and click the Access tab.

3. Click the Users & Groups button.

   An account list drawer appears to one side of the main Workgroup Manager window (**Figure 5.6**).

4. Click the directory authentication icon in the account list drawer and select the appropriate directory database from the pop-up menu (**Figure 5.7**):

   ▲ If you're working on the local directory, choose Local.

   ▲ If you're working on an Open Directory master, choose /LDAPv3/127.0.0.1.

   ▲ If you're connected to another database, select your database from there.

5. To define a new owner, click the Users tab and click-and-drag an account from the user list to the Owner field, or type in the short name of the user (**Figure 5.8**).

Figure 5.6 The Users and Groups drawer opens in Workgroup Manager.

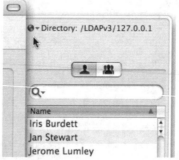

Figure 5.7 Selecting the LDAP domain from the Users and Groups domain list.

Figure 5.8 Dragging a user into the POSIX ownership field for a share point.

Figure 5.9 Dragging a group into the POSIX group field for a share point.

✓ Read & Write
  Read Only
  Write Only
  None

Figure 5.10 The POSIX permission options can be chosen from the pop-up menu.

6. To define a new group, click the Groups tab at the top of the Users and Groups drawer, and click-and-drag an account from the group list to the Group field, or type in the name of the group (**Figure 5.9**).

7. You can use the pop-up menus to the right of the Owner, Group, and Everyone fields to define access rights for any of the three fields (**Figure 5.10**).

8. When you've finished making changes, click Save.

✔ Tips

■ Although it's not recommended, you can also change file and folder permissions by choosing Finder > Get Info. This approach may yield unexpected results, such as not retaining the permissions or ownership you set, so it's always best to change file and folder permissions on Mac OS X Server using Workgroup Manager.

■ You do not need to have a shared (LDAP) domain to set up share points or change ownership and permissions of any share points.

■ Always test access to your item(s) before allowing clients access to them.

Working with ACLs

ACLs further define access to devices or folders by adding fine grain control over the way users and/or groups handle these share points. There is of course the standard read and write, but now additional options are available (**Figure 5.11**). To set these permissions, use the Custom option when selecting a user or group.

To add users and groups to ACLs:

1. Follow steps 1-4 in the previous task.

2. Click the Users folder at the top of the Users and Groups drawer and click-and-drag an account (or accounts) from the account list drawer to the Access Control List field (**Figure 5.12**).

3. Click the Groups tab at the top of the Users and Groups drawer and click-and-drag a group (or groups) from the group list to the Access Control List field (**Figure 5.13**).

   The use of nested groups immediately becomes useful here.

4. When you've finished making changes, click Save and keep Workgroup Manager open to this window.

✔ Tip

- Share point ACLs override POSIX permission and ownership settings.

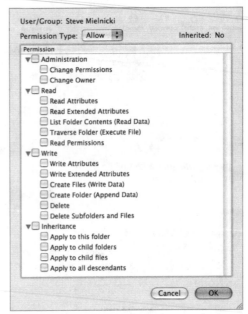

Figure 5.11 The potential options when entering into the Access Control Lists for share points.

Figure 5.12 Drag a user into the Access Control List field.

Figure 5.13 Dragging groups into the Access Control List field.

CONFIGURING FILE AND FOLDER PERMISSIONS

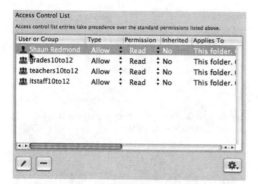

Figure 5.14 Selecting a user from the Access Control List field.

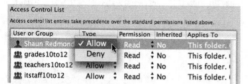

Figure 5.15 Choosing the type of access control for a user, allow or deny.

To set share point ACL parameters:

1. Using Workgroup Manager, select the share point on which you wish to set ACLs.

2. In the Access Control List field, select the user or group whose access you want to edit (**Figure 5.14**).

3. Click the Type tab to select a permission setting from the pull-down menu (**Figure 5.15**).

   The default setting is Allow, and unless you have a *very* specific reason, you should not choose Deny.

continues on next page

CONFIGURING FILE AND FOLDER PERMISSIONS

4. Click the Permission tab to select Full Control from the pull-down menu, since this user will be managing the share point (**Figure 5.16**).

   Full Control allows the user or group total access to do anything to this share point.

   or

   If the user or group needs specific permissions to the share point, select Custom (**Figure 5.17**).

   A dialog opens, showing the four main types of access control (**Figure 5.18**).

5. Select the appropriate check boxes that correspond to the permissions you want the user or group to have and click OK.

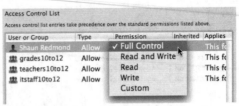

Figure 5.16 Choosing the level of permissions for access control from the list.

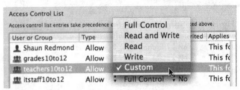

Figure 5.17 Selecting the Custom option from the list...

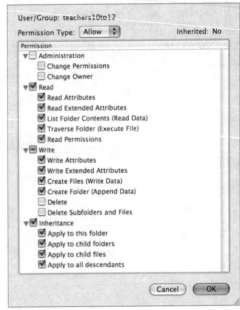

Figure 5.18 ...brings up the Access Control List dialog showing all available options.

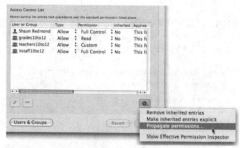

Figure 5.19 Choosing to propagate permissions from the gear menu in Workgroup Manager...

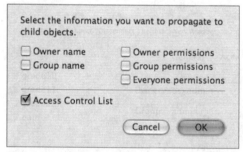

Figure 5.20 ...brings up the dialog allowing both permission types for propagation.

6. If the POSIX or access control settings need to be propagated down all folder levels, click the gear button and select Propagate permissions from the pull-down menu (**Figure 5.19**).

   A dialog opens, allowing you to set the propagation with either POSIX or ACLs (**Figure 5.20**).

7. Click the permissions you want to set and when you've finished making changes, click Save.

8. Thoroughly test the permissions to avoid any conflict due to the fact a user may be in multiple groups.

   Now that you have configured ownership and permissions on your share point(s), you'll need to go over what protocols they are sharing and how to set up those protocols.

The Effective Permissions Inspector

The Effective Permissions Inspector is perhaps the best tool when learning about ACLs. When you have a share point selected within Workgroup Manager, click the gear button and choose Show Effective Permissions Inspector from the pull-down menu (see Figure 5.19). When the Inspector opens, simply drag a username into the Inspector to see the permissions on that given share point (**Figure 5.21**). It's a good idea to view a user's permissions on several share points throughout a folder structure to make sure each user has the proper access.

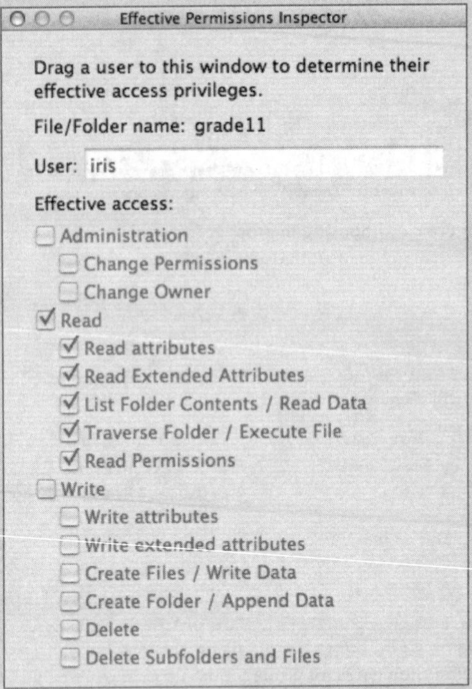

Figure 5.21 The Effective Permissions Inspector is used to review user access control permissions.

Configuring the Apple File-Sharing Service

The primary file-sharing protocol for Macintosh computers is Apple File Protocol (AFP). AFP features file-system compatibility for both Mac OS X and legacy Mac OS 9 systems (although share points mounted by Mac OS 9 clients and earlier cannot take advantage of certain options that Mac OS X clients can). In addition to providing robust sharing services, AFP offers secure authentication and encrypted data transport. AFP share points can also be used for home and group network mounts.

The AFP service requires a bit of overhead to maintain persistent server/client connections: The overhead per connection is quite low, but when you have many connections simultaneously, this overhead can waste valuable server CPU and network resources. To remedy this situation, the server can automatically disconnect clients who are connected to your server but not actively using it. When this functionality is configured, idle disconnections on computers running software older than Mac OS X 10.3 should receive a message that they have been disconnected.

Mac OS X 10.3 AFP Connections

Computers running Mac OS X 10.3 or later handle AFP idle disconnects in a very different manner. Your server still automatically disconnects, but the user shouldn't notice. The share point remains mounted to the client computer, yet the connection is idle. Essentially, the system hides the idle connection from the user. When the user tries to access the share again, the system automatically reconnects to your server. Furthermore, Mac OS X 10.3 or later attempts to reconnect to AFP connections that have been dropped due to network disconnects or sleep/wake cycles.

The following task shows you how to enable basic AFP file services. The remaining tasks in this section offer more advanced AFP options.

To set AFP access options:

1. Launch Server Admin and select the AFP service for your server in the Computers & Services list.

2. Click the Settings tab at the bottom of the screen and then the General tab at the top (**Figure 5.22**).

3. Click the appropriate check boxes:

   ▲ **Enable Bonjour registration** allows Mac OS X 10.2 or newer systems to browse to your server on the local network (sometimes called the local subnet).

   ▲ **Enable browsing with AppleTalk** allows pre-Mac OS X systems to browse to your server on the network using the older Chooser application.

4. In the Logon Greeting window, you may type a greeting that your users will see when they log in (see the "Logon Greeting" sidebar for more information) (**Figure 5.23**).

5. If you don't want users to get the message more than once, click the check box below the Logon Greeting window.

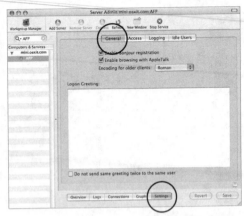

Figure 5.22 Selecting the Apple File Service from Server Admin shows initial options.

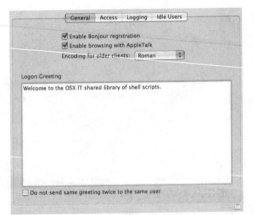

Figure 5.23 Adding a login greeting and managing discovery options for the AFP service.

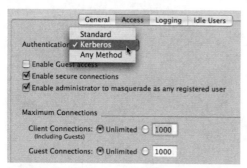

Figure 5.24 Selecting the type of authentication for the AFP service and permitting other AFP service options.

6. Click the Access tab and select an authentication type from the Authentication pop-up menu (**Figure 5.24**):

   ▲ **Standard** uses the built-in AFP authentication.

   ▲ **Kerberos** uses MIT's Kerberos for authentication.

   ▲ **Any Method** uses either of the two other methods of authentication, trying Kerberos first, then dropping to standard.

   See Chapter 3, "Open Directory," for more information about user authentication.

7. To choose AFP authentication options, click the check boxes below the Authentication menu:

   ▲ **Enable Guest access** enables access for users without accounts on the server.

   ▲ **Enable secure connections** enables AFP to be tunneled via an ssh connection (ssh must be turned on for this to work).

   ▲ **Enable administrator to masquerade as any registered user** lets an administrator sign in to the server via AFP using a non-administrator's username but their own administrator's password. This is very useful for testing share points and permissions but should not typically be enabled unless needed.

continues on next page

CONFIGURING THE APPLE FILE-SHARING SERVICE

8. In the Maximum Connections area, click the radio buttons and enter the necessary values to configure the maximum number of concurrent AFP client and guest connections (as seen in Figure 5.24).

You may have a limited number of AFP connections based on your server's software license type.

9. Select the Logging tab and then click the appropriate check boxes to enable both the access and error logs so you can monitor connected users (**Figure 5.25**).

10. Select the Idle Users tab and then click the appropriate check boxes and enter the necessary values for disconnecting idle users (**Figure 5.26**):

▲ **Allow clients to sleep** lets the client computers sleep without counting as an idle connection. Computers sleeping and connected don't produce the extra overhead that running computers with idle connections do. You can set the number of hours you want to let clients to sleep by changing the numeric value.

▲ **Disconnect idle users** lets you disconnect users who have been inactive for more than a set number of minutes. You can change the numeric value as necessary, but you should always click the check boxes (described below) underneath the Except line for idle users who have open files.

▲ **Guests** are any users who didn't authenticate as users to your server.

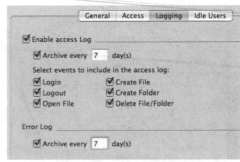

Figure 5.25 Saving all types of AFP service information to the Access log file.

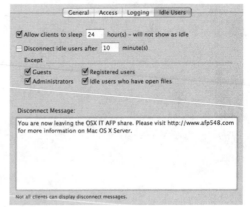

Figure 5.26 Setting idle user options and log out messaging.

▲ **Registered users** are any users who have an authenticated connection.

▲ **Administrators** are any users who have an authenticated connection and are in the admin group.

▲ **Idle users who have open files** are any users who have a file that resides on the server but is open in an application running on their local computer. Severing the server connection while a file is open on the client can corrupt the file—in other words, it's a bad idea.

Selecting the check box next to an exception category allows that user type to remain connected regardless of the idle disconnect settings.

11. Enter a disconnect message, if you want, and when you've finished making changes, click Save.

✔ **Tip**

■ In order to allow guest access, you must also enable guest access for each share point, by checking the box allowing guest access for AFP connections, as seen in Figure 5.28.

Logon Greeting

A *logon greeting* is a string of text that appears as soon as a user attempts to log in from a client computer. Logon greetings can be used for general service information or usage disclaimers for server access. More and more often, users must agree to the legal ramifications of using an employer's computer services. Using a login greeting is perfect for this task, because the user must click the OK button to dismiss the logon greeting dialog and connect to your server. Such logon greetings usually begin with, "By clicking the OK button you agree to...."

Using AFP share-point settings

When you create a share point on Mac OS X Server, it's automatically shared via AFP (as well as FTP and SMB), assuming the AFP service is running. Share points are also automatically configured for both registered user and guest access via AFP. Settings like these are individually configurable for each share point within the Workgroup Manager tool. See the "Configuring Share Points" section earlier in this chapter for more information about creating share points.

To configure AFP share-point settings:

1. Launch the Workgroup Manager tool located in /Applications/Server and authenticate as the administrator if necessary, and then click the Sharing icon and *do one of the following*:

   ▲ Configure an existing share point by clicking the Share Points tab, and then select the share point you want to edit from the sharing browser (**Figure 5.27**).

   ▲ Click the All tab to configure any item on a local server volume.

   ▲ Configure a new share point and select it. See the "To configure new share points" task earlier in this chapter for instructions.

2. Click the Protocols tab and select Apple File Settings from the pull-down menu (**Figure 5.28**).

3. Click the check boxes to allow AFP sharing and guest access for this particular share point.

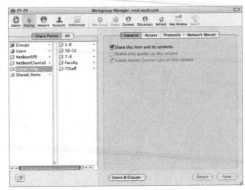

Figure 5.27 Ensuring a share point is active to prepare for sharing over AFP.

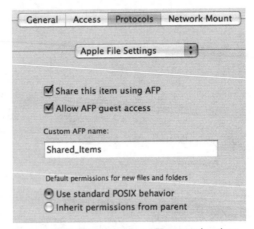

Figure 5.28 Setting the various AFP protocol options.

4. Enter a custom AFP share point name, which can be different from the original share point's name (if necessary).

5. If ACLs are *not* enabled on the volume (Figure 5.28), you can then choose one of the following radio buttons based on your permissions requirements, and then click Save:

   ▲ **Use standard Unix behavior** is the default behavior. New items created in this share point will be owned by the user who created the item, and the group will be set to that user's primary group. See Chapter 4 for more information about primary groups.

   ▲ **Inherit permissions from parent** is an optional behavior. New items created in this share point will have the same permissions as the share point itself. Refer to the "Configuring File and Folder Permissions" section earlier in this chapter.

✔ Tips

- In order for guests to access a share point, its permissions must be set to give everyone read access.

- Disabling guest access to the AFP service in Server Admin disables AFP guest access for every share point, regardless of individual share settings.

- Changing the name of a share point can help disguise a disk as a folder name but can also backfire if the user is looking for the folder's original share name.

To connect via AFP:

1. In the Finder, click the Network icon to browse for your server.

   Mac OS X can browse for AFP servers via the AppleTalk, SLP, or Bonjour protocol.

   or

   To connect directly, select Finder > Go > Connect to Server and enter an AFP address or press Command-K.

2. Authenticate to the server.

   or

   Click Options to configure client-side connection options.

3. Select the share point(s) to which you want to connect.

   Default settings dictate that the share point's icon will mount on the Finder's desktop.

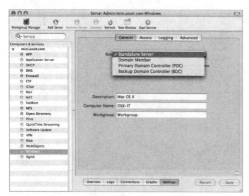

Figure 5.29 Choosing the various Windows server options from the Windows service in Server Admin.

Configuring the Windows File-Sharing Service

Mac OS X Server includes the open-source software Samba to provide Windows services. Your Mac OS X Server can provide a variety of services to Windows clients, including the following:

◆ File sharing via the Server Message Block (SMB) protocol

◆ Print sharing, also via the SMB protocol

◆ Local network browsing via the Network Basic Input/Output System (NetBIOS) protocol

◆ Network browsing and name/address resolution via the Windows Internet Naming Service (WINS) protocol

◆ Network authentication and security services, by acting as a Primary Domain Controller (PDC) or a Backup Domain Controller (BDC) to a Samba PDC

The possible roles of your Mac OS X Server, with regard to Windows services, are chosen by clicking the Settings tab, then the General tab in Server Admin (**Figure 5.29**). Initially, when you enable the Windows service, your Mac OS X Server acts as a stand-alone file server on the network. Windows and Mac OS X computers can discover your server on the local network via the NetBIOS protocol, and SMB handles the connectivity. The following task steps you through the process of enabling this basic configuration.

For more advanced Windows network configurations, see the remaining tasks in this section. For more information about Windows print sharing, refer to Chapter 7, "Printing Services."

CONFIGURING WINDOWS FILE-SHARING SERVICE

To set SMB access options:

1. Launch Server Admin and select the Windows service for your server in the Computers & Services list.

2. Click the Settings tab and then the Access tab and *do one or more of the following* and click Save (**Figure 5.30**):

   ▲ Click the "Allow Guest access" check box if you want to enable Windows guest connections.

   ▲ Select the total number of simultaneous Windows connections. Mac OS X Server doesn't have any licensing restrictions on the number of simultaneous Windows connections.

   ▲ Choose the various authentication mechanisms available for the Windows connections, which are NTLMv2 and Kerberos, NTLM (v1), and LAN Manager.

3. Click the Overview button at the bottom of the window (Figure 5.30).

4. Verify that the Windows service is running, and if it isn't, click Start Service in the Toolbar to activate the Windows server.

✔ Tips

■ To allow guest access, you must also enable guest access for each share point. See the "To configure Windows share-point settings" task later in this chapter for more information about enabling guest access for individual share points.

■ More information about Samba is available at www.samba.org/.

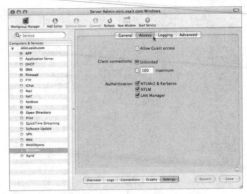

Figure 5.30 Choosing the guest access option and various authentication methods with the Windows services.

To connect Mac OS X via SMB:

1. In the Finder, click the Network icon to browse for your server. Mac OS X client can browse for SMB servers via the NetBIOS protocol.

   or

   To connect directly, select Finder > Go > Connect to Server or press Command-K and enter an SMB address.

2. When the SMB share point pop-up menu defaults to guest connection options, select a share from the menu and click OK.

   or

   Click Authenticate to gain availability to more share points.

   Either button will bring you to the SMB authentication dialog. Default settings dictate that the share point's icon will mount on the Finder's desktop.

To connect Windows clients via SMB:

1. In Windows Explorer, browse to your server as if it were another Windows computer.

   You can also manually add your server using the Add Network Place Wizard.

2. Authenticate using the authentication dialog as you would for any other Windows network connection.

   All the share points appear in the Windows Browser.

CONFIGURING WINDOWS FILE-SHARING SERVICE

About advanced SMB roles

Large SMB networks use an organizational unit known as a *domain* to segregate computers and services. You can restrict access to items inside each domain by enabling domain authentication. Mac OS X Server can join a domain, host a domain by becoming a Primary Domain Controller (PDC), or become a backup domain controller (BDC), all through using the Server Admin tool and managing the Windows service.

When you configure your server as a PDC or BDC, Windows clients can authenticate against your server for access to items inside the domain. Enabling your Mac OS X Server as a PDC or BDC also enables your Windows clients to change their passwords from their computers.

When hosting a PDC or BDC your server must also be hosting a shared (LDAP) database. Windows clients will use the same user accounts hosted in your shared database to log in to your domain. For more information about directory services and Open Directory, see Chapter 3.

By default, your server will act as a Standalone Server and create the workgroup you specify using the NetBIOS protocol. If your Windows domain is complete and does not require any other advanced configurations, enter the server's Description, Computer Name, and Workgroup values.

To enable Mac OS X Server as a domain member:

1. Launch Server Admin and select the Windows service for your server in the Computers & Services list.

2. Click the Settings tab and then the General tab.

3. Select Domain Member from the Role menu (**Figure 5.31**).

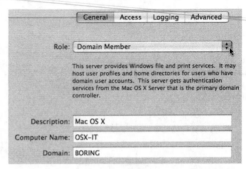

Figure 5.31 Selecting Domain Member from the Role menu.

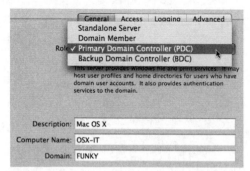

Figure 5.32 Choose Primary Domain Controller from the Role menu.

4. Enter the Description, Computer Name, and Domain for your server in the appropriate fields and click Save.

5. Authenticate as a domain administrator for the Windows domain you'd like to be a member of.

To enable Mac OS X Server as a Primary Domain Controller:

1. Be sure you're an Open Directory Master (see Chapter 3) when you launch Server Admin.

2. Select the Windows service for your server in the Computers & Services list and click the Settings tab and then the General tab.

3. Select Primary Domain Controller from the Role pop-up menu (**Figure 5.32**).

4. Enter the Description, Computer Name, and Domain for your server in the appropriate fields and click Save.

5. When you change SMB server roles, you must authenticate as an LDAP domain administrator for the PDC server.

✔ Tips

- It's best if your server's computer name is the unqualified DNS hostname (xserver, instead of xserver.example.com).

- Windows workgroup and domain names are typically capitalized and can't exceed 15 characters.

- On a Mac OS X (and Mac OS X Server) computer, you can configure SMB network settings, including a specific workgroup or domain for the client, in the Directory Access application.

- Always verify client connectivity after you make SMB server role changes—especially from Windows clients, because domain authentication is vital.

About advanced SMB features

Mac OS X Server provides a variety of advanced SMB features that your Windows users may need. These features include support for alternate languages, improved network browsing, and hosting Windows home folders.

You can also participate in the election of workgroup master and domain master browsers and enable Windows Internet Naming Service (WINS). WINS allows Windows browsing across subnets and facilitates more efficient browsing.

The other option is to enable virtual share points, which provides easier configuration for Windows home directories. If your server is a PDC, a user's home folder automatically mounts when they log in to your domain from a Windows computer. In addition, users have the same home folder for both Windows and Mac OS X.

To enable advanced SMB features:

1. Launch Server Admin and select the Windows service for your server in the Computers & Services list.

2. Click the Settings tab and then the Advanced tab (**Figure 5.33**).

3. To determine which language is used for Windows services, select a language option from the Code Page pull-down menu.

4. Select one or both of the Workgroup Master Browser and Domain Master Browser check boxes to have your server take part in the master browser elections (see the "Master Browser" sidebar).

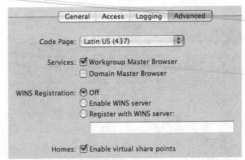

Figure 5.33 Checking these boxes allows your Mac OS X Server to become a workgroup master browser and/or domain master browser.

5. *Choose one of the following* modes for WINS registration:

  ▲ **Off** means that your server has nothing to do with WINS registration.

  ▲ **Enable WINS server** means that your server is the WINS server with which other machines register.

  ▲ **Register with WINS server** means that your server informs other WINS servers that you're providing Windows services. You must enter the IP address(es) of your WINS server(s). You can enter more than one server by separating the addresses with a comma and a single space.

6. Choose whether to enable virtual share points and click Save.

✔ Tips

■ If your server is acting as a PDC, the Workgroup Master Browser and Domain Master Browser options aren't available because a PDC *must* be the domain master browser for that particular domain.

■ On a Mac OS X (and Mac OS X Server) computer, you can configure SMB network settings in the Directory Access application, including the ability for a client to register with WINS servers.

■ You should test these settings thoroughly from both Windows and Mac OS X computers.

Master Browsers

Master browsers are used to facilitate more efficient network browsing when using the NetBIOS protocol. This is the way Windows computers collect and display information when services are shared from Windows computers to Windows computers on a local subnet (local network).

A domain master browser is elected by choosing, one of the master browsers on each local network. This will collect and offer the list of services offered by Windows computers that resided on all the master browsers.

Selecting the Workgroup Master Browser and Domain Master Browser options (see Figure 5.32) doesn't guarantee that your server will become the master browser and/or the domain master browser if other computers are involved in the election.

Using Windows share-point settings

When you create a share point on Mac OS X Server, it's automatically shared via SMB (as well as AFP and FTP), assuming the Windows service is running. Share points are also automatically configured for both registered user and guest access via SMB. You can configure such settings individually for each share point using the Workgroup Manager tool.

To configure Windows share-point settings:

1. Launch the Workgroup Manager tool located in /Applications/Server, authenticate as the administrator if necessary, and click the Sharing icon.

2. In the sharing browser, click the All tab and *do one of the following*:

   ▲ Configure an existing share point by clicking the Share Points tab, and then select the share point you wish to edit from the sharing browser.

   ▲ Configure a new share point. See the "To configure new share points" task earlier in this chapter for detailed instructions.

3. Click the Protocols tab and from the Protocols pull-down menu, select Windows File Settings (**Figure 5.34**).

4. In the Protocols tab, click the appropriate check boxes to configure SMB sharing and guest access and enter a custom SMB share point name that differs from the original folder's name (**Figure 5.35**).

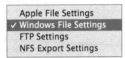

Figure 5.34 Choose Windows File Settings to manage share point options over SMB.

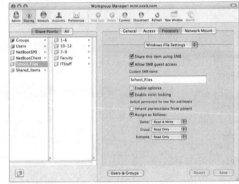

Figure 5.35 Choose a permissions model and guest options for the share point.

5. In the "Default permissions for new files and folders" section, click *one of the following* radio buttons, and then click Save:

▲ **Inherit permissions from parent** will allow new items created within this share point to have the same permissions as the share point itself. See the "Configuring File and Folder Permissions" section earlier in this chapter.

▲ **Assign as follows** is the default behavior, similar to inherited permissions in that the owner and group assigned to each item are the same as those of the parent share point when copied or moved into the share point (however, the owner of a file is still the creator of that file). But you can configure specific access for the user, group, or everyone from the menus.

✔ **Tip**

■ Keep in mind that the general Windows service settings may affect the settings you configure here. For instance, disabling guest access to the Windows service in Server Admin disables Windows guest access for every share point regardless of individual share settings. Remember to verify proper Windows service configuration in both Workgroup Manager and Server Admin.

CONFIGURING WINDOWS FILE-SHARING SERVICE

File Locking

The Windows file service offers a few unique features for managing files that reside on the server but are open on client computers. These file-locking options improve the performance and consistency of open files. You can configure these options individually for each share point.

Once configured, file locks are transparent to the users connected to the server. In addition, file-locking options don't conflict with any Windows service configuration in Server Admin.

To enable file locking:

1. In Workgroup Manager, navigate to a specific share point's Windows service settings.

   See the previous task for instructions.

2. *Choose one of the following* Windows file-locking options and click Save (**Figure 5.36**):

   ▲ **Enable oplocks** lets client computers cache changes to open files locally for improved performance. Opportunistic locking is disabled by default.

   ▲ **Enable strict locking** allows only one user at a time to open a particular file to prevent the file corruption that occurs when applications attempt to edit files that are currently being edited by other users. Strict locking is enabled by default.

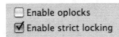

Figure 5.36 Decide on a file locking structure, if you want one.

Configuring the FTP File-Sharing Service

The File Transfer Protocol (FTP) service is by far the most ubiquitous file-sharing protocol available from Mac OS X Server. Almost anything with network access can connect to an FTP server, because FTP is a simple protocol to implement.

However, this simplicity is a double-edged sword. As a default, FTP is highly compatible and easy to implement because it uses clear-text passwords and unencrypted data—a potential security issue if any of your FTP traffic travels through unsecure networks. To compensate for this, Mac OS X Server supports using Kerberos for authentication, thus removing clear text passwords as a security issue. However, sending the data unencrypted is still a problem. A nefarious hacker can easily spot and intercept your FTP traffic. If security is an issue, then your alternative is to use the Secure FTP (SFTP) protocol. When you enable SSH on your Mac OS X Server, SFTP is automatically enabled. You don't need to enable FTP for SFTP to be enabled.

Other limitations of FTP include file-handling issues. Standard FTP can't handle folders because it only supports single file transfers. The FTP service also has problems with the forked files and Unicode filenames that are natively supported by Mac OS X.

You can easily overcome these limitations by using modern FTP client software that automatically archives and/or compresses requested files before they're transferred via FTP. The FTP service provided by Mac OS X Server includes support for automatic file archival and/or compression.

To set FTP access options:

1. Launch Server Admin, select the FTP service for your server in the Computers & Services list, click the Settings tab, and click the General tab (**Figure 5.37**).

2. From the Authentication pop-up menu, choose an FTP authentication method (**Figure 5.38**):

   ▲ **Standard** uses clear-text passwords.

   ▲ **Kerberos** uses MIT's Kerberos authentication.

   ▲ **Any method** is enabled by default.

   See Chapter 3 for more information about user authentication.

3. Select the "Enable anonymous access" check box to enable guest access via the FTP service and click Save.

   For security reasons, anonymous FTP access is turned off by default. *Anonymous access* is another way of saying *guest access*.

4. If you make changes to the FTP service while it's running, you'll be prompted to restart the service; otherwise, when you've finished making changes, click Save.

   Be sure to check for connected users before restarting the service, so you don't kick them off.

5. Click the Overview button at the bottom of the window.

6. Verify that the FTP service is running and if it isn't, click Start Service to activate the FTP server.

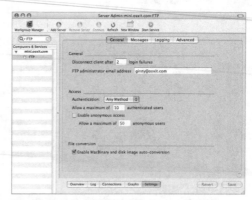

Figure 5.37 Select FTP from the services list of Server Admin to begin the process of setting up FTP service options.

Figure 5.38 The FTP service can be forced to use either standard authentication or Kerberos.

✔ Tips

- In order to allow anonymous access, you must also enable guest access for each share point. Refer to the "To configure FTP share-point settings" task for more information about enabling guest access for individual share points.

- You can limit the number of simultaneous authenticated and anonymous users by entering values in the associated fields. The default of 50 users is a good starting point, because FTP servers are susceptible to performance issues if too many users connect.

Connecting via FTP

Discussing the many third-party FTP clients for Mac OS X could easily fill a book. Try for yourself: Go to www.versiontracker.com/ and type `ftp client` in the search field. You'll probably find about two dozen FTP clients for Mac OS X alone. As tempting as those options are, this book sticks to the FTP clients built into Mac OS X. For SFTP, search for and download Fugu, an SFTP application.

If you prefer the command line, you can use the `ftp` or `sftp` command to connect to your server. On the other hand, if you prefer the graphical user interface, simply follow the first step in the "To connect Mac OS X via SMB" task earlier in this chapter and then authenticate to the server. Mac OS X Client can browse for FTP servers via the Bonjour protocol. As an option, you can have the client computer remember your login.

With FTP, you don't select a share point; you're automatically sent to a default location set by the server's administrator. Default settings dictate that the FTP server icon mounts on the Finder's desktop. You only have read access to an FTP share point when using the Connect to Server option. Use a third-party utility to enable read/write access to the FTP share point.

Creating FTP messages

When FTP was initially developed, all server connections were done through the command-line environment. You didn't just connect to a shared folder; you actually connected to an FTP command-line environment. Upon initially connecting to the FTP server, you were greeted with a banner message and then after authentication, you saw a welcome message.

These messages usually contained information regarding server usage, availability, disclosure agreements, or anything else the administrator wished to communicate to connected users. Although FTP banner and welcome messages are rarely used by modern graphical FTP clients, Mac OS X Server still supports them.

To change FTP messages:

1. Launch Server Admin and select the FTP service for your server in the Computers & Services list.

2. Click the Settings tab and click the Messages tab (**Figure 5.39**).

3. Select the "Show welcome message" check box and enter the desired text string in the field below.

4. Select the "Show banner message" check box and enter the desired text string into the field below.

5. When you've finished making changes, click Save.

6. If you make changes to the FTP service while it's running, you'll be prompted to restart the service. Be sure to check for connected users first, so you don't kick them off.

7. Test these messages via the command line by entering `ftp serveraddress` and then authenticating to the server.

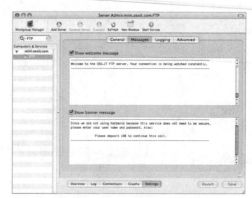

Figure 5.39 Here's where you'll enter your welcome message text and your banner message text.

✔ Tips

- You can disable either the welcome message or the banner message by deselecting the appropriate check box.

- Connecting to an FTP server via the Finder in Mac OS X won't show you any FTP messages.

Figure 5.40 Choose the Advanced tab in the FTP service to change the FTP mount point.

Configuring the FTP user environment

Typically, when an authenticated user connects to an FTP server, they don't get to choose a share point; they're dropped off in a predefined folder. Mac OS X Server lets you configure this aspect of the FTP user environment.

To configure the FTP user environment:

1. Launch Server Admin and select the FTP service for your server in the Computers & Services list.

2. Click the Settings tab and click the Advanced tab.

3. From the "Authenticated users see" menu, *select one of the following options* (**Figure 5.40**):

   ▲ **FTP Root and Share Points** connects users to the FTP root folder (defined in step 4). In the FTP root folder, the system creates symbolic links to your other share points.

   ▲ **Home Directory with Share Points** connects authenticated users to their home folder. They also have access to the other share points. If a user doesn't have a home folder, they're automatically connected to the FTP root folder.

   ▲ **Home Directory Only** connects authenticated users only to their home directory. If a user doesn't have a home folder, they're automatically connected to the FTP root folder.

   continues on next page

4. To specify a custom FTP root folder, enter a new path to the appropriate field and click Save.

   By default, the predefined FTP root folder is /Library/FTPServer/FTPRoot. You can also click the ellipsis button to the right of the FTP root folder field to specify a new folder in a file browser dialog.

5. If you make changes to the FTP service while it's running, you'll be prompted to restart the service. Otherwise, when you've finished making changes, click Save.

   First check for connected users so you don't kick them off.

✔ Tips

■ See the "Connecting via FTP" sidebar earlier in this chapter for more information about various FTP clients.

■ Any administrative account always defaults to its home folder via FTP. However, folder permissions allow administrators to navigate outside their home folder.

■ Because FTP servers often fall victim to hackers, thoroughly test any access configurations you choose. You should also test access from various FTP clients so you know what to expect for your users.

Configuring FTP share-point settings

When you create a share point on Mac OS X Server, it's automatically shared via FTP (as well as AFP and SMB), assuming the FTP service is running. Share points are also automatically configured for both registered user and anonymous access via FTP. You can configure such settings individually for each share point using Workgroup Manager. See the "Configuring Share Points" section earlier in this chapter for more information about creating share points. To configure FTP share-point settings, simply follow steps 1-4 in the "To configure Windows share-point settings" task.

If you ever disable a share point, the symbolic link for FTP functionality may remain in the FTP root folder. You'll have to delete this symbolic link manually after you disable the share point. To do so, move the original item, delete the link, and move the original back. Because FTP doesn't natively support multiple share points, the system creates symbolic links in the FTP root folder that point to your other share points.

Network File System Sharing

The Network File System (NFS) service is very different than all the other file services available. When using NFS, you don't supply a username and password when connecting. Instead the client system determines what permissions a user has on the system.

It's easiest to think of NFS as a locally attached hard drive, as it treats permissions in the same way.

For example, if a user has a UID of 501 on the client system, they will have all of the permissions of the user with the UID of 501 on the NFS server, regardless whether the short names, or even the accounts, are the same. For more information about UIDs, see Chapter 4.

To understand why NFS uses this type of authentication, you have to know where NFS comes from. The NFS service was first used by Unix terminals to access files on mainframe servers. Early Unix implementations relied on a unified directory service to authenticate users to any terminal computer. Because every user had to authenticate to the directory server before they had any computer access, it was safe to assume that once they were logged in to the terminal, they were who they said they were. Thus, NFS requested the UID from the terminal computer.

In today's modern computing environment, which is rife with commodity personal computers, login authentication is often delegated to a local account. Even worse, on Mac OS X computers, the local administrator accounts (UID 501) and root accounts (UID 0) have the same UIDs on your Mac OS X Server. This section discusses a variety of options that let you properly configure NFS share points, called *exports*, and protect them from such security risks.

To set up an NFS export:

1. Follow steps 1-3 in the "To configure Windows share-point settings" task earlier in this chapter.

2. From the Protocols menu, select NFS Export Settings (**Figure 5.41**).

3. Select the "Export this item and its contents to" check box to enable NFS for this share point.

4. To specify via IP address which clients can mount this export, *choose one of the following* from the Export pop-up menu (**Figure 5.42**):

   ▲ **Client** limits this NFS export to a list of specific clients. Click Add or Remove to manage this list.

   ▲ **World** allows any client to access this NFS export.

   ▲ **Subnet** limits this NFS export to a specific subnet of computers. Enter the subnet address and mask in the appropriate fields.

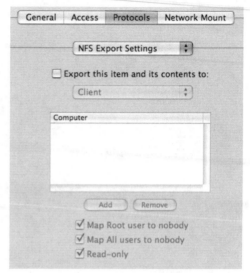

Figure 5.41 After selecting the share point, click the Protocols tab to configure NFS share point options.

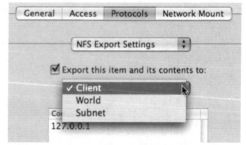

Figure 5.42 Select the "Export this item and its contents to" check box to begin NFS sharing.

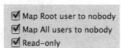

Map Root user to nobody
Map All users to nobody
Read-only

Figure 5.43 You have three options when exporting via NFS.

Figure 5.44 Select the NFS service for your server in the Computers & Services list.

5. To further restrict access to this NFS export, click *any of the following* check boxes at the bottom of the window and click Save (**Figure 5.43**):

▲ "Map Root user to nobody"

▲ "Map All users to nobody"

▲ "Read-only"

Nobody in this case is an actual user with the name "nobody."

6. Launch Server Admin and select the NFS service for your server in the Computers & Services list (**Figure 5.44**).

7. Verify that the NFS service is running. It should automatically start when you configure your first NFS export.

✔ Tips

■ Aside from what you've configured here, all access to this share point is granted based on file-system permissions. See "Configuring File and Folder Permissions" earlier in this chapter for more information.

■ To delete an NFS export, deselect the "Export this item and this contents to" check box, and then click Save.

Connecting via NFS

To connect to an NFS export from a Mac OS X client click the Network icon in the Finder to browse for your server. Mac OS X Client can browse for NFS servers via the Bonjour protocol. To connect directly, choose Finder > Go > Connect to Server and enter an NFS server and path address, or press Command-K. Default settings dictate that the share point's icon mounts on the Finder's desktop.

NETWORK FILE SYSTEM SHARING

Monitoring Sharing Services

Mac OS X Server provides a variety of statistics for monitoring sharing services. Using the Server Admin tool, you can monitor each file-sharing protocol in real time. The information provided by the monitoring tools is invaluable for troubleshooting connection problems and determining if resources are being properly used.

To configure sharing service connections:

1. Launch Server Admin and select the file-sharing service you wish to monitor in the Computers & Services list.

   You can choose to monitor service connections to AFP, FTP, and Windows services.

2. Click the Connections tab at the bottom of the window (**Figure 5.45**).

   A connections frame appears, showing currently connected users for the selected service. AFP is the most extensive of all the file services. Note that idle connections appear grayed out compared to active connections.

3. Click Refresh to force Server Admin to refresh the connected user list immediately.

4. Click a user in the connected user list or Shift- or Command-click to select multiple users.

5. To send a message to a selected user in the AFP connections frame, click Send Message.

6. In the dialog that appears, enter a message to the user (**Figure 5.46**).

Figure 5.45 The connections frame shows currently connected users for the selected service.

Figure 5.46 Send a message to any user you wish.

Figure 5.47 This is the Message dialog that the client sees.

Figure 5.48 You can set the disconnect time and disconnect message.

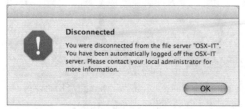

Figure 5.49 The client sees this Disconnect message.

7. Click Send, and the user will be presented with a Message dialog (**Figure 5.47**).

8. To disconnect a selected user, in both the AFP and SMB connections lists, click Disconnect.

9. In the dialog that appears, enter the amount of time before the user is disconnected along with a message to the user (**Figure 5.48**).

10. When you click Send, the user will see the message, and the server will disconnect after the allotted time (**Figure 5.49**).

MONITORING SHARING SERVICES

Monitoring AFP share service throughput

The Server Admin tool provides a graphical interface for monitoring AFP service throughput (kilobytes, megabytes, or gigabytes per second). These graphs provide a visual reference that you can use to monitor your server's resource utilization.

To measure AFP share service throughput:

1. Launch Server Admin and select the AFP service for your server in the Computers & Services list.

   You can choose to monitor service connections to AFP, FTP, and Windows services.

2. Click the Graphs tab to display a graph of the Average Connected Users (**Figure 5.50**).

3. Use the slider below the graph to manipulate the graph's sample timeframe.

4. From the pop-up menu, select Throughput.

   The resulting graph shows average AFP service network throughput (**Figure 5.51**).

5. Click the Refresh button to force Server Admin to refresh the connected user list immediately.

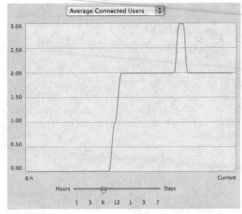

Figure 5.50 Select the service you want to monitor, such as AFP, and use the graph to view your connected user totals.

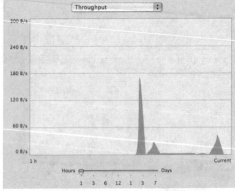

Figure 5.51 This graph shows average AFP service network throughput.

MONITORING SHARING SERVICES

Figure 5.52 Select your share point from the list in Workgroup Manager.

Creating a Home Directory Network Mount

Share points that are configured to automatically mount on your clients at startup are called *network mounts*. (In previous versions of Mac OS X Server, they were sometimes called *automounts*.) It's important to understand that network mounts are always available to any user on the client computer, whereas a share point located in the user's Login Items is available only to that user and is mounted only when the user logs in.

Essentially, network mounts are instructions stored in a directory database that tell client computers to mount certain share points at startup. Thus, the Workgroup Manager tool can configure network mounts only for servers that are part of a directory service system. In addition, your client computers must be configured as clients of the directory service system. (For more information about Directory Services and Open Directory, see Chapter 3.)

Network mounts are an important option because there are certain share points that client computers must have access to at all times.

To create a home directory network mount:

1. Launch the Workgroup Manager tool located in /Applications/Server, authenticate as the administrator if necessary, and click the Sharing icon.

2. Click the Share Points tab above the sharing browser and select the Users folder (**Figure 5.52**):

   The Users and/or Groups folders are common network mounts.

continues on next page

3. Click the Network Mount tab and click the Lock icon next to the directory that will be hosting the mount to view the authentication dialog (usually LDAPv3/127.0.0.1) (**Figure 5.53**).

4. Authenticate as an administrator of the selected directory server (**Figure 5.54**).

   Authenticating as an administrator makes the "Enable network mounting of this share point" option available.

5. Click the "Enable network mounting of this share point" check box (**Figure 5.55**).

Figure 5.53 Select the Network mount tab after clicking the share point.

Figure 5.54 You must authenticate to the selected directory to add the mount point.

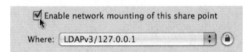

Figure 5.55 Select the "Enable network mounting of this share point" to add the mount point.

CREATING A HOME DIRECTORY NETWORK MOUNT

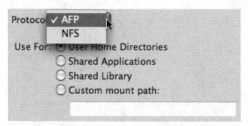

Figure 5.56 Choose AFP as your protocol of choice.

6. From the Protocol pop-up menu, select either AFP or NFS as the share point's protocol (**Figure 5.56**).

 AFP is the generally suggested way of handling network mounts.

7. Select the User Home Directories radio button and click Save.

 See the following section for an explanation of the other options.

8. Restart the Mac OS X computers and verify the network mount.

 Home directory network mounts are found on the local clients at /Network/Servers/*<servername>*/*<share name>*.

✔ Tip

■ To configure individual network users' home directories, see the instructions in Chapter 4.

CREATING A HOME DIRECTORY NETWORK MOUNT

231

Creating additional network mounts

You may find it useful to add other types of share points as network mounts. Examples include the Groups folder, a shared Applications folder, a shared Library folder, or any other share point you want to automatically mount to a specific point on the local client. You can create additional network mounts by repeating the previous task and selecting another share point. To change the mount point on the client, choose from the following network mount options (**Figure 5.57**).

◆ **Shared Applications** will automatically mount to the /Network/Applications directory. The client system will search this folder for available applications.

◆ **Shared Library** will automatically mount to the /Network/Library directory. The client system will search this folder for available resources, including fonts, frameworks, preference panes, or any other application or system support files.

◆ **Custom mount path** will automatically mount to the path specified in the field below.

You can view the network mount details using the Workgroup Manager Inspector (**Figure 5.58**).

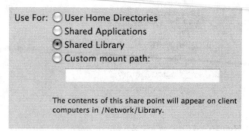

Figure 5.57 The various options when creating a network mount point.

Figure 5.58 Viewing the mount point attributes using the All records tab within Workgroup Manager.

Locally Configured Network Mounts

Instructions for automatic network mounts can be stored in any directory database, including the client's local NetInfo database. From the client in NetInfo Manager, you can add new mount directory entries. You need to add only a few properties and values for each mount entry:

◆ name = <servername>:/<sharepoint>

◆ dir = <localmountpoint>

◆ vfstype = url

◆ opts = net, url==<serverurl>

A typical network mount entry has the following properties (**Figure 5.59**):

◆ name = xserver:/Users

◆ dir = /Network/Servers/

◆ vfstype = url

◆ opts = net, url==afp://;AUTH=_NO%20USER%20AUTHENT@10.1.1.5/Users

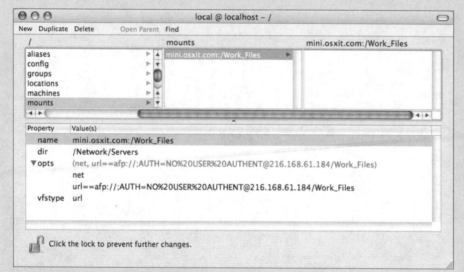

Figure 5.59 Add the mount information in NetInfo Manager.

Network Services Options

What network-related services does Mac OS X Server offer, and how do you go about managing these services? Often, you'll want your Mac OS X Server to do double duty as a router, DHCP server, or DNS server, as well as handling Network Address Translation (NAT). Perhaps you're replacing an older Windows NT server or upgrading an AppleShareIP server. Each of these services extends the functionality of your server. This chapter looks at setting up some of these services and discusses how they will benefit you.

Understanding DNS

DNS is an acronym for both Domain Name System and Domain Name Server. DNS is widely used but widely misunderstood.

The Domain Name System is used to make the Internet easy to navigate. Instead of typing numbers like `http://17.254.0.91`, you type `http://www.apple.com`; both addresses go to the same place, but the second is certainly much easier to remember. In order for DNS to work, Apple Computer must have a computer that is in charge of the DNS domain apple.com, which in turn lists computers under its domain such as www.apple.com, training.apple.com, train.apple.com, and so forth.

Let's back up a bit. Suppose you wish to find a Web site, let's say www.afp548.com. You'd probably start by searching the .com domain, which tells you where afp548.com is, which, in turn, tells you where www.afp548.com is located. That computer is running a Web server and responds to your request by giving you back Web pages. Or you may type in `ftp.afp548.com` in Connect to Server and the same process would take place, finally connecting you to the FTP port (port 21) of afp548.com. This concept works because almost all devices on the Internet that have an IP address associate that address with a name. This, in a nutshell, is how the Domain Name System works.

Registering Your Server

If you don't have control of the Domain Name Server in your organization, ask the administrator to enter both forward and reverse records for your Mac OS X Server. You'll need to give the administrator the following information:

◆ The IP address of your server

◆ The name of your server

The *name* of your server means the *hostname*, as listed in the /etc/hostconfig file. You gave your computer a hostname when you initially set it up. Refer to Chapter 3, "Open Directory," for more information.

What if you have the ability to become your own Domain Name Server? How do you translate the IP address of your computer to its hostname? It starts with the initial setup. If your Mac OS X Server is going to host the example.com domain, then the hostname of the server should be the name of the computer plus the domain. For instance, if the computer is named xserver, and it will be the computer that hosts the example.com domain, then the hostname when setting up the computer is xserver.example.com. You enter this hostname when the server is set up initially.

But just setting up the initial hostname isn't enough. After the server has been through the initial setup, you must run a Domain Name Server on your Mac OS X Server before you promote your server to a master.

About DNS and Mac OS X Server

Mac OS X Server, when running as an LDAP server and a Kerberos Key Distribution Center (KDC), relies heavily on DNS, so it's critical to discuss some key points about how to properly implement DNS on your system. If you are not running DNS on your Mac OS X Server, it is still important that you understand how DNS works. You will need to keep your DNS administrator apprised of any changes to your system so they can properly update the DNS records on their DNS servers.

First, Mac OS X Server can be a Domain Name Server. That is, it can translate its IP address(es) into names and back. If your organization already has a Domain Name Server, it's *imperative* that you have the DNS administrator add zone records for your server. *Zone records* are text files kept on a DNS server that convert names to IP addresses and IP addresses to names.

Many zone records can be used, but this chapter discusses forward and reverse records. If nothing else, you must have both forward and reverse records for your Mac OS X Server if you wish to use it as an LDAP server and a KDC. These particular records are known as *A records* and *PTR records*, and they will be shown later in this chapter.

✔ Tip

■ Before creating an Open Directory master, it is *imperative* that DNS be on one box within your organization and have records for your server (this can, of course, be the server that is the OD master) if you wish to take advantage of everything an Open Directory master has to offer. A good rule of thumb is to get your DNS house in order before turning on any other services or promoting your machine to a master.

To set up simple forward and reverse zone records:

1. Select System Preferences from the Apple menu and click on the Network icon to open the Network Preference pane. Enter the proper IP address, subnet mask, and router address for your server, if it is not entered already (**Figure 6.1**).

2. Launch Server Admin and select the DNS service for your server in the Computers & Services list.

   You'll use Server Admin for most of the exercises in this chapter, so leave it open.

3. Click Settings, select the General tab, and click *one of the following* check boxes (**Figure 6.2**):

   ▲ **Zone transfers** allows for the DNS zone information on this server to be copied to another server, in case this DNS server stops responding.

   ▲ **Recursion** allows for lookups outside of the domain itself and responds with whatever it finds. Recursion is global to the server. If you are running more than one domain and one is internal and one external, you should turn it off for domains that are internal only and turn it on for servers that must face the outside world.

4. Select the Zones tab to configure a basic zone (**Figure 6.3**).

Figure 6.1 Check your network preferences before you proceed with setting up DNS.

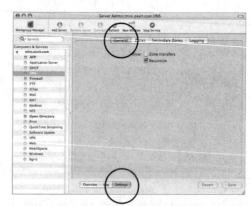

Figure 6.2 Launch the Server Admin tool, and choose the DNS service from the service list.

Figure 6.3 The Zones tab lets you view zone data.

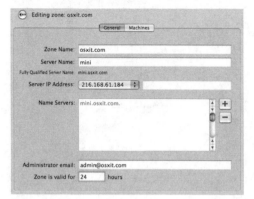

Figure 6.4 Entering default zone data for the DNS service.

Figure 6.5 Adding DNS and search domain information to the Network preference pane.

5. Click the plus button to open the Editing zone dialog, where you can enter the following information (**Figure 6.4**):
   - ▲ The name of the zone you want to add
   - ▲ The name of the machine hosting the zone
   - ▲ The IP address (if the server is configured with more than one) associated with the zone
   - ▲ Additional DNS servers that will host this zone
   - ▲ Administrator email address
   - ▲ The "time to live" for the individual records

6. Click Save and then click Start to start the DNS server.

   You may have to click Start twice the first time you start your DNS server.

7. In the Network preference pane, enter your own DNS server and search domain so that the server can locate itself (**Figure 6.5**).

8. To test your work, open the terminal on your server, type hostname, and press Return.

   This should return the fully qualified domain name of your server. If it doesn't, you may have to stop and start the DNS service and repeat this step again.

9. Type the word host, followed by the result of the hostname command, and press Return.

   This resolves the name to the IP address and should show the proper IP address associated with the name.

10. Type the word host, followed by the IP address result from the first host command.

    This resolves the IP address back to the name, ensuring that both forward and reverse records are functioning properly.

11. If everything resolved correctly, close the Terminal.

UNDERSTANDING DNS

239

Adding extra DNS records

In addition to setting up simple DNS records to become a self-serving Open Directory master (that is, not relying on another server to do DNS for you), having mail services is yet another reason to run DNS. To add a Mail (MX) Exchange record to your DNS service, refer to Chapter 8, "Enabling Mail Services."

There are other services to offer, such as Web, FTP, and AFP, to name a few. You may wish to set up aliases for these records. Aliases allow more than one name in a domain to point to the same IP address. In this fashion you can have www.osxit.com, www2.osxit.com, afp.osxit.com, and so on, all pointing to mini.osxit.com, which is resolving to 216.168.61.184.

There are plenty of other types of records you can have, such as the following:

◆ Address records

◆ Pointer records

◆ Namespace records

◆ Text records

There are several other entries that can be made inside of your DNS zone file, which are beyond the scope of this book. For more information about DNS, you can point your browser to: www.menandmice.com/online_docs_and_faq/glossary/glossarytoc.htm.

Hit Records

The most popular types of zone records are address records, alias records, and Mail Exchange records:

◆ Mail Exchange records are used when you're setting up a mail server.

◆ Alias records are used for other services, (commonly for Web servers).

◆ Address records are used to define other machines.

An abundance of material is available on DNS and the process behind it, called Berkeley Internet Name Domain (BIND). Try the Glossary pages at www.menandmice.com/online_docs_and_faq/glossary/glossarytoc.htm.

Figure 6.6 Viewing the Machine records tab of the default zone file.

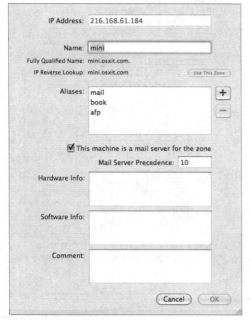

Figure 6.7 Viewing machine record data and associated information.

Figure 6.8. Adding a Web alias to the main zone record.

To add a Web alias record:

1. In Server Admin, select the DNS service for your server in the Computers & Services list.

2. Click Settings and then select the Zones tab and double-click your zone (as seen in Figure 6.3) to open the Editing zone dialog.

3. Select the Machines tab and double-click the record below to view any aliases (**Figure 6.6**).

   A new window appears, showing any aliases associated with that record and giving you options to add more (**Figure 6.7**).

4. Click the plus button and add the name that you want others to type (preceding your domain name) to access your server, and then click OK (**Figure 6.8**).

5. When you've finished making changes, click Save.

UNDERSTANDING DNS

DNS logs

It is important to have DNS logging turned on and active, so that you can troubleshoot DNS issues that may plague your server.

To turn on DNS logging:

1. Select the DNS service for your server in the Computers & Services list, click the Settings button, and then select the Logging tab.

2. Enter a location in the Log Location field and choose Errors from the Log Level pop-up menu (**Figure 6.9**).

3. When you've finished making changes, click Save.

4. Check the Log tab for errors relating to your DNS service, such as a zone file not loading (**Figure 6.10**).

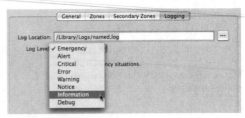

Figure 6.9 The Logging tab lets you change the location of the log file and logging details.

Figure 6.10 Viewing the DNS log file for errors or possible attacks is critical for proper DNS management.

DNS for Life

This isn't the last word on DNS. Setting up and running a Domain Name Server is one of the most critical pieces of a sound network infrastructure. If running a DNS service is one of your primary job responsibilities, take the time to learn more about other options that can affect the security and performance of your DNS server. The Apple interface for setting up and managing DNS (Server Admin) provides a fraction of what can be added and manipulated via the text files that are created when configuring DNS. Those files are as follows:

◆ /private/etc/named.conf tells the DNS service where to find the zone files.

◆ /private/var/named/ (any files inside this folder) is the location of the actual zone files.

UNDERSTANDING DNS

Understanding DHCP Services

Computers, printers, routers, and servers all communicate via IP addresses. But where do these addresses come from? There are routable addresses and nonroutable addresses, or public and private addresses. Chapter 3 discusses these address ranges.

You now need to decide how you can best manage computers connected to your network. Perhaps they will obtain an address from your server; if that's the case, then understanding how to set up DHCP services is an essential piece of Mac OS X Server. Prior to turning on your DHCP service, you need to ask anyone else on your network if their computer is acting as the DHCP server. Having two DHCP servers on the same network can wreak havoc on the network and should be avoided at all costs.

You can also quickly change the setting of any client computer to DHCP and see if it obtains anything but a 169.254.x.x address, or *self-assigned address*, indicating that there is no DHCP server on the local network.

At the bottom of the Server Admin pane, there are four buttons that deal with DHCP:

- **Overview** shows whether the service is running and displays the current number of leases.

- **Log** displays the current log file for the DHCP service.

- **Clients** shows all the client machines that are using an address given to them by the DHCP service.

- **Settings** shows how many network ranges (called *subnets*) you're serving addresses to and what network interface you're using for each range. This tab also lets you set your desired level of logging.

Passing out information via DHCP

Assuming you've done your homework and determined that your Mac OS X Server is going to be a DHCP server for your network, decide which addresses you want to pass out to the client computers. You should also decide whether passing out extra information with the address is necessary for your network. For example, Mac OS X DHCP server can pass out the following information to a client: IP address, subnet mask, router address, DNS addresses, search domains, LDAP information, and Windows WINS information. All this information is transferred from the server to the client when the client asks for an address.

Let's examine what takes place when a DHCP server is on the network:

1. The client machine starts up and searches for a DHCP server.

2. The DHCP server responds to the client and offers the client an IP address and other information.

3. The client formally requests the information from the server, and the server sends it down to the client.

4. The client asks any other computers or printers on the network if the address offered is already taken.

5. If no one responds that they have the IP address in question, the client then proceeds to commit the information to memory. The client is leasing the address from the server.

This process takes place every so often during the day. If you tell your server to give out addresses for eight hours, then your client will ask the server if it can renew the address it has at four hours, or half the lease time.

Figure 6.11 Launch the Server Admin tool, and choose the DHCP service from the service list.

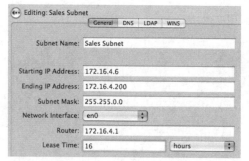

Figure 6.12 Double-clicking the DHCP subnet reveals the four settings tabs for that particular subnet. The General tab allows entry of standard DHCP data.

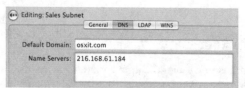

Figure 6.13 Data entered in the DNS tab is pushed down to the client with the IP information.

Having leases that run for six months can be useful when you have only a handful of computers; but if you have laptops that come and go, and people hopping on and off their computers all day, it's better to set the lease time for 8 hours so that you're assured the client computers will ask for a renewal during a standard eight-hour day, thus potentially freeing up addresses for others to use the following day.

Again, before you start the DHCP service on your Mac OS X Server, be *sure* no one else is providing DHCP services on your network.

To change DHCP service settings:

1. In Server Admin, select the DHCP service for your server in the Computers & Services list.

2. Click Settings and then select the Subnets tab (**Figure 6.11**).

3. Click the plus button to open an Editing pane, where you can enter the following information (**Figure 6.12**):

   ▲ Subnet Name

   ▲ Starting IP Address

   ▲ Ending IP Address

   ▲ Subnet Mask

   ▲ Network Interface

   ▲ Router

   ▲ Lease Time

4. Select the DNS tab, and enter the appropriate DNS information you want the client computers to receive (**Figure 6.13**). You may enter more than one DNS and search domain.

continues on next page

UNDERSTANDING DHCP SERVICES

5. Click the back arrow in the top-left corner of the pane to return to the Subnets pane.

6. Click the Enable check box, if it's not already checked (**Figure 6.14**).

7. Click Save and then click Start Service to start the DHCP service.

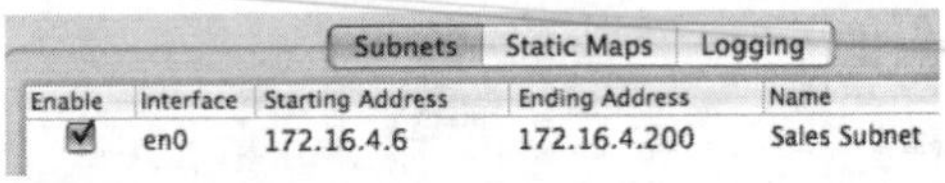

✔ Tip

■ You can set up two DHCP subnets on the same interface. You might do this if you already have a printer or a server within the range of addresses you wish to use. For example, if you have a server or a printer with an IP address of 192.168.1.50, you can have two DHCP ranges—the first going from 192.168.1.2 to 192.168.1.49 and the second range going from 192.168.1.51 to 192.168.1.200, thereby skipping the address users already know.

Subnets	Static Maps	Logging		
Enable	Interface	Starting Address	Ending Address	Name
☑	en0	172.16.4.6	172.16.4.200	Sales Subnet

Figure 6.14 Ensure the Enable check box is selected prior to starting the DHCP service.

The ipconfig Tool

You can always check your server to ensure you're pushing down the appropriate information, but how do you tell from the client side if the information makes it down to the client? When you're utilizing any DHCP server, you can check what information is being handed down to the client by using a command-line tool called `ipconfig`.

You use the command `ipconfig getpacket enx` (where x is the number of your Ethernet connection—en0, en1, en2, and so on) to see what information your DHCP server is sending down to your client. Open the Terminal, type the command, and press Return. You'll see all the information your DHCP server is sending you.

Using `en0` tells the command to look at your built-in Ethernet connection. Use `en1` if you want to look at the DHCP information that's gathered from a computer with an airport card.

Figure 6.15 Starting and viewing the subnet for the DHCP service.

About DHCP and LDAP

You've just learned how to push down IP address information that allows users to connect to your network. But what if your needs are bigger? What if you have home directories on your server and you want the client machines to automatically find them? As discussed in Chapter 3, you can make a Mac OS X Server an LDAP server; one function of that is allowing home folders to exist on the server.

If you have more than 200 client machines, going to each machine to point it to the server is tedious and time consuming. A better way is to allow the DHCP server to push down the information to each client along with the IP address information.

To set up the DHCP service to propagate LDAP information:

1. Select the DHCP service for your server in the Computers & Services list, click Settings, and then select the Subnets tab (**Figure 6.15**).

2. Double-click the subnet to open an Editing pane.

continues on next page

3. Select the LDAP tab and *enter the appropriate information* (**Figure 6.16**):

▲ Server Name is the fully qualified domain name of your server, such as xserver.example.com. This entry is different from those of DNS and should not have a trailing dot at the end of the name.

▲ Search Base is the LDAP search base of your server. In most cases, this looks something like dc=servername, dc=example,dc=com, which parses your domain name into standard LDAP structure. For more information on what to enter here, refer back to the "To create a master directory" task in Chapter 3.

▲ Port lets you enter a port for the information to go over, or leave this field blank to use the default port.

▲ Click the LDAP over SSL check box to secure your connection over Secure Socket Layer (discussed in Chapter 10, "Security").

4. Click the back arrow in the top-left corner of the pane to return to the Subnets pane.

5. When you've finished making changes, click Save.

If the DHCP service is already running, you'll be prompted to restart the service. Doing so implements your changes.

✔ Tip

■ Recall that the LDAP information is needed so the client machine can see the server. In this manner, the client can authenticate against the server and obtain a home folder or other shared folders. If the client machines are already configured to accept a DHCP address, all you have to do is ensure that the LDAP information is passed down along with the IP information.

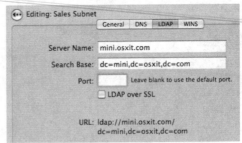

Figure 6.16 Double-click the subnet, and enter the LDAP data to be pushed down to the client.

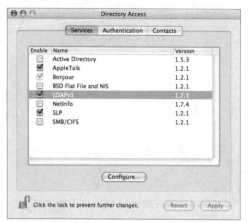

Figure 6.17 Opening Directory Access on a Mac OS X computer to check the LDAP plug-in status.

Figure 6.18 Be sure the "Add DHCP-supplied LDAP servers" option is selected, which allows the client to obtain the LDAP information from the DHCP server.

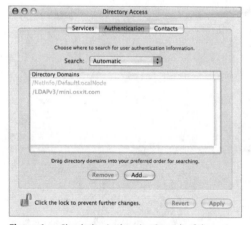

Figure 6.19 Check the Authentication tab of the Directory Access application. LDAP information is being pushed down from the DHCP server.

To set up the client to search for DHCP-supplied LDAP information:

1. On Mac OS X computer(s), launch Directory Access, click the lock in the lower-left corner, and select the Services tab (**Figure 6.17**).

2. Select the LDAP plug-in and double-click it to open a new pane.

3. Click the "Add DHCP-supplied LDAP servers" check box, if it's not already selected, and click OK (**Figure 6.18**).

4. Select the Authentication tab and from the Search pop-up menu, choose Automatic as the path where Open Directory searches for authentication information (**Figure 6.19**).

   Your client machine is now ready to look for LDAP information. If your client machine is getting the DHCP LDAP information, you should see your server's information in the authentication list. If you don't, be sure your DHCP server is sending down the appropriate information.

✔ Tips

■ One other set of data can be pushed down to a client machine: WINS data. Windows Internet Naming Service (WINS) is used by Windows computers to locate one another on a network across subnets. If you have Windows clients obtaining an address from a Mac OS X Server, you configure the DHCP server to push down the WINS information.

■ Using Mac OS X Server as a DHCP server is an excellent way to reduce dependency on an existing Windows server that can now be retired.

Restricting DHCP

There may be a time when you wish to specify which computers receive a certain IP address. For example, you may have computers and printers that always need the same address, yet you do not want your users to set their computers and printers with static addresses. Use the Static Maps tab of the DHCP service to restrict which computers receive a given IP address from a Mac OS X Server DHCP service.

To restrict IP addresses to specific computers:

1. Launch Server Admin and select the DHCP service for your server in the Computers & Services list.

2. Click Settings and select the Static Maps tab (**Figure 6.20**).

3. Click the plus button to open a pane where you can add the hardware address of the built-in Ethernet interface that is associated with the machines that you want to allow or deny an address from the DHCP service (**Figure 6.21**).

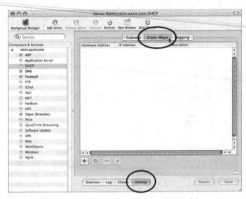

Figure 6.20 Static Maps force a given IP address to a specific device.

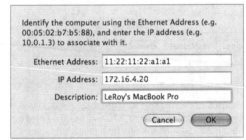

Figure 6.21 Entering data to map a given IP address to a given hardware address.

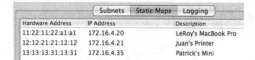

Subnets	Static Maps	Logging	
Hardware Address	IP Address		Description
11:22:11:22:a1:a1	172.16.4.20		LeRoy's MacBook Pro
12:12:21:21:12:12	172.16.4.21		Juan's Printer
13:13:13:31:13:31	172.16.4.35		Patrick's Mini

Figure 6.22 Viewing all mapped hardware addresses and their associated IP addresses.

4. Click OK to return to the Static Maps pane and review your changes to the IP addresses (**Figure 6.22**).

5. When you've finished making changes, click Save.

Your DHCP service will now map given IP addresses to the devices listed in the Static Map window.

6. To restart the DHCP service and have the devices request a new address, restart the devices or unplug the Ethernet cable and plug it back in.

✔ Tips

■ All DHCP service data is stored in the NetInfo database. You can view and edit this information directly by open NetInfo Manager and going to the /config/dhcp/ subnets record.

■ For best results, you should create a DHCP subnet that includes all of your statically mapped addresses.

Network Address Translation

Mac OS X Server can perform NAT, taking requests from machines connected to one network interface and submitting them as if the server had made the request. Enabling NAT doesn't require two network interfaces, but it's suggested.

Any Macintosh that supports Mac OS X Server can perform NAT. This function is also found in inexpensive wireless routers, such as Apple's AirPort Base Station.

There are a few reasons to use NAT:

◆ Shortage of IP addresses

◆ Security

◆ Control

Perhaps your organization doesn't need to have every computer use a public IP address. Using public IP addresses for each computer can, of course, lead to security issues, because every computer can be seen by the outside world. You still need all your computers to access the Internet and send and receive email, but you don't want to take the security risk of having those public IPs. Or, maybe you want to watch all requests to Web sites so you can monitor them for unauthorized use. Perhaps you purchased an Xserve and have no need to purchase many public IP addresses, which can be very expensive. In all these cases, NAT is for you.

Before you begin the next task, be sure your primary network interface is set up correctly and that you can connect to the network properly (**Figure 6.23**). Then set up your secondary network interface with the appropriate IP information for your internal network (**Figure 6.24**). You must have both network interfaces active to make NAT function.

Figure 6.23 Viewing the network information on the built-in Ethernet interface.

Figure 6.24 Entering network information on the secondary network interface.

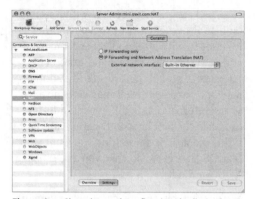

Figure 6.25 Choosing and configuring the limited NAT options from the NAT service in the service list of Server Admin.

To configure NAT:

1. Launch Server Admin, select the NAT service for your server in the Computers & Services list, and then click Settings (**Figure 6.25**).

2. Choose the primary interface to share, click the IP Forwarding and Network Address Translation (NAT) option, and click and when you've finished making changes, click Save.

   The interface you select is the interface that connects to the public network. In most cases, this is the network interface that connects to the Internet. The "IP Forwarding only" option is discussed in the next section.

3. Start the NAT service by clicking Start Service.

4. Choose the Firewall service from the Computers & Services list.

5. Click Start Service again to start the Firewall service.

   The firewall must be running, but it doesn't need to be fully configured for NAT to function.

6. If necessary, start a DHCP server on the network to provide IP addresses to the client machines.

   Client machines can now connect to the Internet, but no device on the Internet can contact your client machines, because they don't really exist on the Internet. As far as other devices on the Internet are concerned, all requests for information are coming from your Mac OS X Server.

NETWORK ADDRESS TRANSLATION

Acting As a Router

Another useful feature of Mac OS X Server is that it can do *IP forwarding*, an option in the NAT service settings that allows requests from one network to be sent to another network. It's necessary when you have a Mac OS X Server with two network interfaces and you want to have information passed from one network to the other. IP forwarding differs slightly from NAT in that your internal network is likely to have public IP addresses, whereas NAT makes all requests as if those requests were coming from the server (the clients have private IP addresses).

When you're deciding how and where a Mac OS X Server should go, one consideration is whether the server will be a link between two different networks. For example, you could have your Mac OS X Server's built-in Ethernet interface go from the server to a switch, and then have the switch connect 40 or so computers that have public IP addresses (they exist on the Internet as separate devices). These computers would use the Mac OS X Server's built-in Ethernet IP address as their router address. All information sent out of those 40 Macs would flow through the Mac OS X Server's built-in Ethernet interface.

Now, perhaps this is an Xserve with a second built-in Ethernet card, or maybe another Macintosh with a second Ethernet card added. Regardless, the second Ethernet interface is probably connected to another network; possibly this interface is connected to the Internet. It has different IP information than the first built-in Ethernet interface. If this scenario is something you want your Mac OS X Server to do, then you'll be enabling IP forwarding.

You've probably already set up your network information to connect you to the Internet. When you want to enable IP forwarding, your secondary network should be below your primary network in the network interface list in your Network Preference pane.

✔ Tip

■ If you can, it's a common best practice to have one Mac OS X Server do NAT, DHCP, and possibly DNS for the secondary network. Another Mac OS X Server may handle IP forwarding, or this function is handled by a router. Other Mac OS X Servers are then placed in the network to handle home directories, Web and mail, and file sharing.

7

PRINTING SERVICES

Modern printers historically fell into two categories: inexpensive local printers that require a host computer, and more expensive standalone shared network printers. For many, sharing fewer high-end printers was a better solution than using individual inexpensive printers. Although they're more expensive, shared network printers are often economically more efficient from a cost-per-page standpoint and are usually technically superior as well, yielding faster and better prints.

But even inexpensive printers can be networked via a number of methods, like inexpensive wireless print servers. So, in small or home businesses without shared printers, people are starting to network printers and running into the same sorts of problems that corporate shared printers have: When shared-printer demand increases beyond the capacity of the printer, resource contention among your users may cause problems. So many administrators use print servers that monitor and manage printer traffic printer resources.

Mac OS X Server can be configured to provide this service. Essentially, your server acts as a traffic cop between your users and the printers. Print jobs are sent to your server, where they're placed in a queue; then, depending on the information in the job, the user, the printer status, and so forth, they're sent to the printer, put on hold, or denied. As the server administrator, you configure how the server handles print jobs. You can manually adjust print jobs, or you can define user print quotas that instruct the server to automatically disable a user's ability to print after their allowance is used up.

The print server also lets you share non-network printers (like small USB laser and inkjet printers), and re-share network printers using different printing protocols than the printers natively support. Specifically, you can create and share a print queue for any printer that Mac OS X can print to. This includes both raster and PostScript printers available to your server via AppleTalk, Windows (SMB), LPR, IPP, HTTP, Bonjour, Bluetooth, USB, and FireWire. Further, Mac OS X Server can share any of its printer queues via IPP, AppleTalk, Windows (SMB), and LPR (with Bonjour) network printing protocols.

Creating Printer Queues

On Mac OS X, when you add a printer to the printer list, you create a local print queue for the computer. Whenever you print from an application, the print job is temporarily stored in the queue until the job is sent to the printer. So in essence, you're a self-contained print server and client. The same is true for Mac OS X Server, only on a larger scale. When you create a print queue on a server, you can then share those queues, allowing other computers to use them. In other words, every printer that is created can be shared and have a queue attached to it.

The default method for setting up printer queues on Mac OS X Server is to use the Server Admin application. Server Admin lets you add printers to the server's printer list and then enable sharing for each printer queue. It is much easier to use the Printer Setup Utility, located in /Applications/Utilities, to configure printers for the print server the same way you would on Mac OS X. (See the section "Configuring Printers on Mac OS X," later in this chapter, for more information about using the Printer Setup Utility.) However, this utility doesn't let you enable the shared queue settings for the server, nor does it easily allow for remote administration of those shared queues.

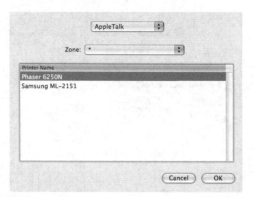

Figure 7.1 In Server Admin, you can add an AppleTalk printer...

So while you can add printers with either the Printer Setup Utility or Server Admin, in order to share the printer, you must use Server Admin. One advantage to using the Printer Setup Utility is that you have more options for connecting your server to the printer than you get from Server Admin. Think of the Printer Setup Utility as totally focused on getting the computer to talk to the printer(s), and Server Admin as focused on not only talking to the printer(s), but also talking to other computers. Also, using the Printer Setup Utility to first create the printers allows the drivers to be chosen automatically under most circumstances, reducing the risk of manually choosing the incorrect driver by mistake.

Before you create any printers, you must understand the different ways a printer can be connected via Server Admin. (Here we're only talking about Server Admin because the Printer Setup Utility is the same whether you run it on Mac OS X or Mac OS X Server):

◆ **AppleTalk** creates a print server queue for an AppleTalk printer (**Figure 7.1**). If your network has AppleTalk zones, select the appropriate zone from the pop-up menu. In either case, AppleTalk printers automatically populate in the list. Select the printer from the list and click OK. AppleTalk printing's great advantage is that it is an "intelligent" protocol, able to relay information not just from the server to the printer, but from the printer to the server too. This allows you to learn more about what's going on with the printer when there's a problem, and allows for automatic configuration of the printer settings.

◆ **LPR** creates a print server queue for an LPR/IP printer (**Figure 7.2**). Enter the IP address or DNS name of the printer. For most printers, you'll leave the "Use default queue on server" check box enabled. However, if the destination printer has multiple queues, deselect the check box and enter the queue name in the appropriate field. When you're done, click OK. The great advantage of LPR is that it's supported by any device that can print on a network.

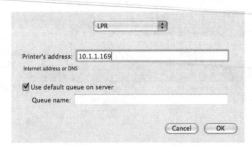

Figure 7.2 ...or an LPR (IP) printer...

◆ **Open Directory** creates a print server queue for a printer listed in a directory system (**Figure 7.3**). While you can put printers in your local NetInfo database, doing so will not automatically share the printer queue to other systems. To share the queue, your server must be either an Open Directory master (or replica) or configured to connect to another Open Directory server. (See Chapter 3, "Open Directory," for more information.) Select the printer from the list and click OK. Open Directory, in this usage, is not a printing protocol per se, but a printer directory. You don't actually use an "Open Directory" print protocol, but you use Open Directory to manage printers that you've already created queues for on an Open Directory master. If you aren't using Open Directory, then you don't need to worry about this.

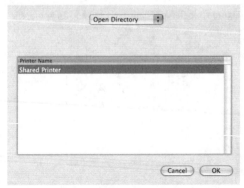

Figure 7.3 ...or an Open Directory printer.

Common Unix Printing System (CUPS)

Mac OS X uses an open source technology known as the Common Unix Printing System (CUPS) to handle printing. CUPS is a standards-based printing system that was written to allow printing to work the same on many different operating systems. Apple first started using CUPS in Mac OS X 10.2. CUPS has many advantages:

♦ Web-based administration via http://_127.0.0.1:631/ (you can also use the hostname of the server in the URL) (**Figure 7.4**)

♦ Command-line administration via the `lpadmin` and other utilities.

♦ A plethora of technical documentation and support, available at www.cups.org. The full CUPS documentation is available from the CUPS URL on every Mac OS X system, both Mac OS X and Mac OS X Server.

♦ A legion of Unix geeks who create hundreds of third-party printer drivers, which are available at http://gimp-print.sourceforge.net

Figure 7.4 You can manage printers using the CUPS Web interface.

Mac OS X Server in 10.3 and earlier didn't use CUPS to manage the print queues. This changed with Mac OS X Server 10.4, and now the Print service uses CUPS for sharing as well. This allows you to have more options for sharing your printers. Thus, if you prefer, you can use the CUPS command-line or Web-based administration tools to create and edit your server's print queues. You use Server Admin to configure sharing for each print queue.

CREATING PRINTER QUEUES

Printer-Sharing Protocols

There are various protocols to share your print queues with others. You can see the options by double-clicking any printer in the print queues window under the Settings tab of the Print Service dialog:

◆ **IPP** shares a queue via the Internet Printing Protocol (IPP). This is the main protocol used by CUPS for printer sharing, and is a new feature for Mac OS X Server 10.4's Print Server. A printer shared via IPP show up as a "Shared Printer" in the Printer Setup Utility, or in the Shared Printers list for printer selection in the print dialogs on any clients (**Figure 7.5**).

◆ **AppleTalk** shares this queue via AppleTalk's Printer Access Protocol (PAP). Make sure AppleTalk is enabled in the Network Preference pane on your server (**Figure 7.6**).

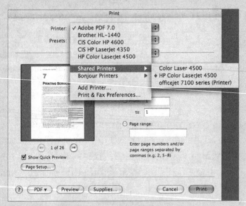

Figure 7.5 Viewing shared printers from the Print menu of an application.

Figure 7.6 Ensure that the AppleTalk protocol is selected on Mac OS X Server if AppleTalk is to be used for printing.

◆ **LPR** shares this queue via the LPR protocol. If LPR is selected, you can then click the "Show name in Bonjour" check box and subsequently browse for this shared queue on Mac OS X 10.2 or newer computers via any Print window (**Figure 7.7**).

◆ **SMB** shares this queue via the SMB (Windows printing) protocol. Make sure the Windows service is also enabled on your server (**Figure 7.8**). (See the section "Configuring the Windows File Sharing Service" in Chapter 5 for more information.)

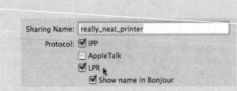

Figure 7.7 Sharing a printer over LPR and as an option, Bonjour.

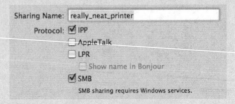

Figure 7.8 Sharing a printer over SMB.

Figure 7.9 Selecting the Print service in Server Admin by using the search bar.

Figure 7.10 The Print queue list is normally empty, unless a printer has been configured using the Printer Setup Utility.

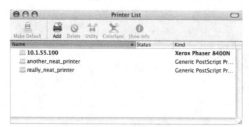

Figure 7.11 Viewing Printer Setup Utility to ensure local printers have been created.

To create a printer queue in Server Admin:

1. Launch Server Admin located in /Applications/Server, and authenticate as the administrator for the server you're going to use as a print server.

2. Select the Print service for your server in the Computers & Services list (**Figure 7.9**).

3. Click Settings at the bottom of the window and then click the Queues tab at the top of the Settings pane.

   For most servers, the print queues list is empty (**Figure 7.10**). On the other hand, any printer connected to your server via USB automatically appears in this list, as do any printers you have already set up using the Printer Setup Utility (**Figure 7.11**).

4. Click the plus button at the bottom of the window.

   The Create Print Queue dialog appears.

   continues on next page

5. Click the Print Protocol pop-up menu, and *select one of the following options* (**Figure 7.12**):

   ▲ AppleTalk

   ▲ LPR

   ▲ Open Directory

   Once you've added the printer queue, the queue Editing window opens (**Figure 7.13**). Again, remember that your goal is to get the printer to talk to the server, and if you prefer, you can use the Printer Setup Utility for this function as well. The major difference is that you don't have Open Directory as an explicit option with the Printer Setup Utility. While it's possible to set up a printer in this manner, setting up a printer with the Printer Setup Utility is the preferred method (as they will show up here to be managed). Please refer to "Configuring Printers on Mac OS X" later in this chapter.

6. In the Editing window, you can change the sharing name of the print queue.

   Note that in the figure, the printer's original name is different from the shared queue's name. Some operating systems or protocols don't allow for spaces or "odd" characters like ampersands in the name of the queue.

7. To enable the shared queue, select one or more of the following protocol check boxes:

   ▲ IPP

   ▲ AppleTalk

   ▲ LPR (Bonjour can also be used on local subnets to advertise an LPR printer)

   ▲ SMB

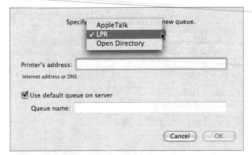

Figure 7.12 Adding print queues via a variety of methods.

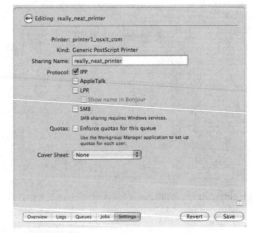

Figure 7.13 Options for editing the queue such as the protocols used to connect to the queue.

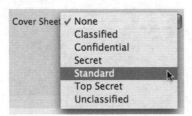

Figure 7.14 Various cover sheets can be applied to each job printed on the print queue.

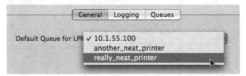

Figure 7.15 Choosing a print queue as the default queue in the General tab of Server Admin.

8. To enable quotas for this queue, select the "Enforce quotas for this queue" check box.

To configure user quota settings, you must use the Workgroup Manager application. Refer to "Enabling Printer Quotas" in Chapter 4.

9. To print a standard cover sheet that identifies the classification status of every document printed via this queue, select the correct option in the Cover Sheet list (**Figure 7.14**).

If you aren't sure whether you need this, you probably don't, and should just leave it set at the default.

10. Click Save and then Back ⊙ to return to the print queues list view in Server Admin.

Setting default print queues

Once a print queue is created, it is advantageous to have a certain queue be listed as the default queue. In this manner the default queue acts as a catchall for users who are not paying attention if (and when) they print via LPR.

To set a default print queue and start the queue:

1. In Server Admin with the Print service selected, click the General tab.

2. From the Default Queue for LPR pop-up menu, select a queue to act as a catchall for any print job not destined for a specific queue on your server (**Figure 7.15**).

continues on next page

CREATING PRINTER QUEUES

3. Click the Overview tab and if the Print service isn't running, click Start Service on the Server Admin Toolbar (**Figure 7.16**).

✔ Tips

■ Printer Sharing, available in the Sharing and the Printers and Fax preference panes on Mac OS X, is disabled on Mac OS X Server in favor of the Print service.

■ If you create a print queue for a network printer, Mac OS X Server can't prevent your users from bypassing this print queue and printing directly to a networked printer, although certain printers allow you to do this via masking on the printer directly. One way to control printing to a given set of printers is to attach them to a separate switch and connect that to the second Ethernet interface on your server, thus turning your server into a pass-through for the hosted printers. Doing so may not permit Bonjour to advertise the printers, based on the networking information supplied to both Ethernet interfaces. This is because Bonjour advertises via multicast, and most organization's routers are configured to deny multicast packets to pass through their routers.

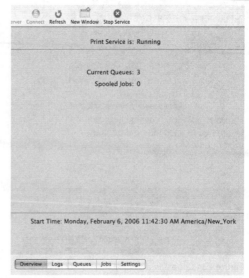

Figure 7.16 The Print service Overview tab of Server Admin shows number of queues and spooled jobs.

CREATING PRINTER QUEUES

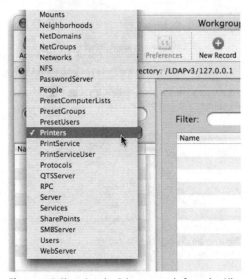

Figure 7.17 Select the LDAP directory database from the pop-up menu.

Figure 7.18 Choosing the Printer records from the All Records tab list.

Configuring Printers in Open Directory

Mac OS X supports discovery of LPR print services via directory services. Any Mac OS X Server that is acting as an Open Directory master can be configured to maintain a list of shared printers. You can configure any printer information you wish in Open Directory, regardless of print server settings. In other words, Open Directory doesn't care where the shared or network printers reside. You use Open Directory to maintain a list of printers that your client computers can easily discover through directory services. Obviously, in order for client computers to discover printers via directory services, they must be configured to access your directory server. See Chapter 3 for more information about directory services.

To configure a printer in Open Directory:

1. Launch Workgroup Manager and authenticate as the administrator.

2. If you haven't already, enable the All Records and Inspector tabs.
   For instructions, see Chapter 2.

3. Click the Accounts icon on the Toolbar and then click All Records on the account types tab.

4. Click the Directory Authentication icon beneath the Toolbar, and choose LDAPv3/127.0.0.1 if it isn't already selected (**Figure 7.17**).

5. From the record selector pop-up menu below the All Records icon, choose Printers (**Figure 7.18**).

continues on next page

6. Click New Record in the Toolbar to add a new printer record initially called untitled_1 and display its attributes and values (**Figure 7.19**).

7. Double-click the first instance of the printer record's name in the Value column to edit the printer record's name (**Figure 7.20**).

8. Click New Attribute.

The attribute-editing dialog appears (**Figure 7.21**).

9. If the default queue for the printer is acceptable, skip to step 12.

10. From the Attribute Name pop-up menu, choose PrinterLPRHost and enter the network address or name of the printer in the Text field. Then click OK to close the dialog (**Figure 7.22**).

or

If you need to define a specific queue, click New Attribute and choose PrinterLPRQueue from the Attribute Name pop-up menu; then enter the queue name in the Text field (**Figure 7.23**).

11. Click OK to close the dialog.

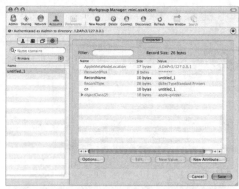

Figure 7.19 The Inspector window shows the default attributes of a new printer record.

Figure 7.20 Change the RecordName value of the new printer record.

Figure 7.21 Open the attribute-editing window of the newly created printer record.

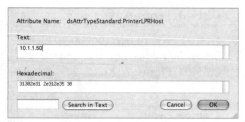

Figure 7.22 Add the PrinterLPRHost attribute IP address for the new printer record.

Figure 7.23 Add the PrinterLPRQueue attribute for the new printer record.

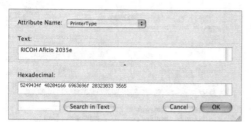

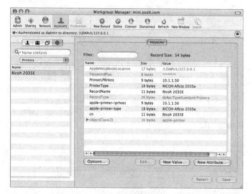

Figure 7.24 Add the PrinterType attribute for the new printer record.

Figure 7.25 The completed printer record looks like this.

Figure 7.26 Viewing the Open Directory printer using the Printer Browser window of the Printer Setup Utility.

12. To specify the printer model driver to use, add another attribute, choose PrinterType from the Attribute Name pop-up menu, and click OK (**Figure 7.24**).

The text you enter here must exactly match the model name used by the PPD.

13. Click Save.

Workgroup Manager will automatically duplicate your settings for directory service compatibility (**Figure 7.25**).

14. On a Mac OS X computer that is bound to the Mac OS X Server (which needs to be running as an Open Directory master), open the Printer Setup Utility.

The printer is now advertised, displaying the attributes with their native names and their Open Directory names (**Figure 7.26**).

15. Select the printer and click Add to add the printer to your local printer list.

This is an extremely efficient way to manage all your printers, whether they are local or global.

✔ Tips

- You can delete a printer record by selecting it and clicking Delete.

- Click Options to adjust how the attribute list is presented.

Configuring Printers on Mac OS X

Mac OS X supports many types of printers, including network and directly connected printers. This section only focuses on using the Printer Setup Utility to add printers shared from a Mac OS X Server. These printers are available to all users on the Mac OS X. There are two parts to the Printer Setup Utility: the Printer List window and the Printer Browser. The Printer List window shows the list of printers added to the local computer, whereas the Printer Browser handles the main browsable printer types, including printers directly attached to your computer. The Printer Browser will also dynamically show AppleTalk, Open Directory (Open Directory can include printers shared via SMB from a Windows computer), and Shared Printers (Shared Printers can include IPP printers shared from another Mac OS X computer).

Mac OS X offers three tools for adding printers:

◆ The Printer Setup Utility

◆ The CUPS web interface

◆ lp commands via the Terminal

The Printer Setup Utility is the easiest and most widely used. In reality, you add printers to your list via the Printer Browser, a separate window of the Printer Setup Utility. The Printer Browser can add printers for the user to print to over the following methods using the Default Browser button:

◆ **AppleTalk**—To select an AppleTalk printer in the Printer Browser, find a printer you want to connect to with a Connection type of AppleTalk. Select the printer and click Add (**Figure 7.27**). A window may appear (depending on the options available for that given printer) while the server communicates with the printer to determine the printer configuration (**Figure 7.28**).

Figure 7.27 Using the Printer Setup Utility's Printer Browser, you can add a printer using the AppleTalk protocol...

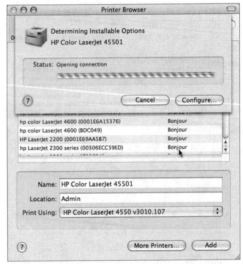

Figure 7.28 ...and a window may appear when the printer is auto-configuring.

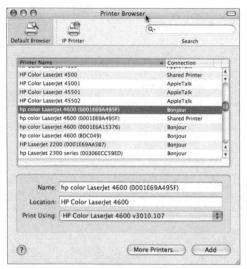

Figure 7.29 Using the Printer Setup Utility's Printer Browser, you can add a printer discovered by Bonjour...

◆ **Bonjour**—To select a Bonjour printer in the Print Browser, select a printer with a Connection type of Bonjour, and click Add (**Figure 7.29**). Since Bonjour can't auto-configure the printer for you like AppleTalk can, if the printer has different options, a window will appear, where you can configure those settings (**Figure 7.30**).

◆ **Shared Printer**—To select a shared IPP printer in the Print Browser, select a printer with a Connection type of Shared Printer and click Add. With a shared printer, a user cannot set the name, location, or the printer type, nor can they change them in the Printer Setup Utility once they've added the printer, because those settings are all determined by the computer sharing the printer, a feature that administrators may want to take advantage of (**Figure 7.31**).

continues on next page

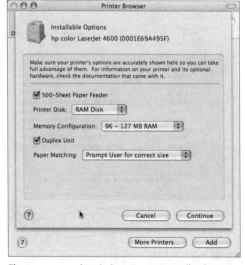

Figure 7.30 ...and a window may appear allowing you to choose printer options.

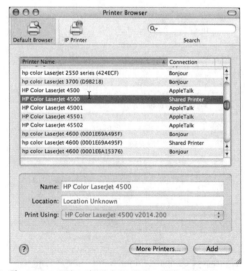

Figure 7.31 Using the Printer Setup Utility's Printer Browser, you can add a shared printer.

CONFIGURING PRINTERS ON MAC OS X

269

◆ **Open Directory**—To select an Open
Directory printer in the Print Browser,
select a printer with a connection type
of Open Directory. If the location and
printer type are set for you, verify that
they're set correctly, and click Add
(**Figure 7.32**). A window appears offering "Installable Options," if there are any
(**Figure 7.33**). Set the options correctly,
and click Continue. In the Print Browser
window, printers being shared via SMB
from Active Directory servers will also
show up as "Open Directory," even
though they technically aren't. If these
printers require authentication, click
More Printers at the bottom of the Print
Browser window to add them.

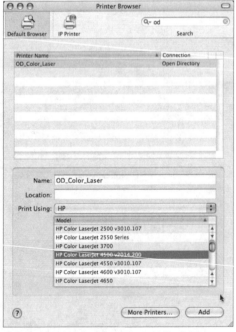

Figure 7.32 Using the Printer Setup Utility's Printer
Browser, you can add a printer discovered by Open
Directory...

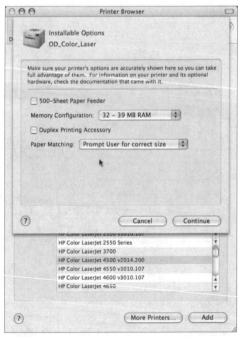

Figure 7.33 ...and a window may appear allowing you
to choose printer options.

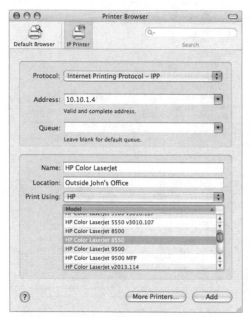

Figure 7.34 Using the Printer Setup Utility's Printer Browser, you can add an LPD (IP) printer.

If the printer is not being advertised by methods that cause it to show up in the Default Browser window, you can also create local printers via other methods. Using any of these three methods requires you to enter the information on the printer manually:

◆ **Internet Printing Protocol – IPP**—To add printers via IPP, enter the printer's IP address or DNS name, and the queue, if needed. Enter a name for the printer in the Name field; this is the name you'll see when you select the printer in the print dialog/sheet. If you don't enter a name, then the IP address or DNS name will be used. Optionally, you can also enter a location for the printer. Select the specific printer type to be used, and then click Add (**Figure 7.34**).

◆ **Line Printer Daemon – LPD**—Use this option for LPR printers. The options are the same as IPP.

◆ **HP Jet Direct – Socket**—Use this option to connect to HP printers via the HP JetDirect protocol. Other than the specific type of printer, the options are the same as IPP and LPD.

✔ Tip

■ LPR and HP JetDirect methods do not talk directly to the printer and request feedback, as other methods do.

If your printer doesn't appear in the browser list, or you have a printer that needs manual/ nonstandard settings, click More Printers to display a menu of various options by printer connection type (**Figure 7.35**).

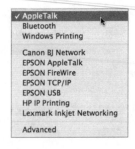

Figure 7.35 This pop-up menu shows various connection options when creating a printer.

◆ **AppleTalk**—If your AppleTalk network is configured with multiple zones, select the appropriate zone from the pop-up menu. In either case, AppleTalk printers automatically populate in the list based on zone (**Figure 7.36**).

◆ **Bluetooth**—If you have a Bluetooth–capable Mac, any Bluetooth printers will show up on this list. Select the printer from the list, verify that the model is correct or pick the correct driver, and click Add (**Figure 7.37**).

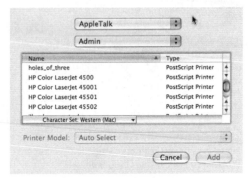

Figure 7.36 Selecting an AppleTalk printer in another zone.

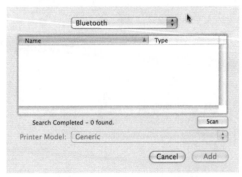

Figure 7.37 You can add Bluetooth printers to the printer list.

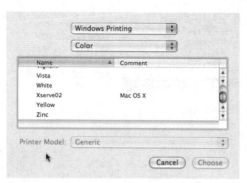

Figure 7.38 Viewing Windows computers with potential shared printers.

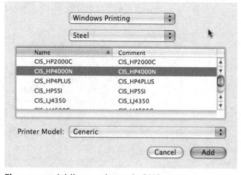

Figure 7.39 Adding a printer via SMB...

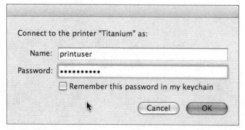

Figure 7.40 ...may require authentication to that particular printer's host.

◆ **Windows Printing**—If your Windows network is configured with multiple workgroups, select the appropriate workgroup from the pop-up menu. Initially you'll be presented with computers running Windows (SMB) printer sharing. Select a computer from the list and click Choose (**Figure 7.38**). Then select the printer from the list, and click Add (**Figure 7.39**).

✔ Tips

■ While you can connect to a printer via SMB in the printer browser via the Open Directory label, if the printer or the Windows computer controlling it requires a password (as most do) you may have problems connecting to that printer (**Figure 7.40**).

■ When printing to an SMB-based printer, you may have to authenticate with a user account and password, as they're often password protected, especially on a large network (as seen in Figure 7.40).

continues on next page

◆ **USB**—With USB printing, plugging in the USB printer is usually enough. You may need to install the printer drivers and printer description files if a CD is included with your printer. Consult the directions and CD that came with your USB printer in that case.

◆ **Other Options**—Depending on the printers you use, you may have other options available, such as Epson AppleTalk or Canon BJ. These are specific to the printer(s) you use, and you should consult the specific documentation for information on using those connection types (**Figure 7.41**).

◆ **The Advanced option**—Sometimes you have a printer you need to add, but it requires a slightly different setup than you would normally see via the Printer Setup Utility. For those printers, the Printer Setup Utility has the Advanced option. This option is normally hidden, as you shouldn't use it casually. To access it, hold down the Option key while clicking More Printers in the Printer Browser window. In the list of available options that appears, you'll see a new entry: Advanced. In the Advanced options, you can manually set up any kind of printer Mac OS X can see. Of all the possibilities, one of the most common is connecting to a printer that uses IPP but via a HTTP URL. This is common with HP Laser printers that support IPP.

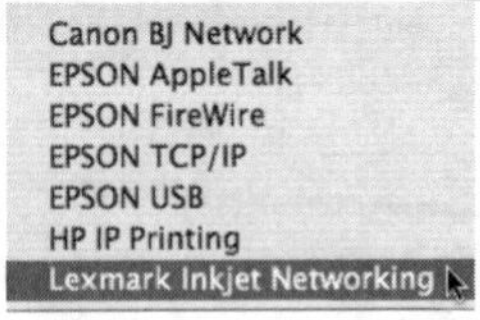

Canon BJ Network
EPSON AppleTalk
EPSON FireWire
EPSON TCP/IP
EPSON USB
HP IP Printing
Lexmark Inkjet Networking

Figure 7.41 Some printers require special drivers, which are installed and viewed separately.

Figure 7.42 Viewing the Printer Setup Utility's Printer List window.

Figure 7.43 Viewing printer options via the Default Browser window.

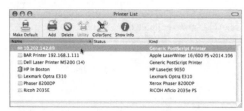

Figure 7.44 Verifying an IP printer is added to the printer list.

To create a printer:

1. On Mac OS X, launch the Printer Setup Utility.

   The Printer List window appears (**Figure 7.42**).

2. Click Add Printer 🖨 on the Toolbar. The Printer Browser window appears.

3. Choose a printer to add to the Printer List from the browser (**Figure 7.43**).

   or

   If you want to connect to a printer via IPP, LPD/LPR, or HP Jet Direct, click IP Printer.

4. Fill out the appropriate information and click Add.

   When you click Add, another window offering "Installable Options" may appear. You can pick any additional options the printer may have, such as extra memory or a duplex unit. Set the correct options for your printer, and click Continue. This will add the printer to the Printer List window in the Printer Setup Utility.

5. Verify that the printer you just selected has been added to your Printer List window (**Figure 7.44**).

6. Quit the Printer Setup Utility.

✔ Tips

- You can delete a printer by selecting it and clicking Delete on the Printer List Toolbar.

- Double-click a printer in the list to view its local print job queue (**Figure 7.45**).

- You can edit a printer's configuration by selecting it in the Printer List window and clicking Show Info (**Figure 7.46**).

Figure 7.45 Double-click any printer to view its queue.

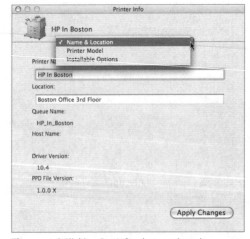

Figure 7.46 Clicking Get Info when a printer is selected shows editable options.

Figure 7.47 Selecting multiple printers in the Printer List window.

Figure 7.48 Creating a printer pool from the selected printer.

Creating Printer Pool Queues

Mac OS X supports a special type of printer queue called a *printer pool*, which can load-balance print jobs between multiple printers. Essentially, a printer pool is a queue that automatically sends a print job to the next available printer on a list you define. It takes only a few steps to enable a shared printer pool on Mac OS X Server.

To create a printer pool:

1. On the server, open the Printer Setup Utility, and add all the printers you wish to pool together.

2. Select all the printers you want to pool by holding down the Command key while you make your selections (**Figure 7.47**).

3. Choose Printers > Pool Printers. The Printer Pool dialog opens.

4. Edit the pool's name, and click Create (**Figure 7.48**).

continues on next page

CREATING PRINTER POOL QUEUES

5. Return to the Server Admin tool's printer queue list to find your new printer pool queue (**Figure 7.49**).

Enable print sharing for the printer pool queue as you would for any other printer. When users print to the queue, CUPS will decide which printer in the pool is to receive the next print job (**Figure 7.50**).

Figure 7.49 Viewing a Printer Pool queue using Server Admin.

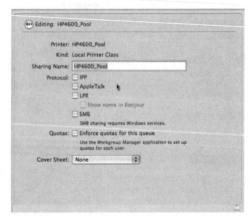

Figure 7.50 Sharing a printer pool is similar to sharing a single printer.

Name	Jobs	Shared via	Kind	Status
10.1.55.100	0	PAP	Xerox Phaser 8400N	
another_neat_printer	0	IPP LPR	Generic PostScript Printer	
really_neat_printer	0	IPP	Generic PostScript Printer	

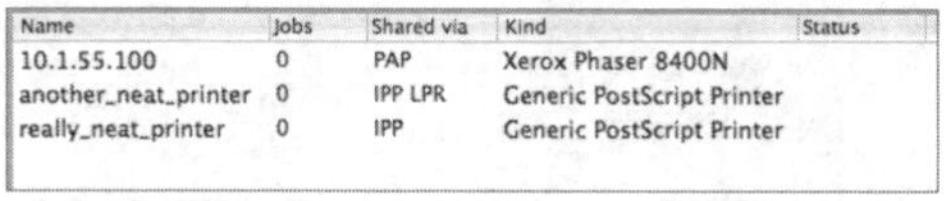

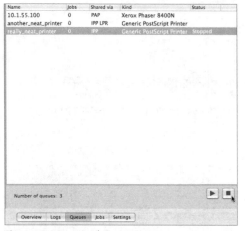

Figure 7.51 Viewing print queues with Server Admin.

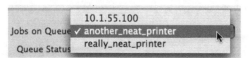

Figure 7.52 Stopping/starting print queues with the appropriate buttons.

Figure 7.53 Selecting a queue to view the jobs within that queue.

Managing Print Jobs

One of the primary reasons to configure a print server is that doing so gives administrators greater control over print jobs. The Server Admin tool in Mac OS X Server lets you monitor every print job that is sent through your print queues. Further, you can hold or delete print jobs waiting in the queue, thus allowing other jobs to print sooner.

To manage print jobs:

1. Within Server Admin, select the Print service and click the Queues tab at the bottom of the window.

   The Queues window appears, showing all your active print queues and the number of jobs in each queue (**Figure 7.51**).

2. *Do one of the following:*
   - ▲ To stop all the jobs in a print queue, select the queue and click the stop button on the lower right (**Figure 7.52**).
   - ▲ Click the start button (the triangle button adjacent to the stop button) to resume the print queue.

3. Select the queue you want to view or manage from the Jobs on Queue pop-up menu (**Figure 7.53**).

continues on next page

4. Click the Jobs tab.

The Jobs window appears, showing the status for all print jobs for a specific queue (**Figure 7.54**).

5. Do any of the following:

▲ To hold a print job, letting other jobs in the queue print sooner, select the job and click the pause button (**Figure 7.55**).

▲ Select a job and click the start button to put the print job back on normal print status.

▲ Select a job and click Delete to delete the job from the print queue.

Figure 7.54 Viewing all print jobs for a particular queue.

✔ Tips

■ Although the Server Admin tool automatically refreshes, it may not refresh often enough for you to see all the jobs. This is because the print server may receive and send the print job in less time than it takes for the Server Admin tool to display the job in the list.

■ In the Queues list you may see the acronym PAP in the Shared Via column. Printer Access Protocol (PAP), a part of AppleTalk, is responsible for communicating between your Mac and a printer or print server.

■ Click the Refresh button on the Toolbar to force the Server Admin tool to refresh the print queue or print job list immediately.

Figure 7.55 Pausing/starting/deleting print jobs within a particular queue using the appropriate buttons.

Viewing Print Logs

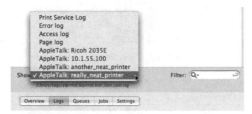

Figure 7.56 Viewing all available print logs using Server Admin.

Figure 7.57 Viewing the Print Service log, the default log when selecting Server Admin.

Figure 7.58 The log file for the selected print queue is displayed in the Logs window.

If you're having printing problems on your Mac OS X Server, your main troubleshooting resource is the print logs. Every time a queue is modified or a print job is processed, the information is written to the print logs, which includes accounting information.

To view print logs:

1. Launch the Server Admin tool and authenticate as the administrator if necessary.

2. Select the Print service, click the Logs tab at the bottom of the window, and view the available log files (**Figure 7.56**).

   The Logs window appears, showing the log for every printer on the server). By default, it shows you the Print Service log (**Figure 7.57**, which includes general print service information, such as adding/deleting print queues, starting/pausing print queues, starting/stopping the print server, and issuing print service error messages.

3. From the Show pop-up menu in the Logs window, select the printer whose log you want to view.

   The Logs window shows the log file for the selected print queue (**Figure 7.58**). This log lists details such as username, print job, and number of pages. Held and deleted print jobs are also reported; however, per-queue logs are only kept for AppleTalk queues.

✔ Tips

- The Server Admin tool is convenient in that you can view log files remotely; however, it lacks some of the log-reading tools available in the Console utility. If you have local access to your server, you can launch the Console utility located in /Applications/Utilities. Note that the location of the print service logs is /Library/Logs/PrintService. If you aren't sure where a log resides, select it in the Logs window, and the physical location of the log on the server will appear just below the name of the print queue (**Figure 7.59**).

- When you're viewing logs from the Console utility, use the Filter field to narrow the log file to the specific items you're looking for.

Figure 7.59 The physical location of the log on the server is displayed just below the name of the print queue.

ENABLING
MAIL SERVICES

8

Although email has changed greatly over the years, the methods used to get email from one location to another have remained rather constant, and it is still a key component for any organization's Internet infrastructure.

The Simple Mail Transfer Protocol (SMTP) is used to pass a single message from server to server until it reaches its intended recipient. Once the message arrives at its destination mail server, the recipient has a choice of two primary protocols to retrieve the content of that message. The Internet Mail Access Protocol (IMAP) is common among users who may access email from multiple computers and want their inboxes to remain on their mail servers. Post Office Protocol (POP) downloads a copy of each message from the server and often deletes it from the server immediately, reducing the amount of resources required on the server. Choosing the right protocol depends on the server infrastructure you're willing to set up and maintain along with the needs of your users. You will have to make many other decisions before you settle on a particular mail access protocol. The good news is that with Mac OS X Server, you can offer many to your users, letting them choose which method is best for them.

Protocol Pros and Cons

When sending mail, Mac OS X Server users must use the SMTP. However, when receiving mail, there are a couple of options. IMAP has numerous advantages. Since your email is stored on the server, you can access it from the same inbox on your desktop at work or your laptop at home. IMAP also offers a wider feature set, including more authentication options. However, while a user is running email client software, a connection typically remains open with the email server. For large organizations, this can necessitate having an extensive server infrastructure to accommodate the simultaneous connections throughout the entire workday.

With POP, once you've connected to your inbox, your email is stored only on your personal workstation. In this situation, you would not be able to see the same email messages from multiple computers, and, unless your workstation is backed up, your email may not have any sort of backup protection. Probably the biggest disadvantage of POP is that it usually uses nonsecure password storage methods. The good news is that there are ways you can safeguard your password through the use of Secure Sockets Layer (SSL), or by using higher-security password systems such as Kerberos.

Mac OS X Server uses open source software to implement many of its services. Mail is no exception. Most of the mail processing is handled by Postfix (www.postfix.org), while the users connect to their inbox through Cyrus (asg.web.cmu.edu/cyrus). Mac OS X Server also comes with SquirrelMail (www.squirrelmail.org) to allow users to connect to their email from a web browser. Mailing list management is handled through Mailman (www.list.org). New in Mac OS X Server 10.4 are even more open source solutions. Junk mail and virus protection are now implemented through a combination of SpamAssassin (spamassassin.apache.org), ClamAV (www.clamav.net), and AMaViS (www.amavis.org). Tiger also offers virtual hosting options, improved mail maintenance tools, and better mail quota support.

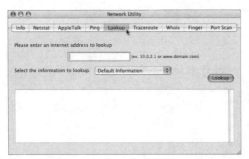

Figure 8.1 Network Utility contains a host of network test tools, including a DNS Lookup tool.

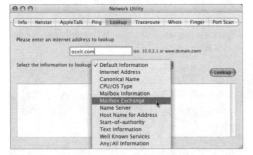

Figure 8.2 Network Utility's DNS Lookup tool can be set to only show Mailbox Exchange (MX) information.

Setting Up Mail Services

Receiving mail from the Internet has a few requirements. First, your server needs to be configured to accept mail by running the SMTP service and opening port 25 in your firewall. Next, everyone else on the Internet needs to know which server receives email for your domain through the DNS mail exchange (*MX*) record. Your domain can (and should) have more than one MX record, each pointing to a different server. Each MX record is assigned a priority. When mail is sent to your domain, the server with the lowest priority number is tried first. If the message can't be delivered to that server, each of the servers referenced in your other MX records will be tried, starting with the lowest priority number.

Ideally, each of your MX servers will be located on different networks and in different locations so your organization continues to receive mail during any outage. Mail relies very heavily on DNS, since half of everyone's email address is the domain name of that user. Since email is such a critical service for most organizations, it's important that you have both a static IP address and redundancy in your DNS service.

To verify your MX record:

1. Launch Network Utility.

   See Chapter 2, "Server Tools," for instructions.

2. Select the Lookup tab (**Figure 8.1**).

3. Type your domain name in the Internet address box.

4. From the "Select the information to lookup" pop-up menu, select Mailbox Exchange (**Figure 8.2**).

continues on next page

5. Click Lookup.

If you don't have an MX record configured for your domain yet, there will be no `ANSWER SECTION` in the output (**Figure 8.3**).

If your MX record is configured, you'll see an `ANSWER SECTION` that contains a line with an `IN MX` record (**Figure 8.4**).

✔ Tip

■ You can also check MX records from the command line by opening the Terminal application and typing `host -t MX` *yourdomain.xyz*.

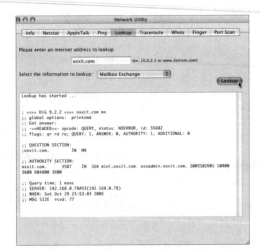

Figure 8.3 The results from an MX record query where no MX record is set.

Figure 8.4 The results from an MX record query where the MX record exists.

Figure 8.5 Select the DNS service in Server Admin.

Figure 8.6 Select your DNS zone in Server Admin.

Setting MX records

You may or may not have control over the DNS records for your organization. If you do not, generally you would send any DNS requests to hostmaster@*yourdomain.xyz*. If you are running Mac OS X Server, the following steps illustrate how to set up your MX record.

1. Launch Server Admin and select DNS from the Computers & Services column (**Figure 8.5**).

2. Select the Settings tab at the bottom of the screen.

3. Select the Zones tab at the top of the screen.

4. Double-click your zone to edit it (**Figure 8.6**).

5. Select the Machines tab at the top of the screen.

6. If you already have a record present for the server that will act as your mail server, double-click that record.

   Or

   Click the plus sign button to add a record.

continues on next page

SETTING UP MAIL SERVICES

7. Make sure that the IP address and name are correct and then create an alias named "mail" by selecting the "This machine is a mail server for the zone" option (**Figure 8.7**).

This allows you to change your mail server without reconfiguring all of your mail clients.

8. Enter a Mail Server Precedence setting.

A setting of 10 allows you to add other machines later with either a higher or lower priority if desired. You need not start at 0.

9. Click OK and then click Save.

10. Verify the MX record using the procedure described in the previous exercise.

You may have to wait for the time to live (TTL) to count down to zero on your zone before the changes you make become visible to your computer (**Figure 8.8**).

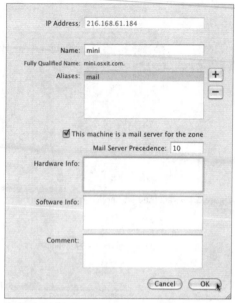

Figure 8.7 Add an alias for your mail server and indicate that this host is a mail server with a precedence of 10.

Figure 8.8 Use Network Utility to check the DNS results. No MX record is shown because the TTL has not expired yet.

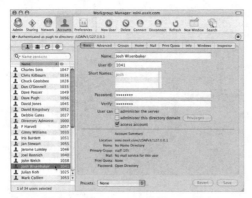

Figure 8.9 Select the user you wish to modify in Workgroup Manager.

Figure 8.10 In the Mail tab of Workgroup Manager, enable mail for this user.

Setting up mail for user accounts

Before your server can accept mail, you have to tell the system that your users are allowed to receive mail.

To set up your account:

1. Launch Workgroup Manager, and in the lefthand column of the window that appears, select the user for whom you want to enable mail (**Figure 8.9**).

2. Select the Mail tab and click the Enabled radio button near the top of the frame (**Figure 8.10**).

   Your fully qualified domain name will likely show up instead of the mail exchange name. This is not an issue but can be changed to reflect the MX record name if you wish.

3. Leave the rest of the options at their defaults for now and click Save.

4. Repeat the previous steps for any other accounts on your system that should be allowed to receive mail.

✔ Tip

■ If you select multiple users in Workgroup Manager, any change will be applied to all of the selected users.

To configure SMTP service:

1. Launch Server Admin.

   You will use the Server Admin tool for the majority of the exercises in this chapter, so you may want to leave it open.

2. From the Computers & Services column, select Mail (**Figure 8.11**).

3. Select the Settings tab and click the Enable SMTP check box (**Figure 8.12**).

4. Make sure the "Allow incoming mail" option is selected.

5. Type your domain name in the Domain name field.

   This is the portion of your hostname that follows the @ sign in an email address.

6. Type the hostname of your mail server in the Host name field.

   This should be the fully qualified version of your hostname, which also includes the domain name. Generally this is the same as the results of a hostname lookup on your IP address (also known as your reverse DNS), although for this exercise, you are seeing the MX record name, which is also acceptable.

7. If your ISP requires you to use its mail relay server, rather than sending email from your server directly to the Internet, select the "Relay outgoing mail through host" check box, type the name of your ISP's SMTP server, and click Save.

8. Select the Advanced tab and then select the Hosting tab.

9. Click the plus sign button to add a local host alias.

Figure 8.11 Select the Mail service in the Server Admin Tool.

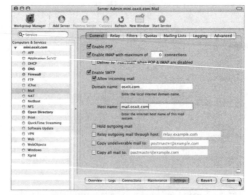

Figure 8.12 Configure and enable incoming SMTP service using the Server Admin tool.

Figure 8.13 In the Hosting tab of the Server Admin tool, list any name that this server might receive mail for.

10. Add your domain name to the Local Host Aliases list.

Local Host Aliases are other names your server may accept mail for. For example, your mail server may accept mail addressed to someuser@osxit.com, someuser@mini.osxit.com, someuser@mail.osxit.com, or someuser@mailserver52.osxit.com. Each possible server alias (the portion after the @ sign) should be listed as a local host alias. Note that each one will usually require an entry in DNS as well.

11. Repeat steps 9 and 10 to add the name of your server, along with any host aliases, to the list so that it contains every possible way mail might address your server (**Figure 8.13**).

12. Click Save and then click the Start Service icon.

✔ **Tip**

■ If you get your Internet service via DSL or cable modem, you may have a host-name that is not trusted by other mail servers on the Internet. In this case, you should always relay your mail through your ISP's SMTP server.

Opening mail ports

Now that you're running an SMTP service, you need to allow other servers to connect to your server. You should already be running a firewall on your server, so you just need to open the mail ports.

To open the firewall for SMTP:

1. From the Computers & Services column, select Firewall (**Figure 8.14**).

2. Select the Settings tab and then select the Services tab.

3. From the Edit Services for pull-down menu, choose any (**Figure 8.15**).

4. Select the "Allow traffic for 'any' of these ports" check box and then select Mail: SMTP (port 25) in the list below (**Figure 8.16**).

5. Click Save.

   At this point, you should be able to send email to your server. You can verify this by sending email to one of the users you enabled in Workgroup Manager. If, after a few minutes, you don't get an error message back, the mail was probably delivered without any problems.

Figure 8.14 Select the firewall service in the Server Admin tool.

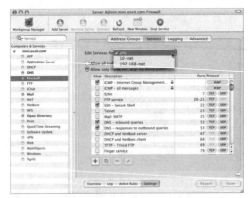

Figure 8.15 Select the any network group in the firewall settings.

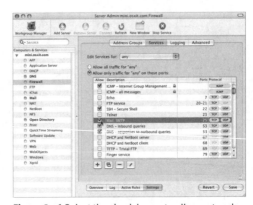

Figure 8.16 Select the check boxes to allow network traffic on the SMTP port.

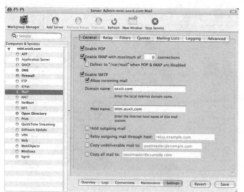

Figure 8.17 Enable both IMAP and POP for your mail server.

Configuring the receiving mail service

Your server can now accept incoming mail, but as of yet, the server may not be configured for users to connect to their inboxes.

To configure your IMAP/POP service:

1. From the Computers & Services column, select Mail.

2. Select the Settings tab at the bottom of the screen.

3. Select the Enable POP and Enable IMAP check boxes, if they aren't already selected (**Figure 8.17**).

4. Click Save.

Free Testing

A number of companies, such as Yahoo and Google, offer free Web-based email. These services are great tools for testing your email system as they are independent email clients that are sending mail to your server from outside of your network. This checks your DNS, firewall, and mail server configurations all with one easy tool.

It is also a good idea to visit a site that will verify your server is not configured as an open relay. There are a number of open relay testing sites on the Internet that will check your mail server for a secure configuration. A quick Internet search will yield numerous options.

Opening the firewall to permit receiving mail

Now that you're running an IMAP and POP service, you need to allow computers to connect to your server. You should already running a firewall on your server, so you just need to open the IMAP and POP ports.

To open the firewall for IMAP and POP:

1. From the Computers & Services column, select Firewall.

2. Select the Settings tab and then select the Services tab.

3. From the "Edit Services for" pop-up menu, choose any.

4. Select the "Allow traffic for 'any' on these ports" check box, and then select Mail: POP3 (port 110) and IMAP (port 143) from the list (**Figure 8.18**).

5. Click Save.

   You should now be able to configure Apple's Mail application to connect to your server using either POP or IMAP to retrieve your mail.

✔ Tip

■ Note that under the current configuration, neither your password nor the mail itself is secure in any way. You'll be taking a number of steps to secure your mail service later in this chapter.

Figure 8.18 In the firewall settings, select the check boxes to allow network traffic on the POP and IMAP ports.

Figure 8.19 Configure quotas to refuse messages larger than 5 MB.

Enhancing Your Mail Service

Now that you have a fully functional email service, you'll no doubt want to make some refinements to its configuration. Mac OS X Server offers numerous mail server enhancements through the Server Admin tool, as well as many that can be configured from the command line via the Terminal application.

Setting mail quotas

You generally don't want your users to be able to accept emails of an unlimited size or to accumulate an excess amount of email in their inbox. Doing so would put a strain both on your server's bandwidth and on the disk space consumed by your mail service. You can control this through the use of *quotas*. Mac OS X Server offers two sets of quotas that you can define for your mail service: per-message size limits that control the maximum size of an individual message as it's received by your server, and per-mailbox size limits, which control the total size of any one user's mailbox.

To limit mail size:

1. From the Computers & Services column, select Mail.

2. Select the Settings tab at the bottom of the screen and then select the Quotas tab.

3. Select the "Refuse incoming messages larger than X megabytes" check box and change the value to 5 (**Figure 8.19**). This will limit the size of any single incoming message to 5 MB or less.

4. Click Save.

You also want to limit the maximum size of any user's mailbox. There are two types of quotas to be applied here. The first is known as a *soft quota*, which is merely a quota warning a user that he or she is approaching (or even exceeding) their quota, but no mail is ever blocked for the user. The other type of quota is a *hard quota*. With hard quotas enabled, once the user reaches their maximum mailbox size, any future emails addressed to that user will be returned to the sender and will be undelivered. Generally soft quotas are preferred since it won't result in email being denied for a user, but if you're tight on disk space or have users who ignore the warnings, you'll want to use the hard quotas.

To enable soft quotas:

1. Click the Quotas tab and select the "Enable quota warnings" check box (**Figure 8.20**).

2. In the settings below, change the values to send quota warnings when usage exceeds 95% and send a quota warning every day.

3. To change the messages sent to users warning them of their approaching quota limits, click the pencil icon next to the "Email server usage is approaching quota" text box.

4. In the window that appears, change the address in the From field (**Figure 8.21**). You can also change the text of the message sent to the offending users.

5. Click Save.

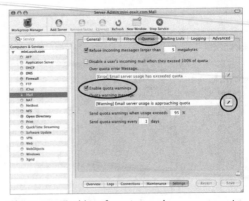

Figure 8.20 Enable soft quota warnings so users get a warning email at 95 percent of their quota.

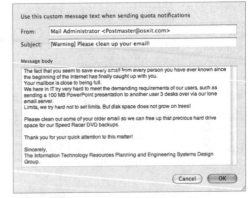

Figure 8.21 Customize the quota email with your administrator's email address.

Figure 8.22 Select the user you wish to modify in Workgroup Manager and change this user's mail quota to 500 MB.

Setting mailbox quotas

The settings you just enabled apply to all users, but by default, users don't actually have a mailbox quota set.

To set the quota for each account:

1. Launch Workgroup Manager, and in the lefthand column, select the user(s) for whom you want to enable mail.

2. Select the Mail tab and change the Mail Quota value to 500 MB (**Figure 8.22**).

   You may wish to adjust this value, depending on the number of users and the amount of available disk space on your mail server. A quota of 0 signifies that the user has no quota (unlimited storage).

3. Click Save.

4. Repeat these steps for any other users that should have quotas applied to the size of their entire mailbox.

Users Postal Over Mail Quotas?

Users generally despise having mail quotas, especially low ones, or ones that result in mail loss. Depending on the types of users you have on your server, simple user education might be sufficient. It's also important to remember that free email providers such as Gmail and Yahoo offer mailboxes with multi-gigabyte quotas. If you need to restrict your mailboxes to smaller sizes than what is offered by the free email providers on the Internet, be prepared to explain both why you did and why users should continue using your service—company security policies, faster connections, and better service—rather than a public Internet service.

Handling junk mail and viruses

One thing you'll want to do for your users is scan their email for spam or other unsolicited junk mail. Mac OS X Server includes SpamAssassin, an open source solution for doing just that. Although SpamAssassin provides a mechanism to scan messages by itself, Apple has chosen to scan mail using another open source solution: AMaViS (A Mail Virus Scanner) calls the SpamAssassin modules internally, simultaneously passing each message through ClamAV, an open source antivirus scanner, while scanning it for spam content—and it all happens automatically as soon as the server receives each message.

To configure your mail server for spam and virus scanning:

1. Launch Server Admin and select Mail from the Computers & Services column.

2. Select the Settings tab at the bottom of the screen and then select the Filters tab.

3. Select the check boxes to scan email for junk mail and viruses (**Figure 8.23**).

4. Select the "Update the junk mail and virus database" check box, change the value to 4 times per day, and click Save.

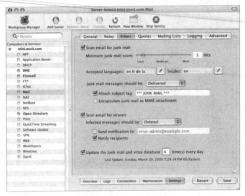

Figure 8.23 Configure junk mail and virus scanning in the Server Admin tool.

Scoring junk mail

There are a number of other customizations you can make on the last screen in the previous exercise. The most visible one is the Minimum junk mail score, which defaults to 5 hits. Every time a message is received by your server, it is assigned a score, based on how many spam tests were matched and the probability of each test indicating that the message is spam. If the score it receives is lower than 5, it's considered not spam (sometimes called *ham*). If the score is 5 or above, the message is tagged as spam. When this happens, the subject line has *** JUNK MAIL *** prepended to it, and some extra headers are added indicating the actual score and the tests that matched. You can, of course, change these options, but the defaults are good ones to stick with until you are more familiar with the operation of the junk mail scanner.

Checking email for spam is a tricky problem. On one hand, nobody likes to receive spam. An even worse problem, however, is when a legitimate message is tagged as spam. This is known as a false positive, and can occur when you have your minimum junk mail score set too low. The default of 5 is a good starting point, but if you discover too many false positives, you may want to adjust this number to be higher.

Junk mail training

One of the best ways to check for spam is using a technology called Bayesian Filters. These filters examine the contents of the message for certain patterns common to spam messages. This filtering process is included as part of SpamAssassin, but first must be trained. If you already have some folders of mail that contain example messages of both spam and non-spam, save them out to two directories, one containing only spam messages, the other containing only non-spam messages. You can perform your initial spam training using these commands in Mac OS X 10.4.0–10.4.3 from the Terminal on your server or a remote ssh connection:

```
sudo /bin/rm -rf /private/var/amavis/
→ .spamassassin
sudo ln -s /private/var/clamav/
→ .spamassassin /private/var/amavis/
→ .spamassassin
sudo -s
su - clamav -c "sa-learn --spam
→ --showdots /Path/To/JunkMail/Folder"
su - clamav -c "sa-learn --ham --showdots
→ /Path/To/NonJunkMail/Folder"
```

You'll also want to continually update the spam training. As messages arrive, the Bayesian database is continually updated. Occasionally, you will receive a message that was mis-tagged as spam or not-spam. When this happens, you'll want to provide a place for users to submit their own samples of messages that are spam or are not spam. For this, create two accounts with special names: *junkmail* and *notjunkmail*. The mailboxes of these accounts are in place for users to bounce or redirect appropriate messages to, and are scanned once a night for inclusion in the Bayesian database.

To create spam accounts:

1. Launch Workgroup Manager and click the New User icon.

2. In the Name field, enter JunkMail, and in the Short Names field, enter junkmail (**Figure 8.24**).
   Leave the User ID at its default (1079).

3. In the Password field, enter a password and reenter it in the Verify field.

4. Deselect the access account check box.

5. Click the Advanced tab at the top of the screen.

6. Deselect the "Allow simultaneous login on managed computers" check box.

7. Set the Login Shell to None (**Figure 8.25**).

8. Click the Mail tab at the top of the screen.

9. Click the Enabled radio button and click Save (**Figure 8.26**).

10. Repeat steps 2–9 but use NotJunkMail for the long name and notjunkmail for the short name.

✔ Tip

- The junkmail and notjunkmail mailboxes are not automatically emptied after their contents are scanned, so you may wish to periodically empty them.

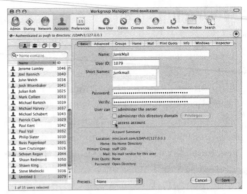

Figure 8.24 Set up the junk mail user in Workgroup Manager.

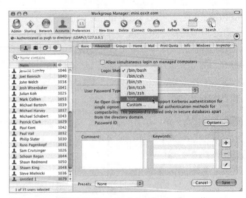

Figure 8.25 Disable the shell for the junk mail user. This will help to secure this account from misuse.

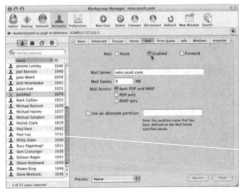

Figure 8.26 Enable mail service for the junk mail user.

Figure 8.27 Enable mailing lists in the Server Admin tool.

Figure 8.28 Set the mailing list service master password and top-level administrators.

Offering mailing lists

Mailing lists, which are sometimes called *listservs*, offer a convenient way for people inside or outside of your organization to form a group identified by one email address. Mac OS X Server provides an open source solution called Mailman, with features such as message archiving, private lists, moderated lists, commands sent through email, and much more. You can manage mailing lists through the Server Admin tool, or users can manage their own lists with a convenient Web interface.

To enable mailing lists:

1. Launch Server Admin and select Mail from the Computers & Services column.

2. Select the Settings tab at the bottom of the screen and then select the Mailing Lists tab.

3. Select the "Enable mailing lists" option (**Figure 8.27**).

4. In the window that appears asking you to create the master password for all lists, type in a password that is not used anywhere else on the system and provide one or more email addresses for the top level mailing list administrators (**Figure 8.28**).

5. Click OK and then Save.

   You'll notice that a default mailing list called "Mailman" was just created. This is also referred to as the master mailing list, and should not be renamed or deleted.

To create mailing lists:

1. Click the Mailing Lists tab and then click the plus button under the Lists column.

   A new window appears asking you to enter the details of the new list you're creating (**Figure 8.29**).

2. Name your list following normal email address conventions.

   For simplicity, it's often best to restrict it to letters, numbers, or hyphens.

3. Type the username (local to this server) or email address (of anyone) that will be administering this list.

4. If you want to allow people to subscribe themselves to this list, check the "Users may self-subscribe" box.

   Otherwise, the mailing list administrator will have to add everyone to the list.

5. Select the default language and supported languages for the list.

6. Leave the Maximum length of a message body at its default of 40 KB.

   Since messages to mailing lists are sent to many people, it's generally good to limit the size of each message. This avoids the problem of someone inadvertently sending a 100 MB attachment to hundreds of people.

7. Click OK.

   Your new mailing list is now created, but currently has no members except the administrator. You probably want to add a few people that you know will be on the list, or perhaps other administrators.

8. In the Lists column, select the name of your new list and then click the plus button (**Figure 8.30**).

Figure 8.29 Create a new mailing list and select its default options in the Server Admin tool.

Figure 8.30 You can use the Server Admin tool to add users to a mailing list.

Figure 8.31 List the local usernames or remote email addresses of the users you wish to add to the mailing list.

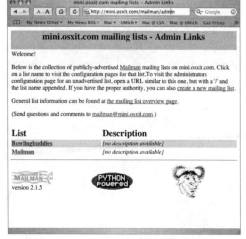

Figure 8.32 Use your web browser to select the mailing list you wish to administer.

9. In the window that appears, type one or more local usernames and/or remote email addresses (**Figure 8.31**).

10. Select the options that should apply to all of those users and click OK.

If you want different options for different users, repeat steps 9–10 for each type of person, or alternatively, add all the users here, then use the main Server Admin window to select or deselect the check boxes for each user.

11. In the main Server Admin window, click Save.

Your mailing list is now ready to use. Assuming you're a member of the list (since nonmembers can't post to it by default), you can send mail to it right away. Nonmembers will have their messages held for approval by the moderator.

ENHANCING YOUR MAIL SERVICE

To set options for your list through the Web interface:

1. In your Web browser, go to http://*yourserver.xyz*/mailman/admin (**Figure 8.32**).

2. Select the name of the list you want to edit.

3. Type a list administrator's password.

   Note that this is not any user's password, but rather the password you typed when you first enabled mailing lists for your server.

   A page is now displayed with many different options you can customize for this list (**Figure 8.33**).

✔ Tips

■ You can view information about lists at the following URL:

http://*yourserver.xyz*/mailman/listinfo

After selecting the list, the archives and subscription information are displayed (**Figure 8.34**).

■ Many options are available to configure and use Mailman to your liking. Please consult www.list.org or the Mac OS X Mail Service Administration manual for more information.

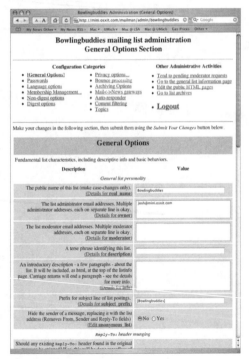

Figure 8.33 Many administration options are available through the Web that are not available in the Server Admin tool.

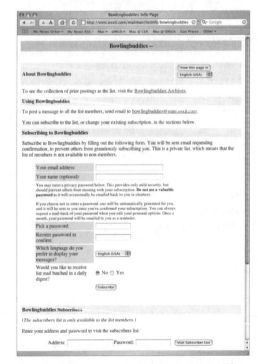

Figure 8.34 Users can use a Web browser to modify their subscription or view the mailing list archives.

Figure 8.35 Server Admin shows where your mail databases are stored. This screen also has a repair button to fix your mail databases.

Storing mail

In the days of older mail systems, mail was simply stored in one file per user. Although this was much simpler to deal with, it was also much slower, particularly for large mailboxes. To alleviate this problem, Cyrus, the mail storage mechanism used by Mac OS X Server, splits the mail up into a large number of files, with an associated database for each user, allowing for faster searching and quicker retrieval of any given message.

To locate the Cyrus mail store:

1. Launch Server Admin and select Mail from the Computers & Services column.

2. Select the Maintenance tab at the bottom of the screen.

3. Click the Database tab at the top of the screen.

Backing up mail

Figure 8.35 shows a typical mail server, where the database of mailboxes is stored in /var/imap, and each mailbox is located in /var/spool/imap. If you have many users, you may also be storing mail in other locations, which will be shown in the window at the bottom.

Numerous configuration and database files are stored in the following locations:

- /var/imap
- /var/spool/imap
- /etc/mail
- /etc/postfix
- /etc/cyrus.conf
- /var/amavis
- /var/clamav
- /var/mailman
- /etc/spam

As with any important data, your mail server should be backed up. Unfortunately, since mail relies so heavily on databases, the mail service should be shut down while the backup is taking place. This avoids problems that might arise from a mailbox being modified after the database for that mailbox has been saved but before the actual mail data has been backed up. The downside to shutting down your mail server when you make backups is that users with IMAP connections will get disconnected. This inconvenience will have to be weighed against the need for accurate regular backups, and, depending on the types of users you support, could dictate the frequency of your mail server backups. Mac OS X Server has no built-in GUI for performing mail server backups. You'll want to create a series of shell scripts that can be automatically run by cron to automate the task of doing mail server backups.

To prepare your system for mail backups, you must first create some directories that will store the backups. Execute the following commands:

```
mkdir -p /var/backupmail/tmp
chown root:wheel /var/backupmail/tmp
chmod 700 /var/backupmail
```

Next, you need to actually save your mail server data in a backup. These commands should be placed in a script, which could be put in /private/etc/periodic/daily so that it's run automatically every day:

```
/usr/sbin/serveradmin stop mail
rsync -exclude=socket -delete -a
→ /var/imap/ /var/backupmail/
→ tmp/varimap
rsync -delete -a /var/spool/imap/
→ var/backupmail/tmp/varspoolimap
rsync -delete -a /etc/postfix/
→ /var/backupmail/tmp/etcpostfix
rsync -delete -a /etc/mail/ /var/
→ backupmail/tmp/etc/postfix
rsync -delete -a /var/amavis/
→ /var/backupmail/tmp/varamavis
rsync -delete -a /var/clamav/
→ /var/backupmail/tmp/varclamav
/usr/sbin/serveradmin start mail
tar -C /var/backupmail -zcpf /var/
→ backupmail/`date +%a`.tar.gz tmp
```

By using rsync, you're only updating copies of files that have changed, thus minimizing the downtime of your mail service. The tar command at the end will compress that day's backup into a file named Mon.tar.gz, Tue.tar.gz, and so on for each day of the week. Consult the date man page for other options you could use.

If you need to restore files from a particular backup, execute these commands:

```
mkdir /var/backupmail/restore
cd /var/backupmail/restore
sudo tar -zxpf /var/backupmail/
→ DAY.tar.gz
```

Once the archive is expanded, you can copy any missing or corrupted files to their appropriate location.

ENHANCING YOUR MAIL SERVICE

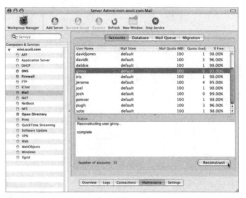

Figure 8.36 Server Admin allows you to reconstruct an individual user's mail database with the click of a button.

Fixing mailbox corruption

Should you run into problems with your mail server, one of the most likely culprits is mail database corruption. Before you restore a corrupted database from your backups, you should first try repairing the existing database.

To fix common database corruption problems:

1. From the Computers & Services column, select Mail.

2. Select the Maintenance tab at the bottom of the screen.

   If everyone is having problems with their mail, or if particular users are having problems receiving mail, it's likely that the problem lies with the database of mailboxes.

3. Click the Database tab at the top of the following screen and click Repair (see Figure 8.35).

   If only certain people are having problems with their mail, particularly if they are reporting that messages are disappearing or becoming corrupted, or that previously read messages are reappearing as new messages, the problem is likely with an individual user's mailbox database.

4. Click the Accounts tab.

5. Select the account you're having trouble with and click Reconstruct (**Figure 8.36**).

Using the Command Line

As with many tasks in Mac OS X Server, you can reconstruct a user's mailbox from the command line through a remote `ssh` connection by typing:

```
sudo -u cyrusimap /usr/bin/cyrus/bin/
→ reconstruct -r user/username
```

Substitute the appropriate short name for *username*.

Keeping Mail Services Secure

Although your mail service is now set up and functioning, it is still far from secure. Internet mail protocols were originally designed in a time when the Internet was a trusting environment, but that's not so today. There are a number of things that can, and should, be done to secure mail for your users.

Advanced mail authentication

The default configuration of Mac OS X Server uses totally clear passwords. This is particularly bad whenever you may be checking email from a wireless link, as it allows anyone else on the same wireless link to quickly and easily obtain your password. Mac OS X Server supports a number of much more secure password transmission mechanisms that are easily enabled.

These are the types of authentication your server supports when an email client authenticates to it. Login, PLAIN, and Clear should all be considered to be completely nonsecure and should be disabled. Authenticated POP (APOP) is better than clear, but should still be considered weak encryption. Challenge Response Authentication Method (CRAM-MD5) is generally sufficient for most needs and should be offered where possible.

Kerberos

Kerberos is an extremely secure authentication mechanism because it doesn't ever transmit the user's password over the network. Instead, the client and server go through a highly secure encrypted exchange of keys that positively identify both the user and the server.

Kerberos is common in many educational institutions, and is also available in a pure Apple Open Directory environment. If it's available, it should almost always be used. If you don't already have Kerberos set up, it may not be worth the hassle to set it up just for mail as SSL provides sufficient security for most people.

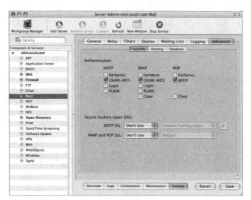

Figure 8.37 If you can turn on authenticated SMTP, you should use CRAM-MD5 authentication.

To enable secure authentication:

1. From the Computers & Services column, select Mail.

2. Select the Settings tab at the bottom of the screen and then select the Advanced tab.

3. Uncheck Login, PLAIN, and Clear in each column.

4. In the IMAP column, check CRAM-MD5; in the POP column, check APOP; and in the SMTP column, check CRAM-MD5 and then click Save (**Figure 8.37**).

✔ Tips

■ Some automated background processes may need to send mail through your SMTP server. With SMTP set to use authentication, you'll need to either have the automated process generating the email authenticate itself to your mail server, or you'll need to add the IP address of the host generating that email to your SMTP server's list of hosts from which to accept SMTP relays.

■ In order for your server to support CRAM-MD5 or APOP authentication, the user's password hash must contain the CRAM-MD5 version of their password.

To enable secure authentication using Open Directory:

1. From the Computers & Services column, select Open Directory.

2. Select the Settings tab at the bottom of the screen.

3. Select the Policy tab at the top of the following screen and then select the Security tab.

4. If you're offering POP mail retrieval, be sure the APOP box is checked and click Save if you made a change (**Figure 8.38**).

To set the options for an account in your local NetInfo directory:

1. Launch Workgroup Manager and select the user from the left column whose password hashing options you want to verify.

2. Select the Advanced tab at the top of the screen and click Security (**Figure 8.39**).

3. In the window that appears, be sure the CRAM-MD5 box is selected (**Figure 8.40**).

4. If you're offering POP service, also be sure the APOP box is selected.

5. Click OK and Save.

✔ Tip

■ Users may have to reset their passwords after you change the different types of password hashes that are stored for them.

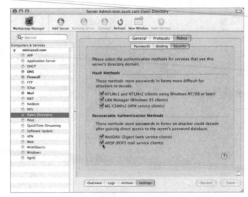

Figure 8.38 Be sure that Open Directory is storing the correct password types for each user.

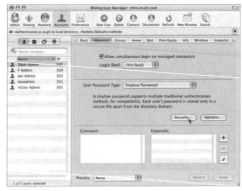

Figure 8.39 If you aren't using Open Directory, click the Security button to set the password types stored for each user.

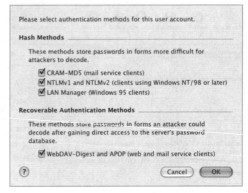

Figure 8.40 Check CRAM-MD5 as an authentication method.

Encrypting mail with SSL

Now that you've enabled stronger security on your mail server, you'll also need to instruct your users to reconfigure their mail clients to use the stronger security.

Although you've just increased the level of security protecting your passwords, the message text itself is still being sent in the clear both when retrieving messages from your inbox and when sending new messages from your client. This is particularly risky in a wireless environment where anyone else on the same wireless link can see the full text of all your email as it is transmitted to and from the server.

To protect against this (and to further protect passwords at the same time), you can implement *SSL* (Secure Sockets Layer) on your SMTP, IMAP, and POP service. This provides the same protection used by e-commerce Web sites that you visit using the HTTPS protocol, and will encrypt the entire traffic path between your email client at the email server. For more information on SSL, see Chapter 10, "Security."

Mac OS X Server comes preconfigured with a Default SSL certificate that you can use for mail services. Though it will provide the same encryption as a commercial SSL certificate that you may purchase, its use will cause each of your mail clients to display a warning dialog each time they connect because the Default certificate installed on each server is self-signed and its authenticity can't be verified by the mail client software. If you'd like to use the Default certificate, or any other SSL certificate that is already installed on your server, skip ahead to the "To configure the mail server to use the certificate" task.

To create your own SSL certificate:

1. Launch Server Admin and select the name of your server from the Computers & Services column (**Figure 8.41**).

2. Select the Settings tab at the bottom of the screen and then select the Certificates tab.

3. Click the plus button (**Figure 8.42**).

4. In the Common Name field of the window that appears, type the name of your mail server exactly how your mail clients will be connecting to it (**Figure 8.43**).

5. Type the rest of the fields as appropriate for your organization and be sure to select a 2048-bit private key size.

6. Click Save.

✔ Tip

- If you'd like to get the certificate signed by a certificate authority, click Request Signed Certificate From CA (**Figure 8.44**). This will usually cost money and take a few days. Once they respond with your signed certificate, click the Add Signed Certificate button.

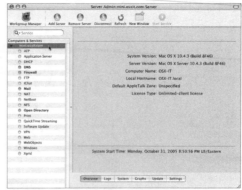

Figure 8.41 Select the name of your server in the Server Admin tool to set options that affect all services.

Figure 8.42 Click the add button to add a new certificate.

Figure 8.43 Type the information that should be stored in the certificate. Be sure to select a 2048-bit private key size for the most strength.

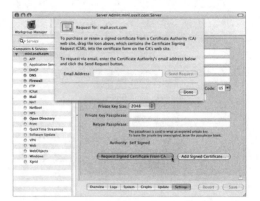

Figure 8.44 Server Admin provides an easy interface to request a signed certificate. Either enter the email address of your certificate authority, or drag the certificate icon to a Web page.

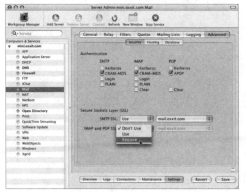

Figure 8.45 Configuring a service to use SSL is easy in Server Admin.

To configure the mail server to use the certificate:

1. From the Computers & Services column, select Mail.

2. Select the Advanced tab at the top of the screen and then select the Security tab.

3. From the SMTP SSL menu, select Use, and from the adjacent pop-up menu, select the SSL certificate you want to use (**Figure 8.45**).

4. From the IMAP and POP SSL pop-up menu, select Require, assuming only normal mail client software will be connecting to your server.

   If you will be using WebMail (described later), select Use instead of Require. WebMail doesn't use SSL to connect, so you must preserve the option to connect without SSL. However, you should firewall off all incoming non-SSL traffic except from your WebMail server.

5. From the adjacent pop-up menu, select the SSL certificate you wish to use and click Save.

✔ Tip

■ A few email clients don't offer SSL encryption for SMTP, so it's usually best to set it to Use, which gives people the option to use SSL but doesn't require it. If you enable SSL for SMTP, be sure to do some extra testing to ensure that your incoming mail, relayed or not, is not rejected for not using SSL. For IMAP and POP, however, SSL is generally available everywhere (except with WebMail), so it's usually acceptable to require it.

KEEPING MAIL SERVICES SECURE

Adjusting the firewall

Although your mail server is now configured to use SSL, you need to make some
adjustments to your firewall since SSL communication is done on a different network
port than non-SSL communication.

To adjust the firewall for SSL:

1. From the Computers & Services column,
   select Firewall.

2. Click the Settings tab at the bottom
   of the screen and then select the
   Services tab.

3. From the "Edit Services for" menu,
   select any (**Figure 8.46**).

4. Select Mail: IMAP SSL (port 993) in the
   list box.

5. If you're offering a POP service, select
   Mail: POP3 over SSL (port 995).

6. Assuming you're requiring SSL for IMAP
   and POP, deselect Mail: POP3 and Mail:
   IMAP (**Figure 8.47**).

   Note that even though WebMail can't
   use SSL, since you're hopefully using it
   from the same host as your mail server,
   its traffic will never be blocked by the
   firewall, so, regardless of whether you're
   using WebMail, you should deselect (block)
   the non-SSL IMAP and POP ports.

7. Click Save.

Figure 8.46 Use the firewall settings of Server Admin
to allow network connections on the SSL IMAP and
POP ports.

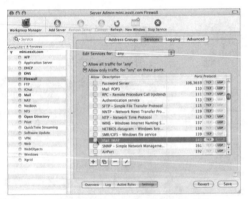

Figure 8.47 You can safely turn off the non-SSL
IMAP and POP ports using the firewall settings of
Server Admin.

Figure 8.48 Scanning for viruses is easy with Mac OS X Server. Just select the option to turn it on.

Detecting viruses

A crucial part of keeping computers secure is preventing viruses from reaching them. Although there are currently no known viruses that can attack Mac OS X directly, there will likely be some eventually. Also, viruses targeted at applications, such as macro viruses, can still infect a Mac because mail traveling through your mail server can contain a virus and could easily infect a less secure computer that might connect to your mail server. Due to this threat, it is in the best interest of mail administrators to scan email messages for viruses.

Fortunately, Mac OS X Server makes this an easy task. ClamAV is included, and can be enabled to easily scan every message that comes into your mail server.

To scan email for viruses:

1. From the Computers & Services column, select Mail.

2. Select the Settings tab at the bottom of the screen and then select the Filters tab.

3. Select the "Scan email for viruses" and "Notify recipients" check boxes (**Figure 8.48**).

   This will send a message to the intended recipients letting them know an infected message was deleted.

4. Select the "Update the Junk mail and virus database" check box and set the value at 4 times per day.

   Since viruses propagate so quickly, it's important to update your virus definitions frequently to minimize the spread of a future outbreak.

5. Click Save.

Using service ACLs

Earlier when you enabled mail access for a user, you did so through Workgroup Manager on a per-user basis. Depending on the type of user management you use and on the size of your organization, this may or may not be an efficient way of controlling who has access to your mail server. As an alternative, you can use *service ACLs* (SACLs, or service access control lists) to control mail access. If you use SACLs to control mail, the per-user mail setting in Workgroup Manager is ignored. One benefit of using SACLs to control mail access is that you can give entire groups of people access to a service rather than having to specify it for an individual user. You can even nest groups (have groups of groups) to make your user management even easier. Note that you'll lose your quotas and forwarding ability if you use SACLs to enable mail as the SACL overrides any mail attributes in the user's record.

To enable mail access through service ACLs:

1. From the Computers & Services column, select the name of your server.

2. Click the Settings tab at the bottom of the screen and then select the Access tab.

3. Deselect the "Use same access for all services" check box and select Mail in the list below (**Figure 8.49**).

4. Select the "Allow only users and groups below" radio button.

5. Click the plus button to open your users and groups drawer (**Figure 8.50**).

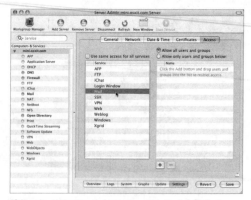

Figure 8.49 You can use service ACLs instead of Workgroup Manager to determine who has mail access.

Figure 8.50 Click the plus button to open the users and groups drawer.

Figure 8.51 Drag users from the drawer into the window to add them to the access list.

6. Click and drag the users and/or groups that you'd like to have access to mail into the access list and then click Save (**Figure 8.51**).

This will automatically enable each user's mailbox and allow them access.

✔ Tip

- Workgroup Manager may indicate that mail is not accepted for a given user. Remember that if SACLs are used, the Workgroup Manager mail settings are ignored.

Understanding physical security

One aspect of security that is often overlooked is that of physical security. You've hopefully taken actions like requiring stronger authentication and SSL for your mail service, but don't forget about the server hardware itself.

Think about physical security in two ways: You should protect the physical integrity of your server to maximize uptime and the authenticity of its contents, and you want to protect the data on your server (the mail messages) from theft or prying eyes.

The simple and obvious solution to most of this is to simply keep your mail server in a locked room and restrict who has access to that room. If someone has physical access to a computer, they can get control of that computer no matter what controls you've put in place. You'll also want to be sure to take the appropriate power, fire, and other environmental precautions. Since your users will always expect their mail to be where they left it, it's always a good idea to place a copy of your mail server backups in an offsite location so that you can quickly bring your mail service back online in the event of a disaster. Keep in mind, though, that those backups on tape or CD contain sensitive information (a copy of everyone's mail) and should also be appropriately safeguarded through the use of a safe deposit box or other physical security means.

Monitoring Mail Services

A key part of any healthy service is monitoring. This includes watching the log files for anomalies, verifying that you have sufficient disk space, and monitoring the function of your mail service daemons.

Watching mail logs

As you already know, your full mail service is comprised of numerous processes. Postfix accepts incoming mail, Cyrus manages connections from mail clients, and AMaViS scans the contents of your messages for viruses and junk mail. Each of these services has a log file. Some have multiple log files with a separate file storing information about a specific function. Each of these logs is available in the Server Admin tool.

Figure 8.52 The Server Admin tool shows you full log details for each of the mail processes.

To access mail logs:

1. From the Computers & Services column, select Mail.

2. Select the Logs tab at the bottom of the screen.

3. Select the log you wish to view from the drop-down menu (**Figure 8.52**).

4. If you wish to adjust the verbosity of the logs, select the Settings tab and then select the Logging tab. Use the drop-down menus to change the desired information (**Figure 8.53**).

Figure 8.53 You can easily adjust the detail of the log files using Server Admin.

✔ Tip

■ The Debug setting provides the most detail, while the Critical setting only shows critical errors. For normal, day-to-day monitoring, you should probably use Notice or Warning levels so your log files only show things you need to see. However, if you're diagnosing a specific problem, it may be helpful to adjust these to their Debug setting.

Figure 8.54 Disk usage is shown in the System tab of Server Admin.

Figure 8.55 Server Admin will show you the amount of space the Mail service is using along with the locations of its files.

Figure 8.56 Disk usage is also available on the command line using df.

Monitoring disk space

For mail to be received, there must be available disk space on the server to save it, so it's important to regularly monitor your disk utilization.

To view available disk space:

1. From the Computers & Services column, select the name of your server.

2. Select the System tab at the bottom of the screen.

   Disk space summaries are shown in the bottom portion of the window (**Figure 8.54**).

3. If you'd like to know how much disk space is used just by your mail service, select Mail from the Computers & Services column.

4. Select the Maintenance tab at the bottom of the screen and then select the Database tab.

   Figure 8.55 shows the amount of space your mail service is utilizing.

✔ Tip

■ As shown in **Figure 8.56**, you can also view your disk utilization from the command line by typing

   df -hl

   The -h option tells df to show the numbers in a human-readable format (30 G for 30 gigabytes), while the -l option tells df to restrict its output to local volumes only.

Quota monitoring

It's also important to monitor the disk consumption of individual users. Some users may find it convenient to just keep all of their mail rather than deleting any of it or keeping it stored on their local computer. Although this might be easier for them, it wouldn't be fair to the other users if someone's mail wasn't accepted due to lack of disk space while someone else had a huge mailbox. This is why establishing quotas is important.

To see individual quota utilization:

1. From the Computers & Services column, select Mail.

2. Select the Maintenance tab at the bottom of the screen and then select the Accounts tab.

3. Click either the Quota Used or %Free column to sort the output (**Figure 8.57**).

   You can click the column again to reverse the listing.

Figure 8.57 Server Admin provides a convenient interface to monitor the disk usage for each mailbox. Clicking on a column header will sort by that column.

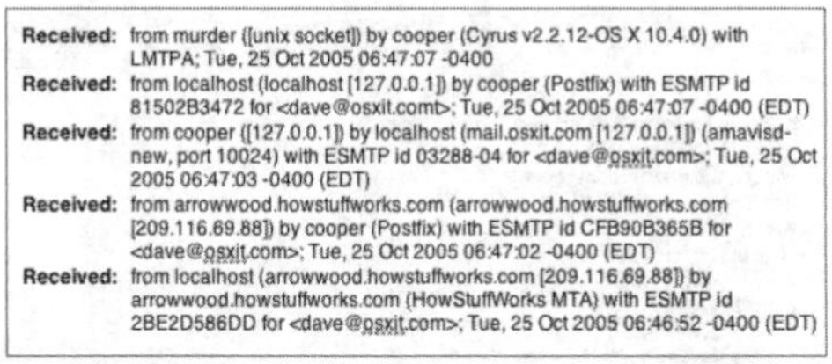

```
Received:   from murder ([unix socket]) by cooper (Cyrus v2.2.12-OS X 10.4.0) with
            LMTPA; Tue, 25 Oct 2005 06:47:07 -0400
Received:   from localhost (localhost [127.0.0.1]) by cooper (Postfix) with ESMTP id
            8150283472 for <dave@osxit.com>; Tue, 25 Oct 2005 06:47:07 -0400 (EDT)
Received:   from cooper ([127.0.0.1]) by localhost (mail.osxit.com [127.0.0.1]) (amavisd-
            new, port 10024) with ESMTP id 03288-04 for <dave@osxit.com>; Tue, 25 Oct
            2005 06:47:03 -0400 (EDT)
Received:   from arrowwood.howstuffworks.com (arrowwood.howstuffworks.com
            [209.116.69.88]) by cooper (Postfix) with ESMTP id CFB90B365B for
            <dave@osxit.com>; Tue, 25 Oct 2005 06:47:02 -0400 (EDT)
Received:   from localhost (arrowwood.howstuffworks.com [209.116.69.88]) by
            arrowwood.howstuffworks.com (HowStuffWorks MTA) with ESMTP id
            2BE2D586DD for <dave@osxit.com>; Tue, 25 Oct 2005 06:46:52 -0400 (EDT)
```

Figure 8.58 Message headers provide a trail of each server the message passed through along with the time and date it was there.

Troubleshooting Mail

Although mail protocols are one of the oldest on the Internet, they are also very complex, and problems will occur. In this section you will look at some simple steps beyond monitoring logs that can help you diagnose a problem.

Examining headers

A lot of information can be gained from a closer examination of an individual email message. While a message is being transmitted across the Internet, each mail server that it passes through will leave something similar to a postmark in the header of the message. This shows you the route the message took, as well as the exact date and time the message was at each server. Most mail software hides these headers by default, but rest assured that the information is still there. For example, in Apple's Mail application, you can view the full headers for a message by choosing View > Message > Long Headers (**Figure 8.58**).

Checking your DNS

If you're unable to receive new mail, the first thing to check is your DNS. You'll want to follow the "To verify your MX Record" task at the beginning of this chapter to verify that your MX record is still present and correct. Be sure to check this from someone else's machine. If you do tests only on your machine, you may be looking at different DNS servers or have information cached that the rest of the public Internet can't see.

Pretending to be mail

If your DNS is configured correctly, you need to find out if your mail service is working. One of the best methods to diagnose incoming mail problems is pretending to be an incoming message. From a command-line session on another machine, preferably outside of your own network, type the following:

```
telnet your.mailserver.xyz 25
EHLO your.full.hostname
MAIL From:<you@yourdomain.xyz>
RCPT To:<someone@yourdomain.xyz>
DATA
```

Now type some message body text. Then type a period on a line by itself and finally, type:

```
QUIT
```

Figure 8.59 shows a sample of this exchange. If there's a problem with your SMTP service, you might figure it out using this procedure.

Figure 8.59 You can use telnet to pretend to be a mail message entering your server.

Figure 8.60 Use Server Admin to select your HTTPS Web site.

Advanced Mail Services

Mac OS X Server comes with SquirrelMail, an open source Web-based interface for users to access their mail. This interface resembles that offered by many of the free Web email services, and is a convenient option to offer your users who may wish to check their email from locations that offer Web kiosks but no way for them to make a direct email connection using IMAP or POP.

It's important to realize that WebMail acts just like an IMAP and SMTP client to your existing mail server. It is not a mail server itself. It does not support POP. Also, it currently does not support making an SSL connection to your mail server. Therefore, you should offer the WebMail service on the same machine as your mail server so that clear-text passwords aren't being passed over the network. You can (and should) use SSL for the Web server itself, though, so that the users' passwords and email content are encrypted between the Web kiosk and your Web server.

To enable WebMail:

1. From the Computers & Services column, select Web.

2. Select the Settings tab at the bottom of the screen and then select the Sites tab.

3. Double-click the site that will host your WebMail service (**Figure 8.60**).

   Since your users will be typing their passwords, this should be an SSL-protected site. See Chapter 9, "Web Technologies" for information on configuring your Web site to use SSL.

continues on next page

ADVANCED MAIL SERVICES

4. Select the Options tab at the top of the screen.

5. Select the Enable WebMail check box and click Save (**Figure 8.61**).

6. To get a command-line session on your mail server, either launch the Terminal utility from the local console or use `ssh` to connect to your server.

7. Type the following command (**Figure 8.62**):

   `sudo /etc/squirrelmail/config/conf.pl`

8. Select option 2 (Server Settings).

9. Select option 1 (Domain) and type the domain (the part after the @ sign in email addresses) that should be used for outbound email (**Figure 8.63**).

Figure 8.61 Check the box on the Options tab to enable WebMail through this Web site.

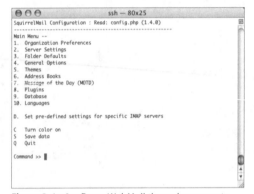

Figure 8.62 Configure WebMail through an easy-to-use text configuration tool.

Figure 8.63 Set the domain name of your server in the WebMail configuration. This setting is used primarily for sending messages through the WebMail interface.

Figure 8.64 Since you disabled weak authentication methods, you must use the text configuration tool to change the WebMail authentication to CRAM-MD5.

10. Select option A (Update IMAP Settings).

11. Select option 6 (Authentication type).

12. Type n since you don't want to detect supported mechanisms.

13. Type cram-md5 (**Figure 8.64**).

14. Type q to quit and y to save when prompted.

    You should now be able to access your mail from this URL (**Figure 8.65**):

    https://*www.yourserver.xyz*/WebMail

✔ Tip

- In the SquirrelMail configuration, don't be tempted to turn on Secure IMAP (TLS). Although SquirrelMail supports TLS (a variant of SSL), it is not currently supported by the PHP build that comes preinstalled on Mac OS X Server.

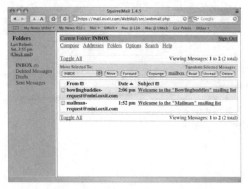

Figure 8.65 WebMail provides an easy-to-use interface to access your inbox from any Web browser.

Creating user aliases

Some users may wish to receive mail addressed to alternate usernames or aliases. This is simple to achieve using Mac OS X Server through Workgroup Manager.

To create user aliases:

1. Launch Workgroup Manager, and in the lefthand column, select the user for whom you want to create an alias (**Figure 8.66**).

2. In the Short Names field, double-click to add a new entry containing the desired alias (**Figure 8.67**).

3. Click Save.

Figure 8.66 Aliases are stored in the Short Names field of a user record in Workgroup Manager.

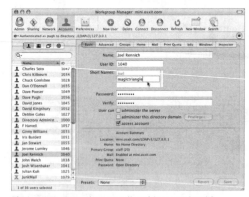

Figure 8.67 Type the new alias this user should receive mail as.

Creating user aliases with Unix

You can also create aliases using the traditional Unix method, which is useful if you want to use an alias to forward mail to multiple people. This effectively creates a group email address, but without the overhead (or features) associated with mailing lists.

To create user aliases with Unix:

1. Use your favorite text editor to open /private/etc/aliases.

   You'll have to do this as root using sudo.

2. Add a new line to the end of the file of this format:

   `desiredAlias: username,username,…`

   Examples might be:

   `magic.triangle: joel,josh`

   `company-leaders: steve@apple.com,schoun`

   `→ teacher: schoun`

3. Save the file.

4. Type `sudo postalias /etc/aliases`.

5. Type `sudo newliases`.

✔ Tip

■ The last two commands update the mail server's alias database. You'll notice in the examples that the recipient list for an alias can consist of just usernames for people on the local server, or it can contain full email addresses to forward the mail to someone outside of your network. Multiple recipients should be separated with a comma.

ADVANCED MAIL SERVICES

Hosting multiple domains

You may wish to use one mail server to host many domain names. It's common for a company to have many variations of the domain name and to want to accept messages from all of them. You can choose from two types of multiple domain hosting: one where all of your users accept mail for a number of domains, and another where some users are in some domains and other users are in other domains.

To set up a host to accept mail for different domains:

1. Launch Server Admin and select Mail from the Computers & Services column.

2. Select the Settings tab at the bottom of the screen and then select the Advanced tab.

3. Select the Hosting tab, then click the plus button next to the Local Host Aliases field.

4. In the window that appears, enter the name of the domain of the host alias and click Save (**Figure 8.68**).

   Once you configure your MX records for the other domains, your mail server will start accepting mail for the other domain using the same usernames that are available for your primary domain. One problem, however, is that messages coming to your alternate domain may not be scanned for viruses and spam. There's an easy solution for that too.

5. Using your favorite text editor, such as emacs, pico, or vi, edit /private/etc/ amavisd.conf.

Figure 8.68 Click the plus button in the Hosting tab of Server Admin to receive mail for other domains.

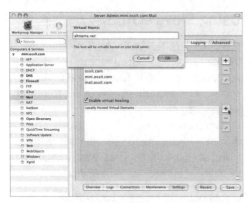

Figure 8.69 Click the add button in the Hosting tab of Server Admin to enable virtual domains on your server.

Figure 8.70 Enter the full email address for users receiving mail from virtual domains.

6. Find this line:

```
@local_domains_acl = ( ".$mydomain" );
→ # $mydomain and its subdomains
```

and add any other alternate domains you may receive mail for:

```
@local_domains_acl = ( ".$mydomain",
→ "myotherdomain.com","domain3.net");
→ # $mydomain and its subdomains
```

7. Save the file.

Hosting specific domains

The second method of hosting multiple domains is a little different. You still have one host accepting mail for multiple domains, but in this case, a given user on your system won't accept mail for all the domains, but only for domains explicitly set for that user.

To set up a host to accept mail for specific domains:

1. Follow steps 1–2 in the previous exercise.

2. Click the Hosting tab and select the "Enable virtual hosting" check box.

3. Click the plus button next to the Locally Hosted Virtual Domains field.

4. In the window that appears, enter the name of the domain of the virtual host and click Save (**Figure 8.69**).

Now you need to tell the system which users will accept mail for this domain.

5. In the left column of Workgroup Manager, select the user you want to add to this domain.

6. In the Short Names field, double-click to add a new entry containing the full email address that user will get mail for, and then click Save (**Figure 8.70**).

Configuring files

The configuration options available through the Server Admin tool only scratch the surface of what you can do with Mac OS X Server's mail service. Hundreds of other advanced options are available to you if you edit the configuration files directly.

If you choose to do so, however, you should be sure to make backup copies of the files you change. Certain configuration files may be overwritten completely if you (or another administrator) uses the Server Admin tool to make a change later. One option to lessen this impact is to use include files where they're supported. Keep all of your local configurations in separate files, and use an include directive in the main configuration file to read your changes.

Unfortunately, not all of the configuration files support file inclusion. Consult the documentation for the specific service to learn more about the options in its configuration file, or simply read through the comments included within the file. Some of the configuration files include:

◆ /private/etc/postfix/main.cf

◆ /private/etc/amavisd.conf

◆ /private/etc/imapd.conf

◆ /private/etc/clamav.conf

Using Sieve scripts

Sieve is a very powerful scripting language for mail servers. The primary use of Sieve is for doing server-side filtering and mailbox sorting. One example use is to automatically move spam messages into a user's spam folder. Users wishing to utilize Sieve must upload their scripts to your mail server using a process called `timsieved`, which must first be enabled by you, the administrator.

Once enabled, there are Perl scripts, WebMail plug-ins, and other ways users can interact with Sieve. Consult the Mail Service Administration manual, or use the Internet archive (www.archive.org) to view the contents of the now-nonexistent www.cyrusoft.com/sieve/ Web site from November 2004.

Using cyradm

`cyradm` is also included with Mac OS X Server. It can be used to interact directly with your IMAP server to create and delete mailboxes, and much more. One common use of it is to modify the permissions on a mailbox for granting other users access to someone's mail. For more information on `cyradm`, consult the man page:

```
man cyradm
```

Figure 8.71 Server Admin can be used to view the mail queue on your server.

Figure 8.72 The mailq command can be used to view the mail queue on your server from the command line.

Clearing the queue

After you've run your mail service for quite some time, you may need to empty your mail queue. The queue holds messages waiting to be delivered. Over time, forged messages from spam may clog your mail server while bounce messages are being redirected to nowhere. You may wish to occasionally check your mail queue for such messages and clear them manually if needed.

To clear your queue:

1. From the Computers & Services column, select Mail.

2. Select the Maintenance tab at the bottom of the screen and then select the Mail Queue tab.

3. Select the desired message and click Retry or Delete, depending on whether you want to attempt to re-send it or just delete it from the queue (**Figure 8.71**).

✔ Tip

■ You can also use the mailq command from a command-line session to check the mail queue (**Figure 8.72**), but it does not have the simple interface to retry or delete messages.

9

WEB TECHNOLOGIES

The Internet is composed of many, many computers directly connected to a publicly available network. Collectively these computers and their content are called the Internet. In Mac OS X Server 10.4, Apple has provided an extensive set of applications and components that can be combined to help you provide content over the Web. These services begin with basic Web site support and continue through to support for dynamic Web page generation, proxy services, WebDAV, and Weblogs (or blogs).

Before you can set up your first Web site, you will need to complete several actions, including configuring files, obtaining a domain name, setting up domain name services (DNS), and building your content. This chapter covers each of those tasks.

Configuring Web Services

It is possible to enable the Web service right out of the box without making any configuration changes. When you choose this route, a default Web site is started that is located at the IP address of your server. If you have a domain name associated with that IP address, the new site is also available using that name. The default Web site provides access to some documentation and a starting point for accessing any blogs you may have enabled.

It is better, however, to configure your Web service prior to enabling it. The general configuration is very simple and primarily allows you to change a few parameters that balance performance and resource use.

To configure Web services:

1. Launch Server Admin, select Web from the Computers & Services list, and click the Settings tab at the bottom of the screen (**Figure 9.1**).

   You will follow this first step for all the exercises in this chapter, so you may want to leave Server Admin open.

2. Click the General tab and choose the options you want to configure:

   ▲ **Maximum simultaneous connections** is the total number of connections to your Web site at any given time.

   ▲ **Connection timeout** is the amount of time a browser will wait for your Web site to transfer the requested page code.

   ▲ **Minimum** and **maximum spare servers** are the number of additional machines that can be used to serve this site to the Internet.

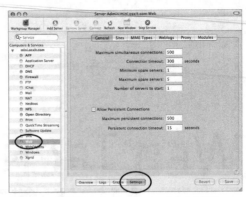

Figure 9.1 The General tab of Server Admin's Web services window.

- ▲ **Number of servers to start** is the number of Web servers to be used.

- ▲ **Allow persistent connections** and its related options function when users connect to your site (usually an active connection via a scripting language such as Java) and leave their browser open for extended periods of time.

  Please note that enabling the Allow Persistent Connections option is not compatible with the performance cache described in the next task.

3. When you've finished making changes, click Save.

4. Click Start Services in the Toolbar to start the Web service.

   Now, any time you make a change to Web services, the service itself will automatically restart after you click Save.

Obtaining a Domain Name

To obtain a domain name, it is necessary to register with a domain name registrar. The fees vary from as little as about $3 per year to as much as about $35 per year.

Some popular registrars include:

- ◆ www.networksolutions.com/

- ◆ www.srsplus.com/

- ◆ www.godaddy.com/

- ◆ www.mactechdomains.com/

When you register a domain name, you must specify the name and/or IP address of your name servers. You should have at least two so that if one name server goes offline for any reason, the other server will still be available. Ideally, the two name servers would even be on different networks in different locations.

Once you obtain a domain name, you must set up DNS for your domain. Again, your ISP will often provide DNS services for you at no additional charge, but if you will be maintaining your own DNS, please refer to Chapter 6, "Network Services Options," for detailed instructions. As for building your content, you are on your own—but if you come up with something wonderful for your Web site, don't forget to mention that you learned how to publish it from this book!

CONFIGURING WEB SERVICES

Setting up a Web site

After you have configured the base Web services, it is time to set up your first Web site. In the beginning of the Internet, there was the HTTP 1.0 protocol specification. In this specification, each Web site had an individual IP address. This began to pose a significant problem when the number of sites exploded. To solve this problem, virtual hosting support was added to the HTTP 1.1 specification in 1999.

The Apache Web server (see the sidebar, "Apache Configuration Files") lets you serve up multiple Web sites with either a basic single-Web site-per-IP-address scheme or virtual hosting of multiple Web sites sharing a single IP address. It is most likely that you will be utilizing virtual hosting for your site, and that is the method explained here. If you need to implement the basic scheme, you can emulate it by having just one virtual host assigned to an IP address.

Apache Configuration Files

For Apple, adopting Apache was a no-brainer. Apache has been around for quite some time, and many Unix administrators are familiar with its configuration files. Apache is a very powerful, efficient, extensible, and secure HTTP Web server because of the open source nature of the server, which allows for constant refinement in an environment of shared programming knowledge.

Although the Server Admin interface is handy, some options are available only in the configuration files:

◆ The main Apache service configuration file is /etc/httpd/httpd.config.

◆ Each Web site has its own configuration file, saved in /etc/httpd/sites/.

You need to remember a couple of rules when you're editing the Apache configuration files. First, always back up any configuration file before you change it! Second, to activate any changes, you must restart the Apache Web service.

Apache is completely free. Legions of technically savvy folks constantly improve the product and can, in turn, help you with yours. For more information, visit httpd.apache.org/.

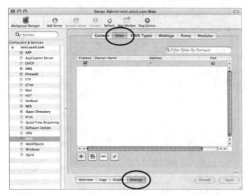

Figure 9.2 The default Sites tab in the Web services window.

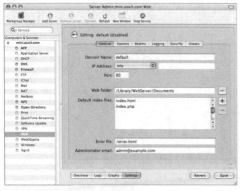

Figure 9.3 The General tab within the Sites tab allows for basic configuration of your Web site.

Domain Name: book.osxit.com

Figure 9.4 Entering the Web site address in the General tab of Web services.

In the following examples, it is assumed you have already obtained a domain name and have configured DNS to associate that domain name with the IP address assigned to your server. First you'll need to create your content and have it stored in a directory on your server.

To add a Web site:

1. After following step 1 in the previous task, click the Sites tab (**Figure 9.2**).

2. Click the plus button and the Editing window will appear (**Figure 9.3**).

   The General tab has been selected by default. The "default (disabled)" text will disappear after the configuration has been completed.

3. In the Domain Name field, enter the domain name to be associated with this Web site.

   You should use the full domain name. For example, notice in **Figure 9.4**, "book" is included (book.osxit.com).

   continues on next page

4. If there is more than one IP address associated with the server, select the specific IP address to be associated with the Web site (**Figure 9.5**).

5. For standard browser access to your Web site, leave the port set at 80.

or

If you have special requirements that require you to use another port, set the associated port number in the Port field.

6. In the Web folder field, select the directory where your Web site is located (**Figure 9.6**).

The default is /Library/WebServer/Documents/.

7. In a simple static Web site, the default page to display when no specific page is requested is named index.html.

If you need to add a specific default index page, click the plus button and enter the name of the additional index page.

While you may have multiple defaults, only the first default that actually exists will be used.

Figure 9.5 Select the IP address for the Web site and then...

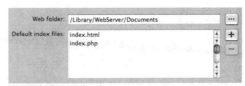

Figure 9.6 ...select the appropriate directory for the Web files and the default file on your server using the browse dialog.

Figure 9.7 Configure the Web site's error file and administrator email.

8. Enter the location of the error page for your Web site in the Error file field.

or

If you do not have an error page, you can leave the default value (/error.html) in place (**Figure 9.7**).

The server will generate a default "404 file not found" error page. Do not clear the field because it causes Apache to generate an erroneous "500 internal server error" error page.

9. Enter the Web site administrator's email address in the Administrator email field (see Figure 9.7).

10. When you've finished making changes, click Save.

You have now configured the basic settings for your Web site.

✔ Tip

■ It's bad practice to leave the default placeholder Web site enabled. That Web page is a good indication to crackers that a server isn't fully configured and is possibly unsecure.

Exploring Web site options

There are, of course, additional options when setting up Web sites. These include accessing Web mail, enabling the performance cache, allowing scripts to run, and creating folder listings. There are some security risks associated with these options, so a thorough analysis is in order (**Figure 9.8**).

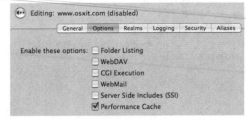

Figure 9.8 Enable any of the optional Web site features.

- **Folder Listing** enables the automatic generation of index pages listing the contents of the requested directory. Enabling Folder Listings can be a great help while developing and debugging your Web site, but you should disable the option for production Web sites. Also, enabling Folder Listings provides a significant amount of information about your Web site to your users, which hackers can use to attack your Web site. Unless you know you need them, you may wish to keep this option disabled.

- **Enabling WebDAV** permits users to connect to your Web site as they would a file server. WebDAV will be covered later in this chapter.

Web Server Scripts

Web scripts differ from regular Web site files in that they're coded instructions that let the server dynamically generate Web page information. Apache, through its extensive modules, supports common open source scripting languages. The most commonly used scripts are CGI scripts written in Perl or Python and PHP scripts:

- **CGI option 1**—The default location for CGI scripts available to all Web sites is /Library/WebServer/CGI-Executables/. In your Web browser, enter http://sitename/cgi-bin/script.cgi.

- **CGI option 2**—If a script will be used by only one specific Web site, you can put it in that Web site's folder. In your Web browser, enter http://sitename/script.cgi.

- **PHP**—Enable PHP script execution by selecting the php4_module in the Web server Modules list. PHP scripts can be located in any Web site's folder. In your Web browser, enter http://sitename/script.php.

Modules and options

It's important to remember that the options settings—alias, redirect, SSL, and realm—must be configured separately for each Web site. However, the module settings—MIME type and content handler—will affect every Web site on your server. And changes to proxy settings won't affect any of your Web site settings.

Also make sure you thoroughly test your Web site options by opening any Web browser and entering the hostname you configured. Modules can be turned on and off via the Modules tab under Settings of the Web service in Server Admin.

Every option and module that you implement can potentially use more RAM, so you may want to keep an eye on RAM usage as you test the various options and modules.

When tweaking the settings for each of your Web sites found under each tab, you may need to enable new Apache modules. These modules, typically installed in /usr/_libexec/httpd/, are coded extensions that add functionality to the Web server. Literally hundreds of freely downloadable Apache modules are available at modules.apache.org:

- mod_macbinary_apple

- mod_spotlight_apple

- mod_auth_apple

- mod_hfs_apple

- mod_digest_apple

- mod_bonjour

- **CGI Execution** enables the execution of Common Gateway Interface (CGI) programs within the Web site. The programs to be executed must have a .cgi filename extension. Unless you know that you need to enable CGI scripts, it is best to disable this option.

- **WebMail** is used for the WebMail application within the Web site. For more information on WebMail, refer to Chapter 8, "Enabling Mail Services."

- **Server Side Includes (SSI)** enables the use of server-side includes within the Web site. SSIs are still a very popular way to build Web site themes or templates. They provide a relatively powerful way to include HTML fragments and even programmatic content in a Web page. Because of this power, they also pose a security threat if used improperly. Unless you know you need them, it is best to disable this option.

- **Performance Cache** loads your Web site into RAM and serves the pages from memory instead of the hard disk. While this may deliver some speed improvements, it requires the Web site to run on a non-standard port, which can cause problems with firewalls. For this reason, and the fact that the speed increase, if any, is completely mitigated by your most likely limited bandwidth, it's recommended that you deselect the performance cache option.

CONFIGURING WEB SERVICES

341

Performing Log Analysis

It is important to always watch Web site logs, as they can reveal information about computers accessing your site, such as the pages visited, the time spent on each page, the IP address of the requesting computer, and so on. There are two main logs to view, the Access log and Error log.

To enable log analysis:

1. Follow steps 1–2 in the "To add a Web site" task earlier in this chapter to navigate to the screen shown in Figure 9.3.

2. Click the Logging tab to display a new set of logging options (**Figure 9.9**).

3. Click the "Enable Access log" check box.

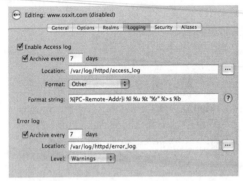

Figure 9.9 The main Web service log setup window.

Apache Log Analysis

Log analysis provides you with lots of information about how your Web site is being used. From the logs, you can gather and report information on the number of requests, the number of visitors, the number and names of the pages requested, and much, much more.

Log analysis is performed by processing the Apache access log. The information stored in the log is aggregated in many ways to be able to provide valuable statistics. It's even possible to use the logs to track a visitor's path through your Web site. This information can be very useful in determining whether your Web site is supporting your organization in a valuable manner.

While log analysis is outside of the scope of this book, the Internet is full of information on log analysis. Do a Google search for "Apache log analysis." Several products (both free and commercial) are also available:

◆ **Wusage**—One of the more popular pieces of Web analysis software

◆ **AWStats**—A free, Web-based, open source log analysis tool: awstats.sourceforge.net

◆ **Webalizer**—Another free, Web-based log analysis tool: www.mrunix.net/Webalizer

◆ **Urchin**—A very popular commercial log analysis suite: www.urchin.com

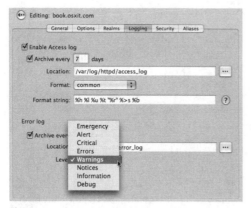

Figure 9.10 The various levels of error log reporting.

Apache Access Log Formats

While Server Admin provides you with a few legacy access log file formats, you will likely find that the defaults available leave your log analysis wanting. Most log analysis programs can work with one of the predefined formats, but you can get better reports by adding additional logging information to your logs.

Also, most log analysis programs will provide you with a recommended log format string. You can enter it in the Format string entry field in Server Admin (shown in Figure 9.10).

For example, you could use this log file format:

```
%h %l %u %t "%r" %>s %b %v
→ "%{Referer}i" "%{User-Agent}i"
→ "%{Cookie}n"
```

One important note here is that the above string includes a reference to the User Tracking Cookie that is provided by the Apache Usertrack Module.

For complete information on the Apache access log file formats, visit httpd.apache.org/docs/1.3/logs.html.

4. To archive the access log, select the "Archive every 7 days" check box and set the number of days between archives.

It's always a good idea to save the log files for later analysis, even if you do not care to review the information now.

5. Enter the path to the log file in the Location field.

The default location is appropriate for most implementations, and you should not change the location of the access log.

6. Use the Format pop-up menu to select from several predefined legacy options for the format of the access log.

or

Click the question mark next to the Format string field to display information about these options.

7. To archive the error log, click the "Archive every 7 days" check box and set the number of days between archives in the Error log section of the screen.

The error log is always enabled for obvious reasons.

8. To change the location of the error log, enter the path to the log file in the Location field.

The default location is appropriate for most implementations.

9. Use the Level pop-up menu to select the level of the error information that will be stored in the log (**Figure 9.10**).

The default level of Warnings is adequate for most implementations.

10. When you've finished making changes, click Save.

Creating Web Site Aliases and Redirects

Web site aliases are often used if you want a Web site to access documents that are on the local server but outside the Web site's folder. Aliases and redirects are easy to set up in Mac OS X Server using Server Admin.

To create Web site aliases and redirects:

1. Follow steps 1–2 in the "To add a Web site" task earlier in this chapter to navigate to the screen shown in Figure 9.3.

2. Click the Aliases tab (**Figure 9.11**).

3. In the Server Aliases field, add any aliases you may have for your Web site by clicking the plus button and entering the appropriate information (**Figure 9.12**).

   These are any other domain names that you have registered that point to the same IP address and that you want to have serve up this Web site.

4. If an alias is all that is necessary, click the Save button when you've finished making changes.

   You may want to also add redirects at this time.

5. Click the plus button beneath the redirects portion of the Alias tab to add a redirect (Figure 9.11).

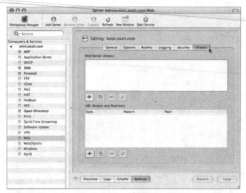

Figure 9.11 The Aliases tab allows for the entry of both aliases and redirects.

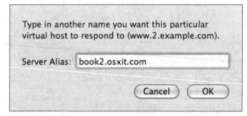

Type in another name you want this particular virtual host to respond to (www.2.example.com).

Server Alias: book2.osxit.com

Cancel | OK

Figure 9.12 Setting the virtual host for the Web site.

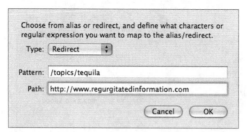

Figure 9.13 Adding a redirect from one path to another Web site.

6. From the Type pop-up menu, select one of the following, enter your redirect, and click OK (**Figure 9.13**):

▲ **Alias**—Maps a site link to a location on your file system

▲ **Alias match**—Maps a given expression from your site to a location on your file system

▲ **Redirect**—Maps a site link to another Web site

▲ **Redirect match**—Maps a given expression from your Web site to another Web site

7. When you've finished making changes, click Save.

✔ **Tip**

■ Make sure you verify that the aliased folder has at least read privileges to the www user or group.

Implementing Secure Sockets Layer Support

Internet security is a very high-profile subject in today's world. Secure Sockets Layer (SSL) support is an important component in ensuring end-to-end security for your Web transactions. SSL provides a basic mechanism for the encryption of data being transmitted over the Internet. This encryption prevents anyone who might acquire your network data from being able to read it.

While the enhanced privacy of SSL may sound wonderful, it comes at a price. Encryption and decryption are expensive operations for a computer. It is wise to only enable SSL on those portions of a Web site that require a high level of privacy.

One approach that has been successful is to implement the secure portions of your Web site using a different URL from your main Web site URL. For example, use www.osxit.com for your main Web site and secure.osxit.com for your secure Web site. This will allow you to separate the two portions, even across two separate servers if necessary.

Additionally, since SSL is implemented at the sockets layer, it is impossible to implement virtual hosting using SSL. This means that each Web site that will be using SSL must have its own IP address.

The implementation of the SSL protocol uses encrypted certificates to share the components of the asymmetric encryption key. Don't worry; you don't have to understand all of the encryption terms to be able to implement SSL for your Web site.

Figure 9.14 Selecting your server in the list within Server Admin.

Figure 9.15 The Certificates tab within Server Admin permits the creation of certificates.

Please note that adding SSL to your Web site does not mean that your Web site is now secure. In fact, the only thing that SSL accomplishes is the encryption of the Web site data as it passes back and forth between the server and the browser.

Before you can enable SSL for your Web site(s), you must obtain or create a certificate. You can either create your own certificate (discussed in the following section) or purchase one from a third-party vendor, such as Thawte or VeriSign.

Generating your own certificates

Mac OS X Server has a convenient way to create certificates and Certificate Signing Requests with the Server Admin tool. You will need to have a fully qualified domain name for your Web site handy.

Self-signed certificates are not signed by a certificate authority. You might want to use them to save money. Deploying self-signed certificates to many computers represents a challenge for administrators, as your client systems will not trust your self-signed certificate by default.

One way around this issue is via the `certtool` command-line tool, which can be used to allow a certificate to be trusted. Please refer to the `certtool` manual page for more information.

To create a self-signed certificate:

1. Select the name of your server in the Computer & Services list (**Figure 9.14**).

2. Click the Settings tab and then the Certificates tab (**Figure 9.15**).

   The screen shows a default certificate that was created when you set up your server, but you can ignore it.

continues on next page

IMPLEMENTING SECURE SOCKETS LAYER SUPPORT

3. Click the plus button at the bottom of the window and fill in the various fields with the following caveats (**Figure 9.16**):

▲ Common Name is the fully qualified name of your site.

▲ City and state names should be spelled out.

▲ Passphrases are used mostly when you are sending the private key elsewhere. However, it is not really necessary to have a passphrase for the private key, since Mac OS X Server already keeps it securely in a system keychain.

4. Click the back arrow when you have finished to see your self-signed certificate is listed in the Certificates tab (**Figure 9.17**).

5. When you've finished making changes, click Save.

6. Launch Keychain Access and view the System keychain (**Figure 9.18**).

See Chapter 2, "Server Tools," for instructions on launching the various tools described in this book.

You will see the public and private keys, and the certificate itself. You can now use the certificate with your Web site.

Figure 9.16 Entering information to create the certificate.

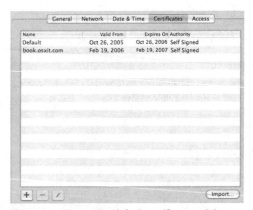

Figure 9.17 Viewing the default certificate and the newly created certificate.

Figure 9.18 The Keychain on the server holds both keys and the certificate for your site.

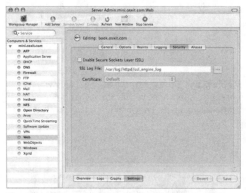

Figure 9.19 The Security tab for a single Web site.

Figure 9.20 Automatic alert indicating the default port has changed for the selected site.

Figure 9.21 Selecting the created certificate from the pop-up menu.

Figure 9.22 The dialog asks you to restart the Web service.

To enable SSL on a Web site:

1. Launch Server Admin, select Web from the Computers & Services list, click the Settings tab at the bottom of the screen, click the Sites tab, double-click on the site you want to edit, and click the Security tab (**Figure 9.19**).

2. Click the Enable Secure Sockets Layer (SSL) check box.

   A dialog appears, notifying you that your Web site will now be available over port 443 instead or port 80 (**Figure 9.20**). This means users will have to type in https:// instead of http:// to access your site. The Web performance cache has also automatically been turned off for this particular site.

3. From the Certificate pop-up menu, choose your newly created certificate (**Figure 9.21**).

4. If you want to change the location of the log file, enter it in the SSL log field and click Save.

5. In the dialog that appears, click Restart to restart the Web service (**Figure 9.22**).

   continues on next page

6. To test your Web site, type the URL in a browser.

You will probably get a message that your browser is unable to verify the certificate (**Figure 9.23**). This is because the certificate you're using was not signed by a provider that your systems trusts by default.

Since you created the certificate, you trust it—you just need to tell that to your browser.

Depending on the browser you use, the next few steps may not be the same, but you can follow along.

7. In the Safari dialog, you would click Show Certificate to see the details of the certificate in the keychain.

8. Click the "Always trust these certificates" check box and click Continue (**Figure 9.24**).

9. Enter your administrator password in the standard authentication dialog that appears to add the new certificate to your System keychain.

10. Reload the site so that you are not notified of the certificate discrepancy again.

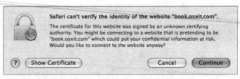

Figure 9.23 Certificate trust warning dialog when entering a site whose certificate cannot be authenticated via a known and trusted certificate authority.

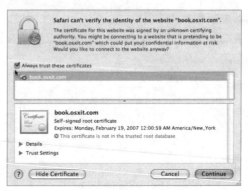

Figure 9.24 Viewing a certificate and placing a check mark in the Always trust... check box.

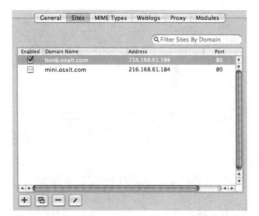

Figure 9.25 Selecting the Web site in the Web services tab of Server Admin.

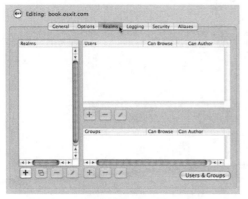

Figure 9.26 The Realms tab is used for creating realms, which are directories within the Web directory that can be restricted.

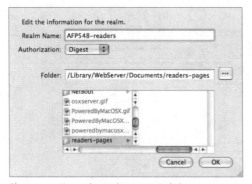

Figure 9.27 Enter the realm name and choose an authentication method and directory.

Setting Up Realms and WebDAV

The Apache Web server uses *realms* to control access to items in a Web site's folder. By default, everything in your Web site's folder can be read by everybody. However, once you specify a folder in your Web site's folder as a realm, you can enable restricted access to those items based on user authentication. Configuring realms is also the first step required to enable secure Web Distributed Authoring and Versioning (WebDAV) support for your Web site.

To add a realm to a site:

1. Launch Server Admin, select Web from the Computers & Services list, click the Settings tab at the bottom of the screen, and click the Sites tab.

2. In the Sites list, double-click the Web site you wish to configure and click the Realms tab (**Figures 9.25** and **9.26**).

3. Click the plus button to open a realm information window and enter a name in the Realm Name field (**Figure 9.27**).

4. Choose an authorization mode from the Authorization pop-up menu.

   Digest authorization is more secure than Basic, as passwords are encrypted before they are sent across the network. Choosing the Kerberos authentication method requires that you have SSL enabled on your Web site.

   continues on next page

5. Specify a directory in your Web site's folder by entering the absolute path to the folder.

or

Click the ellipsis button and navigate to the folder in your directory for which access can be restricted in some fashion.

6. Verify that the realm was created in the window and select it from the Realms list.

7. In the Users area where "Everyone" is highlighted, click the Can Browse check box (**Figure 9.28**).

8. When you've finished making changes, click Save.

While creating a realm in and of itself in this fashion is not readily apparent, you will want to later restrict access to realms.

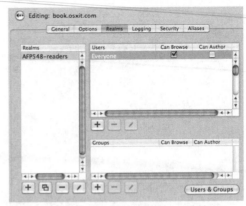

Figure 9.28 Setting the realm to be browsed by everyone.

✔ Tips

■ You can configure as many realms as you want for each Web site, including realms inside other realms. However, you can only define a realm using the Web site's folder or anything inside that folder.

■ You can always use the edit buttons below the Realms list for further configuration.

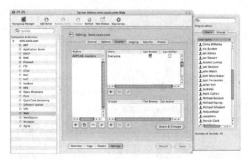

Figure 9.29 Viewing the users and groups drawer in preparation for...

Figure 9.30 ...assigning users to the realm and...

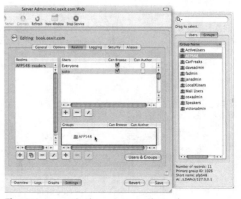

Figure 9.31 ...assigning groups to the realm.

Adding users and groups to realms

The Apache Web server grants authenticated Web site access via any user and/or group accounts known to directory services. For this reason, you must properly configure Directory Access on the server hosting your Web sites. (See Chapter 3, "Open Directory," for more information about directory services.)

To add users and groups to a realm:

1. Follow steps 1–2 in the previous task.

2. Select the realm you want to configure from the Realms list.

3. Click Users & Groups to open a new drawer on the right side of the screen (**Figure 9.29**).

4. *Do one or both of the following* to add a user or group account to the realm:

    ▲ Click the Users tab, and then click and drag user accounts to the realm's Users list (**Figure 9.30**).

    ▲ Click the Groups tab, and then click and drag group accounts to the realm's Groups list (**Figure 9.31**).

continues on next page

5. Deselect the Can Browse option for Everyone, and select the Can Browse option only for user and group accounts that need access to the realm.

6. When you've finished making changes, click Save.

If you aren't prompted by Server Admin, you may need to restart your Web service after making these changes.

7. To test access to your realms, open a Web browser and type in the URL that corresponds with the realm.

An authentication dialog should appear before allowing the user to browse the realm (**Figure 9.32**).

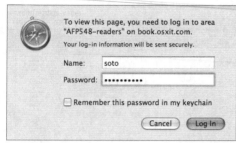

Figure 9.32 The dialog in Safari restricting access to a realm.

Configuring WebDAV access

Many people think Web servers only provide read access to shared items. However, Apache supports WebDAV, which essentially allows users to write changes back to the site. The ability to read and write to a shared destination on a file server makes WebDAV an alternative to standard file-sharing services such as AFP and SMB. Furthermore, WebDAV is an easy protocol to support, because free clients are available for every major operating system and all the network traffic runs across the standard port for HTTP (port 80, which is open on most firewalls).

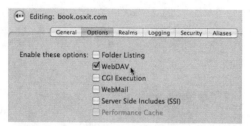

Figure 9.33 Enable WebDAV by checking the box in the Options tab.

WebDAV access is granted based on a Web site's realm configuration. In other words, you must already have realms configured for your Web site in order to use WebDAV. In addition, when you're using WebDAV, you must set special file and folder permissions if you're going to allow users write access to the Web site. You must change the permissions so the group or user www has read and write access to the Web site items because, as a security measure, Apache only has access to items as the system user www and the system group www. (See Chapter 5, "File Sharing," for more information about permissions.)

To configure WebDAV access:

1. Within Server Admin, select Web from the Computers & Services list, and click the Settings tab.

2. In the Sites list, double-click the Web site you want to configure and click the Options tab.

3. Select the WebDAV check box and click the Save button (**Figure 9.33**).

    If you aren't prompted by Server Admin, you may need to restart your Web service after making these changes.

4. Test authenticated access to your realms by accessing them from any Web browser.

Connecting via WebDAV

Connecting to a WebDAV server from a Mac OS X Server involves the following steps:

1. In the Finder, select Go > Connect to Server, and enter a fully qualified HTTP address.

2. Authenticate to the server and, if desired, save your password to a keychain.

Managing MIME types

Multipurpose Internet Mail Extension (MIME) is a standard protocol for defining how a user's Web browser handles files shared from a Web server. Typically, every file on your Web server has a file-type suffix appended to the end of the filename. MIME types define a specific action for a user's Web browser to take when it encounters a certain file-type suffix. Some examples of suffixes configured with MIME types include .htm or .html for hypertext, .jpg or .jpeg for a picture file, and .qt or .mov for a QuickTime video file.

Mac OS X Server's Web server comes with a preconfigured list of standard MIME types. However, you may need to edit or add to your server's MIME types list.

To edit MIME types:

1. Follow step 1 in the previous task and click the MIME Types tab.

   The MIME Types pane displays your Web server's lists of MIME types and content handlers (**Figure 9.34**).

2. Double-click a MIME type or suffix to open an editing window (**Figure 9.35**).

3. Change the path or suffix of the MIME type and click OK to close.

4. Verify your changes in the MIME Types list again and click Save.

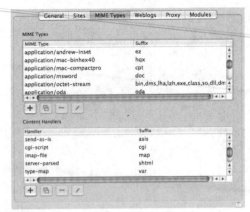

Figure 9.34 Viewing MIME types and content handlers for all Web sites under the MIME Types tab.

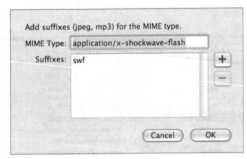

Figure 9.35 Editing MIME types for all Web sites.

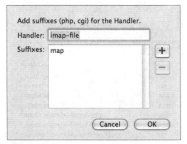

Add suffixes (php, cgi) for the Handler.

Handler: imap-file

Suffixes: map

Figure 9.36 Editing content handlers for all Web sites.

Editing content handlers

Content handlers are programs that define the Web server's response to file requests based on the file-type suffix. Typically, every file on your Web server has a file-type suffix appended to the end of the filename. Some examples of file-type suffixes configured with content handlers include *as is*, which sends the item as it's requested; *bin*, which transfers the file as a Mac Binary file; and *cgi*, which executes the file as a CGI script.

Mac OS X Server's Web server comes with a preconfigured list of standard content handlers. However, you may find it necessary to edit or add to your server's content handlers list. Content handler settings will affect every Web site on your server.

To edit content handlers:

1. Follow step 1 in the previous task.

2. Double-click a content handler or suffix to open an editing window (**Figure 9.36**).

3. Change the name or suffix of the content handler and click OK to close the window.

4. Verify your changes by checking the Content Handlers list again and then click Save.

Enabling Web Proxies

Primarily, Web proxies are enabled to improve the performance of requests made to external Web sites by users on your local network. Many of your users visit the same Web sites throughout the day. A Web proxy caches this external Web site's content; Web browsers on your local network then read the cached content rather than use your slower Internet connection.

Because all client traffic goes through the proxy, you can also use the proxy to restrict access to certain sites.

To enable a Web proxy:

1. Within Server Admin, select Web from the Computers & Services list, and click the Settings tab.

2. Click the Proxy tab to display your Web server's proxy settings (**Figure 9.37**).

3. Click the Enable Proxy check box.

4. In the "Maximum cache size" field, set the maximum amount of space (in megabytes) your Web server will use for proxy cache files (**Figure 9.38**).

5. To specify a cache folder other than the default Web proxy (/var/run/proxy) on the server's local drive, *do either of the following:*

   ▲ Enter the absolute path in the "Cache folder" field.

   ▲ Click the ellipsis button to use the browse dialog.

6. When you've finished making changes, click Save.

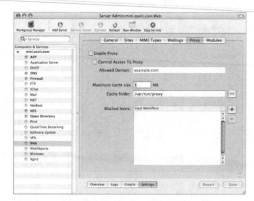

Figure 9.37 Viewing the Proxy tab of Web services.

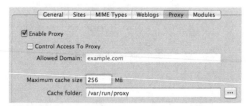

Figure 9.38 Enabling the proxy and setting various options.

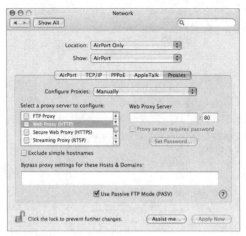

Figure 9.39 Using System Preferences to set the Web proxy on Mac OS X.

Figure 9.40 Entering the Proxy values in the Network preference pane on Mac OS X.

✔ Tips

■ When the cache reaches the maximum size, the oldest files are deleted from the cache folder.

■ For your clients to use the Web proxy, you must configure them to use it. Client computers aren't configured to use a Web proxy by default.

■ If you have a slower Web server and a fast Internet connection, you may be better off without the Web proxy.

To configure Web proxy use on Mac OS X:

1. Choose Apple > System Preferences to open the System Preferences application, and then choose the Network Preference pane.

2. Select the appropriate network location and port configuration.

3. Click the Proxies tab and select Web Proxy in the proxy list (**Figure 9.39**).

4. Enter the address to your proxy in the Web Proxy Server field (**Figure 9.40**).

5. Click Apply Now and quit System Preferences.

ENABLING WEB PROXIES

Configuring blocked Web sites

When you're using a Web proxy, all the Web traffic from your client computers must pass through the proxy server. You can take further advantage of this situation by creating a list of blocked Web site hosts. Doing so prevents your users from going to any Web site that you've defined in the list.

To block Web sites:

1. Launch Server Admin, select Web from the Computers & Services list, and click the Settings tab.

2. Click the Proxy tab to display your Web server's proxy settings (as seen in Figure 9.37).

3. If it isn't already checked, click the Enable Proxy check box.

4. To add hostnames to the "Blocked hosts" list, *do either of the following:*

   ▲ Click the plus button, enter the fully qualified hostname, and press the Return key (**Figure 9.41**).

   ▲ Drag and drop a plain-text file listing the fully qualified hostnames separated by tabs or commas (**Figure 9.42**).

5. When you've finished making changes, click Save.

6. Once the blocked sites have been entered and saved, you should verify that the sites are indeed blocked to your users by testing access to these sites from a browser.

Figure 9.41 Entering names that will be blocked by the proxy.

Figure 9.42 Dragging a text file into the Blocked hosts field.

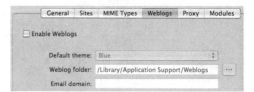

Figure 9.43 Viewing the default values for the Weblogs tab.

Figure 9.44 Changing values for the site's Weblog.

✔ Tips

■ When you're dragging a text file to the "Blocked hosts" window, make sure there is a carriage return at the end of the last hostname in the file. Otherwise, it will be ignored.

■ Mac OS X computers aren't, by default, configured to use a Web proxy. See the "To configure Web proxy use on Mac OS X" task for more information.

■ Any client that isn't configured to use your proxy server can bypass your list of blocked hosts. The best way to prevent this is to use a network firewall that only allows your proxy server to access external Web sites.

Enabling Weblogs

Mac OS X Server now supports Weblogs, or blogs, which let users post items important to them in a log/diary fashion, allowing others to post and discuss them. When blogs are enabled, users with accounts on the server can access and manage their blogs directly from a browser.

To enable blogs:

1. Launch Server Admin, select Web from the Computers & Services list, and click the Settings tab.

2. Click the Weblogs tab to display your Web server's Weblog options (**Figure 9.43**).

3. Click the Enable weblogs check box, choose a color theme, and enter the folder and domain name for the blog users (**Figure 9.44**).

continues on next page

ENABLING WEB PROXIES

4. Click Save to save the changes and make sure that the Web service is running and that at least one Web site is active.

5. In your favorite Web browser, enter the URL of the server and add "/weblog" to the end (**Figure 9.45**).

The screen will show that no blogs yet exist in this server.

6. Enter a user's short name into the field on the right side of the screen and press Return (**Figure 9.46**).

The window changes, showing a default Weblog page and a login option on the right side (**Figure 9.47**).

Figure 9.45 Initial connection from a browser to a site with Weblogs enabled.

Figure 9.46 Entering a user's short name to permit that user's blog to be created...

Figure 9.47 ...and viewed. Customization of the site is done via the Login box on the right that, when clicked...

Figure 9.48 ...shows username and password entry fields.

7. Click Login and enter the Weblog user's username and password in the text fields provided; then click Login (**Figure 9.48**).

A default window appears, allowing the user to customize his or her blog (**Figure 9.49**).

Figure 9.49 Once authenticated, the user can manage their blog.

10

SECURITY

Planning and implementing security is a necessary part of every system administrator's job. Several aspects are involved, among them physical security, password security, firewalls, encryption, virtual private networks, software updates, and log files. Physical security is much the same as it has been since the lock and key were invented, and password security entails using better methods of storing and using passwords. Everything else relates to being connected to a network, because when it comes down to it, a server that isn't connected to a network isn't a server. And while connecting your server to the Internet allows you to provide services reaching the world over, it simultaneously gives miscreants all over the world access to your server. This brings us to two basic security tenets of running a server: Don't turn on services you don't need and don't serve a wider population than you must.

Apple has been very security-conscious with Mac OS X Server. The out-of-the-box configuration has almost no services turned on by default, allowing you to configure your security first and then turn on the services that you need. You'll need some basic services such as SSH over the local subnet to configure your server and remote access to server tools and directory changes. With Mac OS X Server 10.4, Apple provides comprehensive tools to make managing and monitoring the security of your server easier. The underlying services in Mac OS X Server, including Apache, Samba, OpenLDAP, Postfix, and Jabber, are robust, secure, and actively maintained by the open source community and Apple. This combination of tools and services will help you keep your server running securely.

Addressing Physical Security

Keeping your servers physically secure is one of the first aspects of security that you should consider. If a computer can be physically accessed, then with sufficient time it can be compromised. Because servers are shared resources, their security is usually more important because their compromise would more severely affect your organization. There isn't much point in looking after the other aspects of security until you've addressed physical security.

Figure 10.1 Recognizing the Open Firmware Password application icon.

Preventing booting from various other devices

If your server is in an area where others have physical access to it, they could potentially circumvent the login procedure by power-cycling the computer and restarting in a vulnerable mode. For instance, booting from a system CD, a system DVD, a FireWire hard drive, or a NetBoot drive, the perpetrator will have access to all files on the computer. Booting into single-user mode, the perpetrator will have root access to the computer and all items on that computer.

To enable an Open Firmware lock:

1. Launch the Open Firmware Password application, located in /Applications/ Utilities/ on the Mac OS X 10.4 installation disk (**Figure 10.1**).

   For Mac OS X 10.1–10.3.9, you can download the Open Firmware Password application from www.apple.com/support/ downloads/openfirmwarepassword.html.

Figure 10.2 Launching the Open Firmware Password application brings up this dialog.

Figure 10.3 Setting the password for the firmware using Open Firmware Password.

2. In the dialog that appears, click Change (**Figure 10.2**).

3. Click the "Require password to change Open Firmware settings" check box, enter and verify your password, and click OK (**Figure 10.3**).

4. Enter an administrator name and password in the standard authentication dialog and click OK.

5. Quit Open Firmware Password by choosing Quit from the Open Firmware Password menu.

Startup Keyboard Shortcuts

Apple offers the following keyboard shortcuts, which can be executed after the initial startup chime on PowerPCs:

◆ Pressing Option + Command +Shift + Delete during startup attempts to start from a disk other than the primary startup disk.

◆ Pressing C during startup attempts to start from a CD or DVD.

◆ Pressing N during startup attempts to start from a network server.

◆ Pressing T during startup attempts to start in target disk mode.

◆ Pressing Shift at boot (after chime) attempts to start in safe boot mode.

◆ Pressing V during startup attempts to start in verbose mode.

◆ Pressing S during startup attempts to start in single-user mode.

ADDRESSING PHYSICAL SECURITY

Determining rack and room security

If your server is being used for anything other than personal testing, you must limit physical access to it. Ideally, you have a server room with a locking door to which only a small number of trusted people have keys. If you have a shared server room, you can add security by putting your server in a rack cabinet that locks. If you work in an office that is reasonably secure, a locking rack cabinet may be sufficient, but be sure to review all of the people who have access to the space where your server is, and consider the consequences of a compromised server. What if someone breaks into your building? How critical and/or sensitive is the data on your server? These are questions that should be evaluated in deciding the physical location of your server.

ADDRESSING PHYSICAL SECURITY

Open Firmware Password Workaround

Locking Open Firmware is a reasonable deterrent, but it does not encrypt the hard drive(s). This strategy can be defeated by changing the amount of RAM in the computer and zapping the Parameter RAM (PRAM). That's a good thing to know in case you ever lock yourself out. In combination with a case lock (to prevent access to changing the amount of RAM), locking the Open Firmware deters the rapid compromise of a machine. It is a best practice to do this in public access areas, open offices, or wherever unauthorized users may have access to the computer.

Power Macs and recent iMacs can be secured from case intrusion with padlocks or locking cables. Older iMacs, PowerBooks, and iBooks only require a screwdriver to change the amount of RAM, defeat an Open Firmware lock, and gain boot variability to the computer. Though the Xserve has a case lock, it uses a hex key and is primarily intended to prevent accidental intrusions. Xserves are most vulnerable to physical intrusion precisely because they are expected to be protected in a secured rack and/or room.

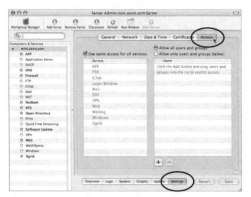

Figure 10.4 Using Server Admin to control access to services.

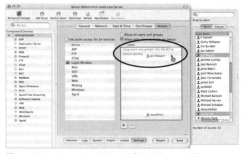

Figure 10.5 Dragging in users from the user list to restrict access to the Login window.

Setting Service Access

Service Access Control Lists (ACLs) are new to Mac OS X Server 10.4. Like the firewall service discussed in the following section, service ACLs are a very powerful security tool—be *very* careful not to lock yourself out of your server! Service ACLs determine which users or groups have access to the services provided by your server. In previous versions of Mac OS X Server, if a service was enabled for one user, it was enabled for all. Service ACLs are an additional security measure that will limit service usage to only those users you define.

The following task shows you how to restrict people from logging into the server, even if they have access to a keyboard and monitor attached to the server.

To restrict access to the Login window:

1. Launch Server Admin and select your server from the Computers & Services list.

   You don't need to authenticate if you have already added your server to the keychain. Leave Server Admin running for the next several exercises.

2. Click the Settings button and then click the Access tab (**Figure 10.4**).

3. Deselect the "Use same access for all services" check box but select the "Allow only user and groups below" check box.

4. Select Login Window from the Service list below and click the plus button to open the Users and Groups drawer on the right side of the window.

5. Click-and-drag your username and any other users from the drawer to the Name list (**Figure 10.5**).

6. Click the Save button to save your changes and permit only the selected users to log in via the Login window.

7. Test access by attempting to log in as a user not included in the access list.

Configuring the Firewall

A firewall offers protection by selectively filtering network packets: you can prevent unwanted inbound traffic from the Internet, and you can restrict outbound traffic from your internal network. The firewall software in Mac OS X Server, IPFirewall (IPFW), is from the FreeBSD organization and is a very powerful and sophisticated tool that offers protection over both IP version 4 and IP version 6.

Fortunately, Apple has made this much more approachable through the Server Admin tool. The best way to set up your firewall is to start with Mac OS X Server's default settings and then create openings only for the network traffic needed by defining a group of IP addresses and selecting the services you want them to be able to access.

What Are the Default Firewall Settings?

Mac OS X Server 10.4 has default firewall settings that will allow you to configure and run your server over a network. Whether you have an Xserve with no monitor or you are configuring a server thousands of miles away, you will need to allow at least some traffic through your firewall. The default settings include special settings, which have a lock icon next to them and cannot be changed, and minimal management settings, which can be changed if you desire. The default management settings are:

◆ SSH—Secure Shell

◆ Server Admin SSL, also Web-ASIP

◆ Remote Directory Access

◆ Serial number support

Serial number support allows traffic to check the legitimacy of your Mac OS X Server 10.4 license; if you deselect the check box for this service, it will turn itself back on. The remaining default services are allowed for any IP address, and may be necessary in order to set up a Mac OS X Server from across the country or from a different subnet. If you will not need such wide access to manage your servers, limit traffic to only the range of IP addresses from which you will be managing them.

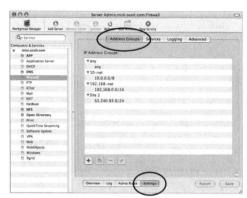

Figure 10.6 Selecting the Firewall group settings in Server Admin.

Be *very* careful when configuring the firewall to not lock yourself out! Make a habit of confirming that you have left the following management services accessible before you save a firewall configuration:

◆ SSH—Secure Shell

◆ Server Admin SSL, also Web-ASIP

◆ Remote Directory Access

It is a good idea to set up a small shell script to flush all the firewall rules every 15 minutes while you test and work on your firewall. This way, if you do lock yourself out, you only need wait until the 15 minutes rolls around and then you can start again.

When you define address groups, you are telling the firewall to adhere to the rules for just that IP range. For servers with only one Ethernet connection and one IP address, you can delete all other groups except the All group; then, no matter what your computer's IP address, you will be managing the firewall for any IP address that the server uses.

To define address groups:

1. In Server Admin, select the Firewall service for your server in the Computers & Services list.

2. Click the Settings button and then click the Address Groups tab (**Figure 10.6**).

continues on next page

Using the Command Line with the Firewall

IPFW can be configured from the command line by using the `serveradmin` command or traditional `ipfw` commands. The `serveradmin` commands essentially give you command-line access to the Server Admin way of doing things, and the `ipfw` commands give you access to the traditional, FreeBSD way. The `serveradmin` commands are useful for tasks such as starting or stopping the firewall service, or checking its status. The `ipfw` commands give you a convenient way to add or modify firewall rules.

It is important to understand how the GUI way and the FreeBSD way interact: Looking in the /private/etc/ipfilter directory, you'll find ipfw.conf, ipfw.conf.apple, and ipfw.conf.default. Viewing the contents of the `ipfw.conf` file will explain the interaction between the GUI elements and the FreeBSD elements.

CONFIGURING THE FIREWALL

3. Click the plus button to open a dialog where you can provide a group name and add addresses; then click OK to return to the main window (**Figure 10.7**).

4. Confirm that the Address range displayed in the lower part of the IP Address Groups configuration drawer is as you intend it to be, and click OK (Figure 10.6).

   Your new address group will appear in the IP Address Groups window.

5. When you've finished making changes, click Save.

Enter the group name and set the address ranges.

Group name: 192.168–net

Addresses in group: 192.168.0.0/16

Figure 10.7 Adding a new group to the Firewall group list.

Figuring Out Subnet Mask Notation

There are three ways you can add IP addresses to a firewall address group. The first is to simply enter a single IP address. But what if you wanted to add more than a single IP address at a time—for example, your company's whole address range? In that case you'd need to define a subnet mask, either using Classless Inter-Domain Routing (CIDR) notation or netmask notation. If you haven't spent a lot of time configuring network settings, this may seem like a daunting task. Consult one of many Internet sites devoted to understanding networking and CIDR notation.

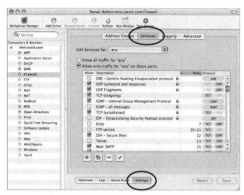

Figure 10.8 Selecting which services are allowed to be accessed through the firewall over the group *any*.

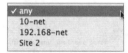

Figure 10.9 Choosing another group over which firewall rules will be applied.

Figure 10.10 Sorting rules by whether they are checked or not.

Allowing access to services

Once you have your IP address groups defined, you can allow services to be accessed by those groups. In the Services pane, you simply select the services you want.

To allow access to services:

1. Select the Firewall service, click the Settings button, and then click the Services tab (**Figure 10.8**).

   The services with the padlock icon cannot be edited or removed.

2. From the "Edit Services for" pop-up menu, select the address group to which you want to add a service (**Figure 10.9**).

3. Select the "Allow only traffic for 'any' on these ports" radio button, and select the service(s) you want to allow below.

4. Click the All column to display selected services at the top of the list (**Figure 10.10**).

5. When you've finished making changes, click the Save button and make sure the firewall is running.

   Your firewall should now allow the traffic for the service(s) you selected for the IP address group you specified.

✔ Tips

- By repeating the process for various other groups (depending on how many interfaces are active on your server), you can provide the services you want to the computers that need them.

- The best way to implement the firewall is to turn off all possible services except the management tools and ssh and then turn on services as necessary. For example, when using Mac OS X Server as a KDC (Open Directory Master), you may not need to open all the services surrounding Kerberos to make secure connections work.

CONFIGURING THE FIREWALL

To add specific firewall rules:

1. Select the firewall service, click the Settings button, and then click the Services tab.

2. From the "Edit Services for" pop-up menu, select the address group for which you want to enable your service.

3. Click the plus button and a new service dialog appears (**Figure 10.11**).

4. Provide a service name, port number, and protocol, and then click OK (**Figure 10.12**).

   Your new service is added to the services list for all of the service groups, but you must select the check box to make that service accessible through the firewall (**Figure 10.13**).

5. When you've finished making changes, click Save.

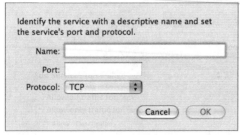

Figure 10.11 Clicking the plus button allows a new service to be listed in the service list.

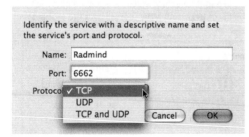

Figure 10.12 Entering data into the new service dialog.

Figure 10.13 Selecting the newly added service in the list.

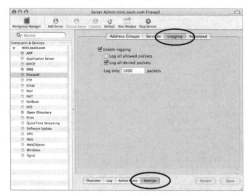

Figure 10.14 Enabling firewall logging via the Logging tab.

Figure 10.15 Viewing the firewall log from within Server Admin.

Figure 10.16 Restricting the log view using the filter.

Setting logging options for the firewall

The logging options for the firewall in Mac OS X Server are quite simple. Generally, you will log all allowed and/or denied packets for analysis or troubleshooting rather than leaving those options selected all the time. Logging every packet can result in some pretty big log files, so be careful! You can limit how many packets are logged, too.

To set logging options:

1. Select the Firewall service, click the Settings button, and then click the Logging tab (**Figure 10.14**).

2. Click the "Log all denied packets" check box and set the value to "Log only 1000 packets" for a relatively small log file.

3. To test the limits you just set, attempt to connect to your Mac OS X Server with a service blocked by the firewall from any other computer.

   For example, type `telnet` `xxx.xxx.xxx.xxx` 115 (the *x*'s represent the IP address of your server; 115 is the port you want to test).

4. Click the Log button at the bottom of the pane to display entries for all denied packets (**Figure 10.15**).

✔ Tip

■ To more easily isolate the packets you are looking for, type a colon (:) followed by the port number of the service you are looking for (**Figure 10.16**).

CONFIGURING THE FIREWALL

Configuring advanced settings and rules

Mac OS X Server's firewall also offers two Stealth Mode advanced options that you can use to give your server a less conspicuous presence on the Internet. When you select the Enable for TCP and Enable for UDP check boxes, packets that your server receives on closed ports are simply dropped; this is the same response an attacker would get if there were no computer present (**Figure 10.17**).

Though Mac OS X Server provides firewall rules for most of the services you will need, there may be times when you need to add your own custom rules. One reason you'd want to make an advanced rule is to allow protocols other than Transmission Control Protocol (TCP) or User Datagram Protocol (UDP)—such as Internet Control Message Protocol (ICMP), Internet Group Management Protocol (IGMP), Encapsulating Security Payload (ESP), or the protocol used to encapsulate static packets in an IP header, IPEncap.

Another reason you'd want to make an advanced rule is to allow different traffic on different network interfaces: All of the entries under the Services tab apply to all the network interfaces of your server. So if you have multiple physical or virtual interfaces defined in your Network preference pane, you can create custom rules under the Advanced tab to set up independent rules for each interface.

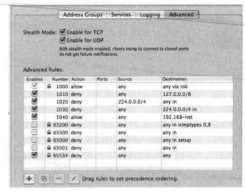

Figure 10.17 The Advanced tab of the firewall settings allows for rules to be moved in order of importance.

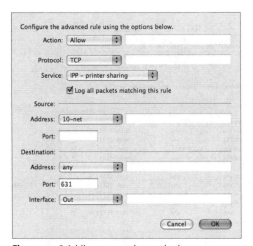

Figure 10.18 Adding a new advanced rule opens this dialog.

To create an advanced rule, you must understand what you want to accomplish. Here are some main options to be explored (**Figure 10.18**):

◆ From the Action pop-up menu, choose Allow or Deny.

◆ From the Protocol pop-up menu, choose the type of protocol affected by the firewall.

◆ Choose a specific service from the Service pop-up menu or select Other if the preset service is not in the list.

◆ In the Source area, the Address pop-up menu provides you with each IP address group from the Address Group tab. You can also enter specific IP addresses or ranges in the field.

◆ In the Port field, you can specify which source port will be used with this specific rule.

◆ In the Destination area, the Address pop-up menu provides the same IP address groups as in the Source area, and the port is sometimes preselected based on your service choice.

◆ From the Interface pop-up menu, choose whether the traffic is coming into or out of your server.

After you set up your customized rule, click OK and then save your changes. You may want to drag the rule higher or lower in the list depending on where you want the rule to fall with respect to your other rules.

Password Security

Password security and physical security share the dubious distinction of often being neglected weak links in a security system. It is frustrating to think how quickly a well-planned security system can be compromised by a poor password choice. With Mac OS X Server, you have the ability to enforce password policies per user or globally for all users. Please refer to Chapter 3, "Open Directory," for more information about password policies.

Recovering from a Lockout

If you are in the unenviable position of being locked out of your server, the firewall will need to be reset to its default settings. All is not lost, but you will need to have physical access to the server, and be able to boot it into single-user mode.

1. Disconnect the server from the Internet.

2. Restart in single-user mode by pressing Cmd+S.

3. Follow the onscreen prompts by typing /sbin/fsck -yf.

4. When the fsck file system check has successfully run, mount the file system:
   /sbin/mount -uw /.

5. Rename the ipfw configuration file and the address groups file:
   cd /private/etc/ipfilter
   mv ipfw.conf ipfw.conf.old
   mv ip_address_groups.conf ip_address_groups.conf.old

6. Flush the firewall rules:
   ipfw -f flush

7. Edit /private/etc/hostconfig to confirm that the IPFILTER setting reads as follows:
   IPFILTER=-YES-

   This will ensure that your server starts with the firewall active.

8. Restart your server and check the firewall configuration.

9. Reconnect your server to the Internet.

Virtual Private Networking

Virtual private networks, or VPNs, extend the reach of your security measures considerably by allowing your remote users to keep their communication with your LAN secure. Not only does that help to protect the data flowing in and out of your organization, but you also don't have to compromise the security of your network in order to provide convenient remote access for your users. VPNs create a secure, encrypted tunnel through which your users can connect to your LAN. Any services that aren't already encrypted will be protected by the VPN.

It also makes it easier for your remote users to access certain resources that are restricted to your LAN, such as services restricted by the firewall to IP addresses on the LAN. In short, a VPN allows a remote computer to behave as though it is directly connected to your LAN.

The VPN service gives you the option of adding other routes to your routing table as well. For example, if you have two different networks at your business and each network has different IP address ranges, you can add these networks to your VPN client information. If you are not sure which IP ranges need to be made available, consult the network administrator at your organization.

There are two methods of connecting to a network via a VPN connection using Server Admin, and each of these contains variances as well. The more secure of the two is Layer Two Tunneling Protocol over IP/Sec (L2TP). The other, less secure method is Point-to-Point Tunneling Protocol (PPTP). L2TP has various options (which will be discussed in the following task). PPTP only offers to add lower 40-bit level encryption to the existing 128-bit encryption.

VIRTUAL PRIVATE NETWORKING

To enable the VPN service:

1. In Server Admin, select the VPN service for your server in the Computers & Services list.

2. Click the Settings button and then select the L2TP tab (**Figure 10.19**).

3. Click the Enable L2TP check box and fill in starting and ending IP addresses to define the range (**Figure 10.20**).

4. From the PPP Authentication pop-up menu, choose either Microsoft's implementation of the Challenge Handshake Authentication Protocol, version 2 (MS-CHAPv2) or Kerberos.

5. In the IPSec Authentication area, select either a Shared Secret (that can be seen when typed in) or a Certificate.

6. To configure PPTP, select the PPTP tab and enter the appropriate information for clients connecting over PPTP (**Figure 10.21**).

Figure 10.19 Select the check box to enable L2TP over IP/Sec for the VPN Service.

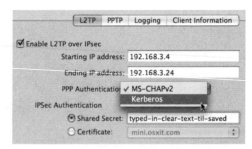

Figure 10.20 Setting various L2TP options.

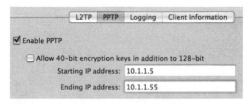

Figure 10.21 PPTP options are minimal.

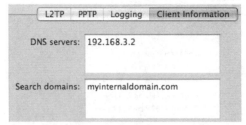

Figure 10.22 Client information can include DNS and domain information and...

Network Routing Definition:		
Network Address	Network Mask	Network Type
172.16.9.0	255.255.0.0	Private
216.168.61.0	255.255.255.0	Public

Figure 10.23 ...both public and private routes that will be added to the user's routing table.

7. Click the Client Information tab and fill in the DNS and search domain so the connecting machine can access internal devices accurately (**Figure 10.22**).

8. Add any public or private routes to be listed in the user's routing table (**Figure 10.23**).

9. When you've finished making changes, click the Save button and start the VPN service.

✔ Tip

- If you are troubleshooting a VPN connection within Internet Connect, select Options from the Connect menu and select the "Use Verbose Logging" and "Send all traffic over VPN connection" check boxes to assist you in locating the issue.

VIRTUAL PRIVATE NETWORKING

Internet Connect application setup

The Internet Connect application also needs to be configured to allow Mac OS X clients to connect to the VPN. When this is done, a new virtual interface is added to the current network location's interface list. If you have more than one location, you should repeat the process that follows for each location, thereby adding the virtual interface to each location.

To configure the Internet Connect application:

1. Launch the Internet Connect application located in /Applications (**Figure 10.24**), and select the VPN icon, if available, in the application's toolbar.

or

Choose New VPN Connection from the File menu (**Figure 10.25**).

2. In the dialog that appears, choose the appropriate connection method and click Continue (**Figure 10.26**).

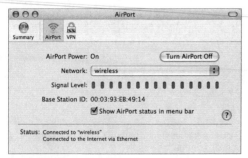

Figure 10.24 Opening the Internet Connect application...

Figure 10.25 ...to add a new VPN connection from the File menu.

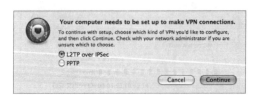

Figure 10.26 When adding a new VPN connection, a new VPN dialog appears.

Figure 10.27 Choosing to edit the new VPN configuration.

Figure 10.28 Entering various data into the new VPN dialog.

3. In the Internet Connect application, choose Edit Configurations from the Configuration pop-up menu (**Figure 10.27**).

4. In the description field that subsequently appears, provide a name for this VPN connection, in case you have more than one to choose from (**Figure 10.28**).

5. In the Server Address field, provide the IP address or domain name of the VPN server.

6. In the Account Name field, enter the short name of the user who will connect to the VPN.

7. In the User Authentication area, select a method of authentication.

   If you are using CryptoCard instead of RSA, contact CryptoCard for information on compatibility at www.cryptocard.com.

8. In the Machine Authentication area, select either a Shared Secret or Certificate.

continues on next page

9. In the Advanced area, you can click the "Enable VPN on demand" check box and then click Options to display a dialog where you can provide a domain name to trigger the connection (**Figure 10.29**).

10. Click OK and then click Connect to connect to your VPN service (**Figure 10.30**).

✔ Tips

■ You can select the "Show VPN status in menu bar" check box in the Internet Connect application to connect to the VPN directly from the menu bar.

■ There are other, more complex connection methods to other types of VPN servers that are beyond the scope of this book.

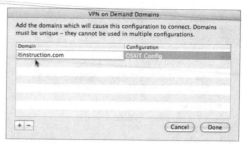

Figure 10.29 Adding a domain to enable VPN on demand.

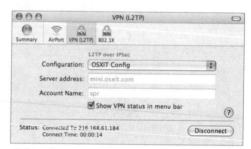

Figure 10.30 Internet Connect showing VPN connection.

Firewall VPN Ports

The firewall should have the following ports open, depending on your VPN configuration:

◆ 500—Internet Security Association and Key Management Protocol/Internet Key Exchange (VPN ISAKMP/IKE)

◆ 1701—VPN L2TP—Layer-Two Tunneling Protocol

◆ 1723—VPN PPTP—Point-to-Point Tunneling Protocol

◆ 4500—IKE NAT Traversal

Always back up your firewall settings with the tear-off configuration plist icon in the lower-right corner of the Settings window so that you can return to a set state, if necessary.

Software Update

Traditional wisdom with software updates is that you wait for other administrators who are clamoring to be first on the bandwagon to install the updates and find out what, if any, issues the updates caused. Once there has been some public testing and it looks as though the update helps more than it hurts, you go ahead and install it.

But now, in this day and age of constant Internet attacks, it is increasingly risky to leave a computer unpatched and vulnerable, especially with respect to security updates. You now have to balance these two approaches carefully. For updates that contain new features and functionality, there is less reason to rush to install, especially on a server. On the other hand, it is probably advisable to install security updates as soon as possible.

Fortunately, because patches are qualified by both Apple and the open source community, security updates are usually timely, reliable, and unlikely to create problems. The Software Update Server can permit users to run the application as they normally would, except for the fact that they are actually connecting to your server. To set up and manage the Software Update service, please refer to Chapter 13, "Client Management."

Another option when you're securing a server is to restrict the users who can access the server via ssh. Since ssh is turned on by default when you install and configure Mac OS X Server, a good password may not be enough to keep others out. You can use open source software contained in Mac OS X Server to generate a key and then give the key to individuals who are permitted to log in via ssh.

To create an ssh key:

1. Launch the Terminal application located in /Applications/Utilities, enter the command `ssh-keygen -t dsa`, and press Return (**Figure 10.31**).

   This command generates the two files necessary for the encryption using the type dsa: the file id_dsa contains the private part of the key, and the file id_dsa.pub contains the public part of the key.

2. In the line that appears after pressing Return from step 1, you do not need to provide a filename. So you can press Return again.

3. On the line that now appears, you can add an optional passphrase to encrypt the private key with Triple-DES encryption for even more security.

4. Copy the id_dsa.pub file to your administrator's home folder on the server. If it doesn't already exist, create a folder called .ssh in the home folder on the server, move the id_dsa.pub file into the .ssh/ folder, and rename it authorized_keys (**Figure 10.32**).

5. On your server, open and edit the /etc/sshd_config file using any command-line editor by changing the following lines from:

   ```
   #PasswordAuthentication yes
   #ChallengeResponseAuthentication yes
   ```

   to

   ```
   PasswordAuthentication no
   ChallengeResponseAuthentication no
   ```

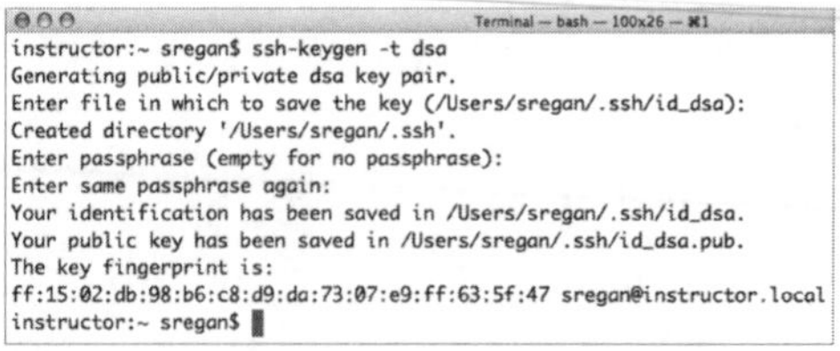

```
instructor:~ sregan$ ssh-keygen -t dsa
Generating public/private dsa key pair.
Enter file in which to save the key (/Users/sregan/.ssh/id_dsa):
Created directory '/Users/sregan/.ssh'.
Enter passphrase (empty for no passphrase):
Enter same passphrase again:
Your identification has been saved in /Users/sregan/.ssh/id_dsa.
Your public key has been saved in /Users/sregan/.ssh/id_dsa.pub.
The key fingerprint is:
ff:15:02:db:98:b6:c8:d9:da:73:07:e9:ff:63:5f:47 sregan@instructor.local
instructor:~ sregan$
```

Figure 10.31 Using the Terminal to create a public/private key pair.

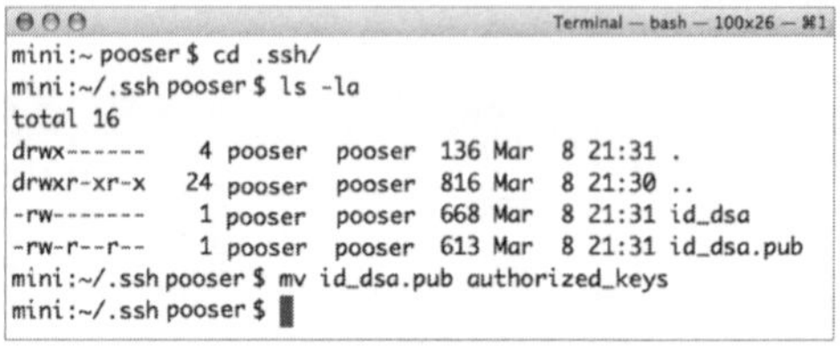

```
mini:~ pooser $ cd .ssh/
mini:~/.ssh pooser $ ls -la
total 16
drwx------    4 pooser  pooser  136 Mar  8 21:31 .
drwxr-xr-x   24 pooser  pooser  816 Mar  8 21:30 ..
-rw-------    1 pooser  pooser  668 Mar  8 21:31 id_dsa
-rw-r--r--    1 pooser  pooser  613 Mar  8 21:31 id_dsa.pub
mini:~/.ssh pooser $ mv id_dsa.pub authorized_keys
mini:~/.ssh pooser $
```

Figure 10.32 Renaming the file on the server.

6. You may want to restart your server at this point because attempting to stop and restart ssh can cause you to lock yourself out of your server.

7. Attempt to log in again from the Mac OS X computer that generated the keys and enter the passphrase when requested.

   Any hackers who attempt to log in using your short name will not be able to log in without the private key on their computer.

✔ Tips

■ It's a good idea to also copy the .ssh directory on your server from your administrator's home folder to root's home folder, thus keeping a direct remote root login safer by restricting it to key access.

■ Make a backup copy of the keys, and install them on all machines that may require other administrators to ssh into the server. You may also wish to copy the authorized_keys file from one administrator account to other accounts or to generate individual keys for each user.

■ If you don't enter a passphrase when you generate a key, then when a user opens the Terminal and attempts to log in with the admin account, they won't be asked for a password or passphrase. This can be dangerous, because the client computer can access the server by opening the Terminal and typing in ssh `admin_name@ip_address`.

Running a
NetBoot Server

At Macworld Expo 1999, then-interim CEO Steve Jobs rolled out a huge cart of 50 iMacs playing the same movie file without a single hard disk among them. He was introducing the first commercially available Mac OS X system, and all the iMacs started up from a single copy of an operating system being hosted by a Mac OS X Server. That's right: One of the first public demonstrations of the future technology to drive all new Apple computers was a Mac OS X Server running the NetBoot service.

A server running the NetBoot service shares disk image files that contain the system software. Client computers, when instructed, automatically find and start up from any one of these disk images across the network. On a fast server with Gigabit Ethernet, more than 50 clients can start up from one disk image. Once booted, a client acts like any other computer that has been started from a local volume. Any changes made while running the NetBoot client computer are not retained upon restart, ensuring consistent system software across all your computers.

This chapter deals with the setup, management, and maintenance of the NetBoot service on Mac OS X Server.

Understanding NetBoot

Upon further dissection, NetBoot is a combination of several different protocols, working in concert to facilitate the remote booting of an operating system over the network. The services required to provide NetBoot include Dynamic Host Configuration Protocol (DHCP) to provide initial IP addressing information, Boot Service Discovery Protocol (BSDP) to advertise the location of the NetBoot server, Trivial File Transfer Protocol (TFTP) to deliver the initial boot files, and either Network File System (NFS) or Web services via HyperText Transfer Protocol (HTTP) to mount the system boot image.

On the client side, the Open Firmware instructions built into the hardware of every modern Apple computer facilitate the NetBoot startup process. While Open Firmware is being replaced by the Extensible Firmware Interface (EFI) on the newer Intel-based Macs, the NetBoot process itself remains primarily the same.

One type of boot image, dubbed an *install image*, can be used to facilitate rapid mass deployment across your network. After you start up a computer, the install image can then automatically install onto the local volume all the software required for your system build. Another potential use for NetBoot is to create an image that contains all your favorite system maintenance and repair utilities.

You can configure the ultimate administrator's toolkit, which is available to any computer on your network at any time—without having to carry a single CD or FireWire disk! Each server can host 25 different images, and you can use as many NetBoot servers as you need on your network. NetBoot servers will even automatically load-balance traffic for high-demand images if the same image is on multiple servers.

Creating a Bootable Image

The System Image Utility is one of the administrative tools included with Mac OS X Server. This application will serve as your main tool for creating boot and install images. Like all the other server administration tools, the System Image Utility can run on your Mac OS X Server or any other computer running Mac OS X.

Before you start the System Image Utility, you need to have access to a mountable volume that contains a copy of Mac OS X or Mac OS X Server. Your choices include the original installation CD or DVD, disk image files created by Disk Utility, or any other available system volume besides the current startup disk.

The System Image Utility essentially creates a copy of any system volume and then performs all the necessary modifications to make it a boot image. This gives you a great deal of freedom, because you can create boot images from any combination of system and application software you require.

What's an Image ID?

The Image ID is a unique number of your choosing that client computers use to identify the boot image. If a boot image will be available from only one server, chose an ID number between 1 and 4095. However, if a boot image will be available from several servers, choose a number between 4096 and 65535.

If a client computer finds an image with the same ID on multiple servers, the client will assume they're identical image files and boot off the first image it receives from any of the servers containing that image. This has the effect of doing rudimentary load balancing between multiple NetBoot servers. The Image ID is entered into the Image Index field of the System Image Utility when creating a new boot image.

To create a bootable image:

1. Choose /Applications/Server/System Image Utility.
   The System Image Utility opens.

2. In the Toolbar, click New Boot (**Figure 11.1**).

3. Click the General tab, if it's not already selected, and enter an Image Name, Image Index (with an Image ID), and Description (**Figure 11.2**).

4. Choose the sharing protocol (NFS or HTTP) and select the final destination (Local or Remote) for the boot image.

5. Click the Contents tab, and from the Image Source pop-up menu, choose the volume, image file, or system CD or DVD you wish to convert to a boot image (**Figure 11.3**).

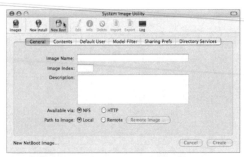

Figure 11.1 Choose /Applications/Server/System Image Utility and click the New Boot button.

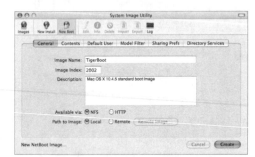

Figure 11.2 On the New Boot Image General tab, fill out the Image Name, Image ID, and Description fields.

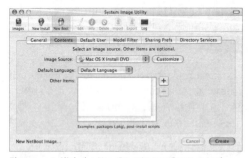

Figure 11.3 Click the New Boot Image Contents tab.

Figure 11.4 Clicking the Customize button allows you to remove certain packages before the image is created.

Figure 11.5 Clicking the plus button and adding other packages to install.

Figure 11.6 Entering the default username and password into the Default User tab.

6. Click the Customize button if you want to modify the list of available packages to be included in the boot image (**Figure 11.4**).

7. If you're creating a boot image from the Mac OS X install CD or DVD, select the desired language from the Default Language pop-up (Figure 11.3).

8. Click the plus button next to the Other Items text area to include installer packages (.pkg), system updates, or post-install scripts in the boot image (**Figure 11.5**).

9. If you're creating a boot image from the Mac OS X install CD or DVD, click the Default User tab and specify the administrator account settings (**Figure 11.6**).

continues on next page

10. You may also click the Model Filter tab and enable specific computers that will be allowed to boot from the image (**Figure 11.7**).

11. *Do one of the following:*

▲ To customize the computer name and hostname of clients booted from this image you are creating, click the Sharing Prefs tab and enter a computer name (**Figure 11.8**).

Computers booted from this image will use the MAC address (without colons) appended to the name you entered.

or

▲ To use unique computer names and hostnames for each machine, use the File Path feature to select a tab-delimited .txt or .rtf file that contains a list of MAC addresses and desired computer names and hostnames (Figure 11.7).

12. Click the Directory Services tab to add directory service settings to your boot image (**Figure 11.9**).

The settings are taken from the machine on which you are currently creating the image. Make sure the directory services settings are configured appropriately (refer to "Directory Access Overview" in Chapter 3 for instructions on how to configure the DHCP service) before proceeding with the boot image creation. Up to this point, you haven't created the image, so you can change almost anything before proceeding.

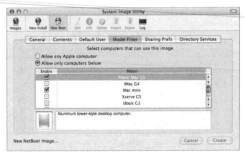

Figure 11.7 Click the Model Filter tab to configure what machines can boot from the image.

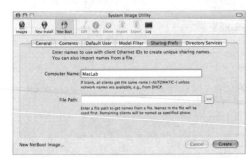

Figure 11.8 Click the Sharing tab to customize the computer name.

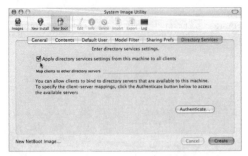

Figure 11.9 Click the Directory Services tab to embed directory service settings into the image.

Figure 11.10 In the Save dialog, choose the destination for the boot image.

Figure 11.11 Click the Log toolbar icon in the System Image Utility dialog to see the New Boot Image process log.

13. Click Create and continue through any other dialogs and license agreements that appear.

14. When the Save As dialog opens, choose the destination for the boot image (**Figure 11.10**).

If you're running the System Image Utility on a server running the NetBoot service, it automatically chooses the NetBoot share point.

15. Click Save to initiate the creation process.

Be patient; it may take a while to create the boot image.

16. Click the Log toolbar button to observe the creation process log (**Figure 11.11**).

✔ Tips

■ Once boot images are created, they take up quite a bit of space. Be sure you have enough free space for your images prior to image creation.

■ The freeware applications Carbon Copy Cloner and NetRestore Helper, created by Mike Bombich, can make boot images. Mike has a number of utilities and tutorials on disk imaging and system deployment, so a visit to his Web site is always a worthwhile trip: www.bombich.com/.

CREATING A BOOTABLE IMAGE

Creating an Install Image

Install images are similar to boot images in that client computers can remotely boot from these image files if they're made available from a NetBoot server. However, when a client computer starts up from an install image, the user is presented with the Installer utility instead of the login window. At this point, the user experience is similar to booting up from the Mac OS X installer CD or DVD: You step through a few simple windows in the Installer utility, and then the system from the install image is installed on the local computer's hard disk.

You can also create an automated install. In that case, having the client boot and choose an install image begins the process of installation. You never have to carry around an installation CD or DVD again.

To create an install image:

1. Choose /Applications/Server/System Image Utility and click New Install in the Toolbar (**Figure 11.12**).

2. Click the General tab if it's not already selected, and enter an image name, image index (with an Image ID), and description.

3. Also, choose the sharing protocol (NFS or HTTP) and select the final destination (Local or Remote) for the boot image (**Figure 11.13**).

4. Click the Contents tab, and from the Image Source pop-up menu, choose the volume, image file, or system CD or DVD you wish to convert to an install image (**Figure 11.14**).

Figure 11.12 Choose /Applications/Server/System Image Utility and click the New Install button.

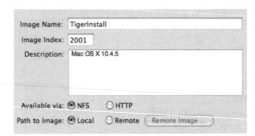

Figure 11.13 On the New Install Image General tab, fill out the Image Name, Image Index, and Description fields.

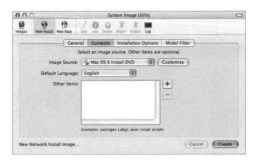

Figure 11.14 Click the New Install Image Contents tab and select an image source, default language, and any additional packages or post-install scripts you want added to the image.

Figure 11.15 Clicking the Customize button allows you to remove certain packages before the image is created.

Figure 11.16 Clicking the plus button and adding other packages to install.

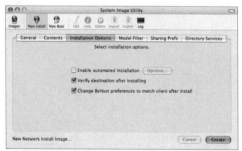

Figure 11.17 Click the New Install Image Installation Options tab.

5. Click the Customize button if you want to modify the list of available packages to be included in the boot image (**Figure 11.15**).

6. If you're creating an install image from the Mac OS X install CD or DVD, select the desired language from the Default Language pop-up (Figure 11.14).

7. Click the plus button next to the Other Items text area to include additional installer packages (.pkg), system updates, or post-install scripts in the boot image (**Figure 11.16**).

8. Click the Installation Options tab and select the following options (**Figure 11.17**).

   ▲ **Verify destination after installing** checks the volume on which the installation took place to ensure the installation went as expected.

   ▲ **Change ByHost preferences to match client after install** takes machine-specific preferences and changes the names of the files to match the volume on which the installation took place.

   The "Enable automated installation" option is discussed in the "Automating Installations" section later in this chapter.

9. Follow steps 10–16 in the previous exercise.

✔ Tips

■ Once install images are created, they take up quite a bit of space. Be sure you have enough free space for your images prior to image creation.

■ If you select the "Verify destination after installing" option on the Installation Options tab, then the installer will verify the integrity of the image after it is installed. This option is only applicable for images created from volume source only. This option also increases the amount of time required to complete the installation.

CREATING AN INSTALL IMAGE

Managing NetBoot Images

NetBoot images are really folders containing all the items necessary to facilitate booting over the network. These NetBoot image folders are easy to spot, because the name of the folder always ends with .nbi.

In order for a NetBoot server to use a NetBoot image, the image must reside in the NetBoot share points. The Server Admin utility automatically creates the NetBoot share points on every server volume in the Library/NetBoot/_NetBootSP# folder. For each different server volume, the # is incremented by one, with the first column number being zero.

You can use the System Image Utility as a centralized utility to manage your NetBoot images. The System Image Utility maintains a list of all your NetBoot images for easy reference. If an image isn't in the System Image Utility image list, you have to add it manually. More important, the System Image Utility can be used to edit existing NetBoot images as your requirements change.

To add to the NetBoot image list:

1. Choose /Applications/Server/System Image Utility and click Images in the Toolbar (**Figure 11.18**).

    A list of images appears.

2. Switch the Finder and navigate the NetBoot image you want to add to the list.

3. Drag and drop the NetBoot image from the Finder to the NetBoot image list in the System Image Utility. The image is now added to the list (**Figure 11.19**).

    Notice that you can also select an image from the list and click Delete in the Toolbar.

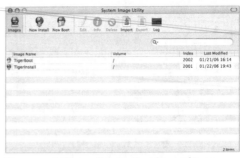

Figure 11.18 Choose /Applications/Server/System Image Utility and click the Images button.

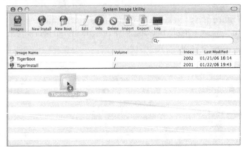

Figure 11.19 Drag a image from the Finder into the System Image Utility Images window.

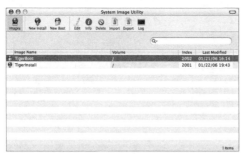

Figure 11.20 Choose /Applications/Server/System Image Utility and click the Images button.

Figure 11.21 Decide whether to create a backup before editing an image.

Figure 11.22 Authenticate as your server administrator.

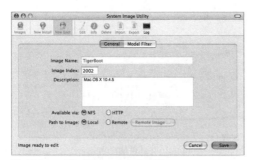

Figure 11.23 The System Image Utility reverts to editing mode. Make changes to the image as required.

✔ Tips

- Don't drag in .nbi folders from remote mounted server volumes.

- Dragging an image into the System Image Utility adds it to the list of images but does not copy or move the image itself. Moving your image to /Library/NetBoot/NetBootSP#/ and launching the System Image Utility will also make it appear in the list.

To modify a NetBoot image:

1. Choose /Applications/Server/System Image Utility and click Images in the Toolbar (**Figure 11.20**).

2. Select the image you want to modify from the images list.

   Note that you can click Info to check the image settings before making any changes.

3. Click Edit in the Toolbar.

   A dialog appears, asking if you would like to back up your image.

4. Click Yes if you would like a backup (**Figure 11.21**).

5. Authenticate as an administrative user (**Figure 11.22**).

6. The System Image Utility reverts to editing mode (**Figure 11.23**).

   You can make any changes to the image as if you were configuring a new image.

7. When you're done making changes, click Save.

Automating installations

Setting up a NetBoot server with install images can be a huge time-saver for administrators who need to install new software on many computers simultaneously. To save even more time, you can automate install images to facilitate a nearly hands-free approach.

To automate install images:

1. Choose /Applications/Server/System Image Utility and *do one of the following*:

   ▲ Click New Install to configure a new install image.

   or

   ▲ Click Images, choose an existing install image from the list, and then click Edit (**Figure 11.24**).

2. In the Backup Image dialog, click Yes if you would like a backup and to authenticate as an administrator (**Figure 11.25**). The System Image Utility reverts to editing mode.

3. Click the Installation Options tab and select the "Enable automated installation" check box (**Figure 11.26**).

4. Click Options and choose from the Auto-Install Options that appear in the dialog, and then click OK (**Figure 11.27**).

5. *Do one of the following*:

   ▲ If this is a new install image, click Create to complete the image-creation process.

   ▲ If you're editing an existing image, click Save to finalize your changes.

✔ Tip

■ If you have enabled the erase target option without enabling the confirmation dialog option, be sure to take great care when using this boot image since data loss can occur when the contents of a workstation's hard drive are automatically erased.

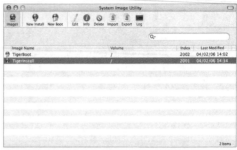

Figure 11.24 Select an existing image, and click Edit.

Figure 11.25 Decide whether to create a backup before editing an image.

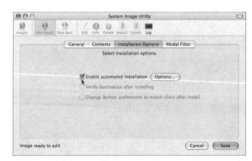

Figure 11.26 Select the "Enable automated installation" check box.

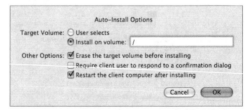

Figure 11.27 Click the Options button, and then select from the list of Auto-Install Options.

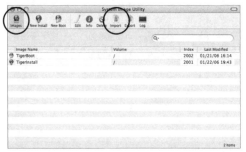

Figure 11.28 Click the Images button and then the Import button.

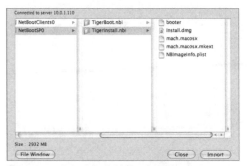

Figure 11.29 Enter the network address and the root user password of the server from which you're importing an image, and click Connect.

Figure 11.30 Select the .nbi files from the server.

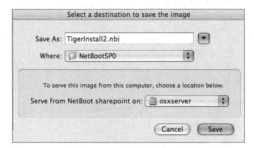

Figure 11.31 In the Save As dialog, choose the destination for the imported image.

Importing or exporting images

The System Image Utility provides a unique function for moving images between Mac OS X Servers. The import and export functions can copy your NetBoot images among servers on the network. This copy service is facilitated through a Secure File Transfer Protocol (SFTP) connection.

To import a NetBoot image:

1. Choose /Applications/Server/System Image Utility and click Images and then Import (**Figure 11.28**).

2. In the dialog that appears, enter the network address and the root user password of the server from which you're importing the image and click Connect (**Figure 11.29**).

3. In the resulting dialog, select the .nbi files from the server and click Import (**Figure 11.30**).

   Typically, the images are stored in /Library/NetBoot/NetBootSP#.

4. In the Save As dialog that appears, choose the destination for the imported image and click Save (**Figure 11.31**).

   If you're running the System Image Utility on a server running the NetBoot service, it will automatically choose the NetBoot share point. NetBoot images are typically over 1 GB in size and can take quite some time to transfer over a network connection, depending on the speed of that connection.

To export a NetBoot image:

1. Choose /Applications/Server/System Image Utility and click Images in the Toolbar.

2. From the image list, select a NetBoot image and click Export in the Toolbar (**Figure 11.32**).

3. In the dialog that appears, enter the network address and the root user password of the server to which you're exporting the image, and click Connect (**Figure 11.33**).

4. Choose the destination location on the server to which you're exporting the image, and click Save (**Figure 11.34**).

   Typically, the images are stored in /Library/NetBoot/NetBootSP#.

✔ Tip

■ The System Image Utility can import and export images to any Mac OS X computer, not just servers. All you have to do is turn on Remote Login in the Sharing System Preference pane and enable the root user in the NetInfo Manager utility.

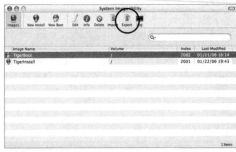

Figure 11.32 Select the image you want to export.

Figure 11.33 Enter the network address and root user password, and click Connect.

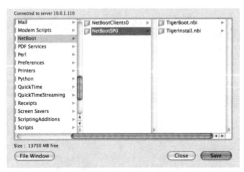

Figure 11.34 In the export location dialog, choose the destination location on the server to which you're exporting the image.

Enabling the NetBoot Service

Enabling the NetBoot server service requires a variety of server configuration changes. The Server Admin tool performs these changes for you, but you must enable a few related services in order for NetBoot to function properly. For example, Network File System (NFS) and (for diskless NetBoot support) the Apple Filing Protocol (AFP) and services must be running in order for you to share your NetBoot images. The NFS service automatically starts when you configure NetBoot via the Server Admin utility, but you must enable the AFP service manually. (Refer to Chapter 5, "File Sharing," for instructions on how to enable the AFP service.)

A properly configured Dynamic Host Configuration Protocol (DHCP) server must also be available on your network in order for the NetBoot service to work. For many installations, the Mac OS X Server will act as the DHCP server. (Refer to Chapter 6, "Network Services Options," for instructions on how to configure the DHCP service.)

What If I Already Have Another DHCP Server?

Many networks have other devices that provide DHCP services. You can still use the NetBoot service in these types of network environments. In previous versions of Mac OS X Server, the DHCP service needed to be running on your NetBoot server because it was responsible for providing the Boot Service Discovery Protocol (BSDP), which allows client computers to automatically find it over the network. However, the DHCP service doesn't have to be running to use NetBoot. To prevent the DHCP service from providing configuration information to the network, choose DHCP from the Computers & Services list and then deselect the Enable check box (**Figure 11.35**).

Figure 11.35 Deselect the DHCP settings' Enable check box.

To enable the NetBoot service:

1. Launch Server Admin located in /Applications/Server, authenticate as the administrator if necessary, select NetBoot from the Computers & Services list, click Settings, and then click the General tab (**Figure 11.36**).

2. From the network port list, select the check box(es) next to the network interface(s) on which you want to enable the NetBoot service.

3. From the volume list, select the check box(es) next to the volume(s) where you want to store the images and the client data. Click Save.

   You must choose at least one volume for each column. The more volumes you enable, the more responsive your server will be.

4. In the Server Admin Toolbar, click Start Service.

   The Server Admin utility will configure the NetBoot server, share points, and user accounts.

5. Populate any NetBoot share points you have with .nbi image files.

   Refer to the earlier tasks on image creation and image management for more details.

Figure 11.36 Select NetBoot from the service list, click the Settings tab, and then click the General tab.

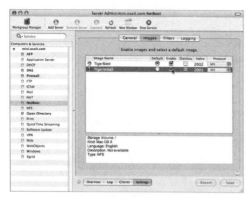

Figure 11.37 In the Enable column, select the check boxes next to the images you want to make available to NetBoot.

Figure 11.38 To view the NetBoot log file, select NetBoot from the Computers & Services list and then click the Log button.

6. Click the Images tab and in the Enable column, select the check boxes next to the images you want to make available to NetBoot (**Figure 11.37**).

7. When you've finished making changes, click Save.

✔ Tips

- You may have to restart the Mac OS X Server in order for NetBoot to function properly.

- If you're experiencing problems with the NetBoot service, check the log file for error messages (**Figure 11.38**). You can view the NetBoot log file in the Server Admin utility by selecting NetBoot from the Computers & Services list and then clicking Log.

- To NetBoot across network subnets, check out the NetBoot Across Subnets utility created by Mike Bombich (www.bombich.com).

Storing Client Images

When any client computer boots from your NetBoot server, a shadow file is created on your server for temporary storage. This file is used to save any changes the user makes from the client computer while it's running. The client images are deleted as soon as the client computer shuts down or restarts. On a busy NetBoot server, a huge amount of data is written to and copied from these client images. You can improve performance by moving the client image storage location to a different disk on your NetBoot server.

To configure the client image location, simply follow steps 1–3 of the previous task. Then, from the volume list in the Server Admin utility, select the check box(es) in the Client Data column next to the volume(s) and click Save (**Figure 11.39**). The more volumes you enable, the more responsive your server will be.

Figure 11.39 Select the volume storage options check box(es).

NetBoot Client Compatibility

Mac OS X Server 10.3 and higher only support NetBoot version 2. Apple computers with Firmware version 4.1.7 or newer are compatible with NetBoot version 2. Computers capable of using Firmware 4.1.7 or later include:

◆ G4 and G5 computers of any kind, except the very first G4 PowerMac

◆ All iBooks

◆ Slot-loading iMacs

◆ PowerBook G3s with FireWire

Beginning with Mac OS X 10.4.4, NetBoot images that support Intel-based Macintoshes can be created using the install DVDs that shipped with those systems.

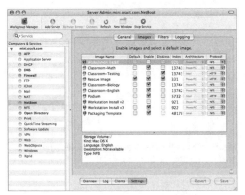

Figure 11.40 In the Default column, select the check box next to the image you want to make the default NetBoot image.

Choosing the default image

To force a Macintosh computer to search for a NetBoot server at startup, hold the N key when you turn on the computer. It always chooses the default image on the NetBoot server. There should be only one default image among all your NetBoot servers, so choose wisely.

To choose the default image:

1. Launch Server Admin located in /Applications/Server, and authenticate as the administrator if necessary. Select NetBoot from the Computers & Services list, click Settings, and then click the Images tab (**Figure 11.40**).

2. In the Default column, select the check box next to the image you want to make the default NetBoot image and click Save.

✔ Tips

- It's a really, really bad idea to configure an automated install image as your default NetBoot image. An unsuspecting user could inadvertently NetBoot a client and end up accidentally erasing important data files on the computer's system disk.

- You can select separate default images for Intel-based and PowerPC-based Macintoshes.

STORING CLIENT IMAGES

Enabling diskless mode

To increase NetBoot system performance, Mac OS X client computers store temporary cache and swap files, sometimes called *shadow files*, on their local hard disks. This performance-enhancing feature of NetBoot can be considered a limitation, because it doesn't allow for a truly diskless client computer. This feature also prevents you from using certain install and repair utilities on the local client's hard disk when you're using a NetBoot server. To remedy these situations, an optional diskless image mode disables shadow files.

To enable diskless mode, follow the first two steps in the previous task and then, in the Diskless column, select the check box(es) next to the boot image(s) and click Save (**Figure 11.41**). You can't enable diskless operation for install images because they're specifically designed to install data on the client's local hard disk. In effect, they are already diskless.

Enabling NetBoot filtering

You can control client access to your NetBoot server by enabling the NetBoot filter. The NetBoot filter can be configured to allow or deny specific client computers based on their Ethernet address. This is useful when you have computers that should *never* be NetBooted, such as other servers.

To enable NetBoot filtering:

1. Launch Server Admin located in /Applications/Server, and authenticate as the administrator if necessary. Select NetBoot from the Computers & Services list, click Settings, and then click the Filters tab (**Figure 11.42**).

Figure 11.41 In the Diskless column, select the check box(es) next to the boot image(s).

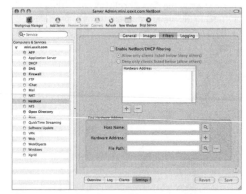

Figure 11.42 Select the "Enable NetBoot/DHCP filtering" check box.

STORING CLIENT IMAGES

Figure 11.43 Click the plus button to manually add a client's Ethernet address.

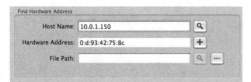

Figure 11.44 Enter a client's hostname and click the spyglass button to have the Server Admin utility query the client for its Ethernet address. Then click the plus button to add the address to your list.

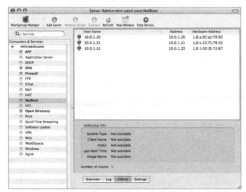

Figure 11.45 You can view a list of NetBoot clients in the Server Admin utility by selecting NetBoot from the service list and then clicking the Clients tab.

2. Select the "Enable NetBoot/DHCP filtering" check box.

3. Choose the appropriate radio button to create the allow or deny filter list.

4. *Do one of the following*:

   ▲ Click the plus button.

   A dialog appears, allowing you to manually add a client's Ethernet address **(Figure 11.43)**.

   ▲ Enter a client's hostname, and click the spyglass button (Figure 11.42) to query the client for its Ethernet address; then click the plus button to add this address to your list **(Figure 11.44)**.

   ▲ Enter a file name (or locate the file by clicking the ellipsis button) that has a list of addresses that you wish to either allow or deny (Figure 11.42).

5. When you've finished making changes, click Save.

✔ Tips

■ Click the Delete (minus) button to remove a client from the filter list.

■ You can view a historical list of all clients that have NetBooted for your server in the Server Admin utility by selecting NetBoot from the Computers & Services list and then clicking the Clients tab **(Figure 11.45)**.

STORING CLIENT IMAGES

409

NetBooting the Client

Figure 11.46 Look for the NetBoot startup globe icon.

After all the hard work involved in setting up your NetBoot server, it's time to NetBoot some clients! There are two primary methods for configuring client computers to boot from your NetBoot server: You can select NetBoot at client startup or from the Startup Disk system preference pane. Selecting NetBoot at startup is only temporary (that is, just for one startup), whereas setting the NetBoot option from Startup Disk is permanent. Also, selecting NetBoot on a lab full of computers allows that entire lab to boot off one image on your server.

To select NetBoot at startup:

1. *Do one of the following:*
   ▲ Hold down the N key at startup.
      or
   ▲ Hold down the Option key at startup to invoke the Startup Manager, select the NetBoot Globe icon, and click Continue.

2. Verify that you're booting from your NetBoot server by observing the Globe icon against the gray background (**Figure 11.46**).

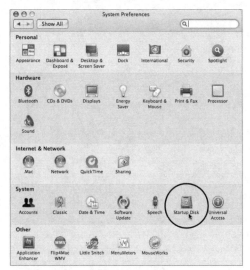

Figure 11.47 Click the Startup Disk icon.

Figure 11.48 In the Startup Disk selection dialog, select the desired image.

To select NetBoot from Startup Disk:

1. Open the System Preferences by choosing Apple Menu > System Preferences.

2. Click the Startup Disk icon (**Figure 11.47**). After a few moments, your individual NetBoot images appear in the Startup Disk window.

3. In the Startup Disk window, select the desired image (**Figure 11.48**).

4. Click Restart.

✔ Tips

- NetBoot clients require 128 MB of RAM and 100Base-T Ethernet connectivity. As always, configurations with more RAM or higher-speed network connectivity will have better performance.

- You can't NetBoot over a wireless network or modem connection.

NETBOOTING THE CLIENT

411

QUICKTIME STREAMING SERVER

Apple has always been at the forefront of authoring audio and video, so it should come as no surprise that the tool used to deliver audio and video media in Mac OS X Server is capable of similarly powerful results. Although it's part of Mac OS X Server, the QuickTime Streaming Server (QTSS) can also be downloaded for free and can be installed on Mac OS X Client. It is provided under a different name—Darwin Streaming Server (DSS)—but make no mistake, it's based on the exact same code. DSS can also be installed on other operating systems such as Red Hat Linux 9 and Windows 2000/2003 Server.

Mac OS X Server provides a suite of three applications focused on streaming. QTSS is the core server, capable of streaming QuickTime, MPEG-4, H.264, MP3, and even 3GPP (streaming to mobile phones) to viewers across cellular networks. QuickTime Broadcast (QTB) is a live encoder application that, when coupled with QTSS, allows for the delivery of live streaming events. Last but not least is QTSS Publisher, which handles media preparation, playlist development, and the creation of Web pages that contain streaming content. QTSS Publisher makes all these common tasks easier to accomplish. QTSS, QTB, and QTSS Publisher make for a terrific triple threat of streaming to help you get started. This chapter teaches you how to set up and run QTSS for your organization.

About QTSS

QTSS is an real-time media delivery server capable of streaming content such as your company's quarterly financials, a video of a rock band's release party for a brand-new album, new employee orientation materials, or training movies required by human resources. A community can even broadcast the unveiling of a new monument live over the Internet.

Beyond the powerful streaming tools, there is one more feature of note in QTSS. Whereas other streaming server solutions require you to pay licensing fees based on the number of viewers connecting to your server, QTSS and DSS apply no "server tax" and do not artificially limit the number of people viewing or listening to your content.

With the top-notch suite of streaming tools and a lack of per-stream or per-user license fees, you can turn your attention toward creating focused and compelling content as opposed to figuring out how to get your streaming server to work.

One note of caution: Please respect the rights of the owners of audio and video material. You should only stream content that you own or for which you have the appropriate copyright approvals. Also, in the case of music tracks from signed recording artists, you should abide by royalty guidelines set down by the American Society of Composers, Authors and Publishers, (ASCAP), Broadcast Musicians Incorporated (BMI), or the Society of Composers, Authors and Music Publishers of Canada (SOCAN).

Understanding Bits and Bytes

Before you can begin streaming audio or video, you should understand the key units of measure related to media files and networks.

Computer 101

Computer files are measured in *bytes*. A byte consists of 8 bits. Generally, audio and video files tend to be large and are often measured in kilobytes (KB, or 1,024 bytes) and megabytes (MB, or 1,024 kilobytes).

When you connect your computer to a network (and by extension the Internet), you do so at a given speed. The speed is measured in bits, *not* bytes. More specifically, network speed is measured in bits per second (bps). Fast networks can be described in kilobits (Kbps, or 1,024 bits per second), megabits (Mbps, or 1,024 kilobits per second), and even gigabits (Gbps, or 1024 megabits). For example, a modem connection can try for 56 Kbps but usually only reaches approximately 46 Kbps. A connection through your high-speed Internet service provider (ISP) can be as fast as 3.5 megabits per second (Mbps), although most such connections top out at 1 Mbps.

Video content being streamed from your server must be properly prepared. For the best viewer experience, it is wise to create two to four versions of your content that match the various types of Internet connections from slow (56 Kbps modem) to fast (768 Mbps DSL/Cable or better). QTSS delivers media in real time. This means your media files must, during delivery, never exceed the maximum amount of data (i.e., Kbps) the client computer can receive at any one moment. Many QuickTime authoring tools provide preset export options for common Internet connection speeds to simplify this requirement.

continues on next page

Review the chart provided (**Table 12.1**) for each connection type (noted in Kbps) and the related media data rates (noted in KB/sec) you should target for that connection type. Also included is a conservative target data rate for problematic network connections.

You must consider not only the connection speeds of your viewers, but more important, the connection speed of your server. If your QTSS server has a 1.5 Mbps T1 connection to the Internet, you can figure out how many viewers at a particular connection speed you can serve simultaneously. If you are serving up an audio stream that requires a 56 Kbps connection, you can quickly calculate that your server can provide 21 listeners with the audio stream (1500 Kbps – 300 Kbps / 56 Kbps = 21 listeners). When calculating maximum server connections, you should allow approximately 20 percent of connection headroom (300 kbps in this case) to avoid overloading you server's Internet connection.

From the previous example, you can see that doing some calculations and planning up front can ensure you have the appropriate media at the appropriate data rate and a server connected to the Internet at a speed ready to handle the challenge. If you don't plan to stream to the Internet at large but are delivering content within your organization (likely using Ethernet or WiFi), the process is much easier. Since Ethernet speeds are much higher (i.e., 10 Mbps, 100 Mbps) than Internet connections, a QTSS server providing content within your organization can service hundreds of simultaneous streams without hitting a server connection speed limit. But even at Ethernet speeds, a balance needs to be struck between quality (i.e., higher data rates) and quantity. It's best to attempt to author and deliver media that clearly gets your message across without requiring an excessively high data rate.

Table 12.1

Bits and bytes

CONNECTION TYPE	CONNECTION SPEED	TYPICAL MEDIA DATA RATE	CONSERVATIVE MEDIA DATA RATE
33.6 modem	33.6 Kbps	3 KB/sec	2.5 KB/sec
56K modem	53 Kbps	4.8 KB/sec	4 KB/sec
384 Kbps DSL/Cable	384 Kbps	35 KB/sec	30 KB/sec
512 Kbps DSL/Cable	512 Kbps	46 KB/sec	40 KB/sec
768 Kbps DSL/Cable	768 Kbps	70 KB/sec	60 KB/sec
1.5 Mbps T1/Intranet/LAN	1500 Kbps	150 KB/sec	100 KB/sec

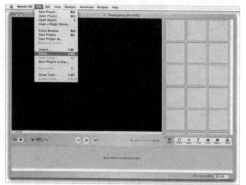

Figure 12.1 Choosing Share from an iMovie HD project is the first step to hinting a movie.

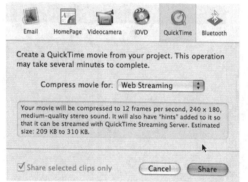

Figure 12.2 Selecting the QuickTime button and the compression for Web Streaming prepares the iMovie HD for streaming.

Hinting files for streaming

Hinting a media file prepares a video or audio file for streaming over a network. A hint track for each valid media is created that provides QTSS with instructions on how to break the media file into smaller parts to send over the network. Hinting a media file literally provides QTSS with a hint (hence the name) on how to best read and deliver a file over the network. Once a media file has been completely authored (captured, edited, compressed), the very last step before copying to a QTSS server is to add hint tracks.

You can hint using a few different tools, some from Apple and some from third-party companies. iMovie HD (which is part of Apple's iLife software suite), for example, provides the ability to hint. QuickTime Pro unlocks QuickTime Player and enables powerful export features, one of which is hinting. QTSS Publisher also provides automatic hinting for media it handles. Apple's Final Cut Pro and many software packages geared toward video compression also offer hinting options.

To hint an iMovie HD project:

1. Open iMovie HD on any Mac OS X computer.

   It is generally located in the /Applications directory, but as the administrator of your Mac OS X computer, you could have moved it anywhere on your system.

2. Open an iMovie HD project and choose File > Share (**Figure 12.1**).

3. When the Share dialog appears, click QuickTime and choose Web Streaming from the Compress pop-up menu (**Figure 12.2**).

Setting Up the QuickTime Streaming Server

The first thing you'll need to do when setting up the QTSS is make a few key decisions. These decisions can always be changed later, but you should always prepare for growth. A Mac OS X Server running other services like DHCP and file sharing and acting as an Open Directory Master isn't the best possible solution for a full-blown QTSS setup. When you're seriously considering multiple connections and high-quality video, you must decide if a separate Xserve running Mac OS X Server with at least 1 GB of RAM is within your budget. Less busy QTSS servers can be run alongside two or three other services with only 512 MB of RAM installed.

Taking a tour of the QTSS setup is easy; you can do so using the Server Admin tool or even a Web browser. After you've launched Server Admin and authenticated as an administrator, choose QuickTime Streaming Server from the Computers & Services list. From there, you have access to the following settings under the Settings tab:

◆ The General tab contains the settings for the streaming media directory, the maximum number of client connections, and the maximum network throughput. When preparing to deploy a QTSS server, make sure the maximum throughput setting is set no higher than the actual network connection speed of your server. The default settings are too high for all but streaming to clients on a local area network (LAN) (**Figure 12.3**).

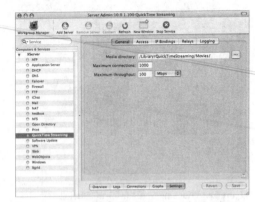

Figure 12.3 Click the General tab under the Settings tab of the QuickTime Streaming Service using the Server Admin tool.

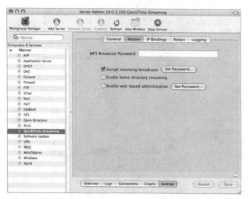

Figure 12.4 The Access tab under the Settings tab of the QuickTime Streaming Service shows the password home directory streaming options.

Figure 12.5 The IP Bindings tab under the Settings tab of the QuickTime Streaming Service permits the binding of the QTSS to more than one IP address.

◆ The Access tab lets you set a password to restrict who can use your server to broadcast MP3 streams (via the bundled Icecast server) or MPEG-4/QuickTime streams. This tab also lets you enable home directory streaming that provides users with accounts on the server the ability to stream files from within their home folder (/Users/<username>/ Sites/Streaming). Here you can also enable Web-based administration, allowing you control QTSS from a remote Web browser (**Figure 12.4**).

◆ The IP Bindings tab provides control over which of your server's IP addresses will be used to provide streaming services. Enabling port 80 streaming allows clients connecting from behind corporate firewalls to have the best opportunity to receive your stream (**Figure 12.5**).

Keep in mind that using port 80 to stream will interfere with any existing Web sites you may be hosting.

continues on next page

◆ The Relays tab lets you create, configure, and delete relays. Relays allow streaming servers to pass a stream from one to another in order to assist with the propagation of that stream. Relays are often used to support streams with a great number of client connections, or to propagate a stream to a remote location that has a limited network connection (**Figure 12.6**).

◆ The Logging tab lets you enable both the Access and Error logs. It is recommended you have Access and Error logs enabled (**Figure 12.7**).

Figure 12.6 The Relays tab shows the currently configured relays.

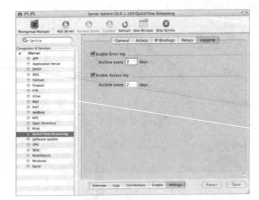

Figure 12.7 Error and access logging are enabled on the Logging tab.

Figure 12.8 Launch the Server Admin tool, and authenticate.

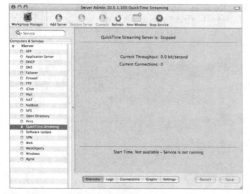

Figure 12.9 The QuickTime Streaming service Overview tab shows the status of the QTSS.

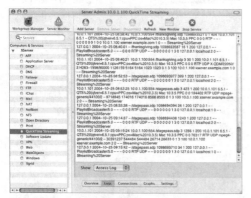

Figure 12.10 The QuickTime Streaming Service Logs tab shows the Access and Error logs.

Once you understand the settings, you can perform the proper configuration to enable the QTSS.

To enable a QTSS:

1. Launch the Server Admin tool from within /Applications/Server, and authenticate as the administrator (**Figure 12.8**).

2. Select the QuickTime Streaming service from the Computers & Services list.

   Notice the five tabs at the bottom of the screen (**Figure 12.9**):

   ▲ **Overview** shows whether the service is running, the current throughput, the current number of connections, and the last time the service was started.

   ▲ **Logs** displays both the Error and Access logs, assisting you in monitoring your QTSS server (**Figure 12.10**).

continues on next page

▲ **Connections** shows, in list form, currently connected users as well as the status of any active relays (**Figure 12.11**).

▲ **Graphs** indicates both the throughput and the number of active users in a chart spanning up to the last seven days (**Figure 12.12**).

▲ **Settings** displays five more tabs, discussed earlier (**Figure 12.13**).

3. Select the Settings tab and then the General tab.

Be sure the movies to be streamed are in the correct directory listed in the Media Directory field (Figure 12.13).

Figure 12.11 Choose the type of connections to be listed using the Connections tab.

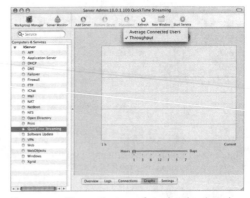

Figure 12.12 Choose the type of graph to be viewed using the Graphs tab.

Figure 12.13 The General tab under the Settings tab shows the path to the movies and the settings for maximum number of client connections and maximum server throughput.

Figure 12.14 Check the IP bindings to be sure the correct IP address is being used for streaming.

Figure 12.15 Enable logging to help troubleshoot and monitor your streaming.

Figure 12.16 Click the Overview tab to view the QTSS's status.

4. Select the IP Bindings tab, and be sure streaming is permitted on the IP address you want (**Figure 12.14**).

5. Select the Logging tab to enable both the Access and Error logs for later troubleshooting and analysis (**Figure 12.15**).

6. Click Start Service in the Toolbar to start the QuickTime Streaming Server service (**Figure 12.16**).

7. View your QTSS's status by clicking the Overview tab.

✔ Tips

■ There are two ways to do QTSS Administration: either through Server Admin or by using Web-based administration. It is wise to be familiar with both methods for administering your streaming server.

■ QTSS provides some sample media files in order to let you test your new server. They are located in the default media directory located at /Library/QuickTimeStreaming/Movies.

SETTING UP THE QUICKTIME STREAMING SERVER

Testing the streaming server

Once your QTSS service is running, you need to make sure it is functioning properly.

To test your QTSS server:

1. Open the QuickTime Player application in the Applications directory.

2. Select File > Open URL and enter a URL to a sample file on your server (**Figure 12.17**).

3. View your stream in the QuickTime Player window (**Figure 12.18**).

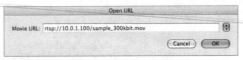

Figure 12.17 In the dialog, enter the URL rtsp://
<hostname>/sample_300kbit.mov, where *hostname*
is the hostname or IP address of your server.

Figure 12.18 The sample video should appear in a new player window.

Figure 12.19 Select the Access tab to locate the Web administration options.

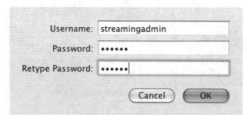

Figure 12.20 Selecting the "Enable web-based administration" check box brings up a user and password dialog.

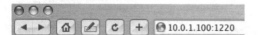

Figure 12.21 Use a Web browser to type in the address and port number of your QTSS server.

Web-Based Administration

Another way to administer QTSS is through the use of a Web browser, such as Safari. Server Admin can be fine for the task of administration, but if you've installed the Darwin Streaming Server on another operating system or Mac OS X Client, you should be aware of Web-based administration.

When Web-based administration is enabled, you have access to the same settings found in Server Admin and QTSS Publisher combined.

To enable Web-based administration:

1. Launch the Server Admin tool from within /Applications/Server, and authenticate as the administrator.

2. Click the QuickTime Streaming Service, click the Settings tab, and then click the Access tab (**Figure 12.19**).

3. Select the "Enable web-based administration" check box.

4. In the dialog that appears, set a username and password for this task (**Figure 12.20**). You may need to click Set Password if this has been done once before.

5. When you've finished making changes, click Save.

6. For security reasons discussed later in this chapter, launch a Web browser of your choice on the server, type in the IP address of the server followed by a colon and the number 1220, and press the Return key (**Figure 12.21**).

   This represents the well-known port number over which the QTSS Web-based administration tool runs.

   continues on next page

7. In the initial Web page that appears, enter the username and password that you entered in step 3, and click Log In (**Figure 12.22**).

Before proceeding to the main admin screens, you may be taken through a simple setup assistant. The options are the same as those available in Server Admin, which we described earlier in the chapter.

You can now manage the QTSS using the Web-based administration tool (**Figure 12.23**).

8. Click any link on the left to view various parameters of your QTSS (**Figure 12.24**). Once you've finished changing settings, always log back out.

✔ Tip

■ It's not a good idea to use the same username and password as your server administrator when you set up Web-based QTSS administration. The Web-based administration tool doesn't currently store the password in the same secure format as other Mac OS X and Mac OS X Server passwords.

Figure 12.22 Enter the username and password in the initial dialog of the QTSS Web-based administration tool.

Figure 12.23 The QTSS Web-based administration tool displays options similar to those of Server Admin.

Figure 12.24 View the log files using the Web-based administration tool.

Administration Security

If you plan to use Web-based administration, you should be aware that no security is provided for the information exchanged between your Web browser and the QTSS server. Security is, however, employed for both Server Admin and QTSS Publisher. Consider using a more general session security technique; for example, when connecting remotely, access your network through a VPN server. Doing so prevents others from gathering information about your QTSS when you use Web-based administration (**Figure 12.25**). You can learn more about VPN in Chapter 10, "Security."

Figure 12.25 While highly useful, the Web-based administration feature does not include any form of security when administering your server.

More Usernames and Passwords

QTSS does not yet utilize Mac OS X Server's centralized Open Directory structure. As a result, any usernames required for use by QTSS are stored outside the reach of Open Directory and require independent creation and maintenance. Since QTSS is similar in design to the open source Apache Web server, the method for managing users (and by extension groups) is much the same. The qtusers and qtgroups files (located at /Library/QuickTimeStreaming/Config/) are used to control access to QTSS Web-based administration and to incoming content, and can even restrict who can view certain media by username and password.

To password-protect streaming media:

1. Launch TextEdit, and then select TextEdit > Preference, and click the New Document tab. In the format section, choose the Plain Text option (**Figure 12.26**).

2. Click the Open and Save tab. In the "When saving a file" section, ensure "Add .txt" extension to plain text files" is unchecked, close the Preferences window, and quit TextEdit (**Figure 12.27**).

3. Relaunch TextEdit, create a new text file and enter the following text:

   ```
   AuthName "QTSS Server"
   AuthUserFile /Library/
   → QuickTimeStreaming/Config/qtusers
   AuthGroupFile /Library/
   → QuickTimeStreaming/Config/qtgroups
   require user viewer
   require group secure-viewers
   ```

4. Select Save from the File menu.

5. Save the text file with the name qtaccess to /Library/QuickTimeStreaming/Movies.

6. Launch the Terminal application located in Applications/Utilities/.

7. Type sudo -s and press the Return key.

8. In the dialog that appears, enter your administrator's password.

9. In Terminal, type the following command:

   ```
   echo "secure-viewers:viewer" >>
   → /Library/QuickTimeStreaming/
   → Config/qtgroups
   ```

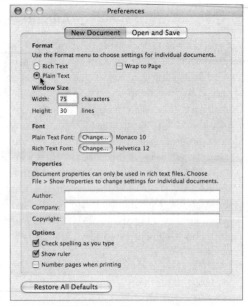

Figure 12.26 Clicking the New Document tab of TextEdit's Preferences.

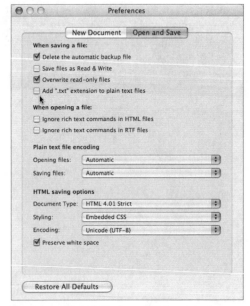

Figure 12.27 Clicking the Open and Save tab of TextEdit's Preferences.

WEB-BASED ADMINISTRATION

10. Press Return.

You have just added the *secure-viewer* group with one user, *viewer*, to QTSS.

11. Type the following command and press Return:

`qtpasswd viewer`

12. In the dialog that appears, enter the password of your choosing.

13. Type `exit`, and quit Terminal.

You have just added the user *viewer* to QTSS.

14. Launch QuickTime Player and select Applications > File > Open URL.

15. Enter the following URL:

`rtsp://<hostname>/sample_300kbit.mov`

where <hostname> is the hostname or IP address of your server.

A password dialog appears in QuickTime Player.

16. Enter `viewer` for username and the password you chose earlier.

17. Click OK.

The stream will now appear.

✔ Tip

- To remove the password restriction, simply remove the file qtaccess located at /Library/QuickTimeStreaming/Movies.

Creating Playlists

Playlists are collections of audio or video files that you want to be streamed. Mac OS X Server includes a few sample files in the /Library/QuickTimeStreaming/Movies directory that you can work with prior to placing your own media files there.

There are two ways to add a playlist: one through the Web-based administration tool, and one using the QTSS Publisher tool. The QTSS Publisher tool will be examined here.

You can create two types of playlists:

MP3 playlists are audio only, based on MP3, and streamed using the Icecast format that can be received by players such as iTunes.

Media playlists can consist of audio, video, or both in either MPEG-4 or QuickTime format. Each playlist you create must contain media of the exact same type (example, all MPEG-4) and must have been encoded the same way (i.e., same data rate, and video frame size, etc). QTSS will review all files in a playlist to ensure they are the same before beginning a playlist stream.

Also, before you can create media playlists, the files in those playlists must be hinted. This includes Advanced Audio Coding (AAC) MPEG-4 files that are simply MPEG-4 files without video. Thankfully, when you add media to your streaming server using QTSS Publisher, the hinting process happens automatically!

To create a video playlist:

1. Launch the QTSS Publisher tool from /Applications/Server, and authenticate as the QTSS administrator (**Figure 12.28**).

2. Click the Media Library icon.

   This window shows all your media files and permits you to sort them based on the column criteria.

Figure 12.28 Launch the QTSS Publisher tool, and authenticate.

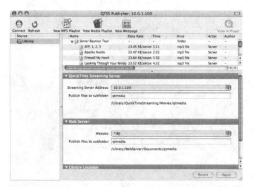

Figure 12.29 Drag your hinted video files into the Media Library window.

Figure 12.30 Create a new media playlist by clicking the New Media Playlist button and entering the appropriate data.

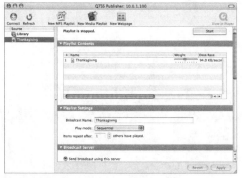

Figure 12.31 Add files from the Media Library to the new playlist and adjust the playlist settings.

3. Drag your video files into the Media Library window (**Figure 12.29**).

4. Click New Media Playlist in the Toolbar.

5. In the dialog that appears, enter the name of the playlist and the URL name (one is suggested for you), and then click Create (**Figure 12.30**).

6. Drag the media file(s) you want to add to the playlist from the media files pane to the Playlist Contents pane and click Apply if necessary (**Figure 12.31**).

7. In the Playlist Settings section, you may choose to change the broadcast name and the play mode.

8. Click Apply to save any changes, and then click Start to start the stream.

continues on next page

9. While you're still working on your server, click View in Player in the Toolbar (see Figure 12.31).

   This will launch the QuickTime Player to test the playlist stream you just created (**Figure 12.32**).

10. After a successful test from your server by using the QuickTime client running on your server, attempt to connect to the stream from another computer connected to the same network. (Perform the test on the same machine you're serving from at first to isolate issues from being network related.)

    The URL for direct access to the stream is provided in the Streaming Link section at the bottom of the current playlist.

Figure 12.32 Test the video stream from a Mac OS X Client using QuickTime Player.

✔ Tips

- It's possible to change the ending part of the URL when creating the playlist so others who have to access the playlist will reduce the chance they will make a typographical error when entering the playlist.

- QTSS Publisher places media files it works with (as well as configuration files) in a special directory located at /Library/Application Support/Apple/ QTSS Publisher/.

Figure 12.33 Clicking on the Media Library shows that all AAC files are now inside the Library.

Figure 12.34 Add a new media playlist.

Creating weighted random AAC playlists

Audio files come in various formats. One format used by iTunes is AAC. An AAC file is simply an MPEG-4 file that contain only audio. With respect to playlists, QTSS Publisher considers them media files and as a result groups them with video MPEG-4 and QuickTime movie files. The end result, however, is the same great audio for your audience to enjoy.

When you're creating files for playlists, you can rate the media in the playlist from 1 to 10 (presented in a slider format), with 10 being the highest rating a file can get. Rating media files in the Playlist Contents section lets media be streamed to the user in weighted random order (not in sequential order), based in part on the rating given each media file. A higher rating means that the media file is likely to be played more often; a lower rating, less often.

To create a weighted random AAC playlist:

1. Launch the QTSS Publisher tool from /Applications/Server, and authenticate as the QTSS administrator.

2. Click the Media Library icon.

   This window shows all your media files and permits you to sort them based on the column criteria. Drag your AAC audio files into the Media Library window (**Figure 12.33**).

3. Click New Media Playlist in the Toolbar.

   In the dialog that appears, enter the name of the playlist and the URL name (one is suggested for you), and click Create (**Figure 12.34**).

continues on next page

4. Drag the AAC file(s) you want to be added to the playlist from the media files pane to the Playlist Contents pane and click Apply if necessary (**Figure 12.35**).

5. In the Playlist Contents section, select each file and drag the Weight sliders left or right to indicate a higher or lower preference for a file.

You're rating your AAC files as you would in iTunes.

6. In the Playlist Settings section, select Weighted Random from the Play Mode pop-up menu.

7. Click Apply and click Start to start the broadcast (**Figure 12.36**).

8. While you're still working on your server, click View in Player in the Toolbar to launch the QuickTime Player to test the playlist stream you just created (**Figure 12.37**).

9. After a successful test from your server to your server (to reduce troubleshooting to mostly non-networking issues, since the stream and the request are on the same computer), attempt to connect to the stream from another computer connected to the same network.

The URL for direct access to the stream is provided in the Streaming Link section at the bottom of the current playlist.

✔ Tips

- It's possible to change the ending part of the URL when creating the playlist so others who have to access the playlist will reduce the chance they will make a typographical error when entering the playlist.

- You create MP3 playlists just like you do an AAC playlist except that you click New MP3 Playlist in the Toolbar instead of New Media Playlist.

Figure 12.35 Create a playlist of AAC files, and specify the name.

Figure 12.36 Drag the weight sliders right for higher a rating or left for a lower rating.

Figure 12.37 QuickTime Player streams the audio broadcast.

Figure 12.38 Send a playlist to another streaming server using options in the Broadcast Server section.

QTSS Publisher Options

When you're using QTSS Publisher to create playlists, you have a few options as to how you can announce the streams.

To send the playlist to another broadcast server:

1. Open the QTSS Publisher application, and select the playlist you want to stream.

2. Navigate to the Broadcast Server section, and click the "Relay broadcast through a different server" radio button (**Figure 12.38**).

3. Fill in the IP address, username, and password of the QTSS or DSS server where you want to send the playlist. Then click Apply.

Creating code for Web pages

Another option is to use QTSS Publisher to create code that you can insert into Web pages you want others to visit. This code can be copied and pasted into the middle of other HTML (Web page) code.

To obtain the code:

1. Open the QTSS Publisher application, select the playlist you want to include in a Web page, and navigate to the Streaming Link section.

2. From the Webpage Action pop-up menu, select what behavior you want your HTML code to perform (**Figure 12.39**).

   The first option will launch the QuickTime Player to stream the playlist, while the other two options will stream the playlist from within the Web page (either after clicking or automatically after the page loads).

3. Click inside the HTML window containing the code, select all the code, and copy it).

4. Switch to your HTML application and paste the code where you want it.

✔ Tip

■ You can also vary the look of the link in both the QuickTime Player and any Web browser when users connect to your streaming server. If you wish to add an image, that image should be a JPEG or GIF image to be compatible with most Web browsers.

Figure 12.39 View the HTML code when selecting a playlist for Web-page streaming.

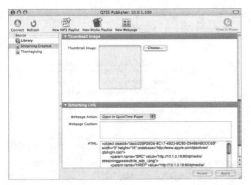

Figure 12.40 The Thumbnail Image section allows you to add a custom image.

Figure 12.41 Select an image for the Web page to show while the stream is playing.

Figure 12.42 Set the caption and custom image.

To add an image to your playlist:

1. Launch the QTSS Publisher tool from /Applications/Server, and authenticate as the QuickTime Streaming Server administrator.

2. Select the playlist you want and navigate to the Thumbnail Image section (**Figure 12.40**).

3. Click Choose and navigate to where the image exists on your server.

4. Select the image and click Open to place it inside the Thumbnail Image window (**Figure 12.41**).

5. Optionally, you can navigate to the Streaming Link section of the playlist and add a caption in the Webpage Caption field (**Figure 12.42**).

6. Click Apply to save the changes.

   You have now added an image to your playlist.

Making use of the image

Once an image is added, you need to choose how it will be used. You have three options, each of which generates different HTML code for use in a Web page:

Open in QuickTime Player allows the image to be embedded so that when you're viewing the stream from a QuickTime Player, the image will appear (**Figure 12.43**).

Embed in Web page places the image in a Web page and plays the stream when the user clicks the image (**Figure 12.44**).

Auto-play in Web page permits the stream to automatically begin playing when the user enters the Web page (**Figure 12.45**).

Remember, each option has different HTML code associate with it. If necessary, you need to copy that code and paste it into the HTML code of your Web page(s).

✔ Tips

- Always click the Apply button after making changes.

- You may need to stop and restart the stream for the changes to take effect.

Figure 12.43 The Open in QuickTime Player option allows the image to be embedded.

Figure 12.44 "Embed in Web page" places the image in a Web page and plays the stream when the user clicks the image.

Figure 12.45 Applying the Auto-play function automatically starts the stream when a user enters the Web page with the link to the stream.

QTSS PUBLISHER OPTIONS

Figure 12.46 Enter the name and URL for the Web page.

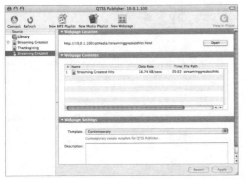

Figure 12.47 Drag a playlist for the source to the Web page section.

Figure 12.48 The Web page appears with the album art, text, and stream controls.

QTSS Publisher Web pages

QTSS Publisher also lets you create preformatted Web pages. These pages include all the code necessary for a Web page to be built so that users can connect and view information about the playlist.

To create a preformatted Web page:

1. Enable your Web site, and start the Web service (see Chapter 9, "Web Technologies," for instruction on starting your Web service).

2. Launch the QTSS Publisher tool from /Applications/Server, and authenticate as the QuickTime Streaming Server administrator.

3. Be sure the playlist you want to create a Web page for is broadcasting (see the "Creating weighted random AAC playlists" task earlier in this chapter).

4. Click New Webpage in the Toolbar.

5. In the dialog that appears, enter the name of the Web page and the URL name (one is suggested for you), and click Create (**Figure 12.46**).

6. Select the Web page you just created from the Source list on the left.

7. Drag a playlist from the Source list to the Web page you just created, also located in the source list, and click Apply (**Figure 12.47**).

8. In the Webpage Settings section, select a Template (Modern is a good choice) and enter a description in the Description area.

9. Click Apply and then click Open.

   Your default Web browser opens and connects to the page you just created (**Figure 12.48**).

✔ Tip

■ A playlist must be running first before being added to a Web page.

MP3 playlist links

MP3 playlists can also be embedded in Web pages and, more important, streamed to iTunes. The setup is similar to that for AAC (.m4a) files and video files; however, there are no options for images in QTSS Publisher. You must edit the Web pages directly to insert album art or other images.

To create an MP3 Web page:

1. Launch the QTSS Publisher tool from /Applications/Server, and authenticate as the QuickTime Streaming Server administrator.

2. Make sure the MP3 playlist is broadcasting (see "Creating weighted random AAC playlists" for similar steps).

3. Click New Webpage in the Toolbar.

4. In the dialog that appears, enter the name of the Web page and the URL name (one is suggested for you), and click Create (**Figure 12.49**).

5. Select the Web page you just created from the Source list on the left.

6. Drag an MP3 playlist from the Source list to the Web page you just created, also located in the source list, and click Apply (**Figure 12.50**).

7. In the Webpage Location section of your Web page, click Open.

   Your default Web browser opens and connects to the page you just created (**Figure 12.51**).

Figure 12.49 Enter the name and URL for the Web page.

Figure 12.50 Drag the MP3 playlist you want onto the Web page.

Figure 12.51 The Web page appears in a browser with all related text.

Figure 12.52 A file is downloaded to your computer.

Figure 12.53 iTunes opens up and the MP3 stream begins.

Figure 12.54 Manually enter a stream URL into the iTunes Open Stream dialog.

Figure 12.55 The Streaming Link section of an MP3 playlist shows the direct URL for the stream.

8. Click the link in the Web page to download the appropriate file (**Figure 12.52**), which iTunes opens automatically (**Figure 12.53**).

✔ Tip

■ To open iTunes directly, choose Advanced > Open Stream, type in the link to your stream, and click OK (**Figure 12.54**). The URL for direct access to the stream is available in the Streaming Link section of the MP3 playlist. Also provided is HTML code you can embed in a Web page (**Figure 12.55**).

QuickTime Broadcaster

QuickTime Broadcaster (QTB) is included with Mac OS X Server, but exists outside Server Admin as a separate application that resides in the Applications directory. QTB is a live encoder application whose primary job is to capture and compress live audio and or video content to a streaming server via the Real-Time Streaming Protocol (RTSP). The Source options in both the Video and Audio tabs are the main considerations for this type of task.

QuickTime Broadcaster was covered briefly in Chapter 2, "Server Tools." To learn how to set up a basic live broadcast, refer to the task "To set up a simple live broadcast" in Chapter 2. This chapter discusses using QuickTime Broadcaster with QTSS.

The following task assumes you're running QuickTime Broadcaster and QTSS on the same Mac OS X Server. You should first have completed the earlier task "To enable a QTSS." You should also have a camera, microphone, or some other supported AV input device connected. If iChat launches when you plug in the device, quit iChat.

To use QuickTime Broadcaster and QTSS to stream live content:

1. Open QuickTime Broadcaster, which is located in your server's Applications directory (**Figure 12.56**).

2. Click Show Details to expand the window.

Figure 12.56 Launch QuickTime Broadcaster.

Live Stream Precautions

Rebroadcasting copyrighted content is prohibited by law. Be sure to check with all parties involved prior to streaming any live audio or video.

Figure 12.57 Set the Network settings in preparation for the broadcast.

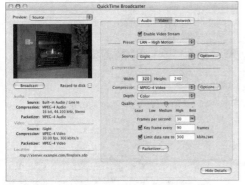

Figure 12.58 View and set the Video settings for the broadcast.

3. Click the Network tab, and complete the following information (**Figure 12.57**):

▲ Leave Transmission set at Automatic Unicast for the type of task being done here.

▲ Host Name is automatically filled in with either the fully qualified domain name or the IP address of your server.

▲ File is the name of the Session Description Protocol (SDP) file used to identify the stream. It's a good idea to use only lowercase letters and numbers—no spaces or other characters.

▲ Username and Password can be used to restrict access to the stream.

▲ Buffer Delay allows for a buildup of data but causes a bigger delay in the delivery of live content.

▲ Broadcast over TCP permits the stream to travel over the TCP protocol, guaranteeing the stream delivered by QTB arrives at the streaming server.

▲ Annotations are used to further identify the broadcast stream. At a minimum, enter a title for your stream to clearly identify it to your viewers.

4. Click the Video tab, and tweak the video input Source details to match the broadcast (**Figure 12.58**).

continues on next page

QUICKTIME BROADCASTER

5. Click the Audio tab, and tweak the audio input Source details to match the broadcast (**Figure 12.59**).

6. Choose File > Save Broadcast Settings in case you wish to use these settings for another broadcast session (**Figure 12.60**).

7. If you've finished tweaking the settings, click Hide Details to reduce the size of the window.

8. Click Broadcast under the video feed to begin the broadcast (**Figure 12.61**).

✔ Tip

■ Prior to beginning the broadcast, you can choose the "Record to disk" check box. When enabled, QTB will (by default) save a hinted copy of the stream on the local hard drive so it can be streamed at a later date. Check the QTB preferences (under Recording) to see where these files are saved.

Figure 12.59 View and set the Audio settings for the broadcast.

Figure 12.60 Save the broadcast settings for later use.

Figure 12.61 Click the Broadcast button to begin the broadcast.

Figure 12.62 Locate the link of a running broadcast.

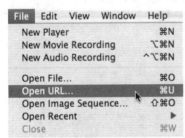

Figure 12.63 Use QuickTime Player to view the broadcast.

Viewing your broadcast

When your broadcast is set up, you should view it on as many machines as possible over different connection speeds to check for variances in quality. For the following task, QuickTime Broadcaster should already be running on your server and reporting audio, video, and CPU usage stats in its main window.

To prepare to view a live broadcast:

1. Locate the stream address in the QuickTime Broadcaster window under Location (**Figure 12.62**).

2. Open the QuickTime Player application in the Applications directory on another computer connected to the same network.

3. Select File > Open URL (**Figure 12.63**). An Open URL dialog appears.

continues on next page

QUICKTIME BROADCASTER

4. Type in the stream address from step 1, and click OK (**Figure 12.64**).

5. View your stream in the QuickTime Player window (**Figure 12.65**).

6. Choose Window > Show Movie Info to open the Movie Info window.

Any annotations you added before the broadcast will appear at the top of this window (**Figure 12.66**).

✔ Tip

■ The Compression settings for both audio and video can be very complex and require background knowledge about color, video, compression, audio and video codecs, and more. When you're changing these settings, it's generally best to test thoroughly on several machines receiving the stream to ensure a quality broadcast.

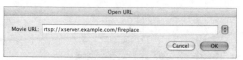

Figure 12.64 Enter the information from the QuickTime Broadcaster Location in the Open URL QuickTime Player dialog.

Figure 12.65 View your video stream using the QuickTime Player from Mac OS X Client.

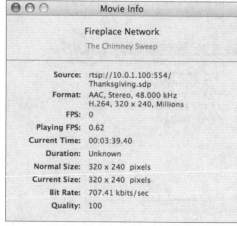

Figure 12.66 Select Window > Show Movie Info to view the properties entered in the QuickTime Broadcaster Network tab as they appear in the final broadcast.

CLIENT MANAGEMENT

Many system administrators believe that a centrally controlled user environment is the ultimate management solution. The concept is simple: Instead of configuring user accounts individually at each computer, management information is centralized on your servers so that you can configure preferences for every account from one central location. For instance, you can prevent a specific user account from launching nonessential applications, restrict printing on an expensive color printer to only a certain group of users, or set a preference that automatically shuts down every idle computer at the end of the workday.

But with such an extensive variety of managed preference options available, this simple concept can become complicated. Fortunately, Mac OS X Server's managed preference settings allow you to micromanage accounts while still working at the macro level. For starters, you can select multiple accounts and simultaneously apply managed preference settings for all of them in one step. Then Mac OS X Server lets you define presets so that newly created or imported accounts are automatically configured with your settings. Most important, you can apply managed preference settings to workgroups or computer lists in addition to individual user accounts.

Now with Mac OS X Server 10.4, you can also manage network views, allowing a managed computer to view only the network settings you want it to view, including specific servers and local computers. This can dramatically reduce the time spent by users when searching large networks for volumes they need.

Prior to implementing managed preferences, consider all the options available and create a plan that will accomplish your administration requirements with the least amount of configuration.

Managing Computer Lists

A *computer list*, as its name implies, is a list of computers. You use computer lists to manage preferences based on computers. In Workgroup Manager, you can add any Mac OS X computer to the computer list based on its hardware Ethernet address or Media Access Control (MAC) address.

You can have as many computer lists as you want, but a computer may be in only one list and each list is limited to 2,000 computers. Any computer outside of a list is automatically in the Guest Computers list. Windows computers have their own list (which is discussed in more detail in "Using Windows computer lists" later in this chapter).

You can configure computer lists on any Mac OS X Server. However, computer lists are only functional on the server acting as an Open Directory master, because such servers are configured to share their directory information with other computers. Also, your client computers must be configured as clients of this directory service system. For more information about directory services and Open Directory, refer to Chapter 3, "Open Directory."

To create a computer list:

1. Launch Workgroup Manager and authenticate as the administrator.

2. Click the Accounts icon in the Toolbar and then click the Computer Lists tab, located with the other account type tabs (**Figure 13.1**).

3. Click the directory authentication icon and select the LDAP directory from the pop-up menu (**Figure 13.2**).

4. Click the New Computer List icon.

   The information in the List window is populated with a new untitled computer list (**Figure 13.3**).

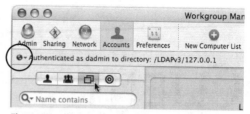

Figure 13.1 Using Workgroup Manager to select the Accounts icon and the Computer accounts button.

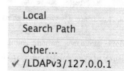

Figure 13.2 Select the LDAP directory database from this pop-up menu.

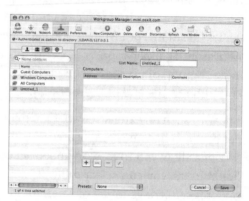

Figure 13.3 A newly created computer list shows up as Untitled_1.

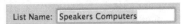

Figure 13.4 The name of the computer list can be used to define physical or logical computer collections.

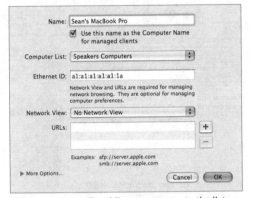

Figure 13.5 Manually adding a computer to the list.

5. Enter an appropriate computer list name (**Figure 13.4**).

6. To add computers to this computer list, *do either of the following:*

 ▲ Click the plus button, and in the dialog that appears, enter the computer's Ethernet address, name, and optional comment in the appropriate fields (**Figure 13.5**). Click Save.

  or

 ▲ Click the ellipsis button (Figure 13.3), and in the browse dialog that appears, select the computer you wish to add to the list (**Figure 13.6**). Click Connect.

7. In Workgroup Manager, verify that the computers have been added to your computer list and click Save (**Figure 13.7**).

Figure 13.6 Browsing all local computers that can be added to the list.

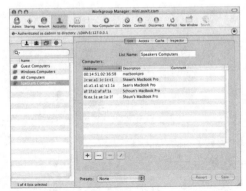

Figure 13.7 Verifying computers were indeed added to the list.

Adding keywords

Once you have added all your computers to their appropriate lists, you may wish to add comments or keywords to various computers, allowing you to search or filter based on keywords.

To add comments and keywords to computer list accounts

1. In Workgroup Manager, click the Accounts icon and the Computer Lists tab.

2. Select a computer from the list and click the pencil icon (edit button) or simply double-click the account.

3. In the dialog that appears, click the More Options triangle to display additional options (**Figure 13.8**).

4. Add your comments in the Comment field (**Figure 13.9**).

5. Select the add/edit keyword button and choose Add Keyword from the pull-down menu (**Figure 13.10**).

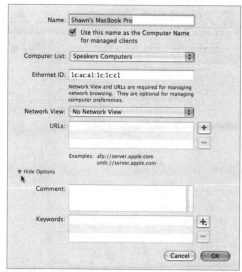

Figure 13.8 Viewing additional options such as comments and keywords.

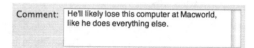

Figure 13.9 Adding a comment to a computer list account.

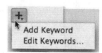

Figure 13.10 Using the button to add keywords to a computer list account.

MANAGING COMPUTER LISTS

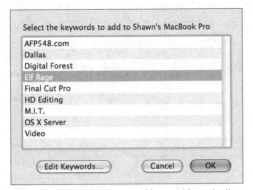

Figure 13.11 Choosing keyword(s) to add from the list.

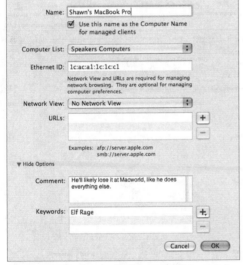

Figure 13.12 Viewing the final computer list account information.

6. Add the keyword(s) in the keyword window and click OK (**Figure 13.11**).

7. In the Computer List settings dialog, click OK to close the dialog (**Figure 13.12**).

8. In the main Workgroup Manager window, click Save to save your changes.

You can change or modify the comments or keywords at any time by double-clicking the computer list account(s) you wish to edit.

✔ Tips

■ You may wish to explore the restricted workgroup access settings, the cache settings, and the managed preference settings for your computer list. Refer to the remaining tasks in this chapter for more information.

■ You can select more than one item in a list by holding down the Shift or Command key while making your selections.

■ As is the case for user and group accounts, you can use account presets to automatically configure new computer lists. See Chapter 4, "User and Group Management," for more information.

Using the Guest Computers list

Any Mac OS X computer that isn't defined
in a custom computer list automatically
uses the settings from the Guest Computers
list. Generally, it's considered bad practice to
allow any of your managed computers to fall
into the Guest Computers list, because you
should reserve this list for computers you
don't want to manage. Take great care with
your choices or you may inadvertently control computers you didn't intend to manage.

To manage the Guest Computers list:

1. In Workgroup Manager, click the
   Accounts icon and the Computer Lists
   tab, and then select Guest Computers.

2. Click the List tab, and choose *one of the
   following options* (**Figure 13.13**):

   ▲ **Inherit preferences for Guest
   Computers**, the default setting,
   allows guest computers to inherit
   their managed preferences from your
   Open Directory server.

   ▲ **Define Guest Computer preferences here** lets you configure specific
   managed preferences, restricted workgroup access settings, cache settings,
   and managed preference settings for
   guest computers (these options will
   be discussed in more detail in the
   "Managing Preferences" section, later
   in this chapter).

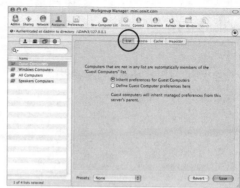

Figure 13.13 Locating guest computer options.

MANAGING COMPUTER LISTS

Figure 13.14 Managing Windows computer list accounts from Workgroup Manager.

Using the Windows Computers list

One of the default computer lists automatically created by the server tools is the Windows Computers list. If your Mac OS X Server is configured as a Windows Primary Domain Controller (PDC), any Windows client supported by your server needs to be in this list. (See Chapter 5, "File Sharing," for more about configuring your Mac OS X Server as a PDC.)

Windows computers can be in only one list. The first time a Windows client joins your server's PDC, it's automatically added to this list. You can also manually configure Windows computers in this list.

To manage the Windows Computers list:

1. In Workgroup Manager, click the Accounts icon and the Computer Lists tab, and then select Windows Computers (**Figure 13.14**).

   Because you can only manage the computer list in the Windows Computers window, the Access and Cache tabs are unavailable. Also, any Windows computer that has already joined your server's PDC is automatically added to this list.

2. To manually add a Windows computer, click the Add button.

   continues on next page

3. In the dialog that appears (**Figure 13.15**), enter the Windows computer's NetBIOS name and an optional description in the appropriate fields. Click Save.

4. In Workgroup Manager, click Save.

✔ Tips

■ You can't modify the NetBIOS name of a Windows computer in the list. You can, however, modify the description by double-clicking the description you wish to edit and entering the new value. When you've finished, press Enter or click anywhere else.

■ To delete a computer from the list, select it from the Windows Computers list and then click the Delete button. Don't delete the entire Windows Computers list!

■ Windows uses NetBIOS names to identify client computers. These names are typically in all uppercase letters and limited to 25 characters.

■ You can try to apply managed preference settings for these Windows computers, but they will ignore your settings. Windows is so different from Mac OS X that Workgroup Manager settings don't apply to Windows computers.

Figure 13.15 Manually adding Windows computer list accounts.

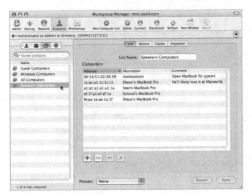

Figure 13.16 Selecting a computer list using Workgroup Manager.

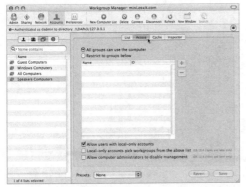

Figure 13.17 Viewing access control options when dealing with a computer list.

Figure 13.18 Viewing the Group drawer from the Computer List Accounts tab within Workgroup Manager.

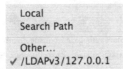

Figure 13.19 Select the LDAP directory database from this pop-up menu.

Restricting login access

By default, any user in any group can log in to any client computer that is connected to your directory system. You can restrict user logins to your computers by combining computer lists with workgroups. In Workgroup Manager, you restrict user login to certain workgroups of users for a computer list. In other words, you assign users to workgroups, and then you assign workgroups to computer lists.

Obviously, in order for this approach to work, you must have already configured workgroups and computer lists. See Chapter 4 for more information.

To restrict login access:

1. In Workgroup Manager, click the Accounts icon and the Computer Lists tab, and then select a computer list that you created (**Figure 13.16**).

2. Click the Access tab to view this computer list's workgroup access settings (**Figure 13.17**).

    By default, any user belonging to any workgroup can log in to the computers in this list.

3. Select the "Restrict to groups below" radio button and click the Add button.

    A window appears in which you can select the workgroups you wish to assign to this computer list (**Figure 13.18**).

4. Click the directory authentication icon at the top of the window and select the appropriate directory database from the pop-up menu (**Figure 13.19**).

    The directory you are currently managing will be the default selection and, most likely, will be the one you want to use.

continues on next page

5. Drag workgroup(s) from the window to the restricted groups list (**Figure 13.20**).

Here, you are restricting the computer list called Marketing to a workgroup called Marketing. It's a good idea to use the same name when you intend to restrict access.

6. To permit access to these computers, select *one or all of the following* options at the bottom of the Access tab:

▲ Click the "Allow users with local-only accounts" check box to let users with local accounts log in.

▲ Click the "Local-only accounts pick workgroups from the above list" check box to let local accounts pick from the workgroup list.

▲ Click the "Allow computer administrators to disable management" check box to let individual administrators disable management for their workgroups.

or

To make restrictions as tough as possible, leave all of these options unchecked.

7. When you've finished making changes, click Save.

Now, when users attempt to log in, their accounts will be compared to the workgroups assigned to the computer list in which the computer resides. If users aren't part of a workgroup allowed to use this computer, then they won't be allowed to log in. If they belong to one of the allowed workgroups, they will continue to log in as normal. However, if users belong to more than one workgroup, they will be required to specify which workgroup they want to use for this session.

✔ Tip

■ To select more than one item in a list, hold down Shift or Command while making selections.

Figure 13.20 Dragging a group from the group list into the Restricted Groups window to restrict that group to using the selected computer list.

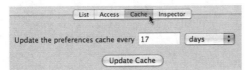

Figure 13.21 Viewing the Cache tab of a chosen computer list.

Figure 13.22 Making changes to the Cache tab for a chosen computer list.

Configuring computer caches

To facilitate computers that may occasionally disconnect from your directory server, like laptops, and to improve directory service performance, managed preference settings are cached locally on client computers. In Workgroup Manager, you can configure how often this cache is automatically updated to the client if any changes are made on the parent directory server. Otherwise, the next time a user logs in to an account, the new account settings will be read, and the local cache file will be updated.

To configure computer cache settings:

1. In Workgroup Manager, click the Accounts icon and the Computer Lists tab, and then select a computer list that you created.

2. Click the Cache tab to view this computer list's cache settings (**Figure 13.21**).

3. To change the cache intervals, enter a different value in the appropriate field, and select a unit of time from the pop-up menu (**Figure 13.22**).

4. To immediately update the cache files on the computers in this list, click Update Cache.

5. In Workgroup Manager, click Save.

   The cache files will be automatically updated based on the schedule you set or whenever a user logs in.

✔ Tip

■ To update the cached preferences on a client computer, hold down the Shift key when you log in. When a dialog appears, click Refresh Preferences to update the cached preference information.

Managing Preferences

By default, Mac OS X Server doesn't have any managed preference settings enabled. Before you begin configuring these settings, consider all of your management options. For starters, Mac OS X Server lets you configure unique managed preferences separately for user, workgroup, and computer list accounts. In other words, you can configure some or all of the available managed preference settings for any account type independently of another account type's settings.

To compound this already complicated situation, each user account can belong to multiple workgroups, and each workgroup account can belong to multiple computer lists. Additionally, computer lists can also have network-managed preferences. That is, a computer that is managed via a computer list can have the network view specified.

With all these configuration options available, situations often arise in which a user account may have conflicting managed preference settings. Mac OS X resolves these conflicts by first narrowing the login to only one of each account type. Obviously, a user account is unique among other user accounts, but computers are also individually unique because they can belong to only one computer list account. The only variable that can occur is when a user is part of multiple workgroups. However, during login, this situation is resolved, because users must choose one workgroup to belong to during their session.

Best Practices for Managed Preferences

A few best practices will help you avoid managed-preference conflict and, as a result, save time:

- Always start with a plan.

- Manage each preference only once at specific account types. For example, manage the Printer List settings only in the computer list accounts.

- Make exceptions only at the user account level. This approach keeps workgroups and your potential confusion to a minimum.

Once the login is narrowed to a single user, workgroup, and computer list account, conflicting managed preferences pan out into one of the following three situations:

◆ A managed setting is configured for only one account type. In this case, there are no conflicts among settings, so the resulting preference is inherited based on the one managed account type.

◆ A managed setting is configured for multiple account types, and the result is overridden based on the most specific managed account type. User account options are the most specific, followed by computer list account options, followed by workgroup account options. Most managed preferences follow this override rule.

◆ A managed setting is configured for multiple account types, and the setting uses list-type options. In this case, the conflicting results are combined based on all the managed account types. The Application Items, Dock Items, Printer List, and Login Items managed preferences follow this combined rule.

When a Mac OS X computer is managed, regardless of whether the management is based on user, group, or computer accounts, there are three areas where these settings are transferred down to the Mac OS X computer, allowing for the management to take place regardless of whether the user is subsequently connected and bound to the server or not. The settings are saved in the local NetInfo database under the Config records, in the /Library folder under managed settings, and in the logged-in user's Library folder. To rid the Mac OS X computer of these managed settings, all three locations must be cleared out and the computer restarted.

✔ **Tip**

■ You may find that an organizational tool such as a group outline or flowchart software like OmniGraffle (www.omnigroup. com) can help you plan the best implementation for your needs.

To configure managed preferences:

1. In Workgroup Manager, click the directory authentication icon and select the LDAP directory database from the pop-up menu (**Figure 13.23**).

2. From the accounts list, (the Groups list is shown here) select the desired user, workgroup, or computer list (**Figure 13.24**).

3. Click the Preferences icon in the toolbar, and depending on whether you chose a user, group, or computer list, you will see slightly different icons in the window below:

   ▲ If you selected a user or workgroup account, the Preferences window appears, in which you can select one of 13 managed preference icons (**Figure 13.25**).

   ▲ If you selected a computer list account, you can choose from one additional managed preference icon (Energy Saver) (**Figure 13.26**).

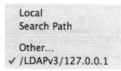

Figure 13.23 Select the LDAP directory database from this pop-up menu.

Figure 13.24 Choosing the appropriate group for managing preferences.

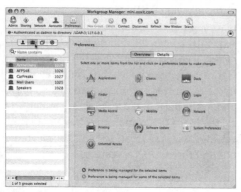

Figure 13.25 Available preferences for user and group accounts.

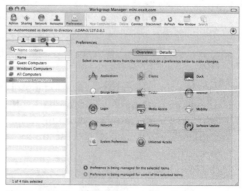

Figure 13.26 Computer list account preferences include Energy Saver.

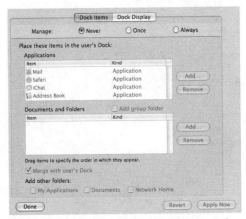

Figure 13.27 Selecting a preference reveals most of the managed options.

Figure 13.28 Most preferences can be managed three ways: Never, Once, and Always.

4. Click the preference you wish to manage to reveal the available options (**Figure 13.27**).

5. Depending on the preference you chose, you may select *one of the following options*, which appear at the top of every managed preference window (**Figure 13.28**):

   ▲ **None**—The default setting for every managed preference. For the selected account, this preference isn't managed.

   ▲ **Once**—Available for all managed preferences. For the selected account, this preference is managed the first time a user logs in. Afterward, the user may configure their own custom preferences.

   ▲ **Always**—Available for every managed preference. For the selected account, this preference is always managed; the user can't make any changes to this setting.

6. To discard your changes, click Revert.

   or

   When you've finished making changes, click Apply Now.

continues on next page

7. Click Done to return to the managed preferences icon view.

The arrow icon next to a preference icon indicates that managed preferences are configured for this item. The changes you've made will automatically be updated to the client computers based on the cache schedule set in the computer lists or whenever the user logs in next.

✔ Tips

■ Each managed preference is saved in the same manner. Refer to tasks later in this chapter for more specific information on each managed preference.

■ To configure managed preferences for Mac OS 9 computers, you must use the Macintosh Manager service and configuration tools.

■ As is the case for group and user accounts, you can use account presets to automatically configure new computer lists. See Chapter 4 for more information.

About the Applications managed preference

Before you read the following sections on different types of managed preferences, be sure you're familiar with the concepts discussed in the previous task. The figures in these sections show a variety of managed preference configurations. They are only examples and should not be interpreted as the most appropriate configuration for your needs.

MANAGING PREFERENCES

Figure 13.29 Choosing what applications can be launched via the Applications managed preferences.

The Applications managed preference icon lets you restrict the launching of applications on Mac OS X computers. You can do the following (**Figure 13.29**):

◆ Specify a list of approved or unapproved applications.

◆ Restrict the launching of local applications.

◆ Restrict approved applications from launching other applications.

◆ Restrict the use of Unix tools.

You should test before restricting Unix tools as many applications make calls to Unix executables (what Apple calls *tools* here). If you restrict Unix tools, you may find that some applications that are permitted to run will not function properly.

Except where noted, all of the managed preferences discussed in the following sections are available to user, workgroup, and computer list account types. You can't manage these preferences just once, because most are either unmanaged or always managed. If there are conflicting account settings, the resulting lists will be a combination of all the settings. Otherwise, all conflicting account settings for these managed preferences follow the override rule.

✔ Tip

■ Workgroup Manager automatically finds applications on the computer it's running on; therefore when you're creating the applications list, it's best to use Workgroup Manager from one of the clients you'll be managing.

About the Classic managed preference

The Classic managed preference icon lets you configure the Classic environment and restrict access to Classic-related items on Mac OS X computers. In the Startup tab you can do the following (**Figure 13.30**):

◆ Require that Classic launch after user login.

◆ Warn the user before Classic attempts to launch.

◆ Specify a custom location for the Classic system items.

On the Advanced tab, you can do the following (**Figure 13.31**):

◆ Allow special Classic startup modes.

◆ Restrict access to Classic Apple menu items such as the Chooser and Network Browser.

◆ Specify the amount of time before Classic can go to sleep when idle, thereby saving both memory and CPU usage.

✔ Tips

■ Classic managed preferences work only if a copy of Mac OS 9 is installed or available as a disk image on the Mac OS X computer.

■ If you restrict access to the Classic Startup application using the Applications managed preference, users won't be able to launch Classic.

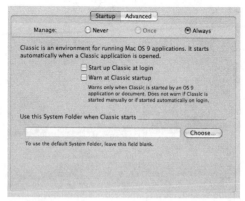

Figure 13.30 The Startup tab of the Classic managed preferences permits Classic to start up at login.

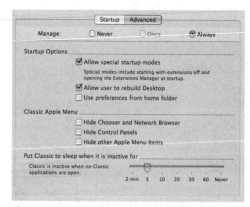

Figure 13.31 The Advanced tab of Classic managed preferences permits hiding certain classic Apple menu items.

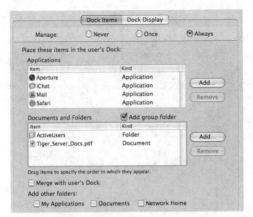

Figure 13.32 The Dock managed preference lets you define the contents of the Dock and define the Dock's visual settings on Mac OS X computers.

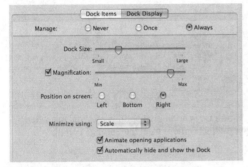

Figure 13.33 The Dock Display tab of the Dock managed preference window offers additional options.

About the Dock managed preference

The Dock managed preference icon lets you define the contents of the Dock and define the Dock's visual settings on Mac OS X computers. In the Dock Items tab you can do the following (**Figure 13.32**):

◆ Populate the Dock with applications or documents.

◆ Restrict the user from modifying the contents of the Dock.

◆ When managing group preferences, you have the additional option of adding the group folder to the Dock.

◆ Merge the Dock with the user's existing Dock.

In the Dock Display tab, you can do the following (**Figure 13.33**):

◆ Specify all the visual aspects of the Dock, including its size, location, and magnification.

◆ Specify the minimize window animation.

In addition to leaving this preference unmanaged, you can manage it once or always.

✔ Tip

■ Make sure any item you add to the Dock Items list is accessible to the client computers. Otherwise, those items will show up with a question mark icon in the Dock.

MANAGING PREFERENCES

About the Energy Saver managed preference

The Energy Saver managed preference icon lets you define the power-saving features for both desktop and portable Mac OS X computers. In the Desktop tab, you can do the following to both Mac OS X and Mac OS X Server (**Figure 13.34**):

◆ Specify the amount of time the computer waits before it enters various sleep states.

◆ Specify various wakeup options by choosing Options from the Settings pop-up menu (**Figure 13.35**).

On the Portable tab, you can do the following (**Figure 13.36**):

◆ Specify the amount of time the computer waits before it enters various sleep states.

◆ Specify various wakeup options by choosing Options from the Settings pop-up menu (**Figure 13.37**).

◆ Specify unique Energy Saver settings for either using the power adapter or battery power.

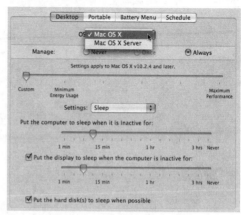

Figure 13.34 The Energy Saver managed preference lets you define the power-saving features for both desktop and probable Mac OS X computers.

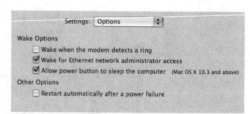

Figure 13.35 Additional options are available when you select Options from the Settings pop-up.

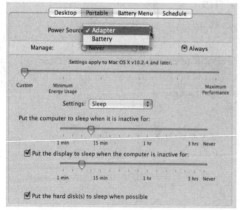

Figure 13.36 The Portable tab has choices when running portables on either battery power or plugged in.

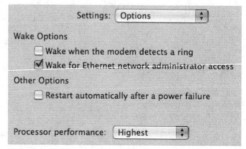

Figure 13.37 The Portable tab also has additional options available when you select Options from the Settings pop-up.

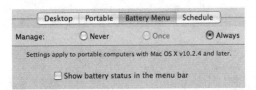

Figure 13.38 The Battery Menu tab permits the battery icon to be added to the menu bar.

Figure 13.39 The Schedule tab is used to manage startup, sleep, and shutdown times.

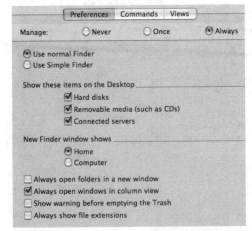

Figure 13.40 The Finder managed preference lets you define the Finder interface options for Mac OS X computers.

In the Battery Menu tab, you can enable the battery status for portable computers (**Figure 13.38**). In the Schedule tab, you can specify daily startup, sleep, or shutdown times for both Mac OS X and Mac OS X Server (**Figure 13.39**).

Unlike the other managed preferences discussed previously, the Energy Saver managed preference is only available to computer list accounts.

✔ Tip

- All of the Energy Saver managed preferences work only with Mac OS X 10.2.4 and above. The Schedule settings work only with Mac OS X 10.3 and above.

About the Finder managed preference

The Finder managed preference icon lets you define the Finder interface options for Mac OS X computers. In the Preferences tab, you can do the following (**Figure 13.40**):

- ◆ Choose between normal or the more restrictive Simple Finder modes.

- ◆ Specify the items that appear on the Desktop.

- ◆ Specify various Finder view options.

In the Commands tab, you can do the following (**Figure 13.41**):

◆ Allow or restrict various Finder volume commands, such as ejecting disks or connecting to servers.

◆ Allow or restrict the Go To Folder command.

◆ Allow or restrict shutdown and restart commands.

In the Views tab, you can specify icon and list view settings separately for the Desktop, Default, and Computer views (**Figure 13.42**).

In addition to leaving settings in the Preferences tab and Views tab unmanaged, you can manage these settings once or always. Settings in the Commands tab are either unmanaged or always managed.

✔ Tips

■ Removing access to the Restart command only allows users to shut the machine down and start it back up with the power button. This may help flush stubborn temporary files that may linger if you simply restart.

■ Removing access to the Go To Folder command reduces the chances that a user will go poking around in the hidden directories, such as /private, /usr, /bin, and others.

■ Forcing the Desktop view to show icons as large as possible, snapped to a grid and organized by some attribute, is a great way to discourage users from saving files to their Desktop folder.

■ The Simple Finder is a limited interface that is great for new computer users or kiosk computers that are open to the public.

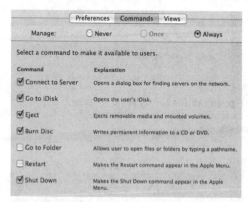

Figure 13.41 Additional options are available on the Commands tab...

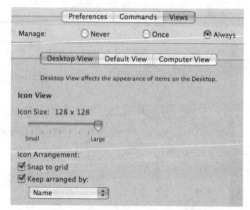

Figure 13.42 ...and the Views tab, most of which are self-explanatory.

Figure 13.43 The Internet managed preference lets you define email settings on Mac OS X computers and...

Figure 13.44 ...the Web tab provides additional options such as application preference and home page.

About the Internet managed preference

The Internet managed preference icon lets you define the Internet settings on Mac OS X computers. In the Email tab, you can do the following (**Figure 13.43**):

◆ Specify the default email application.

◆ Specify the user's email account configuration.

◆ Specify email server and protocol information.

In the Web tab, you can do the following (**Figure 13.44**):

◆ Specify the default Web browser application.

◆ Specify home and search Web pages.

◆ Specify the local location for downloaded files.

In addition to leaving this preference unmanaged, you can manage it once or always.

✔ Tips

■ Be sure you allow access for the applications you define as the default email and Web browser if you're also using Applications managed preferences.

■ The Email Address field should be managed only at the user account level. You can, however, leave it blank if you wish to manage other email settings, such as incoming and outgoing mail server information.

About the Login managed preference

The Login managed preference icon lets you define the Login window options for Mac OS X computers. Four types of login management are available, and only one is available to be managed via user, group, and/or computer list accounts (Login Items). The other three managed preferences devoted to login (login and logout scripts, login window interface variables, and auto-logout and Fast User Switching management) are only available to be managed via computer lists accounts. In the Login Items tab, you can do the following (**Figure 13.45**):

◆ Create a list of applications to launch, server volumes to connect to, or folders to open after the user logs in.

◆ Restrict users from adding their own login items and temporarily disabling login items by holding down the Shift key at login.

◆ Add network home share points (if they are not automounted) and merge listed login items with the user's existing items; this option will only be available when setting managed preference for the initial login (Once).

In the Scripts tab, you can do the following (**Figure 13.46**):

◆ Have scripts run at login and logout, regardless of user.

◆ Include local scripts on Mac OS X computers.

✔ Tips

■ Trusted binding must be used for the scripts to work. (Refer to Chapter 3 for more information.)

■ The root com.apple.loginwindow property list must contain a key EnableMCX-LoginScripts and be set to True for the scripts to work.

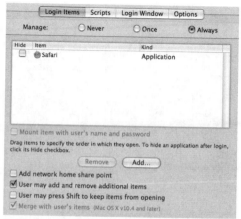

Figure 13.45 The Login managed preference lets you define login items and potential mounts when a user logs in.

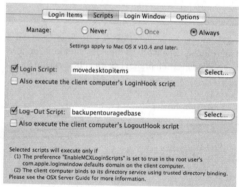

Figure 13.46 Login scripts can be managed efficiently by choosing a group or computer list account to which to apply these settings.

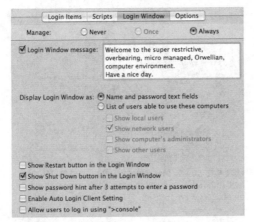

Figure 13.47 The Login Window tab permits text and manipulation of other content on and surrounding the Login window.

Figure 13.48 The view of a Login window on a Mac OS X computer that is being managed.

Figure 13.49 The Options tab allows or denies access to fast user switching and auto-logout.

In the Login Window tab, you can do the following (**Figure 13.47**):

◆ Choose login window message and view options for listed users.

◆ Remove the auto-login setting.

◆ Disable other login window features such as Restart and Shutdown buttons and console login. Login window text appears the next time a user who is a member of that computer list starts up a bound computer (**Figure 13.48**).

In the Options tab, you can do the following (**Figure 13.49**):

◆ Enable fast user switching.

◆ Configure the amount of idle time that can pass before the system automatically logs out the user.

✔ Tips

■ Be sure you allow access for the applications in the Login Items list if you're also using Applications managed preferences.

■ The Auto Log-Out settings work only with Mac OS X 10.3 or later.

About the Media Access managed preference

The Media Access managed preference icon lets you define controlled access to removable media on Mac OS X computers. In the Disk Media tab, you can do the following (**Figure 13.50**):

◆ Completely restrict access to optical disk media, or require administrator authentication.

◆ Completely restrict access to recordable optical disk media, or require administrator authentication.

In the Other Media tab, you can do the following (**Figure 13.51**):

◆ Completely restrict access to internal disks, or require administrator authentication.

◆ Completely restrict access to external disks, or require administrator authentication.

◆ Force removable media to be ejected when the user logs out.

✔ Tip

■ The only instance where you should completely restrict access to the internal disks is if your client computers start up from a NetBoot server.

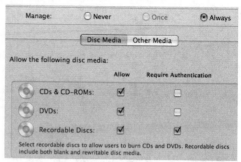

Figure 13.50 The Media Access managed preference lets you define controlled access to removable media on Mac OS X computers.

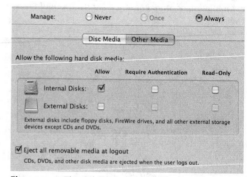

Figure 13.51 The Other Media tab offers additional options, such as making a device mount as read-only.

MANAGING PREFERENCES

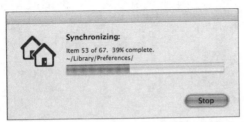

Figure 13.52 The window that appears after you log in with a username and password; but before the Desktop appears.

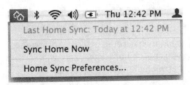

Figure 13.53 Manual syncing of the local and network home folders via the Home Sync menu item.

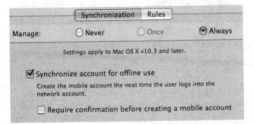

Figure 13.54 The Mobile Account managed preference lets you enable the mobile user account option on Mac OS X computers.

About the Mobile Accounts managed preference

A typical network user account requires that the client computer be always connected to the directory server and the home folder share point. On the other hand, mobile accounts are special network user accounts that don't require a persistent connection to your servers. The first time a mobile-account user logs in to a computer, a new home folder is created for this user on the client computer's local startup volume based on the user template on that client computer. The user's account information and managed preference settings are cached in the client computer's local user database.

A mobile-account user can disconnect from your network at any time, and all their account settings remain intact on the local client computer. Any time the computer is on your network and the user logs in, the account information and managed preference settings caches are updated (**Figure 13.52**). The user's home folder can be synchronized and various options exist on how that synchronization takes place, such as through a logged-in user's menu bar (**Figure 13.53**). Synchronization will be discussed later in this section.

The Mobile Account managed preference icon lets you enable the mobile user account option on Mac OS X computers, including the following (**Figure 13.54**):

◆ Enable the Mobile Account option.

◆ Require administrator authentication to create the Mobile Account home folder on the local computer.

In the Rules tab, the Login & Logout Sync and Background Sync tabs permit the following (**Figure 13.55**):

◆ Decide what directories should be synced and—more important—should *not*.

◆ Specify whether to merge with the users settings

The Rules tab lets you specify how often you want synchronization to occur when using background syncing (**Figure 13.56**).

When you set up active syncing, take care to note exactly what Apple does not sync. Apple chose not to sync 13 items (all set to the full path of the final directory or file). When you add to this list, you can use the up/down arrows (shown in Figure 13.55) to choose how to locate items that should not be synced. Your choices appear in the pop-up menu (**Figure 13.57**).

✔ Tips

■ The Mobile Account settings work only with Mac OS X 10.3 or later; synchronization of accounts works only with Mac OS X 10.4 or later.

■ Choosing the Once option when doing login/logout and/or background syncing allows users to choose when they sync from that point on, from the menu bar. This approach can backfire, as users may not be diligent about syncing their directories.

■ It is wise to not sync users' Music, Pictures, and Movies folders unless absolutely necessary, due to the potentially large file transfers that may occur.

■ If users are using Entourage, be aware that the entire Entourage database will be synchronized each time the synchronization process takes place. This file can become quite large, and in a managed environment with several hundred users, the synchronization process can cause a significant increase in network traffic.

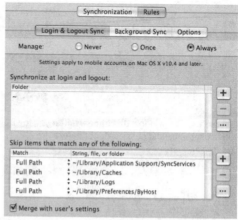

Figure 13.55 The Mobile Account managed preference Rules tab lets you choose how, when, and what is synchronized between the client and server.

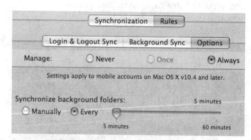

Figure 13.56 When syncing client and server home directories, you can choose how often the automatic syncing takes place, or you can allow manual syncing.

Figure 13.57 Parameters used to define how to locate items to be synced.

MANAGING PREFERENCES

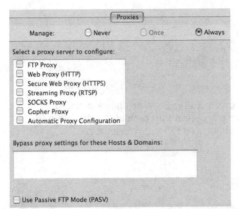

Figure 13.58 The Network managed preference sets proxy information for a variety of sources.

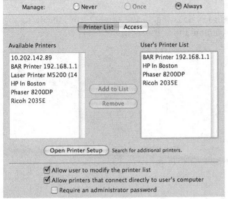

Figure 13.59 The Printing managed preference lets you define controlled access printers on Mac OS X computers.

Figure 13.60 The Access tab provides additional options such as default printer and access control.

About the Network managed preference

The Network managed preference icon lets you define proxy settings on Mac OS X computers in the following ways (**Figure 13.58**):

◆ Specify the proxies, if any, for FTP, Web, Secure Web, Streaming, and others.

◆ Bypass proxies for specific domains, such as internal or external mail servers.

About the Printing managed preference

The Printing managed preference icon lets you define controlled access printers on Mac OS X computers. In the Printer List tab, you can do the following (**Figure 13.59**):

◆ Specify the printers available in the Printer list.

◆ Restrict the user from adding new printers to the local computer's Printer list.

◆ Completely restrict access to directly connected local printers, or require administrator authentication.

In the Access tab, you can specify the default printer and require administrator authentication on a per-printer basis (**Figure 13.60**).

✔ Tips

■ Workgroup Manager automatically finds printers in the Printer list on the computer it's running on, not the server if Workgroup Manager is running remotely.

■ When you're creating the Printer list, it's best to use Workgroup Manager from one of the clients you'll be managing if running it directly on the server is not feasible.

■ Printer quotas are managed in each user's account settings. See Chapter 4 for more information.

About the Software Update managed preference and Software Update service

The Software Update managed preference lets you restrict access to where bound Mac OS X computers search for software updates by directing them to your Mac OS X Server instead of Apple's server (**Figure 13.61**).

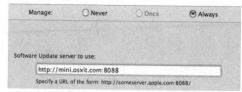

Figure 13.61 The Software Update managed preference points the computer to the correct location to receive software updates.

Forcing the location of the Software Update server will not function properly unless you turn on the Software Update service, which you do via the Server Admin tool. When selecting the Software Update service, you have some choices as to how the updates are handled.

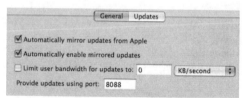

Figure 13.62 Using Server Admin to decide how to implement the Software Update service.

System updates are then managed in two different fashions; updates are downloaded to the server and do not mirror Apple updates automatically. This enables you to push out specific updates you choose but not automatically download new updates until you click Check Now under the Updates tab in the Software Update service.

The second method is to automatically enable mirrored updates, enabling users to get the latest updates from your server without you checking them first. They still come from your server, so bandwidth is conserved, but you do not discriminate on which updates they are allowed to install (**Figure 13.62**).

Figure 13.63 Locating the Software Update service using Server Admin.

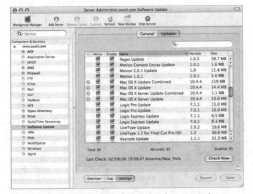

Figure 13.64 A large collection of software updates from Apple are stored locally on the server for download by bound Mac OS X computers.

Figure 13.65 Check boxes in the Software Update service permit the mirroring of Apple downloads and the option to enable those downloads.

To enable the Software Update service:

1. Open the Server Admin tool, authenticate as the administrator, and select the Software Update service (**Figure 13.63**).

2. Select the Updates tab and click Check Now (**Figure 13.64**).

   Depending on your Internet connection, be prepared to wait as the Software Update service downloads almost every conceivable update to your server.

3. Click the General tab and choose how to enable the service, as mirrored or not mirrored, and if mirrored, whether to enable all mirrored updates (**Figure 13.65**).

4. You then decide whether or not to limit bandwidth to a given speed and what port to choose.

   Use port 8088 if you do not want to reconfigure all your Mac OS X computers to look over another port.

continues on next page

MANAGING PREFERENCES

5. Click the Updates tab again and deselect the updates that are not germane to your Mac OS X computers (**Figure 13.66**).

6. Make sure you have managed accounts in one fashion or another (user, group, computer list) and enable the Software Update managed preference to point to your server (**Figure 13.67**).

7. Click Start in the toolbar of Server Admin to start the Software Update service.

   or

   You can also run this via the command line by navigating to the /usr/local/bin/ directory and running the swupd_syncd daemon.

✔ Tips

- All downloaded updates are located in the /usr/share/swupd/html/ directory.

- You can view the Software Update log file by using Server Admin and clicking Software Update service, then clicking the Log tab at the bottom of the window.

- Should the Software Update service not behave as expected, remove the downloaded updates and click Check Now again to re-sync the updates.

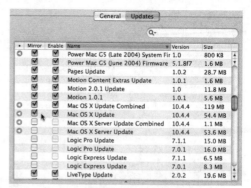

Figure 13.66 Disabling nonessential downloads.

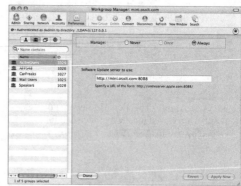

Figure 13.67 Setting the location of the software update service server in Workgroup Manager.

MANAGING PREFERENCES

Figure 13.68 The System Preferences managed preference lets you restrict access to System Preferences panes on Mac OS X computers.

About the System Preferences managed preference

The System Preferences managed preference icon lets you restrict access to System Preferences panes on Mac OS X computers. In particular, you can specify a list of approved System Preferences panes and hide all other Preferences panes from the user (**Figure 13.68**).

✔ Tips

- ■ If you restrict access to the System Preferences application using the Applications managed preference, then users won't be able to use any System Preference panes.

- ■ Unless absolutely necessary, you should disallow access to the QuickTime preference pane if you have a QuickTime Pro license. Any user can click on this preference pane and retrieve the name and serial number, making theft of another user's serial number a very easy task.

MANAGING PREFERENCES

About the Universal Access managed preference

The Universal Access managed preference icon lets you define settings that help users who have physical limitations that impair their ability to use Mac OS X computers. In the Seeing tab, you can do the following (**Figure 13.69**):

◆ Enable and specify screen zoom options that magnify the screen image.

◆ Enable grayscale and inverted color options.

In the Hearing tab of the Universal Access managed preference, you can specify that the screen flash whenever the audible alert sounds (**Figure 13.70**).

In the Keyboard tab, you can do the following (**Figure 13.71**):

◆ Enable and specify Sticky Keys options that hold the modifier keys.

◆ Enable and specify Slow Keys options that create a delay between when a key is pressed and when its input is selected.

Figure 13.69 The Universal Access managed preference lets you define settings that help users who have physical limitations that impair their ability to use Mac OS X computers.

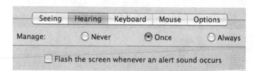

Figure 13.70 Additional options are available on the Hearing tab...

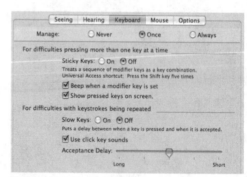

Figure 13.71 ...the Keyboard tab...

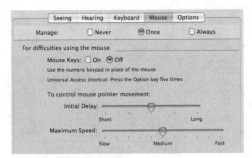

Figure 13.72 ...the Mouse tab...

In the Mouse tab, you can enable and specify Mouse Keys options that let you control the cursor using the number keypad (**Figure 13.72**). In the Options tab of the Universal Access managed preference, you can enable the Universal Access keyboard shortcuts that let you toggle Universal Access features using various keyboard shortcuts (**Figure 13.73**).

Figure 13.73 ...and the Options tab.

MANAGING PREFERENCES

MCX Is Behind the Scenes

Managed preference settings, like all other account settings, are stored in your Mac OS X Server's Open Directory database. However, due to the complexity of these settings, they go beyond the standard attribute/value data specification.

Managed preference settings use a format known as Machine Control XML (MCX) (some say it also means Managed Client for X). (More fun with acronyms—XML is short for Extensible Markup Language.) These MCX files consist of text formatted in a certain manner that is understood by the preference system on the client computers. In fact, the MCX text file format is similar to the format used for other Mac OS X preference files called *property lists*.

You can directly view and edit the MCX settings by using the Inspector view in Workgroup Manager. Take great care when editing this information directly, because human errors can cause some serious problems. See Chapter 4 for more information about using the Inspector.

Understanding Preference Files

You have probably seen the preference files created by Mac OS X applications. They appear in a user's Library/Preferences folder and are named similar to this: *com.apple.Dock.plist*.

This naming convention can be viewed in reverse, as Top level domain (TLD-com in this case), company (Apple), and application (Dock). When applications follow this method of saving their preferences, those applications may also be able to have their preferences managed similar to that of Mac OS X managed settings, like the Dock.

To view the preference files, first click the Preferences icon in the Toolbar of Workgroup Manager and then click the Details tab adjacent to the Overview tab (**Figure 13.74**). When viewing a preference, such as the Dock, you can see that various parameters can be changed that are not present in the user interface of Workgroup Manager. Some keys are not even shown or listed, but can be added to further manage these items. For example, if you click the Dock item and click Edit, you are shown three sets of settings: one for Once, one for Always, and one called Often (**Figure 13.75**).

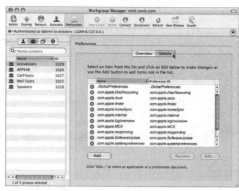

Figure 13.74 Clicking the Details tab reveals managed preference property lists.

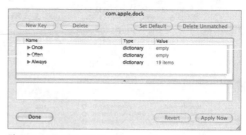

Figure 13.75 Viewing the three main settings in a property list.

Often Enough?

The Often setting is a bit ambiguous. When keys are used in the Often setting, the logged-in user can change those settings, but when they log out and log back in, the settings are returned to the default and any modifications the user made to the preferences while they were initially logged in are not saved.

Figure 13.76 Clicking the disclosure triangle displays all the keys for that setting.

Figure 13.77 Adding a key that did not previously exist.

Depending on your method of management, you will see several keys beneath one or more of these sets. In this example, you can see that the Always set has several parameters (**Figure 13.76**).

One aspect of these files is the ability to add keys that do not exist yet. In the case of the Dock, you can click New Key to add a key called pinning, where the String is *start*, *middle* (default for Mac OS X), or *end*. This places the Dock in the corner of your screen, depending on what side your Dock is on (**Figure 13.77**).

Another extremely useful aspect of preferences here is the Preference Manifest, which allows other applications to actually have their preferences managed. This has great potential, as application developers write their preferences to Apple's manifest requirements. One of the first applications to take advantage of using manifests is Safari.

To add Safari Manifest to the Preference/Manifest list:

1. In Workgroup Manager, select the LDAP directory from the directory list.

2. Click the Preference icon in the Toolbar, select the user, group, or computer list accounts that you wish to manage, and click the Details tab in the main Preferences window (**Figure 13.78**).

3. Click Add, navigate to the /Applications folder, and select Safari.

   Two additional items have been added to the manifest list (**Figure 13.79**).

4. Select *com.apple.Safari* from the list and click Edit.

5. Click the disclosure triangle next to the Often text and select a line of text (**Figure 13.80**).

   There are several keys that will be set for multiple users.

6. Click Done to close the window and return to the Details tab.

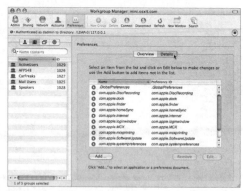

Figure 13.78 The Details tab is also where Preference Manifests can be viewed and edited.

Figure 13.79 Selecting a preference manifest from the list.

Figure 13.80 Choosing an attribute in the Preference Manifest.

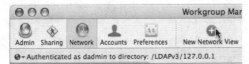

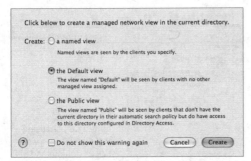

Figure 13.81 Creating a new network view with Workgroup Manager.

Figure 13.82 The three options for creating a new network.

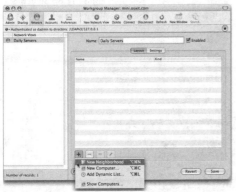

Figure 13.83 Adding a new neighborhood to a named network view.

Using network views

Often users get frustrated when clicking the Network icon because several domains and servers present themselves. In most cases, you want all users to search the entire network for the relevant servers. But what if users only go to a fraction of those servers? Waiting for the list to fully download and searching that entire server list can be tedious. It also may be unsecure as there may be some servers you do not wish others to see. With network views, you can decide what can be seen and how it can be seen.

To add a network view:

1. In Workgroup Manager, click the Network icon in the Toolbar and click the New Network View icon (**Figure 13.81**).

   Several types of views can be set (**Figure 13.82**):

   ▲ **Named view**—These are views with names you specify.

   ▲ **Default view**—If a client is not part of any computer list but still bound to the server, this is the view they see.

   ▲ **Public view**—Clients are not bound to the server but do have access to the directory.

   You can have many Named views but only one Default view and one Public view.

2. Click the Add button to add a Network Neighborhood, if desired (**Figure 13.83**).

   continues on next page

3. Give the neighborhood a name directly in the window (**Figure 13.84**) and then decide what type of computers to add to the view: specific and/or local.

   Local computers are on the local subnet or advertised via SMB (**Figure 13.85**).

4. To restrict a network view to a specific computer or computer list, click the network from your list and choose Show Computers from the plus button pull-down menu (**Figure 13.86**).

   A window appears showing all of the previously added computers (**Figure 13.87**).

5. Select the computers you want to see in this particular network view and drag them into the main window (**Figure 13.88**).

Figure 13.84 Naming the new neighborhood.

Figure 13.85 Choosing local discovery services such as Bonjour and SLP.

Figure 13.86 Selecting the Show Computers option...

Figure 13.87 ...reveals a drawer that lists all computers within any computer lists.

Figure 13.88 Dragging over selected computers into the main Settings window.

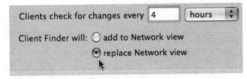

Figure 13.89 Choosing how the new network view will be displayed on the bound Mac OS X computers.

Figure 13.90 Viewing the final list for a specific network view.

6. Decide how you want the network view to update and whether or not to replace or add to the existing network view; then click Save (**Figure 13.89**).

Test from a Mac OS X computer that is both bound, and then unbound, to the server (depending on the network view configuration).

✔ Tips

■ When properly implemented, network views can have a tremendous impact in segregating servers based on logical roles, rather than alphabetical or cryptic names (**Figure 13.90**).

■ Keep in mind that when setting up network views, planning plays the most critical role. For views that show specific servers, it's best to ensure a written policy is in place before implementation goes to the final stage.

INDEX

C

N